EXPERIENCE AND CONTENT

For Alice and my parents

Experience and Content
Consequences of a Continuum Theory

W. MARTIN DAVIES
Visiting Scholar in Philosophy
The Flinders University of South Australia

Avebury
Aldershot • Brookfield USA • Hong Kong • Singapore • Sydney

© W. Martin Davies 1996

All rights reserved. No part of this publication may be reproduced, stored in a retrieval system, or transmitted in any form or by any means, electronic, mechanical, photocopying, recording or otherwise without the prior permission of the publisher.

Published by
Avebury
Ashgate Publishing Limited
Gower House
Croft Road
Aldershot
Hants GU11 3HR
England

Ashgate Publishing Company
Old Post Road
Brookfield
Vermont 05036
USA

British Library Cataloguing in Publication Data

Davies, W. Martin
    Experience and content : consequences of a continuum theory. - (Avebury series in philosophy)
    1. Experience
    I. Title
    128.4

ISBN 1 85972 342 X

Library of Congress Catalog Card Number: 96-86402

Printed in Great Britain by Antony Rowe Ltd, Chippenham, Wiltshire

Contents

Figures and tables   vi
Acknowledgements   vii
Preface   viii

Introduction   1

Part One: Experience and content   11

1 Observations and inferences   13
2 A continuum theory of content   41
3 Experience and language   61
4 Experience and belief   77

Part Two: Experience and structure   101

5 Sensational content   103
6 Idealised and naturalised experience   131
7 Animal experiences   151
8 Modularity and insularity   167

Part Three: Experience and science   191

9 Experience without Feyerabend   193

Part Four: Experience and mind   223

10 Sellars's myth   225
11 Experience eliminated?   257
12 Experience and subjectivity   307
13 Experiencing the 'manifest' image   335

Bibliography   343

Figures and tables

Figure 1: A Taxonomy of Content   50

Figure 2: Ambiguous line groupings   112

Figure 3: Ambiguous dot array   113

Figure 4: The Muller-Lyer Illusion   171

Acknowledgements

This book began life as a doctoral dissertation at The Flinders University of South Australia. My thanks go to Rodney Allen, Philip Cam, George Couvalis, Frank Jackson and Chris Mortenson for their encouraging, yet critical, comments. Stephen Hardy, David Joyner, Michelle Short, Dale Lambert and Som Prakash commented on various early versions of the manuscript and Roger McCart proofed the penultimate version making important improvements in matters of style and substance. Flinders University provided a overseas study grant and an Amy Forwood travelling award to allow me to write some of the material at the University of Edinburgh, and a further grant in order for me to prepare the manuscript for publication. An Australian Post-Graduate Research Award supported me in the initial stages of the project. My wife Alice provided gentle encouragement throughout the entire writing process.

My thanks to Oxford Press, Cambridge Press and Routledge Press for permission to publish.

Preface

This book is about experiential content: what it is; what kind of account can be given of it. I am concerned with identifying and attacking one main view - I call it the *inferentialist proposal*. This account is central to the philosophy of mind, epistemology and philosophy of science and perception. I claim, however, that it needs to be recast into something far more subtle and enriched, and I attempt to provide a better alternative in these pages.

The inferentialist proposal holds that experiential content is necessarily underpinned by sophisticated cognitive influences. My alternative, the *continuum theory,* holds that these influences are relevant to experience only at certain levels of organisation and that at other levels there are contents which such features do not capture at all. Central to my account is that there are *degrees* to which cognitive influences affect experiential content; indeed, for the most part, experience is an amalgam of both inferential and non-inferential features. I claim that the inferentialist proposal is fundamentally flawed and deserves replacement, and I argue that my alternative fills the hollow that remains.

The book is divided into four sections. In Part I, Chapter 1, I introduce two traditionally rival views of experiential content. In Chapter 2, I develop my continuum alternative. Chapter 3 assesses the relationship between experience and language, while Chapter 4 explores the relationship between beliefs and experience. The overall argument is that it has been a mistake to understand experience simply in inferential or non-inferential terms.

In Part II, I examine the structure of mental content. Chapter 5 is concerned with the kinds of experiences which escape the inferentialist analysis. Chapter 6 considers Kant's metaphysic of experience counterpointed to Lorenz's reading of his work in the light of evolutionary biology. Chapter 7 treats animal experience in relation to the continuum view I am developing, while Chapter 8 reviews Fodor's contribution to perceptual psychology. It is argued that the view of experiential content being developed is both consistent with empirical data on informationally local perceptual sub-systems, but also accords well with evolutionary theory and a naturalist interpretation of Kant's taxonomy.

Part III deals with inferentialism in the philosophy of science. In Chapter 9, I assess the theory dependence of observation thesis as it is advanced by Paul Feyerabend. I bring out of his account a subtle confusion concerning the importance of inference in the context of scientific inquiry.

Part IV deals with the issue of experience in the philosophy of mind. In Chapter 10, I look at Wilfred Sellars's attack on sense data theories. Chapter 11 confronts Paul Churchland's treatment of 'folk psychology' while Chapter 12 isolates the issue of experiential qualia and the position of property dualism. I offer a critical review of Thomas Nagel's work in this chapter and claim that his position can be read in a way which is consistent with the continuum account I am developing. I conclude the book in the usual fashion with a summary of the central claims.

Introduction

'Frankly, I do not understand even now how you unravelled this case.'
Holmes leaned back in his chair and put his fingertips together.
'My dear fellow, there was no great difficulty in the problem. The facts were obvious enough, but the delicacy of the matter lay in the need that the murderer himself should confirm them by some overt act. Circumstantial evidence is the bane of the trained reasoner.'
'I have observed nothing.'
'You have observed everything, but failed to reason.'

'The Adventure of the Sealed Room'
The Exploits of Sherlock Holmes
A.Conan-Doyle and J. D.Carr

Introducing the problem

In *Remarks on the Philosophy of Psychology,* Wittgenstein distinguishes 'purely optical' aspects of experiences from those '*mainly* determined by thoughts and associations.'[1] The reference occurs in the context of his discussion on 'seeing as' but, as is customary with Wittgenstein's work, the passage is not developed in detail. Regardless, the remark may be of historical importance as an early statement of an issue which now runs orthogonally through much of the contemporary writing and problems central to the philosophy of science, perception and cognition.

The issue is whether experiential content is, in any full-blooded sense, inferential, and thus, dependent on high-level theories, concepts and background knowledge ('associations', as Wittgenstein would have it), or whether such content is non-inferential, coming entirely from input on the sense organs (Wittgenstein's 'purely optical' aspects).

Given the differences in the experiences of Sherlock Holmes and Watson, it would seem obvious that the content of an experience cannot simply be obtained from the latter source: to make *meaningful* observations it is not sufficient to receive purely optical inputs; it is also essential that one be trained to form

---

[1] L. Wittgenstein, *Remarks on the Philosophy of Psychology*, §960-1017.

appropriate associations, and this seems to require inferential abilities. This is, in fact, the orthodox philosophical line on such an issue. The routine ability to perceive, according to most current views, seems to rely on perception being fully informed by *reason*.

However, there are aspects of perception that this strongly inferential line misses out on: it seems true to say, for instance, that experiences have some content even when not completely informed in this manner. Watson did experience *something,* though admittedly, not as much as his more astute friend. Doubtlessly, he perceived material relevant to the case in question even without complex inferential abilities. But it also seems true to say that completely uninformed experiences have content too. They must have content because some organisms (dogs, cats, conceptually unsophisticated infants) do not seem to possess the kind of reasoning that is required in order to make complex perceptual judgements. It is to this kind of underdeveloped content, perhaps, that appellations like the 'purely optical' apply.

If one inclines to each and all of these views, however, one is faced with an uninviting philosophical dilemma: how can individuals perceive anything if they fail to form associations of any kind? But equally, how can the forming of such associations alone be *necessary and sufficient* for seeing?

Neither of the traditional perspectives on this issue are very comforting. On the one hand, the content of reasoned perception must consist of inferential abilities drawing upon various degrees of *theory* (it was this ability that Holmes's partner seemed to lack). On the other hand, the content of uninfluenced perception must consist, not in the possession of networks of complex theoretical associations, but in information derived from a non-inferential source. Thus, one view insists that all experiences are highly *epistemic;* the other emphasises what are allegedly *non-epistemic* features. One view leads to a highly propositional and representational view of perceptual content; the other turns to proximal information that impinges on the sense receptors. Both approaches traditionally admit of hidden agendas, and both approaches seem too extreme. For this reason alone it seems likely that neither account in its current form will do. (Interestingly, Wittgenstein's qualification, 'mainly', may offer a solution here which has not been noticed by philosophers when considering this issue.)

The preoccupation with the structure of perceptual content has historical affinities to Kant's work in epistemology. The issue has also been informed by sense data theories of perception advanced in the early twentieth century. The tradition stemming from Kant argues that the sensation/inference threshold collapses with inference taking the dominant organisational role. The opposing view, stemming from positivism and the sense-data theories, claims that the reverse is the case. Articulated in these terms, the issue is firmly in the domain of the epistemologist and the philosopher of perception. And, articulated in these terms, the issue generally leads to a philosophical stalemate - a polarisation of opinion between views which eschew the importance of inference entirely and those which take the importance of inferential abilities to extraordinary lengths. As mentioned, the present consensus of opinion in philosophy is broadly in the latter camp.

There are, however, more contemporary ways of approaching the matter of experience and content than simply along these traditional philosophical lines.

One of these ways even claims to provide a principled way of resolving the matter of the extent to which inference affects experiences.

Recent discussions concerning perceptual content have looked at the processing capabilities of the perceptual apparatus and has drawn upon psychological data on perceptual illusion and cognitive responses to ambiguous stimuli. Some theorists, notably Fodor, have suggested a multi-level conception of perceptual structure, where only some content is (properly) inferential, and other content is not, due to the operation of relatively autonomous, locally responsive, perceptual sub-systems, operating incidentally to higher-level cognitive mechanisms.[2] Perceptual content, on Fodor's account, is *modular* and available to the influence of inferential abilities only at certain levels. This work has been influential in support of functional theories of the mind, but is not without interest in other areas of inquiry.

In this book, the modular view will be modified substantially and accommodated within a multi-level philosophical theory of experience that has not been considered before. A multi-level view of perception will provide a way of adjudicating between traditionally rival positions on the issue of experience and content.

There are several reasons to be optimistic about employing the results of investigations in the visual sciences. The modularity hypothesis, unlike standard philosophical theories of perception, is an empirical theory and is thus open to empirical confirmation or rejection. With modifications, it is also a means of having our inferential cake and eating it too. As shall be argued, it suggests a way of reaching a decision about how inference affects experience without compromising the integrity of the more traditional approaches which either ignore inference entirely or take its influence to absurd lengths. The view that there might be limits to the extent to which cognitive processing influences experience inspires a philosophical theory of content which shall be called the *continuum theory*.

But there is also a more general reason for taking heed of such strategies. The reason is that the problem seems to *require* a compatabilist solution. It seems likely that the prima facie separate approaches of Kant, the sense data theorists, and Fodor, have more in common than has otherwise been accorded by philosophers. It is plausible to suppose, for instance, that the observational-inference dispute is not only a metaphysical, but also an empirical problem. A fully adequate account thus must take account of both philosophical speculation and the experimental and psychological facts about the perceptual system. Neither approach on its own is intrinsically very satisfying in the long term. And it is important to bring these considerations together because the two approaches are obviously complementary, and are, in any case, often interdependent: one often gives rise to new considerations about the other. For example, what Kant's a priori views in epistemology did for perceptual theories in the 18th century and developmental psychology much later were as important as what experimental work in perception is doing for epistemology now. It is clear that there should be no boundaries on approaches to this issue. Both speculative and empirical considerations must be addressed. And, as shall be

---

[2] J. A. Fodor, *The Modularity of Mind;* 'Observation Reconsidered.' *Philosophy of Science,* 51 (1984): pp. 23-43.

shown later, by taking such an approach to the problem, these very different ways of looking at the issue can usefully inform each other.

I want to consider how these very different approaches might overlap in this book. The issue is the bearing of inference upon experience, and the extent to which experiential content is explained in such terms. The central focus of the attack will be various forms of, what shall be called, *inferentialist* views, which stress not only the primacy of inference over sensation, but the *redundancy* of the latter. The price of these inferentialist views has traditionally been to rule out of court *sensational properties of experiences*. This consequence arises out of current theories of perception because content is seen exclusively in terms of inferential abilities with no allowance for features which cannot be captured in inferential terms. On current views, all that is needed to capture the content of perception is to specify the various inferential associations that perceivers routinely perform. However, it can be shown that this stress on the reasoning abilities of perceivers has been to the detriment of other kinds of content which cannot be captured in such terms.

The kind of content that might escape the inferential net is what philosophers sometimes call *qualia:* the 'felt' aspect of mental states - the redness of a colour, the loudness of a sound and so on. Capturing the quale of an experience is important to any adequate story about the evolution of perceptual systems. It shall be argued that qualia typically have a causal role in perception and do some important epistemic work. It is thus essential that any view of experiential content must give some account of them. The continuum account developed in this book is designed to accommodate such features of perceptual content.

By contrast, there are many important contemporary views which ignore or reject the importance of sensational properties of experiences altogether. The work of Churchland and Sellars are explicit in their rejection of all but an inferential content to perception; the work of Feyerabend is quite covert in this regard but offers a similar view. Philosophers as varied as Hanson, Armstrong, Harman and Davidson have been sympathetic to an inferential view of content at some stage in their philosophical development. There has certainly been no lack of opposition to the idea that experience possesses non-inferential, qualitative aspects. The voices against this view can also be traced to the important philosophical influence of Descartes and Kant who left enduring legacies to this tradition. Each of the philosophers mentioned have ignored or refused to admit content which cannot be captured in inferential terms - thus, they have been largely responsible for an *inferentialist theory of experience* and the consequences that flow from such a view.

The present work will chart some of these 'consequences'. It will also examine the consequences of rejecting the inferentialist story. The book will suggest that, in large measure, the full-blooded inferentialist picture of content is false - good intentions and long traditions notwithstanding. I shall examine the implications of the inferentialist view and highlight its problems. But a negative critique is not the only outcome - a positive account is also attempted. In rejecting inferentialism, I suggest we should end up with a continuum account which legitimates several kinds of non-exclusive content. Unlike inferentialist views, the continuum account allows that at some levels there is more to content than proximal stimulations, though rather less than a fully inference-based account allows. The position proposed in this book is that experiences might well be 'determined by thoughts and associations' to some important degree, but, as Wittgenstein would have it, the operative word here is 'mainly'; there are also other kinds of content to consider which have non-inferential and sensory aspects. The continuum view is thus an attempt at bringing together the various kinds of views mentioned, empirical and speculative, into some sort of integrated approach. It is this attempt at an integrated approach that is largely the aim of this book. Another aim, however, is to come to some conclusions regarding the importance of experience in the context of some of the wider issues in contemporary thought. Some of these issues shall now be outlined.

The bearing of perceptual content on issues in contemporary philosophy has a number of levels of focus which need to be looked at. As already mentioned, it certainly features in how philosophers stand on the important issue of qualia; the (supposedly) irreducible and immediate qualitative 'rawness' of phenomenal states experienced while undergoing acts of perception. This is an issue in which philosophers fall clearly into two distinct groups: the 'qualia freaks' and those that 'quine' them (as Dennett would have it) by denying that there is anything which could amount to irreducible 'felt' properties of such states which cannot be 'explained away' by inference, elimination or reduction.[3] This dispute has created imaginative points of interest, with Thomas Nagel arguing that no amount of physical information about the constitution of bats and their experiential states will tell us 'what it is like' to be one, and Frank Jackson arguing that an omniscient neurophysiologist of colour vision confined to a black and white room can't ever know how colours *look*.[4] The burden of such examples is supposed to suggest that physicalism, reductionism and eliminativism are simply false when it comes to the content of experiences.

This is an issue which is importantly tied to the question at hand, since only if such contents are *not* fully inferential, can there be any room for argument over what other kinds of content there might be. (And 'qualia freaks' being, for the most part, anti-inferentialists tend to regard this extra content as being ineluctably *experiential* in some sense.) Alternatively, Churchland, Sellars, and others, argue that there is no such additional content to speak of, for there are no perceptual qualia in a view of experiential content shot through with inference. The problem of perceptual content is thus firmly bound up with one principal divisive issue in the philosophy of mind today: the existence and nature of experiential qualia. The suggestion here will be that, because there are genuine problems with the inferentialist view of experience and content, and because low-level content seems to have a genuine causal role, there are reasons for taking the qualia theorists seriously. It is true, I shall argue, that not all features of experiences can be captured in inferential terms. However, this does not mean that the opposing position which eschews the importance of inference altogether is correct. Rather, the view proposed in this book is that experiences

---

[3] See D. C. Dennett, 'Quining Qualia,' *Consciousness in Contemporary Science*; Rpt. in Lycan, *Mind and Cognition: A Reader*, pp. 519-545. See also: 'Qualia Disqualified', in *Consciousness Explained*.
[4] Thomas Nagel, 'What is it like to be a Bat?', *Philosophical Review* 83, (1974): pp. 435-50; Rpt. in Nagel, *Mortal Questions;* Frank Jackson, 'What Mary Didn't Know', *Journal of Philosophy* 83, (1986): pp. 291-5.

possess two broad kinds of content: one which can be captured in inferential terms and one which cannot. Within the context of the philosophy of mind, my position shall be that an interactionist property dualism is still a serious option; indeed, much of the thesis that follows can be read as a sustained argument in support of this form of property dualism. In defence of this, I shall also endorse an argument which avoids the counterintuitive consequences of epiphenomenalism as an account of experience and content. The legitimation of a property dualist theory of mind is an important consequence of the rejection of inferentialism.

The issue of experience in the philosophy of science is also central to this book. The point of most interest is the recent discussion of whether observations are *theory dependent*. Does theory-dependence provide a inferentially neutral basis for scientific observations in the context of theory change? This issue has ramifications far beyond the inferential nature of experience to the nature of science itself: whether, for instance, the scientific enterprise is so thoroughly embedded in theory that it might proceed unencumbered by the need for making any observations at all. Paul Feyerabend seems to think that it is likely and desirable to have a 'science without experience', and Fodor has recently claimed that having experiences is but only one way whereby scientists can achieve 'cognitive self-management.'[5] The issues here are, of course, central to the methodological procedures of scientific inquiry, but they intersect too with any adequate account of perceptual experience generally, quite independently of the implications they have for the nature of paradigms, theory change and incommensurability. Any approach to the very general issue of experiential content will have to say something about how it bears on the parallel issue in the philosophy of science. As will be shown, there is much confusion on this matter, and this leads to a heavy-handed emphasis on inferential abilities. The claim here will be that, for similar reasons to those enunciated in relation to the philosophy of mind, science needs at least two broad levels of experiential content - that which is captured by inferential abilities and that which isn't. The inferentialist view, I shall argue, is as unsatisfactory as an account of the mechanics of science as it is as an account of the ontology of mind.

There is, then, a single theme to this book and two main foci. The theme is a rejection of inferentialism and a statement of a continuum theory of experiential content. The foci are experience as it features in the philosophy of mind and in the philosophy of science. The aim of the book is to develop a theory of content which considers the influence of stock philosophical views and current empirical work as contributing features to understanding the nature of perceptual experience.

The issues mentioned are linked in more ways than one as this book will show. The inference/non-inference dichotomy is one way of measuring the dispute, but there are others. Implications for an account of animal and infant cognitive development is another, quite different, yardstick. Inferentialism with respect to perceptual content, qualia, the theory dependence of observation, and

---

[5] See: P. K. Feyerabend, 'Science without Experience', in *Realism, Rationalism and Scientific Method;* J. A. Fodor, 'The Dogma that didn't Bark (A Fragment of a Naturalised Epistemology)', *Mind,* 100 (1991): pp. 201-230.

so on, goes alongside any account of cognition which is sophisticated and epistemically high-level. Hence, we have Feyerabend ruling out the possibility of observations without theory in any 'sensing subject', and Davidson and Stich arguing that animals, in effect, can't have cognitive content if they can't use a language, or, at least, have cognitive states which can't be fully isomorphically matched by those of language users.[6] Many other recent theorists, including Geach, Malcolm and Bishop, have taken a similar (essentially Cartesian) line about animal cognition.

It shall be argued that views which have such consequences are examples of inferentialism running wild. The importance of inference to cognitive content should be divorced from such claims. Language, of course, presupposes a highly permeable network of relatively accessible cognitive information of a symbolic nature, and is indisputably inferential in a complex sense. However, it is not clear that it is the *only* influence on content. It is plausible to suppose that though there might be significant causal penetration of the sensory aspects of experience by language and theory, this does not mean that there is no sensory content *without* language and theory. As has been stated recently: 'sensory information has a certain priority over theory ... denying the obvious when it has an immediate sensory impact on one is a recipe for a short life.'[7] Clearly one should be able to keep the importance of inference without subscribing to a fully inferentialist view, and one must do this if one wants to preserve the intuition that animals and pre-linguistic infants have experiential content in some important sense. The trick, however, is to work out a way of keeping the intuitively plausible idea that experience requires inferential abilities without buying into such deeply counterintuitive views as those mentioned above. I resolve this problem simply by admitting qualia as part of the experiential continuum.

The treatment of the above issue in this book blends well with the modular view of perception mentioned earlier. This view argues that low-level structural sub-systems might be just as important to cognition as the higher level systems. Not enough blending of these very different approaches to the problem is attempted in the literature. This book will attempt to do just that. The continuum account advanced here is an attempt to reconcile the tensions between some of these very different approaches to the issue of experience and content. The application of mechanisms of inference to animal and infant experience is one such source of tension. The approach given will be to reject inferentialist views and to allow different levels of content to feature in the experiences of differentially sophisticated organisms. The attempt to reconcile the two kinds of influence along naturalist grounds thus leads to a strongly evolutionary line on the development and the nature of perceptual systems.

Philosophical theories and concepts must be kept within the constraints of evolutionary theory. I do not conceal my biases on this point. Metaphysical speculation must ultimately be in keeping with the Darwinian model of the conditions for species selection and phylogenetic similarity and divergence.

---

[6] Donald Davidson, 'Thought and Talk', in S. Guttenplan (ed.) *Mind and Language*, pp. 7-23; Stephen P. Stich, 'Do Animals have Beliefs?', *Australasian Journal of Philosophy* 57, (1979): pp. 15-28.

[7] C. Mortensen and G. Nerlich, *Aspects of Metaphysics*, p. 7.

This, at least, will be an unargued assumption in this book. Any model of perceptual content should thus be broadly in keeping with such principles and not run against them. As I will try to show, however, the important relation between high-level content (incorporating such inference-based abilities as language) and the selective importance of low-level, non-inferential content has often been ignored in keeping to the letter and spirit of what I have called 'inferentialism'. But there is a good case for keeping a low-level experiential content for basically phylogenetic reasons: reasons which are parsimonious and plausible in evolutionary terms. Such naturalist grounds are consistent with a philosophical theory of content which allows for low-level sensory content as well as high-level inferential content.

The inferential/non-inferential dispute should not, like other staid philosophical dichotomies, be seen in terms of mutually *exclusive* influences. At least, that is what shall be argued here. Instead, the emphasis should be on a continuum account of content: inferential influences at one extreme and non-inferential influences at the other extreme - with all sorts of graded possibilities in between. It will be argued that this is entirely consistent with an evolutionary approach. The point to be noted about the move away from the dichotomised to a continuum view of content is that the whole issue of experience has been hamstrung by something of a false option: a *choice* between inference and non-inference. I want to say, by contrast, that there are both inferential aspects and non-inferential aspects to such contents. I also want to suggest that the idea that either influence alone explains the nature of experiential content is an error. Both the inferentialist approach and the sense-data approach tend to suggest this, but ultimately neither view is satisfactory on its own. This book, instead, will try to charter a position which includes both inferential and non-inferential aspects without falling into the extreme views mentioned. Each approach has insights to offer, but that they fail to integrate these insights into a satisfactory overall account, which I think my view supplies.

I will be drawn to suggest a multi-level structure to experience, and hence, side with the qualia theorists to the extent that there must be some perceptual/sensational content which is 'extra' to that explained through mechanisms of inference. I shall also be endorsing a view of modular cognitive processes. Kant's views will also be compared favourably with the modularity story. The empirical evidence for modularity is impressive in any case, quite independently of the argumentative supports philosophers offer for it. And, I think all of these claims can be sustained as *complementary* attitudes in evolutionary terms. By adopting the continuum view of experiential content, the merits of each of these approaches can be satisfactorily combined and the counterintuitive implications the inferentialist proposal has for low-level animal and infant experiences can be successfully avoided.

Claiming that there are contents to experience which are low-level and non-inferential is not to claim that there is no room for defending the importance of inference in any adequate view of experiential content and structure. There obviously is a role needed for inference in any account of experience. The point is that only if one assumes an already *dichotomised* conception of inference/non-inference is there a case for saying that these influences are mutually exclusive. I won't be asserting such a view, and I shall be explicitly arguing against the sense data theories, which insist that non-inferential sense data can be held alongside the claim that they are *epistemically* structured. As Sellars has pointed out, this view involves a substantial confusion. The position to be taken in this book will be that low-level experiences can have content too, a content in a low-level sense - a sense which is significantly deficient in such things as high-level beliefs, theories and background knowledge, but which is nonetheless, by strength of reasons, not entirely *empty*. This is a tautological claim, but I think an informative one, because the view to be attacked does not admit of a non-exclusive way of treating the issue.

To summarise: this book endorses a continuum account of experiential content, and rejects a fully inferentialist view. The arguments advanced to support this draw upon several different approaches to the relationship between inference and sensation, both empirical and speculative, in both the philosophy of science and the philosophy of mind. The account also considers the unsophisticated experiences of animals and infants and keeps the issues in check with the constraints of evolutionary theory. The major claim is that all of these considerations and the various approaches to the problem can be sustained as complementary attitudes if one adopts the continuum account suggested. But if one does this, then by necessity one forfeits a heavily inferentialist view in which experience depends on the imposition of the content of theories, concepts and background knowledge. However, as it is advocated that a non-dichotomous relationship is in order here, this does not mean that we thereby have to abandon the importance of inference entirely. I suggest that there is certainly a place for inference in experience, both within the philosophy of mind and the philosophy of science, but that *inferentialism* is actually false. There is still a place for 'purely optical' aspects in a content which may be 'mainly' determined by thoughts and associations.

Part One
EXPERIENCE AND CONTENT

1 Observations and inferences

We may not have prayers in public schools, but by G-d we will have a distinction between observation and inference - Fodor's Granny.[1]

Preliminaries: setting up a view

Experience and knowledge

This book is about experiential content, so let's consider the following case study. Sherlock Holmes, Private Investigator, enters a room and experiences the following scene: Before him lies a body on a blood-stained carpet and near the body lies a cigar-band. A moment's reflection has Holmes realise that a murder has been committed, correctly identify the perpetrator of the crime, the weapon used, and the approximate time of the victim Jones's death.

A first consideration about such an experience might be this: Holmes did not extract all these details from the visual scene before him; he inferred most of it, cleverly, from available perceptual information. Nonetheless, he did immediately and reliably identify certain objects and relations in the world - a dead body, a cigar-band, a relation of 'nearness' etc., despite not having come across them in exactly the same way before. That he could have done this must indicate that he had *prior knowledge* of what constituted such things as a dead body, a cigar-band, etc. Such things were already concepts for Holmes before he arrived on the murder scene.

Experiences are related in some important sense to concepts and, in particular, to knowledge states as they usually occur within the context of knowledge claims (one often identifies an experience of something by identifying an object of purported knowledge or belief). But then again, when we experience something for the first time it is not obvious that full knowledge is involved, though of course we bring to bear epistemic concepts (in the form of background knowledge) on new experiences to make sense of them.

---

[1] J.A. Fodor, 'Observation Reconsidered,' *Philosophy of Science,* 51 (1984): p. 23.

(Suppose, for instance, that Holmes recognised a stray cylindrical paper object that he *inferred* was a cigar-band on the basis of what he knew about the habits of the suspected perpetrator who smoked cigars.) In any event, whether a first time experience for Holmes or not, it seems true to say that he would have had to identify some known object or other on the basis of prior concepts, so it does seem as if experiences are saturated by background information in some sense.

There is a traditional view of perceptual content which takes this 'saturation' thesis very seriously. On this view, it is *necessarily true* that Holmes must have brought to bear some fairly sophisticated background knowledge to have the experience he did: He must have known that the object in question was made of paper, he knew a suspect that smoked cigars, he had the concept of a cigar, a dead body, a murder, and so on. To have the *full* experience he did, he would have even had to have made an inferential link between the cigar-band and the suspected perpetrator of the crime. On this view, we might even say that he needed a *theory* that linked the cigar-band to the suspect. So, even though a 'first time' experience for Holmes, it was not an experience without the very substantial influence of background knowledge, concepts and theories. On this view, Holmes could not have had the experience he did have without carrying out this explicit or implicit *reasoning*. These sophisticated background influences shall be called the 'high-level' influences on experiences. On the view being examined, high-level epistemic information *penetrates through* experiential content, and experiences can be characterised in terms of *inference from* such background information.

It is clear that the high-level influences of background knowledge and concepts are linked to an adequate understanding of experiences. That there is more to perception than meets the eye is rather old news. But what constitutes 'high-level' influences, and what kinds of experiences are in question here?

In Immanuel Kant's opinion, experiences are only possible if concepts like permanence, identity, relation, space and time are in place, so epistemic categories are crucial to experiences on his account. Kant assumed that the imposition of high-level influences was a *necessary condition* of having experiences, and he took this claim to its extremes. On one reading of Kant, even an implicit knowledge of Euclidean geometry was *a priori* relevant to experiential content. On this account, the nature of high-level influences were *very* sophisticated, and applied to *all* cases of experiences; intuitions without sophisticated concepts, according to Kant, are blind. Taking these two doctrines together - the 'background knowledge' story and the Kantian approach - the traditional view to be examined holds that sophisticated high-level concepts, theories, background knowledge as well as an implicit imposition of spatiality, temporality and relation, are *necessary* features of experiential content. Just as Kant argued space, time, permanence, identity and relation made experiences possible so too do concepts, theories and inference from background knowledge.

Yet it is clear that not all experiences are like the ones Kant discusses. Specifically, it is not clear that for experiences to have content, they *must* be informed by sophisticated high-level influences. A simple example brings out this point. If a dog entered the same room at the same time as Sherlock Holmes and experienced the same visual scene, it is unlikely that it could have 'picked out' the same perceptual information. The dog might have brought to bear some background information to his experience, yet it is clear that it would not have been very complex information: certainly not Euclidean geometry, and perhaps not even concepts like 'cigar-band' or 'murderous event'. The experience of the dog would have been very unlike the experience of Sherlock Holmes in some sense. If it involved high-level features at all, then they could not be of the kind that Sherlock Holmes brought to bear on his experience, for, compared to Holmes, the dog is a conceptually *unsophisticated* creature.

In fact, dogs, cats and other animals (and very young babies for that matter) can't be said to possess conceptual knowledge in the sense that Holmes does - or, if they do, they are very primitive concepts (i.e., not 'high-level' ones). Yet, these creatures clearly have experiences of the world in some sense, even if they are simply aware of certain aspects of their environment: colours, shapes and so on. Perhaps it is true to say that animals and infants bring *some* high-level factors to bear on experiences - such as spatiality, temporality and relation - but not much more. (The dog might have perceived the cigar-band near Jones's body, even if it had none of the appropriate concepts to identify those objects.) Indeed, the main influence on animal experiences might not be just 'high-level' factors, but instead, purely visual or optical features of the observational situation, such as properties of colour, light and hue - along with some high-level features, such as spatiality, temporality and so forth. We can say then that some experiential content arises as an awareness through action on the senses as well as through the influence of background knowledge, concepts and theories.

The above case seems genuinely different from the Sherlock Holmes example but does it raise a problem for the general account under consideration?

One thing is clear: the view mentioned does seem too blunt to allow for such distinctions. It tends to lump all experiential content as being influenced by such high-level factors *ne plus ultra*. However, the case of unsophisticated animal and infant experiences does not seem to fit with such a story. In such cases, there is a clear sense in which experiential content depends on features of the observational situation rather than the various features of high-level inference.

This book claims that there is a *confusion* as to the degree to which high-level influences are brought to bear on experiences. Instead of holding that all experiences can be understood only in terms of high-level features, it is argued that there might be *degrees* to which such considerations influence content. The first aim is to describe a view which emphasises only high-level features and then compare it to another kind of view which emphasises only observational features. The second aim is to contrast it with the alternative account developed in this book. In the process, several different accounts of experiential content which mostly emphasise only high-level features will be examined and criticised.

Belief fixation and the inferentialist proposal

There is more to seeing than meets the eyeball.[2]

Experiences are importantly connected to the notion of a belief. Experiences tend to fix beliefs of various kinds. (Seeing the cigar-band or a red spot often

---

[2] N. R. Hanson, *Patterns of Discovery*, p. 4.

seems tantamount to believing that there is a cigar-band or a red spot that one sees.) There is, on some views of perceptual content, even the temptation to define experiences in terms of high-level belief acquisition.[3]

The view I have been discussing here could likewise be put in terms of how experiences fix beliefs. Some questions to be asked here are: are beliefs about things (say, some object being a cigar-band) fixed via inference from concepts and knowledge previously held, even guided by them; or, as in the case of Kant's categories, made possible by them? Or are beliefs fixed mainly by observation?

There are clear reasons for adopting the first view in preference to the second. The belief-by-knowledge case will clearly support the puzzling case of how experiences can originate at all given that they are always underdetermined by sensory arrays - where any number of observations can be compatible with a wide variety of perceptual *causes*. In this case, background knowledge is essential for sorting the many possible observations from the relevant ones. So, Sherlock Holmes *can* infer the criminal from the stray cigar-band and from knowledge he has about his suspects. By background knowledge, idle observations come to be fixed into beliefs about the criminal from a lot of peripheral information.[4] This is one good reason why high-level influences are relevant to the fixation of beliefs and why experiences must, at least partly, originate with prior knowledge. If Holmes brought *no* background knowledge to the murder scene, (not even some general knowledge about objects and relationships between them) it is doubtful whether he could have experienced anything at all. If one continues with this line of argument, one ends up with the 'high-level' account of experiential content I have been presenting.

There are simple reasons why this is a plausible attitude. For supposing that experiences originate with observations and there is nothing theoretical or conceptual involved in *seeing* an object, makes it hard to see how we can fix our beliefs about an experience in this manner. It seems we can't do this at all, for it is unclear, for a start, how we can say that we are acquainted with any sort of *object,* if we rule out the influence of high-level considerations altogether. H. I. Brown has spelt out this point clearly:

> Consider a relatively common, everyday instance of perception such as my seeing my typewriter. Now, in order to see that this object is a typewriter it is not sufficient that I just look at it; it is necessary that I already know what a typewriter is. Simply glancing at objects with normal eyesight will undoubtedly stimulate my retina, initiate complex electro-chemical processes in my brain and nervous system, and perhaps even result in some conscious experience, but it will not supply me with meaningful information about the world around me. In order to derive information from perception it is necessary that I be able to identify the objects that I encounter, and in order to identify them it is necessary that I already have available a relevant body of information.[5]

---

[3] D. M. Armstrong has one such view. It will be presented in Chapter 4.

[4] I owe this example to Fodor, op. cit., pp. 31-32.

[5] H. I. Brown, *Perception, Theory and Commitment,* pp. 81-2.

'Relevant body of information' and 'meaningful information' surely means certain sophisticated concepts (in this case 'typewriter'). Only if one is already possessed of such high-level background information of the sort of thing a typewriter *is,* can one say that a certain thing in one's visual field is a typewriter. But the need for sophisticated recognitional abilities in the process of belief fixation goes even further than this. For, the act of recognising the typewriter as an object distinct from its surroundings, *itself* presupposes high-level abilities. One surely needs to be able to recognise a *certain* object, but - even more fundamentally - one first needs to distinguish one thing from another in one's visual field. Basic conceptual information such as 'object' thus needs to be already a part of one's conceptual repertoire *before one can even get going.* It is probable that because we are so familiar with such objects as typewriters that we fail to acknowledge that seeing a typewriter is not a brute fact of observation; rather, it is an experience which involves high-level influences. For one thing, a typewriter is *represented* in a certain way as a certain object; for another thing, it is *conceptualised* and linked with a good deal of background theory. As shall be pointed out later, because one usually labels the content of an experience with a word or phrase, there is even a case for saying that in every experiential act a perceived object or event has a certain tokened, expressible form in a mental *language.* 'High-level' influences are clearly important features of everyday experiences if any or all of the above claims are true. Even ordinary experiences, it seems, involve very sophisticated forms of reasoning.

To neglect such influences, moreover, is to neglect Kant's important insight that concepts beget categorisation, and a categorisation scheme, in his view, is necessary to spot anything at all. And, at the very least, we need to 'distinguish delivery trucks from fire trucks and paper towels from napkins.'[6] So there is more to experiencing anything than simply opening one's eyes; experience also involves what will later be called (in deference to Kant) theoretical, representational and linguistic-propositional *judgments.* These terms shall be defined later.

Kant's idea that a conceptual base was fundamental to having experiences, it seems, leads naturally to the idea that making distinctions in experiences is not possible without a background of high-level influences. Such influences are also fairly sophisticated features. They include not just concepts, but also background knowledge and theories and possibly even language. Moreover, they seem to occur together: saying that an experience captures certain features which can be described in some way, say, as a 'typewriter', already assumes that the rest of the high-level features are in motion, filtering, organising and labelling the experience. (One cannot describe an experience unless one sees an object corresponding to the description; one knows what a typewriter is; one represents a certain object gestalt, and so on.) It seems once some high-level features are seen to be involved, the rest follow naturally. Moreover, the high-level features seem to be not just central to experiences but *necessary* for them.

Could we learn these sorts of distinctions between objects without such features? Hardly. It is not clear how, without the various features of high-level inference, we could make the fundamental divisions first. This seems,

---

[6] Ibid., p. 82.

moreover, to be as much a case for ordinary run-of-the-mill kinds of experience involving *concepts* as cases in the laboratory involving scientific *theories*. Perhaps even more so in the latter case. For just as one cannot identify things like 'scientist', 'laboratory' or 'experiment' unless one possesses the appropriate background concepts, so one cannot see what is going on when a scientist conducts an experiment unless one is familiar with their specialist knowledge. That is, even if we can get over the first problem and observe that *something* is going on, we can't see what the scientist is doing unless we understand the theories behind the practice. One can't, for instance, make the jump from (i) measuring the oscillations of a piece of iron with a mirror to (ii) measuring the electrical resistance of a coil unless one knows a bit about electrical theory.[7] On this view, high-level influences are bound up as *necessary conditions* for observational experience in rather the same way that a problem is necessary for a solution. Sellars isolates something like this kind of response to the issue when he says:

> [I]f the ability to recognize that x looks green presupposes the concept of *being green,* and if this in turn involves knowing in what circumstances to view an object to ascertain its colour, then, since one can scarcely determine what the circumstances are without noticing that certain objects have certain perceptible characteristics - including colours - it would seem that one could not form the concept *being green,* and, by parity of reasoning, of the other colours, unless he already had them.[8]

Of course, 'knowing what circumstances in which to view an object to ascertain its colour' presupposes that (a) one represents an object, (b) one knows what it is, i.e., that it is conceptualised in some way, (c) the object is linked with large-scale epistemic connections, (for instance, that medium-sized objects are generally coloured), and (d) the object can be described as a (coloured) thing and named accordingly. So the influence of various high-level features are tacitly assumed even in this simple example.

The central point is that, on the story being outlined, we need some sort of high-level conceptual ability to make *anything* out of our sensations at all. To experience anything like a typewriter or green or the electrical resistance of a coil, one needs to bring to bear fairly sophisticated background knowledge, concepts and theories. And, to apply such information assumes that experiences are already invested with high-level content.

There is a point of emphasis to be noted here. The kind of view presented so far holds that *all* the various features of high-level inference are necessary for experiential content. Kant's view is an extreme version of this position with the imposition of the entire range of sophisticated *a priori* categories of cognition. However, even simple examples such as experiencing a coloured object or a typewriter seem to involve all the high-level features mentioned as well.

---

[7] Hence Hanson's remarks: 'The visitor [to the laboratory] must learn some physics before he sees what the physicist sees.' op. cit., p. 17. Learning some physics, of course, amounts to learning *concepts* and *terms* in the appropriate technical *language*.

[8] W. Sellars, 'Empiricism and the Philosophy of Mind,' in *Science, Perception and Reality*, p. 147.

There is a second point of emphasis to be noted here. It is one thing to say that experiences mostly originate with such high-level influences; it is another to say that they *must* originate with them. Again: the more radical idea being considered claims that sophisticated background knowledge, concepts and theories are *necessary conditions* for having experiences. On this view, there is no sense in which we can *have* experiences unless we can conceptually filter out some things, and this depends on inference from background knowledge and high-level concepts and theories. As mentioned, Kant had something like this kind of story to tell with his famous categories of the understanding: experiences are only possible if one can identify relationships, causality and so on. 'Appearances' are underdetermined by the 'manifold of intuition' but the 'categories' of cognition somehow sort all this out.[9] A similar view has recently been expressed in terms of the 'theory ladenness of observation' thesis in the philosophy of science. It is probably time now to put a label on this view. I shall call this radical form of the belief-by-knowledge case - where inference from sophisticated high-level knowledge is necessary for the having of experiences - the *inferentialist proposal*.

There is a third point of emphasis to be noted here which sharpens the issue even further. In the hands of Kant, the inferentialist proposal says that high-level features are necessary for experiential content. However, in the hands of some contemporary theorists, the inferentialist proposal amounts to an even stronger thesis: namely, that high-level features are both necessary *and sufficient* for experiential content. Unlike Kant's view, where a sensory manifold and high-level input was required for experience (but where the high-level categories were necessary for the organisation of the manifold), some recent theorists claim that there is no need to speak of a sensory manifold at all - for them, the only thing of importance for experiential content is high-level input: theories, concepts and background knowledge. The differences in emphasis here shall be addressed later. It should be noted here that both views, strictly speaking, are examples of what has been called the inferentialist proposal. Both are radical doctrines - one only sightly more radical than the other - and both have been endemic in recent philosophical thought. Moreover, both of them hold that *all* the high-level features are crucial for experiential content.

I have set up this position - the inferentialist proposal - because I want to reject it in place of a better account of experiential content. We have already seen one problem with this view. If what has already been said is true, then there is a serious confusion in the terms of the inferentialist proposal. A dog might bring to bear *some* high-level factors, like spatiality, temporality and identity, yet not possess concepts such as 'cigar-band', 'dead body' and 'murderous event' - let alone a *theory* which connects them. So it seems not *all* high-level influences fix appropriate experiential beliefs. Moreover, some experiences do not seem to require the various high-level features by necessity: Animal and infant experiences simply do not seem to contain some of the high-level features stipulated by the inferentialist proposal. The *way* unsophisticated animals and infants experience things is not like the way clever private investigators like

---

[9] I. Kant, *Critique of Pure Reason,* passim. At least this is the *orthodox* view of Kant's work. A rather different account shall be presented in Chapter 6.

Holmes experience things. Yet, for reasons mentioned earlier, it seems plausible to say that for most experiences, some kind of recognitional ability is required: experiences must be *organised* in some sense and not conceptually empty. There is a sense in which even a dog must bring some kind of high-level organisational schema to his experiences, even if not a sophisticated one. How can these claims be reconciled?

An alternative view: the observational account

Clearly there must be more to the story of how experiences originate than the inferentialist proposal allows. The view just described seems to be deficient in some respects. Beliefs seem to be fixed not just by the imposition of high-level background concepts etc., but by *mere observation* in the case of animals and infants, and there are very good reasons for our beliefs to be fixed in this manner as well. As Fodor has noted:

> For one thing, observationally fixed beliefs tend, by and large, to be more reliable than inferentially fixed beliefs. This is primarily because the etiological route from the fact that P to the belief that P is metaphorically - and maybe literally - *shorter* in observation than in inference: less is likely to go wrong because there's less that *can* go wrong ... our rational confidence in our knowledge claims depends very largely on their ability to survive observational assessment.
> Second, the observational fixation of beliefs plays a special role in the adjudication and resolution of clashes of opinion. When observation is not appealed to, attempts to settle disputes often take the form of a search for premises that disputants share. ... [and] [s]ince observation is not a process in which new beliefs are inferred from old ones, the use of observation to resolve disputes does not depend on a prior consensus as to what premises may be assumed. The moral, children, is approximately Baconian. Don't think; look. Try not to argue.[10]

The sort of 'observationally fixed beliefs' that Fodor refers to are expressed in predicates like 'is red' or 'occupies more of the visual field.' That these sorts of *low-level* experiences are not inferred from previous beliefs but 'directly' somehow seem 'homely truths'[11] but the idea that seeing must come from knowing has been traditionally sufficient to dampen enthusiasm for any observationally-based alternative to how experiences originate at all. The view which holds that only the observational situation is relevant to how experiences originate will arise in a different context in later pages. To contrast it with the inferentialist proposal, I shall call it the *observational account*.

There are essentially two elements to Fodor's remark in support of some kind of observational account:

Firstly, there is the implicit suggestion that evolutionary considerations may be important in the fixation of certain beliefs. Some perceptions have to be quick and reliable. Such, presumably, would be the case for low-level

---

[10] Fodor, op. cit., p. 24.
[11] Loc. cit.

experiences like 'red' and 'occupies more of the visual field.' (In these cases, the identification of features of complicated things like objects may not necessarily be involved.) Cases in point would perhaps be the kinds of experiences that simple animals and conceptually unsophisticated infants have, which don't seem to be accounted for on the terms of the inferentialist proposal; here high-level influences are simply not *needed*.

Secondly, there is the point that the inferentialist proposal may lead to an overly conservative view of theoretical progress. On both points, non-inferential 'looks' (as opposed to high-level inference) should not depend in any necessary way on background knowledge and theories. For one thing, this is because some basis must be available for sorting out how and where beliefs and theories differ, and for another thing, because evolution requires that some experiential beliefs simply do not need or require the input of high-level inferential mechanisms. Belief fixation, it is suggested, might go on at both levels. Despite the good sense of such considerations, however, the inferentialist proposal, not the observational account, has traditionally loomed large in discussions about experience and content.

Observationally-fixed beliefs clearly have some value where animal and infant experiences are concerned because they seem to capture aspects of experiential content in a way which the inferentialist proposal cannot do. However, can experiential content be understood *without* the significant imposition of high-level influences at all? And, what does a commitment to the observational view mean for an account of experience and content?

A brief digression: What has been called 'the observational account,' of course, has a familiar history. Particularly, the doctrine has its roots in the views of the empiricists and the logical positivists. The former held an epistemological thesis, that knowledge was derived from sense-data or 'impressions' which were direct and unmediated; the latter held a methodological thesis in the philosophy of science - that there was a fundamental distinction between observational evidence and theories and that science was built up from a non-theoretical, empirical foundation. Brute features of observation - colours, shapes, and so on - were supposed to be a means of providing inductive support and verification for theoretical propositions, and, in at least one view, the propositions had to 'mirror' these features of observation not only if they were to claim any support at all, but also if they were to be in any way meaningful.

Observational facts, on such views, were highly specific: the observational fact that 'there is red at a certain place and time' could be expressed in a single specific predicate, and the whole of scientific theorising had ultimately to be pinned on such 'factual' foundations. To a similar degree, sense-data theorists (equally taken with brute unmediated observations, though less interested in providing foundations for factual and meaningful, scientific propositions), used the idea to substantiate the belief that empirical support could give a basis for *knowledge* through *sensation*. Observations, after all, involved sensations, and if anything seemed non-theoretical, unmediated, non-inferential and direct, then sensation was surely a serious candidate.

Sensation, of course, was mostly taken to mean *sense-data* here. History has interpreted the observational account as expressing the view that experiential content is fixed by sense-data. On this version, there were qualities of 'red' perceived which were not wave-lengths or actual red objects, just as the sense datum of a bent stick in water was not the actual stick. A sense-datum was something directly perceived 'in between' the object and physical impression on the sense organs. It was a *particular;* a quasi-object of appearance. This was an odd notion, but it at least avoided the matter of inference in determining the content of perceptual structure.[12] There were, however, several severe problems with this kind of observational account.

Wilfred Sellars, for one, roundly rejected the observational approach of the sense-data theory for good reason. He declared that the sense-data theorists confused the idea of non-inferential particulars being sensed with inferential knowledge, giving the impression that sensing sense-data made 'epistemological knowledge rest on a 'foundation' of non-inferential matters of fact.'[13] This, however, was a 'mongrel' view, and could not be sustained. A 'particular' was not, by definition, inferential and could not be an item of knowledge; and knowledge of a 'fact' involved inference - the sense-data theorist wanted to have a bit both ways. Sellars also pointed out, somewhat more contentiously, that saying something *looked* red amounted to saying that something *was* red, specifically: 'knowing in what circumstances to place an object if one wishes to ascertain its colour by looking at it.'[14] This, in his view, amounted to already having 'a whole battery of concepts'[15] about such an object such that the *looks* relation made sense. He further claimed that any *looks* relation could be captured in terms of propositional content of a sentence which was true or false. Sellars's view was that 'seeing,' to some important extent, presupposes 'knowing.' So, Sellars attacked the sense-data view on the sophisticated 'high-level' terms of the inferentialist proposal. Sellars advances a complicated argument to this conclusion, which shall be dealt with in Chapter 10. Suffice to say for now that such criticisms slowly strangled the notion of sense-data historically, though the notion of observationality - that experience was in some important sense concept-free and 'given' remained.

There is an exegetical point to make here. It is clear that though it may have *influenced* the tradition of the observational account, the sense-data theory does not fully *characterise* it. This is a reason for distinguishing these doctrines by name. One can legitimately hold the view that some aspects of experiences are observationally fixed in some sense without holding that all observations have to be characterised by sense-data. The claims are, at least, *logically* separable. In the chapter on Sellars's inferentialist critique of the sense-data view much shall be made of this point. Let it be said for the time being that though positivism and the sense-data theory were historical antecedents of the observational account, there may be ways of keeping the idea that experiences are observationally fixed in some sense without simultaneously being

---

[12] Hence, Harman's summary of the innovation here: 'Many philosophers ... [say that such] data are about how things look, sound, taste, smell, feel and so on .... [they] go on to say that in ordinary cases of (visual) perception one does not *infer* that something is there, one simply *sees* that it is there ... there is no conscious reasoning in ordinary perception.' G. Harman, 'Epistemology', in E. C. Carterette and M. P. Friedman, *Handbook of Perception*, p. 53.
[13] Sellars, op. cit., p. 128.
[14] Ibid., p. 146.
[15] Ibid., p. 148.

committed to either view.

The observational account has been also closely allied thematically with *foundationalism,* though it need not have been. The reason for this association was mainly the stress that logical positivism and, particularly, the sense-data theory gave to the idea that knowledge was inevitably grounded on information derived from the senses. Sellars's attack was directed at this consequence of the observational account.

Another important point to be made here is that just as the observational account need not be taken together with the sense-data theory, likewise it need not logically embrace foundationalism. To say that experience is direct and not dependent in any necessary and sufficient way on the features of 'high-level' inference, *is not to say* that the senses provide the foundation of knowledge. It is entirely conceivable to claim that there is a sense in which experiential content is observationally fixed, without saying that knowledge is so fixed. Later discussion will bring out the importance of this point. Later discussion will also require a distinction to be made between different levels of knowledge corresponding to different levels of informational content.

The idea that experience is observational and not dependent on the various features of high-level inference can be seen to have a basis in these sorts of positivist and empiricist supports. And, Sellars's rejection of sense-data theories notwithstanding, the idea fits somewhat with intuitions too: for there doesn't seem to be anything sophisticated involved in one's seeing that an object looks red or looks longer than another. It wasn't obvious then, and it is still not obvious now. As mentioned previously, it seems even less obvious when unsophisticated animal and infant experiences are considered, because it seems hard to say that animals make conscious inferences from high-level background beliefs, concepts and theories etc., in the sense required. High-level features just do not seem to capture the kinds of contentful experiences had by such creatures. Rather, it seemed intuitive to refer to low-level animal and infant experiences as simply *sensational* experiences. Whether the observational account is true or not, Fodor's remarks about the value of observationally-fixed beliefs seemed to capture an important insight.

However, the terms of the inferentialist proposal push our intuitions in the opposite direction. For it is hard, on reflection, to see how observations or sensations *could* provide a basis for how experiences originate unless they involved inference from high-level features such as concepts and background knowledge. Sellars, and others, had an important point as well. The now orthodox view that experience *needs* high-level inference has been expressed in somewhat defiant terms:

> Knowledge of the world is based on inference. If there is knowledge of the world in perception, then there is inference in perception. If one is not conscious of the inference, then there is unconscious inference. If it would have to have been instantaneous, then inference takes no time. If one was not aware of the premises, then one can make inferences without being aware of the premises of those inferences.[16]

---

[16] Harman, op. cit., p. 54.

Of course, such a claim does not stipulate that all the previously mentioned high-level features are necessary for perception. However, as shown earlier, once some of the high-level features are embraced the rest follow naturally. The point for now is that the issue of the nature of experiential content seems to come down to a choice: either adopt the observational account with its unfortunate historical stress on positivism, the sense-data theory and foundationalism, or adopt the inferentialist proposal with its historically heavy stress on the importance of high-level influences as necessary and sufficient conditions of experiential content.

Which story is true: the observational account or the inferentialist proposal? Given that there are good *prima facie* reasons for adopting an observational account, and given that there are cases which do not seem to fit the inferentialist analysis, it seems natural to adopt an observational account of experiential content. Yet there did seem to be good reasons for keeping the terms of the inferentialist proposal as well. If - on the observational account - no high-level influences are needed, it is hard to see how Sherlock Holmes could have experienced anything meaningful at all. However, perhaps we don't need to make a choice: perhaps neither view is true and something else entirely is the best means of explaining experiential content. Perhaps it is best to try and have our cake and eat it too on this issue. It shall later be argued that there are more plausible reasons for adopting a third kind of view which combines the insights of both accounts.

It will be suggested later that there may be high-level and low-level *aspects* to experiential content, and that full-blooded knowledge and mechanisms of high-level inference etc., arise at only one level. Experience might be best understood in terms of an *amalgam* of several levels of observationally-fixed and inferentially-fixed content. In the passage above, Fodor seems to argue for experiential belief fixation going on at both levels. My question here is: why can't this be true of experiential content generally? Why, indeed, can't elements of both the inferentialist proposal and the observational account be true?

Experience and propositional content

We should be clear about the commitments of the inferentialist proposal at this point. As it turns out, there is more than a passing interest in this view: its commitments are many; its history is long and distinguished. It also implies more in the way of high-level features than has been mentioned up until now.

I have given the case for observationally and inferentially fixed beliefs. On the inferentialist proposal, inferential belief fixation involves more than just background knowledge. Beliefs, if not fixed by observation, must be fixed by various degrees of theory. Theory, in turn, presupposes *propositional* content which theories can be true of, and about which parties may claim agreement. Experiences, on this view, have contents which can be true or false. Thus, perceptual experience can be said to be inexorably propositional; or, at least, minimally theoretical in the required sense, where 'the required sense' amounts to involving *semantic* as well as epistemic features. Millar's treatment of perception being analogous with belief states is a useful statement of this view:

> The relation between experience and perception is in some ways

> analogous to that between belief and knowledge ... One can believe that *p* without knowing that *p* and so also one can have an experience of a ø without perceiving a ø ... In view of these analogies, it is tempting to regard experiences as being, like beliefs, intentional states, that is, states which have a *representational* content specifiable by means of propositional clauses. To say that a subject has an experience of a ø before him is to say that it seems or appears to the subject *that there is a ø before him*.[17]

Experiential content is certainly representational in some sense. Objects, like cigar-bands, are discriminated as being in certain spatial relationships to other objects; being a certain shape, going fast or, otherwise, being stationary. Experiences are 'gestalt-like' constructions of the world. But what of the alleged intentional or propositional features that experiences possess?

Experiences can be said to involve intentional states because one can undergo experiential states in the absence of the thing in question. Thus, according to some theorists, just as it makes sense to say that one can happen to believe that Beijing is in China while lacking all information about China, so it makes sense to say that one can seem to experience a ø while being absent from a ø. This situation would arise, for instance, in circumstances of perceptual mistakes or hallucinations; one can be convinced that one is experiencing a ø (it might seem to the subject that there is a ø before him) even if such a thing was not actually in one's field of view. Nevertheless, there still might be some sense in which one's experiential state in this case can be true or false even if one was not experiencing the thing in question. It is this sort of argument that provides reason for thinking that experiential content, like the content of beliefs, is actually *propositional* in some sense.

There is even a reason for saying that experiences might *necessarily* involve such propositional features, just as they are said to necessarily involve background knowledge and concepts. The reason is that just as several people might believe the same thing, they might also undergo an experience of the same logical type. So there must always be some common feature of beliefs (and experiences) by virtue of which a particular belief (and experience) could be commonly true or false. The intentional features of the belief (experience) must therefore 'point' to some recognisable or distinguishable *state*. David Armstrong has expressed this argument in the following way:

> Suppose, for instance, that nine men believe that the earth is flat. We have nine different beliefs. There is A's belief, B's belief, C's belief ... there are nine numerically different *states* .... In the case of the nine men, what is thought is the same thing in each case: that the earth is flat. It is just such a case that philosophers, at any rate, describe by saying that what the nine men think or entertain is the same *proposition*.[18]

Admittedly, Armstrong does not refer to experiential content here, but, for reasons mentioned earlier, if the argument goes through for the content of

---

[17] A. Millar, 'What's in a Look?,' pp. 83-4.
[18] D. M. Armstrong, *Belief, Truth and Knowledge*, pp. 38-9.

beliefs, it will go through for the content of experiences. On this argument, and on the inferentialist proposal, to be capable of a common response, experiences must be characterised by having some kind of intrinsic propositional content, just like that of the content of commonly held beliefs. Armstrong is actually one of those who thinks that the intentional content of experiences can be *equated* and *defined* in terms of beliefs. As he puts it: 'the intentionality of perception reduces to the intentionality of the beliefs acquired.'[19] So, on this view, to experience p is just to have a high-level belief about p. On Armstrong's version of the inferentialist proposal, high-level beliefs are both *necessary and sufficient* to capture experiential content. Armstrong's views shall be discussed later. The point made here is simply that if experiential states are said to be like belief states, then there is reason to think that they are, likewise, *propositional*.

Propositional contents are, of course, usually understood in terms of a *language*.[20] For something to seem ϕ is for it to be represented in ϕ *terms* - as a clause that such-and-such seems ϕ. That experiences can have tokenings in a language makes it possible for experiences to be true or false when a subject is not, in fact, perceiving the thing in question. So even if Holmes was under the influence of some potent hallucinogenic drug, he still might have had the experience of a cigar-band near Jones's body, because things might have been represented in some propositional way which he could express with language. One might say, in response to this kind of argument, of course, that there is a confusion between experience and language here; indeed, this is what shall be argued later on. It shall be argued that there is a confusion in the application of sophisticated 'high-level' features to experiential content generally. Objections aside for now, the point of this kind of move on the inferentialist view is simply to preserve the idea that if experience is propositional in some sense, it is also closely allied with the notion of a *language*.

There is, then, implicitly more to the inferentialist proposal than simply high-level knowledge and inference from high-level beliefs, concepts, theory, etc. As well as involving such things, experience requires representational features and this involves notions like propositions which can be expressed in the predicates of a language. So we might say that all experiences require elements of a language: an experience of a ϕ necessitates the concept of a ϕ, attendant background beliefs about ϕ and so on, as well as clauses in a language which represent ϕ when it seems to the subject that ϕ is the case. This is clearly a complicated addition to the inferentialist proposal but, on the above view, it is a necessary addition if it is to capture the similarities in the relations between experience and knowledge. For, on this view, experiential states, like knowledge states, clearly represent some expressible state of affairs the content of which is invariably fixed into sentences. The following kind of claim is symptomatic of this whole approach to the content of experiences, where high-level factors, especially the propositional content of language, are isolated as the *bearers* of experiential content:

---

[19] D. M. Armstrong, *A Materialist Theory of the Mind*, p. 211.

[20] As Armstrong notes: 'The etymology of 'proposition' suggests that it is fundamentally a linguistic notion. It is something proposed, something put forward, and so something asserted.' (1973) op. cit., p. 42.

> Let me ... call attention to the fact that the experience of having something look green to one at a certain time is, *in so far as it is an experience,* obviously very much like that of seeing something to be green, in so far as the latter is an experience. But the latter, of course, is not *just* an experience. And this is the heart of the matter. For to say that a certain experience is a *seeing that* something is the case, is to do more than describe the experience. It is to characterize it as, so to speak, making an assertion or claim, and - which is the point I wish to stress - to *endorse* that claim. As a matter of fact ... it is much more easy to see that the statement 'Jones sees that the tree is green' ascribes a propositional claim to Jones's experience and endorses it, than to specify how the statement *describes* Jones's experience.[21]

We can see now how the terms of the inferentialist proposal can gain a firm foothold on experiential content. If the high-level features are taken to be *necessary* features of experiences (or both necessary and sufficient features), then there is little resistance to the move of *conflating* experiential content with things which are demonstrably unlike experiences (e.g., language). Much shall be made of this conflation in Chapter 3. As we shall also see later, just as Sellars equates experience with the propositional content of a language - the process of 'making an assertion or claim' - so other theorists equate experience with *theories* and *representational* or *epistemic* states; 'high-level' features rather than low-level *sensations.* We have seen how Armstrong conflates experiential content with belief states. We shall see later how Churchland and Feyerabend closely align experiences with theory-ladenness. Indeed, a good number of recent materialist philosophers insist on claiming that the imposition of high-level features of one kind or another is both necessary and sufficient to capture contentful experiences. By 'capturing' contentful experiences, they mean that there is no observational or experiential residue beyond the imposition of high-level features.

In the passage just quoted, of course, it happens to be the propositional content of language which is seen as important to experiences, not how the experience is described as *looking.* As we shall see in Chapter 10, there is, on Sellars's view, nothing 'residual' which remains of such an experience beyond how the propositional content of a sentence is endorsed. The view that high-level features are the *only* features of interest in experiential content will be disputed in this book.

Itemising and distinguishing the features of experiential content

Several threads of the inferentialist proposal has been distinguished so far. On this view, experiential content is characterised by the possession of high-level factors: concepts, theories, background knowledge. Such contents can be characterised in other terms too: notably, by being representational states and

---

[21] W. Sellars, op. cit., p. 144. See M. Pendlebury for a contemporary defence of the experience as proposition view. 'Sense Experiences and their Contents: A Defence of the Propositional Account,' pp. 215-230. For a recent reaction to this view, see: W. Bechtel and A. Abrahamsen, 'Beyond the Exclusively Propositional Era,' in *Epistemology and Cognition.*

language-like propositional states. On the terms of the inferentialist proposal, all these things are necessary features of experiential content.

It is worthwhile itemising them briefly, from lesser to greater degrees of sophistication:

(i) *Representational content:* Objects and events have a certain projected, gestalt-like focus. We can discriminate objects because they do not (normally) merge with their surroundings, they reflect light, are stable, permanent features, spatio-temporally located and so on. This is as much a part of experiential content as our knowledge or interest in it. We can localise epistemic features of interest because our experiences have a certain representational content. Moreover, a content can be representational without being *recognised* as an object of a certain informationally specifiable sort. One can, for instance, vaguely recognise an object in the corner of a room *qua* object, but not be able to say exactly what that object might be.

(ii) *Background knowledge:* Experience needs background knowledge on the terms of the inferentialist proposal because experiences are underdetermined by available sensory information. To discriminate any perceptual scene one needs to localise features of epistemic interest, not just their representational features. (To Sherlock Holmes, it was the interest in evidence at the murder scene, not the colour of the walls or the ash in the fireplace - though these could have been of epistemic interest if Holmes had been inclined to note them. If Holmes did not bring to bear certain background knowledge to his experience, he might have non-selectively noted *everything* about the visual scene, which would mean that he would, in effect, have noted nothing of importance at all.)

(iii) *Concepts:* Perceived objects and events are mostly identified as things of certain kinds and labelled accordingly. Concepts allow experiences to be *determined* as objects of certain specifiable sorts. The cigar-band near Jones's body was identified and described (thought of) as a certain object. Concepts are means of applying *descriptive* meanings to certain features of the world. (More will be made of this in Chapter 2.) Because we see the world as being represented in a certain way, and we know what such-and-such is, we can label our experience as an experience *of a* ϕ. Holmes needed to bring some conceptual information to bear on his experience simply to (say) identify *this* represented object as being a dead body, etc. (Concepts obviously form part of background knowledge, though not an exclusive part. It is possible to bring to bear background knowledge to an experience, without being able to identify certain features of an experience conceptually - this is the phenomenon of *learning* new things. It is not possible, asymmetrically, to identify a thing conceptually and not bring background knowledge to bear on experience.)

(iv) *Theories:* Concepts and background knowledge are linked implicitly by theory and theories have the role of relating such items internally by means of inference. (The cigar-band was linked to the smoking habits of the assassin Holmes remembered who had been arguing with Jones prior to the murder scene, seen by an informant to be carrying a large ice-pick, etc.) Of course, theories also involve external relations - contingent laws and their implications. But in the sense relevant to this example, they have a distinct importance in making and utilising large scale epistemic connections which are useful for the fixation of experiential content.

(v) *Intentional/Propositional content:* Experiences are *states* of the mind in some sense and can be undergone in the absence of the thing experienced. According to some theorists, this intentional quality is propositional, and since propositions are often associated with language, experiential states are language-like in some sense. This implicit feature of the inferentialist proposal was outlined in the previous section. A more detailed and refined taxonomy of all these features will be outlined in the next chapter.

There are other features which influence experiential content which have not yet been mentioned but which deserve brief comment here. A main feature is what Sibley refers to as *focus of attention*. This is to be distinguished on his view from the physical condition when the eye muscles are in a certain state of optical focus on a certain object. As he notes, it is possible to experience something differently when what is optically out of focus is then experienced by attending to that thing. It is also possible to be optically focussed on something and not attend (and hence not 'see') it at all. This gives reason to think that, over and above the high-level influences on experiential content mentioned and the physical fact that one is focussed on and looking at an object, there is also the fact of *attentiveness* which can substantially affect how things are seen:

> Direction and focus [in perception] normally shift with shifts of attention; if attention is taken by something near and to one side while one is focusing on something distant and ahead, the eyes are likely to turn to the new object of attention and refocus on it. But with effort, we can, to some extent prevent this coordination of direction and/or focus with attention. We can deliberately attend to objects towards the periphery of our vision (and to how they look, blurry, of uniform colour, etc.) without turning our eyes; or, while focusing on the distant trees through the window, attend, without refocussing, to the (blurry) appearance of a scratch on the window pane. ... If we are physically focused on the trees a hundred feet off, we will ordinarily not notice scratches on the window through which we are looking, even though they are certainly visible to us *at that focus*. ... there are [also] cases where attention, even to whatever is in perfect optical focus, ... diminishes or is entirely absent. While listening intently, concentrating on a problem, or daydreaming, our attention may be partly or wholly engaged elsewhere, or engaged nowhere.[22]

Such cases are an important consideration for any account of experiential content. Something can look different (e.g., scratches on a window) depending on whether we are attending to it or not. But, as shall be argued much later, they do not support an inferentialist story, but rather, something far more subtle.

I have been trying to paint a certain picture of experiential content - the view of the inferentialist proposal. From what has been said so far, experience can be characterised in terms of the strictly high-level features discussed. Such features are linked to experiences as necessary and sufficient conditions, and it is not possible to speak of experiential content without implicitly employing features such as the above. As we have seen, 'high-level' features can include

---

[22] F. N. Sibley, *Perception: A Philosophical Symposium*, pp. 93-95.

background knowledge, concepts and theories, representational and propositional states, and even the notion of a language.

Of course, the various high-level elements of the inferentialist proposal can be distinguished and separated. It is plausible, for instance, that while inference from background knowledge may be necessary for an experience, there need not be a propositional content in any sense requiring clauses in a language. There *might* be such features in some circumstances, but equally, there need not be. A dog, for instance, clearly perceives things in terms of their spatial location, though one would be hard-pressed to say that a dog's experience involves language-like propositional features. In the sense in which 'proposition' was used in Sellars's claim previously, the word seems closely allied with the endorsement of *statements,* but obviously, animals like dogs do not use or endorse statements or claims, so it hardly seems as if propositional content *in this sense* can apply to their experiences. We shall see another sense in which 'proposition' may be used in this context below. For now, it is suggested that the 'high-level' propositional feature, at worst, does not apply to some experiences at all; at best, the notion stands in serious need of clarification. However, just as some experiences have propositional content and others do not, so some experiences are not *informational* experiences in the same way as Sherlock Holmes's experience of the cigar-band. Despite this, such experiences are still inferential in some important sense. Again, this objection can be levelled at the inferentialist treatment of animal experiences. Dogs, for example, clearly *learn* things about spatial location - they carry out avoidance behaviour; they bury objects and retrieve them. So there must be some kind of inference from background knowledge going on, even if - in the case of the dog's experience - there may not be judgement-like intentional features such that it seems to him *that* ø, in the same sense in which Holmes experienced *that* there was a cigar-band next to Jones's body. (If this example is unclear, consider the experience of an even less sophisticated animal such as a bee or a dragon-fly.) Such animals might experience the cigar-band in the sense of representing them as objects, but not represent them as anything informational.[23] The point is: there is a sense in which not all high-level features go together. For one thing, inference can be separated from informational content, and propositional content as it is expressed in terms of a language may, it seems, be involved in some cases, though not necessarily in other cases.

Some features of human experiences can also be separated like this too: an experience that something is 'to the left of' something else, for instance, scarcely requires a language-like propositional content, yet it is clearly *representational* in some sense. Even in the case quoted above, some aspects of a tree being experienced may not be captured propositionally - say, for instance, the tree seeming to be a certain distance from another object in one's visual field, or the tree occupying more of the visual field than another object. In this case, the experience has a certain representational content, yet there seems to be more to the experience than that. I will return to this example in Chapter 5 and

---

[23] 'Informational' here, of course, is ambiguous. Well-trained animals might represent some objects informationally, but not *judge* them as cigar-bands etc., in the sense which requires a linguistic ability. I shall expand on and distinguish such subtleties in Chapter 2.

look at it in some detail.

But there are yet still more complex cases: when one looks at an assemblage of objects with one eye closed and then looks at the same assemblage with both eyes open, it is clear that what is represented has not changed, though there seems to be something quite different about the experience. So, there seems more to an experience than simply what is represented and what is captured in terms of propositional content or background concepts and theories. Binocularity enables a considerable refinement of the perception of objects in terms of their depth relationships than does monocular vision - yet the high-level categories mentioned are of little help in capturing the content of the experiences. It is likely that other experiential features can be separated off and distinguished in a similar way. Such examples will later provide good reasons for accepting an alternative to both the observational account and the inferentialist proposal. It shall be suggested later that if high-level considerations do not influence experiential content *en bloc,* it may be better to consider a *weaker* view of the relation between experience and 'high-level' factors.

There is, however, yet another reason to consider some high-level features in isolation from the rest. This reason concerns the notion of a propositional content. The idea of a prepositional content in the context of a belief or an experience might not always be said to be captured by *linguistic* features at all, but in other terms. Propositions may not *necessarily* be tied to language use as is commonly supposed. The notion of a proposition is, admittedly, notoriously unclear, so we can easily accept this suggestion. One might even continue to agree that beliefs and experiences require some high-level propositional features but not propositional features in the character of a *language.*

Armstrong, for one, has argued just this - holding that perception requires beliefs and concepts and propositional content in the manner stipulated by the inferentialist proposal.[24] But he has also been careful to disassociate himself from the view that propositions are essentially *linguistic.* 'Propositions' he notes, 'have no special connection with language.'[25] Instead, Armstrong seems to closely attach the notion of a proposition to a representational state of some kind, not the tokenings of an experience in the form of a language.[26] Of course, animals clearly have a representational component to their experiences, so in this sense their experiences *can* have propositional content: most animals, even fairly unsophisticated ones, we would assume, do represent *something* in their

---

[24] Note, for instance, his remark: 'Perception [is] nothing but the acquiring of true or false beliefs ... To perceive that there is something that is red before us is to acquire the (true) belief that there is something red before us as a result of the causal action of that red thing on our minds .... Beliefs involve concepts. Acquiring the belief that a particular object is red involves the possession of the concept of red. Possession of the concept entails a general capacity of the perceiver ... to distinguish between things that are red and things that are not red. And so, a perceptual belief, which involves capacity for selective behaviour ... entails the possession of *higher-order* capacities.' op. cit., Armstrong, (1968) p. 339, italics mine.

[25] Ibid., p. 202.

[26] Armstrong actually claims that propositions are 'simply features of belief states' which function 'neither referringly nor predicatively.' See: Armstrong, (1973) op. cit., p. 46-7. Recently, Armstrong has been developing an ontology of 'states of affairs' to which propositions belong. See his paper 'A World of States of Affairs'.

experiences, even if we might well query whether or not their experiences had an *informational* content in the same sense as Holmes's experience.

Propositions need have no 'special connection' with language for a number of good reasons. Armstrong was right to distinguish propositional content from language. In *Belief, Truth and Knowledge,* Armstrong argues that high-level beliefs and thoughts are logically independent of the words that they are expressed in (see his Chapter 3). But the other important reason he advances to avoid this connection is that animals and pre-linguistic children have such things as beliefs and yet they do not have a facility with a language. So, the propositional content of *their* beliefs, at least, can't be language-like. By parity, of course, their experiences too might involve a propositional content which is not language-like. The relevant sense in which both beliefs and experiences might be fixed by high-level propositional features does not then *necessarily* hang on the acquisition of a language - one might hold the inferentialist proposal without it. This seems especially plausible in the case of colour experiences like that of red or green; for it is quite unclear how the propositional content of such an experience *could* be language-like (if, indeed, such experiences can be characterised as being propositional at all). Once again, it seems, such 'high-level' features can easily be distinguished and separated.

The point here is not that *no* high-level features are brought to bear on experiences, just that it is unclear to what *degree* they are relevant. If high-level features are relevant to experiences only by degrees, then this amounts to a much *weaker* version of the inferentialist proposal than that expressed earlier where *all* the high-level features were seen as both necessary and sufficient for experiential content. However, it may be that this position is wrong: it may be that no such high-level features are *necessary* for certain kinds of experiential content at all, even if all the high-level features are generally present together in normal *human* experience. Moreover, if high-level features are only relevant by degrees and can be effectively stripped from experiences, then there may be a case for claiming that the individuation of each leaves behind an experiential residue. If so, then the various high-level features are not necessary *and sufficient* for content at all. I shall try to argue for both these points later on.

The point just mentioned enables distinctions to be made between various forms of inferentialism. If someone like Armstrong, for instance, can agree with the thrust of the inferentialist proposal and yet eschew the matter of language, then it would seem that some of the various features of high-level inference (in this case, propositional content and language) are logically separable: one can plausibly claim that *some* experiences are propositional and attached to the endorsing of certain statements (Sellars's view) or one can claim that some experiences are propositional in some other sense not involving language (Armstrong's view). Moreover, some experiences might be taken as representational and yet not *informational* in any sophisticated sense at all (e.g., a rats or a dragon-fly's experience of the cigar-band near Jones's body). Indeed, there seem to be several possible combinations in the ways in which high-level influences can be brought to bear on experiential content, and - correspondingly - several possible degrees of inferentialism.

One of the important points to be brought out of the above discussion is this: What was described as being fairly uncontentious before (that propositional contents are language-like) can now be seen as a matter of serious debate, even among theorists who are otherwise sympathetic to the terms of the inferentialist proposal. This issue is worth spending more time on before continuing.

The continuum idea

Armstrong's concern, in the earlier passage is with the content of belief states, not experiences. According to Armstrong, belief states can be characterised as propositional states. But, as we have seen, on the inferentialist proposal the case of beliefs and the case of experiences actually run parallel: because experiences fix belief states, what can be said of the one kind of content can rightly be said of the other. So if one accepts the inferentialist proposal and the view that propositional content is characterised by language, it seems that one could hold that the content of experiences, like the content of beliefs, are likewise characterised by language. But such a view would then make nonsense of the idea that animals and infants have experiences in any important sense. Although this argument clearly follows on the inferentialist proposal, it seems that it would leave anyone who held this view in a rather absurd position.

However, as we have seen, this problem can be overcome easily: by saying that *some* propositional contents are language-like and some are not. So again: some high-level features are easily separated from others. Someone sympathetic to the propositional requirement of the inferentialist proposal, might thus take the line that there are two senses of 'proposition': one that is closely tied to language and one which isn't. It might also be suggested that the propositional content of animal/infant beliefs and experiences are *inferior* to the propositional content of adult beliefs and experiences for just this reason. Someone who wanted to keep the emphasis of the inferentialist proposal might take this *inferiority* line on animal and infant beliefs and experiences - ruling as insignificant or irrelevant any content which did not possess the required high-level features specified.

But a question can be raised here: does the argument that animals and infants might have propositional contents which are not language-like necessarily rule as *inferior* or *irrelevant* these kinds of beliefs or experiential contents? Armstrong, for one, does not think so. Attacking the possibility that animals and children might have 'logically secondary' cases of beliefs because of this deficit, he advances the view that such creatures might 'lie along a certain scale or continuum'[27] with language-using humans on one end of the scale and amoebas at the other. Although it might be clear where to attribute linguistic competence on such a scale, it is less easy to see where to attribute notions like beliefs. But this doesn't rule such beliefs as thus having a necessarily *inferior* content. To suggest otherwise would be to already assume the proposition-as-language-like model. Instead, in a marginal note, Armstrong tentatively advances the idea that belief content attribution can be understood as being ascribable by *degrees* (hence, the 'continuum' idea). The point here is that the high-level propositional requirement of belief states, which is built into the inferentialist proposal, may well be too strong.

Presumably, the same would go here *mutatus mutandis* for experiential content: *if* one assumes that experiences require a high-level background of

---

[27] D.M. Armstrong, op. cit., (1973) p 30.

propositional features, then such features cannot be language-like unless one is prepared to rule out animal and infant experiences. And one can't do this on pain of begging the question in favour of the bias towards language. But there may be a way of ascribing significant experiential content to animals and infants by dropping the inferentialist proposal and adopting a more graduationist account; allowing experience to feature by degrees - in terms rather like a *continuum*. On this revised account, experiential content may be characterised in a number of different ways, not simply and exclusively in terms of features of high-level inference, and, in particular, propositional content. Such high-level considerations may be *part* of the story, but not all of it. Moreover, using only high-level features as criteria for experiences may be as dangerous and misleading as using language-like propositional content as a full and adequate characterisation of the nature of beliefs.

This point can be linked to the previous concern about the strictly 'high-level' emphasis given by the inferentialist proposal in the context of outlining an account of experiential content. What seemed a plausible analysis for the experience Sherlock Holmes had of the cigar-band near Jones's body, we saw, did not seem plausible for the dog's experience of the same scene. True, the dog must have spatially represented something, and formed inferences from previous experience, memory, etc. Even so, here it did not seem appropriate to label all experiential contents as being influenced by all the sophisticated high-level factors mentioned; it did not seem plausible that the dog underwent the appropriate *reasoning*. Rather, it seemed that where some high-level features were relevant to the dog, others were not. This seems particularly plausible in the case of propositional contents having the character of a language, for such things are obviously not a feature of dog experiences. It does seem that the inferentialist proposal has taken things too far: there might be rather less in some experiential contents than the inferentialist proposal would have us believe.

This argument is plausible even in this very rough form. What it might indicate is that something is wrong with the proposal that necessarily and only attributes high-level contents to the low-level experiences of unsophisticated organisms. Such categories simply do not always capture the experiences of such creatures. What it also shows is that comparisons with cases of high-level influences which legitimately capture the experiential content of sophisticated creatures who *can* use language is inherently unfair: it is something of a category mistake; an error in explanatory overkill. Moreover, just because an account of how experiences originate in terms of high-level considerations doesn't altogether capture animal and infant experiences, does not mean that they have no experiences, or that their experiences are inferior in some sense. Even though some experiences might be characterised in terms of high-level features, these features may not simultaneously capture *low-level* experiences which might escape such an analysis. The model we are using of experiential content - the inferentialist proposal - may be faulty, or just plain wrong.

What we have looked at in the previous sections is an account of experiential content in terms of high-level inferential features. It seems now, however, that a serious alternative is emerging to the view that experience *necessarily* involves the imposition of such features, or the observational view that experiences require no such input at all. This alternative holds that the high-level features are relevant by *degrees,* and thus, do not necessarily underpin experience at all levels - only experiences of a greatly sophisticated kind. So, although Sherlock Holmes's experience of the cigar-band near Jones's body may be, in some sense, fully characterised in terms of inference from background knowledge, propositional content and representational features, this sort of analysis might not be altogether possible of very unsophisticated animal experiences or of the difference in our experience of an assemblage of objects viewed with one eye and then both eyes. The nature of such experiences seems to require a far more subtle and elaborate account of the bearing of the so-called high-level influences on experiences.

The point of this section is not to argue that propositional content must be non-language-like, or even that propositional content is necessary for experience as the inferentialist proposal assumes. It is unclear what propositions are, and this difficult question will be avoided in this book. The point about propositions has been raised only to bring out Armstrong's suggestive analogy of a continuum. Armstrong's suggestive remark will be used here as an idea which needs development in the context of an account of experiential content.

The useful thing about this notion is that it might allow us to think of the content of experiences as being at interestingly distinct levels without having to say that one kind of content has to be inferior to another 'higher-level' content. It may even give us reason to think that the inferentialist proposal, as it stands, is actually *false.*

Rationality and the inferentialist proposal

It is not sufficient, on the terms of the inferentialist proposal, that only *some* experiences involve propositional features, representational features or inference from background knowledge. It is also not appropriate that the various high-level features can be separated and individuated in the way which we have seen. On the proposal being examined, it must remain true that *all* experiences require *all* the high-level features specified. The inferentialist says that the combination of such high-level features - background knowledge, theory, propositional and representational features - are either necessary conditions of experiential content, or both necessary and sufficient conditions. Experiences are, on this view, propositionally specifiable, representational states, necessarily underpinned by inference from background knowledge, concepts and theories.

Part of the reason the inferentialist proposal is so inflexible is that it is a doctrine that has strong historical roots. The view goes back to Descartes' rationalism and his stress on the uniqueness of the human species. The human species was unique in Descartes' view, centrally because of its ability to employ a language. The human beings' greater knowledge and theoretical base also distinguished them intellectually from animals. On this view, such high-level intellectual abilities were the deciding features of an organism's claim to *rationality*. Along with rationality came the fruits of human beings' superior understanding and experience of the world around him. For Descartes, where animals were merely mindless automata responding to stimuli from proximal cues, human beings could actually *discern* features of the world, discriminate amongst them and use things in the world to their own ends. Part of the reason why human beings were superior to animals was that only they could *experience* the world, not merely *respond* to it. And the key to this difference was their knowledge, theoretical understanding and, particularly, their facility with language - in other words, the 'high-level' features mentioned above. [28]

Much later, Kant expressed a similar view of the importance of high-level intellectual attributes when giving his account of human rationality. Keeping a deferential tie with the stress Descartes gave to language, his view became an explicitly *judgement-focused* analysis of human rationality as well as human experience. Humans were rational and could experience the world because they made intellectual judgments. Kant thus shared Descartes' view that the human species could be individuated as vastly superior creatures compared with animals because language, intellect and knowledge distinguished them from the 'lower' species.

Kant was far more explicit about how these high-level features distinguish human beings from other animals. More particularly, he saw there to be 'a logical connection between 'intuition' and 'understanding', that is, between sensory and intellectual capacity.'[29] This insight formed the basis for his account of epistemology and philosophy of mind as well as his account of experience. For him, the intellectual input from the understanding was logically connected with the sensory capabilities of a sophisticated organism, because without this, an organism would be unable to make relationships and form inferences from one moment to the next. Such features then, operated as necessary *a priori* conditions for manipulating the material of sense. Kant called these intellectual features 'categories' of the understanding and called the operation of these categories in each individual case 'judgements'. For Kant, of course, making a 'judgement' involved bringing to bear the whole gamut of high-level *a priori* knowledge to bear on experience - Euclidean geometry, space and time - the works. In this sense, Kant's philosophy constituted an important extension of rationalist thought.

Both Descartes and Kant were major players in developing what has been called 'the inferentialist proposal', so it was very natural that the importance of both *language* and *intellectual manipulation* were retained as necessary features separating the rationality, and the experiences, of man from animals.[30] Both became *a priori* necessary features of experiential content. The importance of such high-level features has persisted and can be found as a theme in the work of the early Wittgenstein, Davidson, Armstrong, Feyerabend, Sellars, Churchland, Hanson and Stich, to name but a few. Even a cursory glance at much of contemporary analytic philosophy will bear out this point.

---

[28] For an exposition and an attack on Descartes' views on animals, see: J. Cottingham, '"A Brute to the Brutes?": Descartes' Treatment of Animals', pp. 551-9. See also, by the same author: *Descartes*, pp. 107-110.

[29] J. Bennett, *Rationality*, p. 41.

[30] Routley points out that this tradition may well have been a product of 'a long, vigorous, and perhaps, dominant, tradition in Western Philosophy, ... which though weakened in the empiricism of Hume and Bentham, reaches current philosophy through both (Cartesian) rationalism and through idealism.' He cites Hegel, not Kant, as a representative of the latter influence: 'What distinguishes man from the beasts is *the faculty of Thought* manifested and first laid down in ... human language.' Hegel's *Science of Logic*, p. 39. See R. Routley: 'Alleged Problems in Attributing Beliefs and Intentionality in Animals', p. 412.

Donald Davidson, for instance, has recently argued that only language users can have concepts like beliefs, and S. P. Stich has echoed this view by suggesting that belief attribution is possible only in situations where all the features of such beliefs can be 'isomorphically mapped' in terms comprehensible by language users.³¹ To isolate *language use* as a criterion for conceptual sophistication is to make a substantial commitment to the terms of the inferentialist proposal. Similarly, as we have already seen, Wilfred Sellars has argued that all mental content attributions, including that of perceptual experience, can be captured, without residue, in terms of propositional contents which can be true or false. Armstrong has also claimed the same for perception in terms of the propositional content of belief states.[32] Feyerabend, to take a different case, has declared that the idea of a 'sensing subject' without the mediation of *theory* is 'incomprehensible.'[33] And, somewhat in sympathy with Feyerabend, Churchland has contended that mental content is, by nature, a *theory* which can be discarded and replaced wholly with scientific descriptions.[34] Much earlier, of course, Wittgenstein was famous for saying in the *Tractatus:* 'Whereof we cannot speak we must pass over in silence.'[35] The stress on language, theory, representational states and propositions is obvious.

The emphasis in each of these cases conveniently displays how the several high-level features of the inferentialist proposal have made their mark on contemporary approaches to the issue of mental content and experience in general. Moreover, the various high-level features are mostly found together: Churchland's eliminative materialism, for instance, stresses the theoretical dependence of mental content, but he also claims that any such theory is held as a network of integrated *sentences* which are held true as a pattern of integrated holistic beliefs. Sellars holds to the view of *psychological nominalism:* that there is no awareness outside what can be expressed in the terms of a theoretically and epistemically loaded language. Feyerabend has claimed, counterintuitively, that the only difference between a blind man and a seeing man is that 'one uses a different part of [a] theory (or some of the consequences of [a] theory) as his observation language.'[36] Each of these views shall be examined in detail in subsequent chapters.

Such views demonstrate what might be called the rationalist origins of the inferentialist proposal. The stress placed on the high-level aspects of experiential content will be obvious when they are considered later. The point should be made here that all of these views take a *pejorative* line on content which cannot be captured in the high-level terms mentioned. In this sense, they approach the issue as an inferentialist might approach the issue of animal and infant cognition - they view any other approach as tapping an inferior, irrelevant

---

[31] D. Davidson, 'Thought and Talk', in S. Guttenplan (ed) *Mind and Language,* pp. 7-23; S. P. Stich, 'Do Animals have Beliefs?,' pp. 15-28.

[32] W. Sellars, op. cit., D. M. Armstrong. *Perception and the Physical World,* passim.

[33] P. K. Feyerabend, 'Science Without Experience', in *Realism, Rationalism and Scientific Method.*

[34] P. M. Churchland, *Matter and Consciousness.*

[35] L. Wittgenstein, *Tractatus Logico Philosophicus,* § 7.

[36] P. K. Feyerabend, op. cit., p. 33.

or even a non-existent resource. This will be obvious when Churchland's views are considered; less obvious in the other cases.

It was mostly this rationalist background to the inferentialist proposal which, as Bennett says, makes it possible to 'swallow in a greedy and undigested lump, the Kant-Wittgenstein stress upon language.'[37] One might add to this lump the other high-level features specified, since it is clear that the rationalist influence contains much more than just a stress on language. Also, as will be recognised from some of the above views, the 'undigested lump' has come to signify more than simply the distinguishing features of rationality and a way of separating the province of man and nature, but also a way of understanding what any account of experiential content must fulfil. Such a view holds that the distinguishing and essential features of *all mental content attributions* are the 'high-level' features stipulated. And these features turn largely on the early importance Kant and Descartes jointly gave to language and high-level intellectual manipulation.

It is partly this rationalist influence on the nature of experiential content which will be questioned in this book. The aim is to show how high-level features, which influence the having of experiences, can be detached from their association with the rationalist origins mentioned. Rather than adopting the inferentialist proposal *holus bolus,* it is better to keep elements of it in the form of a substantially modified account of the relation between experience and content.

I have already mentioned three reasons for making this move; reasons which shall later be developed as arguments.

Firstly, as we have seen, it does seem obvious that sophisticated high-level features need not feature in dog experiences, let alone in the experiences of organisms lower down the phylogenetic tree. So there seems little case for insisting that the inferentialist proposal be adopted as an *overall* strategy for understanding how experiences are engendered. There may, instead, be a case for combining elements of the observational account with elements of the inferentialist proposal.

Secondly, since each of the high-level features can be individuated and separated, it seems unlikely that the various high-level features can *jointly* account for the nature of experiential content - something a more subtle account might achieve. The point is not that because the various features can be separated the inferentialist proposal cannot account for experiential content (for wholes can have properties over and above their parts). The point is that if it can be shown that each of the high-level features are neither necessary nor sufficient for certain experiences, then there is a case for claiming that individuating each leaves behind an experiential residue. It will be argued that any account of the relation between experience and content has to be seen in the light of evolutionary principles and the nature of the complexity of differing species and their species-specific cognitive architecture. Furthermore, there is a need for low-level *sensational* experiences when this is considered. (This, in turn, will provide a connection between an attack on the inferentialist proposal and a legitimation of property dualism.) A graduationist account will more readily include these considerations.

---

[37] Bennett, op. cit., p. 2.

Thirdly, it has been intimated that there is a more general problem with the inferentialist proposal as a fully-fledged account of experiential content. If the inferentialist proposal is true, then there is hardly any sense in which experiential content can be observationally fixed. All experiences should, instead, presuppose theory, knowledge, concepts and propositional contents, even - experiences like the experience of the colour red. This seems less than obvious. Such things seem to have more to do with the observational situation than high-level influences like knowledge, theories and language. Indeed, there is a good case for claiming that 'observational' features of low level experiences such as colours have survival value too, independent of such influences. If the inferentialist proposal claims that such high-level features are *necessary and sufficient* precursors to any kind of experiential content, then something may well have gone astray.

These themes shall be taken up in the following chapters. In Chapter 3, it will be revealed just how things may have gone astray by showing how experience has been conflated with language. This conflation is premised on a simple philosophical error. In Chapter 4, it will be examined whether experiential content can be fully captured in terms of representational content; specifically, in terms of the propositional content of belief states (I will be looking in detail at the views of Armstrong in this connection). In Chapter 10, Sellars's claim that rejecting sense-data theory automatically goes with accepting an inferentialist account heavily dependent on the propositional content of statements is assessed. In Chapters 9, and 11, the ways in which experiential content has been said to be theory dependent will be questioned.

My response to the inferentialist proposal, finally, is not to rule out the application of such high-level features, but to modify and limit their influence. Chapter 5 argues the case for the experiential residue that escapes the inferentialist analysis, whereas Chapter 7 takes up the issue of animal experiences. The claim arising from these chapters will be that there is still an important sense in which experience can be said to originate observationally. The revised account I shall be making - the continuum account - will rest convincingly well with a modular view of mental content which is outlined in Chapter 8, and a property dualist theory of the mind which is outlined in Chapter 12. It will also reconcile the traditional dichotomy of the inferentialist proposal and the observational account and will provide grounds for a more subtle reading of Kant's views in Chapter 6.

Conclusion

In this chapter, the case for the inferentialist proposal was presented. This account emphasises the importance of the high-level influences on experiences. It was demonstrated that this view has had a long history stemming from early rationalism. Each of the high-level features were itemised and shown to be important features of experiential content on this view. An alternative to this view was also described briefly and was counterpointed to the inferentialist view. Each of these approaches has some merit. Just as it seems necessary for experiences to be organised conceptually, so too does it seem necessary that some aspects of experiential content depend on features of the observational situation rather than wholly cognitive factors. The case of conceptually unsophisticated animal and infant experience was discussed in this connection. The claim here is that the nature of content need not be understood in terms of a dilemma: either entirely inferential or non-inferential. Instead, a broader combinatory position needed to be sought. It was argued that a combinatory position might best be developed by taking Armstrong's suggestion of a continuum seriously.

A final point: the inferentialist proposal stipulates 'high-level' features as either a *necessary* condition or a *necessary and sufficient* condition for experiential content. The distinction here is taken to be degrees of emphasis of a single radical doctrine. However, the importance of this distinction for any attempt to abandon the inferentialist proposal was not explored in detail.

It is clear that the distinction is an important one. The *necessary condition* thesis is a legacy of Kant's views, and a rejection of this claim on its own is not enough to successfully attack the claims of the inferentialist proposal. On Kant's account, the sensory manifold was available in experience prior to its integration and synthesis by the forms of intuition and the categories. So, on Kant's view, there is more to experiential content than simply 'high-level' features; there is also a sensory manifold. However, the high-level features were necessary for experience on this view, because the manifold itself was unformed and unstructured. What remains after separating the high-level features from the sensory manifold is not any kind of *content*. To Kant, experiential content amounted to sensory manifold *plus* the imposition of the categories and forms of intuition.

By contrast, the *necessary and sufficient* thesis is a view common to many recent materialist philosophers such as Churchland, Armstrong, Harman, Sellars and Feyerabend. This amounts to the view that *all there is* to experiential content are the high-level features specified by the inferentialist proposal. There is no unformed sensory content outside the imposition of the high-level features. Although this more radical view shall be examined in the following chapters I shall also treat the Kantian position in some detail in Chapter 6.

The necessary condition thesis should not be confused with the necessary and sufficient condition thesis. However, the arguments to be advanced against the inferentialist proposal shall strike at both views. It shall be claimed that there are *contentful experiences* that do not contain the high-level features emphasised by the inferentialist proposal. So, low-level experiential content can be importantly separated from high-level content. Claiming this enables me to hit the necessary condition side of both targets. Against the necessary and sufficient condition thesis, it will be argued that there is more to experience than high-level features; against the necessary condition thesis, it will be argued that low-level experiences are actually *contentful*.

2 A continuum theory of content

[Man is] a mixture of all things and an orderly combination of contraries.[1]

A taxonomy of experiential content

Introduction

In the previous chapter it was suggested that an adequate account of content should acknowledge that high-level influences can occur in degrees, rather than in all-or-none terms. It was also suggested that conceptually unsophisticated animal and infant experiences need some sort of account too. The burden of the theory of content that is advocated here takes as its starting point that there are low-level features as well as high-level features of experiences. Experiences can occur in degrees of sophistication anywhere along a content continuum.

An otherwise sophisticated 'high-level' experience, of (say) a cigar-band being near Jones's body, can also have low-level aspects which can't be captured in any of the high-level terms mentioned. The continuum account thus holds what shall be called a *complexity* thesis: some experiences have low-level aspects *and* high-level aspects. Moreover, the relationship between high and low-level aspects is asymmetrical: an experience need not have high-level aspects *but all experiences have low-level aspects*. Several levels of experience will now be distinguished in some detail.

Linguistic propositional judgements

We have seen the problem that arose with the characterisation of a proposition in relation to experiential content. We can use this confusion as the starting point for our taxonomy. On the one hand, it seemed plausible that Sherlock Holmes could have been in some state which was explicitly tokened in a language and which could thus be true or false in absence of the thing

---

[1] M. Aurelius, *Meditations*, VII, 48.

experienced. In this version, the experience had propositional content in a sense which was *language-like*. On the other hand, it also seemed plausible that the notion of a propositional content need not be so closely tied to a language. This was especially so because some (lower) animals might also represent their experiences propositionally in some sense, though without tokening their experiences in a language. Both of these views (and much else besides) can be true on the account presented.

We can begin by defining some experiential contents as having content explicitly tokened in some kind of language (or a language-of-thought).[2] Call this level a *linguistic propositional judgement.* An example of this kind is Sherlock Holmes and his experience of the cigar-band near Jones's body. For Holmes, having the experience meant that he then underwent some kind of tokened, expressible, representational state. It is not that his experience put him *in* this tokened state; rather, the experience brought about his tokening of that state, because it necessarily involved the imposition of 'high-level' propositional factors. His experience had content which was expressed (or thought) in words (or tokens) such as 'cigar-band', 'Jones's body', etc., and this involved the imposition of background knowledge, concepts, theory and so on. To avoid confusion, the term 'proposition' shall be used only in relation to this level of content and no other. The account being developed will not make extensive use of this notion. 'Proposition' is defined as a strictly *linguistic* feature of content.

Representational judgements

Holmes's experience was also *represented* as certain structural features in his visual field; that is, as certain discernible things distinct from their surroundings. This, presumably, is precisely the way in which fairly sophisticated animals like dogs might perceive such scenes. This level shall be called the level of *representational judgements.* This level of content can be distinguished from the linguistic propositional judgement in the respect that it is not explicitly tokened in a language or a language of thought, though it is implicitly structured by virtue of being an organised perception of some kind. (This, of course, can occur in degrees - a rather less sophisticated organism, for example, a dragon-fly or a bee, might structurally represent rather less in its visual scene than Holmes or a dog does, because it has less sensitive perceptual equipment - or more sensitive depending on the kind of experience in question.)

This kind of 'gestalt'-like structuring of experience which is not linguistically tokened, was presumably what Armstrong had in mind by his use of the term 'proposition.' Armstrong's rejection of this term in relation to *linguistic* propositional judgements was mentioned earlier. His claim was that propositional content is not necessarily tied to the notion of a language. As

---

[2] The essentials here do not matter for my account. The language-of-thought hypothesis might be true, if by it, is meant that one can represent certain *aspects* of one's experience in some tokened form or other. This might be true of aspects of animal experiences as much as ours. (A dog might have some mental token ø, by which he represents 'master'.) Where I diverge from this is in how less sophisticated aspects of experiences can be represented. (It does not seem obvious that all aspects of experiences need to have mentalese tokenings, but more on this below.)

mentioned, however, the use of the term 'proposition' will be reserved for the strict linguistic sense only; I shall be using the term 'representational judgement' to capture Armstrong's sense of 'proposition.' The distinction between linguistic propositional judgments and representational judgements is thus important because it avoids the ambiguities in the term 'propositional content.'

It is not being suggested that by making these distinctions both kinds of 'judgements' cannot occur jointly. Demonstrably, they *can* occur jointly. It seems obvious, for instance, that Holmes may form a representative judgement (have a certain gestalt-like experience) as well as token such features in a language. For some organisms, and in some circumstances, both kinds of judgements can occur together. Of course, by parity, they need not: Holmes might, for instance, have experienced certain structurally organised features, without tokening them *explicitly* in a language as certain types of things, even if he *represented* them implicitly as organised features in his experience. He may have been day-dreaming or concentrating heavily on having a conversation with Watson, for example. (This brings out the important influence of *attention* in fixing features of experiential content, but more on this later.)

The distinction made between linguistic propositional judgments and representational judgements is not meant to suggest that subjects are always fully *conscious* of the contents of their experiences. Linguistic propositional contents do not correspond exactly to 'conscious' experience and representational contents do not correspond exactly to the converse. A representational judgement may be a conscious experiencing in which certain structural features represented are explicit. Holmes, or his dog, may consciously discern certain spatially represented objects in certain places etc., by the very act of experiencing some scene. But a representational judgement may also be of another character entirely: i.e., as a projection which is not explicitly conscious; i.e., as an implicit - and only partly conscious - 'noticing'. For instance, someone might project a visual array in space without being completely cognisant of what it is that is being projected. Something like this seems to be going on in 'tactile vision' experiments. In a similar way, features of an experience need not necessarily be consciously tokened in a language, but may, nonetheless, be represented in linguistic-propositional form.

Although some very sophisticated organisms (such as Sherlock Holmes) *might* unconsciously token their experiences, (Holmes might *think* 'cigar-band' in some way in 'mentalese' without noticing he did or intending to do so), there is a sense in which an experience can also be left untokened but nonetheless 'represented' in some other way. (Presumably other animals do this and so might Sherlock Holmes in certain circumstances were he distracted or otherwise occupied.) Consider also the example of waking up in a strange place: in such a situation one might project certain spatially represented objects without tokening them as objects of certain types (a 'thing' in a vague direction to the left of another 'thing'). There is thus a clear need to distinguish linguistic propositional judgments from representational judgements.

Informationally representational judgements

There are two distinguishable senses of experience so far - a linguistic propositional content and a representational content. Further complications arise, however, when one considers some of the high-level influences on experiences beyond that of representational and propositional content. Such considerations force us to extend the taxonomy. Consider, for example, concepts and background knowledge. It would seem likely that an experiencing organism such as Holmes might form a representational judgement without bringing to bear a concept or background knowledge of that particular thing. (He might recognise, for instance, that the cigar-band is *near* the body without recognising the objects as a cigar-band and a body.)[3] In another circumstance, of course, he *may* bring such specific information to bear on the experience. To take the opposite extreme, a very unsophisticated animal might not have the conceptual equipment to bring such information to bear on its experience at all - it may be only able to represent certain features of its experience without conceptualising or knowing what they are in any way. (Consider a dragonfly's experience of Jones and the cigar-band.)[4] To enable a distinction to be drawn between such clearly less sophisticated cases, and the representational judgement case mentioned above, call an experience which *does* involve these features, an *informational representational judgement* and call an experience which doesn't involve such features simply a *representational judgement*. This allows the possibility that some experiences can involve more or less representational content than others.

Consider also the influence of *theory* in this context. Obviously, some experiences which are linked with background knowledge can also be crucially linked with theory. That is, an experience with informational content can also be linked with *large scale* epistemic connections. Such connections might involve a good deal of complicated references to historical information or analogies, or - in the case of Holmes - just plain off-the-cuff ingenuity. Such large scale connections are clearly not possible in the experiences of unsophisticated animals and infants, but equally, it need not be so in the case of Holmes's less astute partner, Watson. Watson may 'miss the point' of experiencing the cigar-band so close to Jones's body and not make the theoretical connection between the murder and the suspected perpetrator of the crime. For some organisms, then, an experience can involve *theoretically informational judgements,* in the sense that large scale epistemic connections, or theories are involved.

Again, however, this need not be always so. Even Holmes, at times, (say, when he is sleepy or tired) may not bring to bear this theoretical input on his experience, even though he may still identify the cigar-band as a certain informational content and represent the cigar-band as a certain object (he may also 'token' it in a linguistic propositional judgment simultaneously).The

---

[3] He has the concept of 'near' in this case of course, but this is saying something rather less sophisticated than saying that he forms a representative judgement of the cigar band near Jones's body.

[4] Though again: a more sophisticated, well-trained animal such as a dog might be able to know (conceive of) features of its experience (e.g., its master). It is not being suggested that only humans can make such determinate judgements, but that experiential complexity trails off by degrees, from more to less sophisticated content with respect to their degree of phylogenetic sophistication. On the most plausible story, most lower animals bring rather less 'high-level' input to their experiences than humans do to theirs, but this should not rule out that some animals, in some circumstances, can localise some cognitively sophisticated experiential features.

continuum theory allows that sometimes an experience can have certain degrees of high-level content at different times, or different degrees of content at the same time for equal or distinct experiencing organisms such as Holmes, Watson and the dog.

The above cases have considered the various 'high-level' features and their connection with experiential content. They are obvious considerations, but surprisingly, the inferentialist proposal has traditionally not admitted such distinctions. This is reason enough to make them plain now. Linguistic propositional judgements have been distinguished from representational judgements, and informational representational judgements from theoretically informational ones. Since there seem to be good reasons for saying that each and all of these kinds of features can occur in experiences (sometimes in one and the same experience), it is suggested that we call these features, high-level *aspects* of experiential content. On the continuum account presented, experiential content can have varying degrees of such high-level content specificity. It remains to be seen if there is any other kind of content that can be present in experiences which is not exclusively 'high-level'.

Non-representational aspects

We can also extend this kind of taxonomy in the opposite direction, and consider different degrees of *low-level* content specificity. A few examples of this should suffice, since these kinds of features will be treated in more detail later. For now, the suggestion is that at this low-level of content, an experience can have, what shall be called, *non-representational* or *sensational* aspects. Take the case, once again, of Holmes's experience of the cigar-band near Jones's body. Even though Holmes may be said to make a certain representational judgement in this instance, (and perhaps even a linguistic propositional judgement simultaneously), it can also be true that his experience has features which cannot be captured in any such representational/propositional terms.

Perhaps, for instance, Holmes registers certain colour hues of the visible objects he sees which suddenly change (become brighter) when a shaft of light enters the window, or perhaps he surveys the scene first with one eye open and then opens the other. In either case, something about the experience changes, and it is not what can be captured in the high-level terms already mentioned. Further, consider what an unsophisticated creature such as a rat might experience in the above situation. Presumably it experiences nothing theoretically representational or informationally representational, and certainly nothing linguistically propositional. The creature does not (plausibly) make a 'judgement' about certain objects in certain relationships in any of the senses given above. It does not employ any of the high-level features we have been considering. Yet the creature might undergo some experience or other, however unsophisticated - perhaps it experiences only lightness or darkness, or only responds to such features in the same way as a knee will reflexively respond to being hit in a sensitive place.[5]

---

[5] The 'experiences' of very unsophisticated creatures such as *stentor caeruleus* (a ciliate - a unicellular organism) might well best be described in this behaviourist, stimulus and response terms. However, somewhat more sophisticated creatures such as rats surely experience something actually informational, even if it is only degrees of brightness and darkness. The

However, such an experience, although not representational and judgemental, might still be *informational* in some sense. Later, the experiences of a congenitally blind person having their sight restored by a tactile vision substitution system is considered as an example of informationally *sensational* features. It shall be clear from this sort of case that we need another category beyond that of the high-level features mentioned. These features shall be called *non-representational, sensational aspects* or *purely sensational aspects* depending on the context. The context stipulated is this: When an otherwise representational judgement has some sensational aspects, the experience will be said to have 'non-representational, sensational aspects' (better: 'impurely sensational aspects'); when an experience with no representational features at all has sensational aspects, the experience will be said to have 'purely sensational' aspects. It is clear that although very primitive creatures might not be able to represent certain features in their experience, they might still have an experience with informationally sensational content. Similarly, a congenitally blind person who has had their sight restored, might well be able to represent things in some sense, yet, for the most part their experience is informationally *sensational* rather than informationally representational.

It is clear that an otherwise representational judgement can have non-representational, sensational aspects (consider the hue changes in Holmes's experience of the cigar-band as the sun moved slowly past the window). Such experiences can, in some sense, be *informational*, yet not be captured in representational terms. And an experience which is not representational at all can still have sensational aspects (consider the *purely* sensational aspects of the 'experience' of the rat.) These sorts of features too can occur in degrees, and equally, can be present in some circumstances and not in others. It will later be suggested that the sense in which a person like Holmes is responsive to the representational features of his experience and not the sensational features, is largely a function of his attentiveness; his ability to *concentrate* on one or other aspect of his experience. Finally, where some experiences have *purely* sensational content, *all* experiences have at least *impurely* sensational content. So the continuum view is in serious disagreement with that of the inferentialist proposal which claims that experiences are *necessarily* underpinned by only 'high-level' features; where high-level features are necessary and sufficient for content. On the continuum account, there can be contentful experiences that do not contain the high-level features specified by the inferentialist proposal.

Three theses

There are some important things to note about this view of experiential content: For a start, the account is quite literally continuum-like. It is claimed that there are several degrees of *content* for experiencing organisms which lie along a perceptual gradient. At each end of the gradient are the polarities of the 'high-level' and the 'low-level.' The 'purely sensational' excludes the high-level; however, the high-level does not exclude the low-level. The high-level thus always contains low-level, impurely sensational aspects. What make the

---

fact that the responses of some creatures are best accounted for behaviourally does not contradict an account of experience which allows for different levels of sophistication to occur at the polarities of high and low-level content.

continuum are the degrees of constraint and conceptual organisation from the low-level to the high-level - i.e., the presence of differently organised low-level content *in all experience.*

This continuum account admits of several distinct elements which should be distinguished. These elements capture the relationships between the various kinds of content mentioned These elements can be isolated as distinct theses:

> (i) *The continuum thesis.* This is simply the fact that several distinguishable levels of organisation can be discerned in experiences as previously explained. Particularly, this refers to the 'impure' low-level content reaching through all experiences (see diagram below).

> (ii) *The complexity thesis.* This claims that there are several different aspects to contentful experiences *within each level.* Experience is mostly an *amalgam* of several low and high-level aspects A purely sensational experience, by definition, excludes high-level aspects but *all other experiences contain both kinds of features.* (Since human beings are sophisticated creatures, their experiences usually have the character of being 'impure': i.e , an amalgam of several kinds of content.)

> (iii) *The asymmetry thesis.* This follows from the previous thesis. Because (ii) stipulates experiential amalgams, and as the purely sensational is excluded from this, the continuum is asymmetrical. There are varying degrees of (impurely) sensational content in high-level experiences, but there is no high-level content in purely sensational experiences. Experience should thus best be seen in terms of *degree-additions to low-level content,* rather than degrees of high-level content. At the very bottom end of the continuum no high-level aspects feature but moving toward the upper end of the continuum, both high-level and low-level aspects feature to varying degrees in every experiential complex.

In addition, the point about *focus of attention* must be included. This can be seen to feature in terms of how an experiencing organism discriminates between the various aspects of an experiential amalgam. As will be clear from the preceding discussion, a perceiver may or may not focus their attention specifically upon (say) a change in hue, but there remains a sense in which the visual system registers the hue. The hue change (whether focussed on or not) remains a part of experiential content.

With these classifications and distinctions included, the taxonomy of experiential content has become considerably more complex than the high-level features itemised in Chapter 1. The relationships between the various degrees of content specificity can, however, be reproduced schematically to show the connections between them:

Linguistic propositional

Theoretically informational

Representationally informational

Representational

Non-representational
(Impurely sensational)

Purely sensational

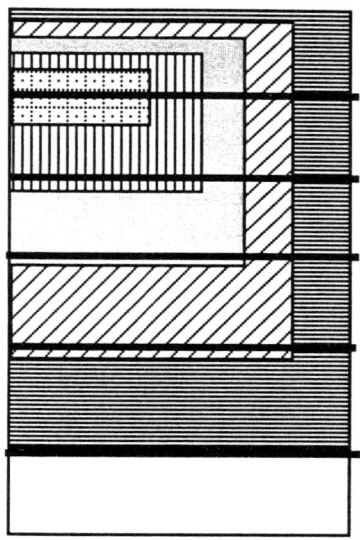

In this schematic view, various levels of experiential content are depicted as shaded blocks. Working from below, an experience with *purely sensational* aspects (no representational features at all) might belong to primitive animals only (say, some invertebrates which experience (are responsive to) only darkness and lightness). Further, something can be experienced as having *non-representational, sensational* aspects jointly with (some) representational features. A *representational* experience can be experienced as being *informational* as a certain conceptualised object or merely representational *qua* object distinct from its surroundings (in either case, it can be experienced as having non-representational, sensational aspects). Further, a determinately representational experience can be experienced as having *theoretical* content (again with or without experiencing non-representational features and non-representational, sensational aspects), while a theoretically representational experience can have *linguistic propositional* content in addition to the other kinds of content (again, with or without experiencing non-representational, sensational aspects). The schema here is subject to three general rules or theses: (1) there is a continuum between high and low-level experiences including varying degrees to which high-level features are realised at varying levels of experience (the *continuum* thesis). (2) there is always a multi-aspect or multi-level nature to high-level experience - i.e., it can simultaneously involve different levels of experience (the *complexity* thesis) and (3) there are (often) independently identifiable low-level contents in high-level experiential amalgams, but whether identifiable or not, low-level sensational contents are present in all experiences no matter how straightforwardly high-level (the *asymmetry* thesis).

Figure 1 A taxonomy of content

In what has been argued in setting up the inferentialist proposal, only 'high-level' aspects of experiential content are considered to be *necessary* features of perception. However, if the view being developed is true, then experience can also have low-level *sensational* aspects too. In fact, on the *asymmetry* thesis, experiences must have low-level content, even if - given the *complexity* thesis - this is not always separable from the overall experiential complex, or isolated via the focus of one's attention (sensational content is, thus, mostly 'impure' and non-separable). It shall be assumed that, for the most part, the distinctions above are clear and will not need further elaboration in terms of how they relate and can be distinguished as taxonomic features, though more time shall be spent on elucidating the sensational aspects of experiential content in Chapter 5.

Definitions

Experience, perception and 'aspects'

At this point, the terms used shall be defined more precisely. The word 'experience' is used as a generic term encompassing the various kinds of ways in which *contentful properties* appear to sensing organisms. 'Perception,' a species of this, might be defined as a *mechanical achievement* by which an organism may come to have an experience *using the sense organs*.

This definition is a little unorthodox, but there needs to be a rough and ready distinction here: it is clear, for instance, that not all experiences are *perceived* (consider, for instance, the case of gravity - always experienced yet rarely perceived) and not all *perceptions* are experienced (consider the case of having one's retina stimulated by EM light waves but still going through a red light; psychological experiments where the subject is unaware that she is responding in ways consonant with exposure to previous signals, etc.) The distinction between experience and perception is supposed to capture the sense in which experiences are sometimes *conscious* perceptions.

In this book I also speak of *aspects* of experiences, as the chief aim is to highlight the point that some features of experiential content cannot be captured by the inferentialist proposal. 'Aspect' means those features of content which can or cannot be captured in terms of linguistic propositional, theoretically informational and representational judgements. Following Peacocke,[6] these aspects shall be divided into two broad groups: 'representative' aspects of experience - by which I shall mean those that have a discernible representational/propositional content (as Sherlock Holmes had when he discovered a cigar-band near Jones's body) and 'non-representative' or 'sensational' aspects of experience which do not have a discernible representational structure, but which has *qualitative* content. Occasionally these broad kinds of content shall be referred to as being 'descriptive' and 'sensational', respectively. Given the continuum account an essentially sensational experience can have some determinate/representational aspects to it, even if it can't be fully captured in such terms. There is no suggestion here that an experience can't have *both* aspects (in fact, regularly they do) but this does not tell against the point that there are aspects of experiences which are not entirely inferential in the high-level sense required by the inferentialist proposal. The two divisions are meant to legitimate two broad senses in which experiences have content, not to suggest that they either have one kind of content or the other. The argument here is *against* a dichotomous treatment of the issue.

There are convenient reasons for the distinction above. As shall be shown

---

[6] C. Peacocke, *Sense and Content: Experience, Thought and its Relations*, pp. 5-7.

later, we can be *aware* of aspects of certain experiences without this aspect being necessarily 'representative' in content. On the other hand, it is possible that we can have high-level *theories* about some things without being (necessarily) aware of anything at all. (One could, for instance, be a brain-in-a-vat believing that the earth was round.) So it seems on the face of it that there is a genuine conceptual distinction here.[7]

The legitimation of low-level sensational aspects to experiential content will allow me to reject the inferentialist proposal. It will be here where an evolutionary argument inserts its wedge. There must be such low-level content to account for why we react to such experiences in the ways that we do, and why experience seems constrained in the manner it is, and this for essentially *phylogenetic* reasons: experience, at all levels of sophistication, *needs* to have a content because it typically needs to fix beliefs. Something must be going on when conceptually unsophisticated creatures experience things like colour aspects and visual field enlargements, and that 'something' is a kind of experience as good as any other. But the point is that it is not clear that these kinds of structured, low-level experiencings are captured by beliefs in the sense which involves representational, theoretical and propositional linguistic judgements.

So, for stronger reasons, there seem to be *two* broad ways in which experience can have content: one which can be properly captured on the terms of the high-level features of the inferentialist proposal; the other which cannot be captured in such terms, but which is still structured and, in evolutionary terms, *useful*. Correspondingly, there are two distinguishable senses of experiential belief-fixation. Such claims will provide reasons for the view that not all experiential content originates with high-level influences.

Four caveats

There are four important *caveats* to note about the view of experiential content presented:

1. In saying that sensational features of experiences are *useful,* I am not making any reference to the sense data theory. This view claimed that conscious sensory experiences were not experiences of real objects or events in the world, but were properties of, for example, intervening coloured patches. It is not being claimed, however, that the sensational content of experience can't be represented as belonging to objects in the world. Such a view is not plausible in an evolutionary sense: intervening coloured patches cut no evolutionary ice unless they can be projected onto real events and objects. (What would be *selectively* important about an intervening red patch, for example?) The claim, rather, is that conscious sensory contents mostly do have a representational aspect which projects them on to objects, but this is not the only content they

---

[7] This example is not as insipid as it seems on first blush: recent theorising in the philosophy of science has it that science can be carried on without experiencing things at all: i.e., simply by plugging theories into computers and having other computers reading off the result. This kind of view makes a substantial commitment to saying that investigations about the world are not importantly observational. See Paul Feyerabend, 'Science Without Experience' in *Realism, Rationalism and Scientific Method,* Philosophical Papers, Vol.1. Feyerabend's views are treated in detail in Chapter 9.

have. A vitally important evolutionary function of experience is that they can have a *felt* quality for the perceiver. And this is so simply because projected experiences may, on some occasions, be wrong. So, there might be a survivalist reason for why there must be 'something that it is like' to have conscious sensory experiences in addition to any representational, descriptive, high-level judgements that something looks like this or that. When confronted with an object speeding before one, for example, it is survivally more important to be aware of an enlargement in the visual field, than seeing what seems like a balloon (in fact a sharp missile) is speeding before one. My attachments to this kind of argument will later allow me to link my thesis with a property dualism of the kind adumbrated by Nagel. Far from the views of Dennett, for whom 'thrown into a causal gap, a quale will simply fall through it',[8] I want to argue that qualia actually fulfil a genuine causal role - by providing low-level informational content to experiencing organisms.

2. Related to this point, it is stressed that sensational aspects of experiences are *informational awarenesses* in some sense and, as such, are not epistemically idle. 'Felt' experiential properties do yield some informational content for perceivers. However, this kind of content is not anything which would be similar to the claims made for sense data. Sensational aspects of experiential content are not epistemically foundational, nor incorrigible, even though they may be, in an informational sense, *sui generis* to high-level judgements. The claim is that, concurrently with representing one's experience or forming a theoretically informational or propositionally linguistic judgement, one might also experience aspects of that experience which cannot be captured in high-level terms. However, there is nothing epistemically fundamental about such experiences; they can be overridden and ignored as a function of attention. (One can either notice a certain hue or fail to, even if one's visual system may register the hue.) The sense of 'informational' here should be seen in survivalist terms: having a felt aspect of one's experience is probably more to do with a biological story about how we have evolved, than a perceptual story about how the visual system processes information and directs us to items of particular epistemic interest. More will be said about the epistemic function of low-level content later.

3. It is not claimed that high-level considerations are not brought to bear on experiential content at all. It seems highly likely in fact that the various elements of the inferentialist proposal can be individuated, and said to be relevant to various degrees. The point is only that *some* aspects of experiential content are not captured by such features. If so, it would seem that the inferentialist proposal is false as it stands, and a more subtle and elaborate account of the relation between high-level considerations and experiential content needs to be developed.

A more refined version of the broad kinds of content mentioned earlier would be this. There may be a *three-way* manifestation of experience to the organism: proximal stimulations (psychologically non-inferential); low-level sensational contents (experienced qualitatively, perhaps partially inferential - depending on the organism in question)[9] and representative descriptive experiences

---

[8] Epigraph to 'Qualia Disqualified', in D. C. Dennett, *Consciousness Explained,* p. 369.

[9] Unsophisticated animals are less likely to have the latter aspects but more than likely to

(structured conceptually, highly inferential). It is the second sort of experience that will be crucial. Throughout this book, it shall be separated from the third level of experience.

On the inferentialist proposal, experience is taken to be primarily exhausted by the third form listed above. By contrast, the 'observational account' of the classical empiricist and the sense-data theorist take experience to be exhausted by the first type (of course for these theorists, the first type was *more* than just 'proximal stimulations'). On the continuum account, the second option *as well as* the first and third, are required for a fully adequate account of experiential content. It is not claimed that experience can be exhausted by its representational or inferential content. The option is thus not entirely inferentialist; not entirely specified by an application of background epistemic, representational and propositional features. There is something about the content of certain aspects of experiences which is strictly *observational and sensational* and there is something about the content of other aspects of experiences which is fully representational and can be explained and captured in the terms of the inferentialist proposal. There are also a number of possibilities in between these two options (see below). This kind of situation is implausible under any view of experiential content other than the continuum view.

4. Finally, it is claimed here that experiences need to be fixed by beliefs. Belief is usually understood as a 'high-level' epistemic feature - a representational state or a belief-*that* in Armstrong's terms. This would seem to conflict with the claim that experience has aspects which do not depend on high-level features. Later, a continuum view of *belief* is outlined which rests well with my several levels of experiential content. This allows low-level, sensational experiences to fix certain low-level beliefs ('look' beliefs, as I call them). In the view being presented, just as experience can have varying degrees of sophistication, so beliefs can too. So the claim that experiences fix beliefs does not conflict with the continuum theory because on this view not all beliefs can be characterised in high-level terms. The issue of experience and beliefs is dealt with in detail in Chapter 4.

The continuum theory

The continuum theory asserts the following: *there are several levels in which contentful properties can be presented to experiencing organisms which may, in evolutionary terms, be differentially sophisticated.* Thus, one can speak of high-level descriptive content, which has aspects which can be captured in terms of the inferentialist proposal, and low-level sensational content which has aspects which cannot be captured in such terms. There are, of course, a range of possibilities in between. Consistent with the notion of a continuum, we can also speak of sub-descriptive experiential content, which has some representative

---

have the former (in varying degrees, of course). Again, the possibility of graduations of difference here is central to the continuum account. (It is noted in work on invertebrate perception that bees, for instance 'can distinguish between different colours ... [but] they have a very limited ability to distinguish shapes.' See: P. A. Meglitsch, *Invertebrate Zoology*, p. 653. Moreover, some contents can be lost and others gained: certain species of fish, birds and butterflys, for instance, are able to perceive UV radiation - an ability lost in primates. (My thanks to Roger McCart for this point.)

content, but perhaps not enough to qualify as being propositional or theoretical. The experience that a dog has of spatial location does not require very high-level features, although it still requires some inference if the dog is to negotiate and remember this region. By contrast, the experience of a cigar-band being spatially located requires yet more high-level conceptual and representational features, whereas the experience of a spatially located object having a certain relationship to Jones's dead body has yet more high-level (theoretically informational; propositional linguistic) features and so on.[10]

Moreover, some experiential content exhibit none of these 'high-level' features. Such experiences harness structured sensational features of experiential content which have discernible qualitative features, but very little else; certainly nothing that can be captured in the high-level terms of the inferentialist proposal. The various contents of experience thus occur in degrees from highly sophisticated features to very primitive features in something like a linear or ordinal sequence.

That there can be various degrees of cognitive penetration of the mechanisms of inference, background knowledge, theories and language can be plausible only if the inferentialist proposal is false. For inferentialism requires that all experiential content necessarily has such 'high-level' influences (in the views of some, such influences are necessary and sufficient for experiential content).

A graduationist thesis like the one suggested makes evolutionary sense. It seems plausible that the detection of some low-level features like colours is experientially and perhaps cognitively prior to how such things are expressed in the linguistic propositional judgements and prior to how they are developed in high-level theories. The former may be possessed by pre-linguistic creatures to aid survival; the latter may be a symbolic vehicle employed by cognitively sophisticated organisms which have evolved in complex ways and have transcended, to some degree, such basic survivalist requirements. Between the extremes, mechanisms of inference may be operational in the detection of objects, relations and so on, which, although involving inference, may not involve high-level concepts and propositional features, and so can't be captured fully on the inferentialist account.

That there can be a graduation of such influences does not rule out the intrinsic value of Kant's idea that experiences and the mediating function of the intellect are typically closely linked; it does rule out the idea that experiences must be so mediated. On the continuum theory, some intuitions without concepts may well be 'blind', but whether this is entirely true depends very much on one's initial focus of interest. The consequences the continuum view has for the traditional interpretation of Kant's account is outlined in Chapter 6.

Other terms and miscellanea

There are a couple of other words and phrases which should be defined

---

[10] To push the example I have been using: Holmes's dog usually brings rather less in the way of inferential sophistication to the visual scene than Watson, who brings rather less (inductive/theoretical) input than Holmes. This need not *always* be the case: if the object perceived was a leash or a slipper the dog might make somewhat stronger inferences than either Holmes or Watson - i.e., expectations of future behaviour. (My thanks to Roger McCart.)

precisely. The important terms 'inferentialism' and 'inferentialist' are to be used synonymously with 'the inferentialist proposal': the doctrine that all experiential content necessarily draws upon high-level influences *en bloc*. The term 'inference' shall be used to mean the psychological transition between high-level psychological states. It is possible on my account for an experience to involve inference yet not be explained entirely in the strictly high-level terms of the inferentialist proposal. The terms 'high-level' and 'low-level' refer, respectively, to the features of experience captured entirely in terms of the inferentialist proposal and those sensational features that cannot be so captured. I shall later be calling *beliefs* which correspond to such influences on experiences as *inferential* beliefs and *look* beliefs respectively. For simplicity, *visual* experiences shall be the main focus, although what will be said about these cases should be taken as applying, equally well, to the other senses. Later discussion will clarify the issues that these terms raise.

Another word about the Inferentialist Proposal: The inferentialist proposal, as it is expressed here, is something of a philosophical fiction. No theorist has argued explicitly for this view by name, nor has one claimed to have been influenced by it. However, to the extent that it has been assumed, it is claimed that this position has the character of a myth; a myth which has pervaded contemporary thought and which needs to be examined. Later on several views on experiential content shall be treated which closely characterise this doctrine. All of them need to adopt a more subtle account of experience which sees the relation between elements of high-level inference as underpinned by other important considerations; namely, the evolutionary and observational considerations mentioned.

There is one final distinction to mention. It concerns the application of *concepts* to experiences. Since the various high-level features are characterised by a sophisticated *conceptual* ability of some sort, what is needed here is an account of conceptual content. The next two sections, accordingly, will deal with the nature of concepts. Out of this, the ambiguous nature of concepts is outlined. It is suggested that sensational experiences can be 'conceptual' and yet not commit us to the overly sophisticated terms of the inferentialist proposal. This is done by turning to a treatment of 'concept' unavailable on the terms of the inferentialist proposal. The claim is that, just as there can be several levels of non-exclusive content to experience, so one may speak of several distinguishable senses of concept.

Descriptive concepts

What concepts are in this connection is very problematic. We could define a concept as 'the mode of presentation of a property.'[11] It is a vague definition, but I know no better. And it fits the purpose for the inferentialist account. Many concepts are usually understood as *descriptive* modes of presentation of a property, and descriptions are high-level *epistemic* notions. The definition is somewhat Fregean, so we can use a somewhat Fregean example. 'Temperature' and 'Mean Molecular Kinetic Energy' (MMKE) are presentations of the same property; however, they are *described* in a different way, and so thereby

---

[11] Peacocke, op. cit., p. 89.

constitute different *representations*. By 'Temperature' we employ a different epistemic/semantic description from 'MMKE'. The concepts are different because the descriptive mode is different, but in this case the reference or property represented is the same. And we fix our beliefs about these concepts partly through their location in the descriptive/theoretical net. The property in this case is subsumed under certain high-level descriptions which fit our broad-based theories about how we represent the world, and this descriptive mode amounts to the concepts, respectively, of 'Temperature' or 'MMKE' depending on the degree to which we understand and apply theoretical physics. Such concepts are *descriptive* concepts as they put a label on certain properties via the possession of certain theories. Descriptive concepts are properties *subsumed* under theories.

This account of the nature of concepts is plausible, and it fits with the inferentialist account of how concepts are needed in fixing experiences. Because experiencing the world amounts to the detection and identification of certain properties, it is clear that such properties are also *described;* our experiences are usually *of* something. Holmes's experience was *of* the cigar-band next to Jones's body. Moreover, experiences need *descriptive* concepts in this sense, if they are to fit with our theories, and Sherlock Holmes is an expert in manipulating such concepts precisely *because* he is a good theorist. Theoretical, propositional and epistemic factors, it seems, hang together with an essentially descriptive conceptual glue.

Having concepts in the *descriptive* sense means the following: to make experiences from observations, we need to describe a presented property in certain informed ways; ways which fit in with our theories and background knowledge. Allan Millar has called this 'the concept principle.' To have an experience of a certain type one must possess the concept (so to have an experiential belief that one's cat is Russian Blue, one must have the concept of Russian Blue).[12] Properties are thus subsumed under such descriptions: 'Mean Molecular Kinetic Energy' is subsumed under the description it is because of a certain knowledge of physics. That this follows is a plausible extension of inference from background knowledge as mentioned. However, the claim of the inferentialist is not that this is so occasionally: the claim is that *all* stock observations are subsumed under concepts in this manner, even typical sensory properties like 'green' or 'blue', and subsumption under descriptive concepts presupposes the inference from background knowledge, theories and the propositional contents of a language. Commenting upon what he sees as the heretical idea of the 'given' in experience, Sellars notes that:

> [E]ven such 'simple' concepts as those of colour are the fruit of a long process of publically reinforced responses to public objects (including verbal performances) in public situations. ... *instead of coming to have a concept of something because we have noticed that sort of thing, to have the ability to notice a sort of thing is already to have the concept of that sort of thing and cannot account for it.* [13]

---

[12] Allan Millar, *Reasons and Experience*, p. 20.
[13] W. Sellars, *Science, Perception and Reality*, p.176.

Inferentialism with a vengeance. But, as it will be clear from the preceding discussion, it does not only presuppose a concept; it also tacitly presupposes linguistic, propositional and representational judgments. If true, on all levels, (even the lowest) there *is* more to seeing than meets the eye, and that the essentials of the observational account are fundamentally flawed. There is no form of observational 'noticing' without the prior application of high-level descriptive concepts, background knowledge, representational states, propositions and theories.

All this fits together very well with the inferentialist package outlined. The idea that experiences involve high-level features of various kinds rests rather well with an account of concepts as *descriptive* modes of presentation of properties. Just as it was clear that Sherlock Holmes needed to involve some epistemic information to have an experience of the cigar-band, (or that he needed to token his experience linguistically, or represent it judgementally) it also seems clear that these concepts had to identify essentially *descriptive* features. The problem of how to regard concepts on this analysis thus has a natural solution: the solution must be that experience requires descriptive concepts to fix appropriate perceptual beliefs. So, if one takes on board the inferentialist proposal, it is very easy to say here that all experiences involve descriptive concepts. Such an account of concepts is grist for the inferentialist's mill. However, one can say this only on the assumption that concepts can *only* be of a descriptive kind. *Query:* are there modes of presentation of properties - concepts - which are *not* essentially descriptive in nature?

Sensational concepts

I think there are, and think this helps to have an account of experiential content without putting too much stress on propositions, representations, theory, knowledge, and high-level inference. Some modes of presentation of properties can simply have sensational features - aspects which are not descriptive in character and which can't be captured in any such high-level terms. Christopher Peacocke puts the point thus: 'One way to think of the physical property of having high temperature is by a mode of presentation we can employ because we are capable of having sensations of heat.'[14] It seems plausible to suppose that conceptually unsophisticated animals (like rats) can utilise these sorts of *sensational* concepts though (perhaps) not the former descriptive kind. The point is that none of the sophisticated high-level concepts seem relevant here, so there might be a case for claiming that not all concepts provide grist for the inferentialist's mill. Some concepts harness sensational aspects of experience, not aspects which can be captured by descriptions.

This is not to say, of course, that there are only sensational concepts and no descriptive ones; it just means that some concepts might be best *characterised* in sensational terms. Just as one does not fully capture the experience of heat by describing it in a certain (physical) way, there might be some concepts that capture certain ways by which things are felt or sensed, whereas others best capture descriptions of things. With some experiences, of course, it might be genuinely unclear how they are best characterised (does experiencing something

---

[14] Peacocke, op. cit., p. 89.

spatially located have descriptive representational features or is it simply sensational, for instance?)[15] However, it is best in an overall sense to claim that experiences can have both descriptive and sensational *aspects* and human beings at least can concentrate on one or the other (it is a moot point whether animals have *descriptive* concepts at all because they don't make linguistic, propositional judgments).[16] It is, therefore, not the case that only by high-level *descriptive* concepts can experiences be characterised.

This point can be applied to other experiencing creatures. Animals, including humans, are presented with features of thermal temperature and wavelengths of light; we experience these as contentful heat and colour sensations respectively. There are also more sophisticated examples of such modes of presentation, like that of shape, the appearance of largeness or smallness in the visual field, or length.[17] There are also examples which seem to be both descriptive and representational and which *also* have sensational features. An example might be the stereoscopic view of an assemblage of objects *vis-à-vis* a monoscopic view of the same scene.

The point is that sensational concepts can isolate features which are not descriptive in nature, but are only *felt* properties. There is some *felt* sense in which the stereo/mono experience changes, just as there is a sense in which some experiences, such as colours, have an indescribable *look*. Such aspects of experiences isolate *sensed* features and, in an important sense, have nothing to do with background, high-level beliefs and propositions.

It is not the case that such features *can't* be described if one focuses on them in a certain way (one clearly can); rather, it would seem that there are 'aspects' of such experiences which are not descriptive in the way in which other experiences can normally be captured by descriptions, yet these features are concept-like. They are concept-like because such experiences are not like James's 'blooming, buzzing confusion'; they seem to have an intrinsic structure. These features of experience will be called *sensational aspects* or (to change the terminology for variation) *primordial contents*. Such concepts are sensational because they seem to capture essentially 'felt' aspects of experiences; they are primordial because they are concepts which are unavailable on the high-level descriptive terms of the inferentialist proposal. Because experiences may be fixed by sensational as well as descriptive content, we do not need to take on board the inferentialist proposal *holus bolus* - a better strategy is consider better ways of formulating the relation between experience and content. To suggest that the only concepts which are relevant to the fixation of experiential content are *descriptive* concepts might already be to beg the question in favour of the inferentialist proposal.

There is a sense in which the inferentialist proposal does not capture *all*

---

[15] As will be argued in Chapter 5, this example is a particular problem case for the congenitally blind 'seeing' with the aid of a tactile vision substitution system.

[16] It is a moot point because though they don't have a language, they may have descriptive concepts even if they lack one of our ways of *giving expression* to how they take things to be.

[17] Length would seem to be a clear case of a *descriptive* capacity, which depends on an *inferential* background. Fodor has supplied an example which makes this seem doubtful. (See Chapter 8).

aspects of experience. The various high-level features seem distinguishable. A dog's experience, for instance, might involve representational factors, but very little else; a very low-level experience of a pre-linguistic infant might not involve even that. The experience of looking at some objects with one eye, then both, may result in the representational features of the experience remaining the same but something else about the experience noticeably shifting. Such cases are much more ambiguous and unclear than the case of Sherlock Holmes and the cigar-band. In the latter case descriptive concepts fixing appropriate representational features seem mostly relevant but in the cases just mentioned, the experiences are marked by a variety of influences, of greater and lesser degrees of sophistication. If the various high-level features can be separated from experience there might be a case for claiming that none are *necessary and sufficient* for content, and thus, there may be a case for claiming that they leave behind an experiential residue.

By joining the account of concepts above with the elaborated taxonomy of experiential content, we can say that at some very low-level degree of sophistication, some aspects of experiences are just *felt,* not described and not represented; they are conceptualised as 'sensed' aspects. Such is the case with the monocular/binocular visual scene above. There seems to be a qualitative feature to such an experience which is not captured on any of the high-level terms delineated. Such also might be the case with aspects of the experiences of unsophisticated animals and infants. Indeed, that there might be a *graduation* of kinds of ways in which experiential content might be fixed, may give support to the continuum view, not to the inferentialist proposal *nor* the observational account. The sense in which we seemed to be faced with a choice between *either* inferential factors and non-inferential factors at the beginning of this book, may have been an overly *superficial* way of looking at the issue of experience and content. Once this is admitted, of course, one begins to take seriously the continuum account advocated.

The continuum account doesn't assert that there is no fully-fledged descriptive content brought to bear on experiences. It says that there can be *aspects* of experiences which are not descriptive but sensational. Also, it doesn't assert that all sensational contents are entirely non-inferential. It suggests that *some* features of such experiences are simply not in this category. All the view advanced claims is that there are a number of different ways in which differentially sophisticated organisms are presented with properties and a number of ways in which such properties are fixed into concepts, and only some of those ways have aspects which are properly descriptive or inferential. It is claimed here that most of the arguments for the radical inferentialist account do not, in effect, rule out the case for the continuum possibility. It is only by the latter that we can shorten what we earlier saw Fodor call the 'etiological route' between observation and knowledge. The usual story is put in either/or terms: either experiences are made possible by the imposition of high-level features of cognition (the inferentialist proposal) or experiences are 'built up' from non-inferential sense data (the observational account). However, I claim this kind of dichotomous treatment of the issue is superficial and misleading.

A further preliminary point that needs to be made is this: utilising the notion of concepts which are not descriptive, only sensational, translates naturally to a similar view of *beliefs*. It is suggested animals and infants might largely fix beliefs about some low-level experiences like colours etc., largely through concepts of this *sensational* kind. There are, then, possibly more than two ways in which experiences can be said to originate, and more than two ways in which experiences are fixed into beliefs: not only through inference from background knowledge involving descriptive concepts or through a supposed non-inferential direct action on the senses. There may be a middle road here. Perhaps some primitive animal or infant-like experiences are underpinned by qualitatively different sorts of concepts and different sorts of beliefs - concepts and beliefs which have very little to do with high-level linguistic propositional and representational judgements but everything to do with *sensational appearances*. Perhaps these concepts and beliefs act as evolutionary constraints upon the structure of our experience and high-level concept development, learning and so on. If this can be established then perhaps experiences can, after all, be said to be observational in some important sense. This will be a welcome conclusion. For it seems fairly obvious that experiential concepts are, at some level, simply observational and sensational to a degree regardless of what some philosophers say.

Conclusion

Three central reasons have been given for reconsidering the claims of the inferentialist proposal:

(1) High-level features (like linguistic propositional judgements) are not always present in experiences of unsophisticated creatures like animals and infants.

(2) The terms of the inferentialist proposal can be individuated and separated, so there seems to be grounds for considering a more subtle account of the relationship between high-level factors and experiential content.

(3) Observationally-fixed experiential content would *prima facie* seem to have survival advantages over inferentially-fixed experience.

These points raise three key issues: the separability of the features of high-level inference; evolutionary considerations; and the matter of the rationalist underpinnings of this account of experience and content. Various degrees of high-level input have been outlined: linguistic propositional judgements, theoretically informational and representational judgements and non-representational or impurely sensational aspects. It was claimed that because such features can be distinguished, there are grounds for reconsidering the terms of the inferentialist proposal.

3 Experience and language

There is a 'linguistic' factor in seeing ... Unless there were this linguistic element, nothing we ever observed could have relevance for our knowledge. We could not speak of significant observations: nothing seen would make sense, and microscopy would only be a kind of kaleidoscopy. For what is it for things to make sense other than for descriptions of them to be composed of meaningful sentences?[1]

Language, meaning and experience

Introduction

In the last two chapters, the inferentialist proposal and the observational account were outlined as rival views of content. A continuum view of content was compared with these more traditional views.

There was a common theme in these introductory chapters. When undertaking both tasks, it was shown how important the imposition of high-level features were to an adequate account of experience. As argued, unless perceptual experience involved high-level features, the discrimination of objects and events in the world would not be possible. It is on this kind of argument that the inferentialist proposal relies, and it is enough of an argument to cast in doubt any fully observational account. Moreover, it is probably the intuitive acceptability of this kind of argument along with the influence of early rationalist thought and the unacceptable consequences that the observational account has in legitimating positivism, foundationalism and the sense data theory, that has made the inferentialist proposal the received dogma in much of contemporary thought.

There is another reason why the inferentialist proposal has become the received dogma. The inferentialist view of content has come about by conflating the high-level nature of language with a full and complete understanding of experience. This mistake has given the notion of content its present epistemic and propositional bias. This has come about because a positivist account of observational *terms* has been unable to offer a fully adequate account of how

---

[1] N. R. Hanson, *Patterns of Discovery*, p. 25.

such terms get their *meanings*. Attempts to suggest a better account of the meanings of observational terms has made theory-ladenness a necessary condition of meaningful language use. However, as an unforeseen consequence of this move, language and theory-ladenness has come to be associated with observational experience. This, in turn, has amounted to the conflation of high-level descriptions in a language being said to capture the nature of observational experience. This move will be criticised in this chapter, as it is one of the weak links in the inferentialist's position. But to make this criticism, it is first necessary to go into the issue of the relation between observational and theoretical terms.

Observational and theoretical terms

It is not obvious that our ideas about observational predicates need to be revised. It is less clear why theory-ladenness needs to be incorporated in an account of the meaning of observational terms. If theory-ladenness is seen to be a necessary condition of the use of observational predicates, then the oft-used and familiar distinction between observational and theoretical terms would seem to collapse. The reason for this is not obvious however, as the differences between observational and theoretical terms seem so great:

> *Prima facie* it looks as though there is an important difference between such putative O- [observational] terms as '... is warm.' and such putative T-[theoretical] terms as '... is an electron'. One can grasp the meaning of '... is warm' without having to learn any scientific theory and one can apply the term on the basis of one's perceptual experience with a high degree of justified confidence. By contrast, to learn what is meant by 'electron' one has to have at least partial mastery of a complex scientific theory. And furthermore, one does not sense the presence of electrons in the way that one senses that something is warm. One has to use sophisticated equipment to detect the presence of electrons and one's judgement that one has detected electrons is risky in that it presupposes a host of theoretical assumptions.[2]

It would also seem that O-terms are semantically and epistemically privileged whereas T-terms are not: '... is warm' (or, at least, '*feels* warm'), can be given through ostensive training and in eventually being able to make such discriminations one can be said to 'know' such things through direct experience. It is not the case that T-terms can be experienced or learnt in such a 'direct' manner.

There are other good reasons to preserve the distinction which would seem well-motivated: the meaning of O-terms would presumably remain constant through theory change if the two ('O' and 'T' terms) were genuinely different.[3] Tied to the immediacy of experience, observational terms such as '... is warm' would remain unaltered even if the composite superstructural scaffolding of T-terms surrounding it happened to shift. They could thus have a role in

---

[2] W. Newton-Smith, *The Rationality of Science*, p. 22.

[3] This is what Fodor hints at - see quotation, p. 20.

adjudicating and resolving clashes of theoretical opinion. This seemed to be a safe way of keeping some bedrock of knowledge in the face of the whims and fancies displayed in the motions of theoretical progress. Also, the separation of the two avoids having to presuppose theoretical assumptions in the articulation of observational terms: being supposedly theory-neutral, these could be rendered free of such corruptions and, hence, could be the foundation for resolving disputes at the higher (theoretical) level.

As Newton-Smith notes, the difference here between such terms was defended as a 'difference in kind and not a difference in degree.'[4] But the sharpness of this difference simply did not hold up to close scrutiny: the characterisation of an observational term as something which had its meaning obtained without the aid of theoretical assumptions amounted to a term which could be understood without the aid of technical instruments, but, instead, *directly in experience.* This is far from true, however, as the example of the weight of an object makes clear.

Problems with the observational account of meanings

If we say that an object can be determined as having a certain weight, it is unclear that this can be said without reference to some scale or other technical device. Even if we restrict ourselves to weight as a mere sensation, say, the 'feel' of a heavy pair of boots on our feet, we do not thereby explain the meaning of 'weight.' In fact, we risk, thereby, ruling out as weightless, objects which were not felt in this manner, and which we would surely wish to say have weight in some important sense. If we thence appeal to that property observed through the medium of technical instruments as instead, some general feature of the world, we have then no reason not to admit *other* properties obtained in this manner (like 'fields', 'electrons', 'forces', 'quarks', and so on), which are usually deemed 'theoretical' terms and also mathematical descriptions of them ('weight' becomes, then: $w=mg$). If there is a difference between observational and theoretical terms then it is not a difference in kind, because the 'observational' terms collapse ultimately into theoretical ones.

The complete rejection of the sharp distinction here, for those that opted for its rejection, admitted the idea that all observational terms are *theory-laden.* If observational terms and theoretical terms were not easily separated then it would seem that what went for the one, went for the other. Just as 'is a quark' needed a systematic body of theoretical beliefs and generalisations, so did terms referring to weight, colour and so on which were usually considered 'observational' or 'sensory', and the dependence on this theoretical superstructure was a matter of degree. For instance, a person had to see weight as a relatively stable property and not something which didn't change depending on the colour of the object considered or didn't alter in wet weather or on certain odd-numbered days of the year. But if this was so, then the closer an observational term was to the centre of a theoretical network, the more likely it was to change or be revised by a change in theory.

The long term implication of observational terms being theory-laden was that, *all observation reports are revisable,* even such banal reports as: 'the counter

---

[4] Newton-Smith, op. cit., p. 23.

now reads 4'; and, being revisable, more likely than not there was a case for thinking that such observation terms could not be compared with each other (the notorious doctrine of 'incommensurability'). Just as such theoretical terms as 'mass' in different theoretical structures did not mean the same thing (*cf.* Newtonian and Einsteinian theory) so too terms like 'weight' or 'the counter now reads 4' could mean different things in different theoretical circumstances. This seems counterintuitive, but is a plausible inference from the rejection of positivism and the conflation of observational and theoretical terms.

But there was another, less intuitive, consequence. Observational *reports* being theory-laden came to mean, for some, that observational *experiences* were so as well. Hence, we have Feyerabend arguing:

> The only difference between a blind person and a seeing person consists in the fact that the first one uses a different part of a theory (or some of the consequences of the theory) as his observation language.[5]

This sort of move presents inferentialism in a new dress. The theory-ladenness of observational terms has come to signify the legitimacy of the idea that there is no observational experience outside making high-level theoretically informational judgements and propositional linguistic judgements. So, on this view, not only is the observational account seen as flawed because it ignores the importance of high-level categories in fixing experiential content, it also seems that this assumes the essential distinction between observational terms and observational experiences where the inferentialist conflates this distinction. The rest is recent history.

The issue of the rejection of the positivist account of observational terms and the consequences this has for an adequate account of experience will be dealt with in Chapter 9. For now it should be noted how the inferentialist proposal arrives at this view, and how, in the hands of those imbued with the spirit of the inferentialist proposal, it can lead to startling consequences.

Experiences and meanings: the sleight of hand unveiled

The comparative merits the inferentialist proposal had over the observational account were presented in an earlier chapter. Now there is an additional claim made in support of inferentialism. Not only is some conceptual ability necessary for the observational recognition of objects, observational terms also require high-level concepts. However, it is here that we have struck a snag. For if it is admitted that all observational terms are theoretically laden and if we admit that high-level features are important for experiential content, it seems an easy move from this to saying that all observational experiences are theoretically laden, and this seems nothing short of a fallacy. It also leaves us with the kind of counterintuitive remark that Feyerabend makes about the sighted and the blind.

This move is clearly far too swift. The idea that the *language* of observational reports should be theoretically imbued is explicitly tied to *experiences themselves* being theoretically imbued and vice versa. But surely there is some

---

[5] P. K. Feyerabend, 'An Attempt at a Realistic Interpretation of Experience', in *Realism, Rationalism and Scientific Method,* Philosophical Papers, Vol.1, p. 33.

confusion here: observational language is not observational experience, just as the token expression of a pain ('pain') is not a pain. Whether observational terms are theory-laden or not seems a shortfall from the claim that observational experiences are so as well. *Experiences are not meanings.*

There do, in fact, seem to be several ambiguities concerning the theory-ladenness thesis in relation to experience and observational terms. This may explain some of the confusion. On the one hand, the theory-ladenness thesis seems to say that one sees only what one has theoretically structured linguistic concepts for. On the other hand, it seems to say that one can only see what one expects to see as determined by one's background theory. (The Feyerabend quote above seems [literally!] to imply this second interpretation). But clearly, the theory-ladenness of observational terms, at best, only implies the *first* application to experiences, not necessarily the second. The second application seems to require much *stronger* argument. (This seems to require that language, in some sense, precedes or occurs concurrently with content.) A second ambiguity here concerns the assumed equivalence between the meaning of observational terms and the experiences that such terms stand for. Given the several levels of ambiguity, what *can* be legitimately asserted from all this?

The point of any conflation between experience and the theory-ladenness of observational terms has a simple explanation. In order to communicate about anything one needs to have a basis of recognition; for example, the scientist experimenting with electrical currents will recognise aspects of phenomena which the non-expert does not. The recognition amounts to the phenomena having a recognisable meaning for the scientist and not the non-scientist. 'Having a recognisable meaning' in part, of course, requires *sharing the same theory.* (For a scientist who knows about theories of electricity, certain experiences will mean more.) Thus, all significant experiences must have a theoretically-imbued *meaning* to be experiences for us. So, language, or at least *meaning,* is crucially involved in having experiences. H. I. Brown has argued this point by drawing an analogy with reading a text:

> [We must] recall that we are concerned with perception as a source of information: whatever it is that we 'really see' when we are reading, it is only the meaning of what we see that can become part of our knowledge, just as when I observe familiar objects or laboratory phenomena it is only the meaning of these objects that is relevant to what we know. If there are bare, meaningless data, the very fact that they are meaningless makes them non-significant and irrelevant to knowledge.[6]

As a claim that experiences can be meaningful, this seems fairly uncontroversial and uninteresting. However, this claim can be read in another way; namely, that experiences are like meanings in some sense. And this seems rather less than obvious. Here Brown could be interpreted as making the stronger claim - ruling as 'non-significant' any experience which is not meaning-like. Read in this way it is a very odd argument indeed. Would the experience of 'red' be significant or non-significant on Brown's view? It would seem that he must be committed to saying that it was non-significant, a view which seems rather paradoxical. For,

---

[6] H. I. Brown, *Perception, Theory and Commitment,* pp. 88-9.

why is the term of significance here the high-level factor of *meaning?* When animals and infants experience colours isn't their experience significant in some sense even though they have no facility with language? If not, it would make animals and infants experientially *in vacuo.* Yet this seems far from obvious; it seems indeed to be an argument for some kind of linguistic chauvinism. The extent of this chauvinism and its implications for animal experiences will be outlined in Chapter 7.

The point here is not that Brown is committed to a view like this, but simply that given the multiple levels of ambiguity concerning the theory-dependence of observational terms, the claim could be read in this way. It could be read in a way which legitimated a *very strong sense* in which features of high-level inference are necessary for experiential content. It could, for instance, be read in a way which stipulated perception as being propositional in some way which was language-like. (Such a view seems to lie behind Hanson's remarks at the beginning of this chapter and Feyerabend's comment cited earlier.) My point is that, given the levels of ambiguity, it is easy to fall into the trap of the inferentialist proposal, and assert that observational experiences, not just observational terms, need to be invested with high-level features such as propositions, representations, theory and background knowledge.

There is, of course, a historical reason for meanings, language and theory-ladenness having been tied up with experience, and it has largely been due to a subtle but pervasive confusion. The historical reason is as much a contributing factor to the inferentialist proposal as the rampant rationalism discussed in Chapter 1. (I owe some of the following points to G. J. O'Brien.)

When W. V. O. Quine was busy attacking the positivist movement earlier this century, he was attacking the idea of the 'building block' approach to semantics, where 'simples', expressions which denoted facts, could be piled up on top of one another to yield meaningful sentences. On some views of science, these statements could be *independently* verified by virtue of their empirical atomic structure. Quine claimed that this was the wrong sort of picture: the unit of meaning of science, particularly, was a holistic network where observational terms 'face[d] the tribunal of sense experience not individually but only as a corporate body.'[7] In this case, the theoretical/observational distinction in language was an elastic distinction, and, like every other facet of language, amenable to large-scale review and adjustments to the overall network of scientific discourse. Observational and theoretical terms were properly distinctions of 'degree' in having a certain proximity in the network, either closer to, or farther from the outer sensory field. The important thing to note is that here the theoretical-observation distinction was a feature of *language* and was not confused with experience. Unfortunately, however, the important innovation of meaning holism did not stop there.

The conflation of experience and high-level descriptions

This view of theoretical and observational terms and experience was not the same in Hanson's work some time later. The issue of observational terms in language clearly became *conflated* with observational experience:

---

[7] W. V. O. Quine, 'Two Dogmas of Empiricism,' in *From a Logical Point of View*, p. 41.

> Our visual sensations may be 'set' by language forms; how else could they be appreciated in terms of what we know? Until they are so appreciated they do not constitute observation: they are more like the buzzing confusion of fainting or the vacant vista of aimless staring through a railway window. Knowledge of the world is not a *montage* of sticks, stones, colour patches and noises but a system of propositions.[8]

Language, on this view, was the *bearer* of content; it became a necessary and sufficient condition for observational experience. The observational situation doesn't bring about experiences unless 'set' by language. Paul Churchland has a similar view when he says that our experiences, our 'perceptual judgments', are structured and organised by an underlying conceptual framework given by a language; a framework rooted:

> ... not in the nature of the perceptual environment ... but rather in the structure and content of our common language, and in the process by which each child acquires the normal use of that language.[9]

A significant move has been made here and might easily go unnoticed. The holism thesis, with very little pushing, tells two very *different* stories. The idea that the systems of beliefs that a person holds might be expressed in the statements of a language lying at remote distances on 'an infinite connected graph'[10] is one thing. The idea that these statements can simultaneously be construed as the (now familiar) idea that each location or 'node' on the graph corresponds to 'the entailments of [a] theory [and the] semantically significant relations that hold among its theorems; inferential relations, evidence relations, and so forth'[11] is quite another. However, the upshot of this view is that since experiences are fixed into beliefs by theory and so on, experiences are inexorably *theoretical* and not *observational*. Experience, in Hanson's, Feyerabend's and Churchland's view, is importantly holistic in this second, stronger sense: to be actually bound up, without residue, with the nature of our linguistic *descriptions* and the conceptual and theoretical network that contains such descriptions. Once this move is made, it is a relatively easy jump from this inferentialist construal of the situation, to the following more typical consequences that are often said to hold between observational terms, the underlying framework of such terms and observational experiences:

> Meaningful observational terms, therefore, will always be embedded within some set of assumptions. And ... those assumptions will always be speculative and corrigible. Meaningful observational terms, we seem bound to conclude, will always be laden with theory.[12]

> [T]he meaning of the relevant observation terms has nothing to do with

---

[8] N. R. Hanson, op. cit., p. 26.
[9] P. M. Churchland, *Scientific Realism and the Plasticity of Mind*, p. 7.
[10] J. A. Fodor, 'Observation Reconsidered,' p. 26.
[11] Loc. cit.
[12] P.M. Churchland, 'Perceptual Plasticity and Theoretical Neutrality,' p. 183.

the intrinsic qualitative identity of whatever sensations just happen to prompt their non-inferential application in singular empirical judgements. Rather, their position in semantic space appears to be determined by the network of sentences containing them accepted by the speakers who use them.[13]

[T]he view that the meaning of our common observation terms is given in, or determined by, sensation must be rejected outright, and ... we are left with networks of belief as bearers or determinants of understanding.[14]

The 'ineffable' pink of one's current visual sensation may be richly and precisely expressible as a '95Hz/80Hz/80Hz chord' in the relevant triune cortical system...This more penetrating conceptual framework may even displace the common sense framework as the vehicle of intersubjective description and spontaneous introspection. Just as a musician can learn to recognize the constitution of heard musical chords, after internalizing the general theory of their internal structure, so we may learn to recognize, introspectively, the n-dimensional constitution of our subjective sensory qualia, after having internalized the general theory of *their* internal structure.[15]

The emphasis does not really need to be spelt out: the examples here show how quickly and easily features of high-level inference have percolated through perceptual content. The quotations above begin with an innocent enough claim about the theory-ladenness of observational terms and then go on to reject sensation as being the bearer of *semantic* content. With sensations 'rejected outright', however, the claims then move from the idea that networks of beliefs (as expressed in sentences) are the bearers of understanding, to the suggestion that *sensations themselves* are replaceable by internalising new belief networks or theories. Observational experience is thereby replaced with *descriptions* in the context of high-level beliefs, theories and language. The astounding claim is made here that because sensations do not bear on content at all, a common sense language of sensational content can be replaced by a better theoretical basis. Both language *and* sensations are thereby seen as replaceable by better descriptions. But this is not an isolated view: Hanson. Churchland and Feyerabend are not alone in making this philosophical sleight of hand; Sellars is in this camp too, as previous passages quoted have shown. And there are many others.

The turning point for this sleight of hand seems to be the factor of language, but once this has been embraced, other high-level features - theoretically informational judgements, descriptive concepts, etc. - follow. The flaw here is that once sensations are seen as being linked with high-level features, such as theories and language, and if theories and language are taken to be holistic and not immune from revision, the next step is to see sensational experiences

---

[13] P.M. Churchland, op. cit., (1979) pp. 11-12.
[14] Ibid., p. 13.
[15] P. M. Churchland, 'Some Reductive Strategies in Cognitive Neurobiology,' p. 303.

themselves as theoretical and revisable. This move naturally leads down the slippery slope of eliminative materialism and to the rejection of the view that there is any content to sensory experiences at all.

The implications of such passages should be noted: it must be remembered that descriptive concepts which are expressed in the propositional content of a language are a crucial feature of one important and influential approach to the fixation of experiential content. Such passages then not only belie a confused connection between language, experience and meanings, they also wholeheartedly embrace the tenets of the inferentialist proposal. And, if the inferentialist proposal is true then animals and infants are experientially *in vacuo* and experiences cannot be fixed observationally. Instead, experiences necessarily require the input of high-level features. These points were mentioned earlier. The suggestion now is that the collapsing of the theory-dependence of language with the theory-dependence of experience is rather less than satisfactory, if it is meant to be a *justification* of this position. It seems, instead, a rather simple and obvious philosophical error. What has happened here is that various philosophers have confused the point that high-level features (such as language) are *important* for experiences at one level, with the inferentialist's stress that high-level features generally are both *necessary and sufficient* for any kind of content at all. However, in view of what has already been said in support of a continuum account of content, this seems to be a very unconvincing move. What seems to have gone unnoticed here is that (i) experiences are not exclusively language-like, and (ii) though important for experience, high-level features generally are not thereby necessary and sufficient for *content*.

Consideration of cognitively unsophisticated animal and infant experience is surely enough to question the conflation of language and experience, thereby undermining the inferentialist proposal. Consideration of low-level content is enough to challenge the idea that all experiences are high-level. Neglecting point (i) above would be to commit oneself to something like a Kantian account of content (and a Cartesian view of animals); neglecting (ii) would be to go some way towards supporting an eliminativist thesis which seems *prima facie* untenable. Both of the above points need to be considered in any adequate account of experience. The inferentialist proposal, it seems, has neglected both of them with its conflation of language and observational experience, and therefore, needs serious revision.

Consequences of the inferentialist proposal

The subtle confusion between the theory-dependence of observational terms and the theory-dependence of observational experience has been outlined. It has also shown how this confusion lends superficial support for the terms of the inferentialist proposal. However, adopting this move uncritically leads to counterintuitive outcomes. One of the outcomes is that animals and infants have to be seen as creatures without experiences (rationalism); another is that since experiences are seen as being language-like, they are also seen to be replaceable by better descriptions of content (eliminativism). Conflating language and experience is clearly a move that has considerable ramifications.

This whole story has major ramifications for the distinction between theory and observation, and its bearing on experiential content. For if the view that no theoretical description of experience is immune from revision is bound up with the view that experience has no content outside the internalisation of theories, then 'the speculative tail can wag the ... observational dog.'[16] A change in theory ultimately translates into a change in experience and there can be *better* theories about experiential content and also *worse* ones. No fixed points of revisability means, in effect, no qualitative, non-theoretical content. In other words, the observational dog has been lost to its theoretical tail. A better metaphor for this, perhaps, is Campbell's 'great Gippsland worm, with head and tail merging in one continuous, homogeneous structure.'[17]

As stressed before, the inferentialist proposal is not entirely faulty. Some of it is substantially correct. The *meanings* of our observational *terms* are inferential in the required sense, because 'meaning' is, inevitably (even trivially) propositional in form. However, it doesn't follow that perceptual *experiences* are entirely inferential or propositional and necessarily involve 'high-level' considerations. There are plausible reasons for being cautious here. The taxonomy of experiential content offered in the previous chapter suggests that these influences can actually be separated. Propositional content can be disjoined from representational content and sensational content can be separated from other high-level features. The intuition that experiential content is observationally fixed is, in a way, legitimised. Observational content, in my view, is importantly *sui generis* to high-level inferential content in some sense. Moreover, this has major ramifications for one's philosophy of mind and perception, leading us from the inferentialist proposal to a *continuum* view of content.

It seems that we must say this because the inferentialist proposal leads us inevitably to absurd conclusions. From the above brief analysis, it is clear that the relationship between experience and high-level factors has become what might be called *inferential linguisticism:* the doctrine that experience is dependent on a theoretical background of *language*. This, as we have previously seen, is part of the high-level content and a mainstay of the inferentialist proposal. It is also clear that this view cannot be true, if it is considered in relation to the experiences of animals, pre-linguistic children and us, when we undergo certain low-level experiences. (In what sense, after all, does the experience of one object being next to another require language?) It does not seem that theoretically informational or propositional, linguistic judgments have much to do with experiences in such cases, though they seem experiences with content nonetheless. The fully inferentialist story in such cases seems simply wrong.

An alternative picture is far more plausible. To remove the absurdities from this view that high-level features, such as language, are necessary for experiential content, something like a phylogenetic argument must be made. This appeal places experiential content of all creatures along an evolutionary continuum, and claims that the various high-level factors influence experiential content to various degrees. An argument against the thrust of the inferentialist proposal in relation to animal experiences has been recently expressed by

---

[16] K. Campbell, 'Philosophy and Common Sense', p. 164.
[17] Loc. cit.

Mortensen and Nerlich:

> [I]t is very hard to believe that a sensory experience amounts in the end to something whose information content is wholly verbalisable. For one thing, it makes it difficult to explain how homo sapiens is an evolved creature. Dumb animals, from which we are descended, are known to have similar sensory-processing apparatus to ourselves, certainly at the cortical level.[18]

Reasons why the sensory is 'radically unlike the verbal' will be looked at in later chapters. Cases where the sensory is unlike the other features of high-level content will be examined as well. My claim will be that engaging the importance of evolutionary considerations in this context is a necessary way of keeping the relationship between high-level considerations and experiential content in some sort of perspective.

The inferentialist proposal is underpinned by the assumption that the imposition of features of high-level inference is more important to experience than the qualitative content of sensation. This certainly explains the impetus behind the philosophical sleight of hand outlined - a kind of rationalism is once again rife in contemporary circles. Moreover, if the historical characterisation of experience and language mentioned is a correct one, then it also explains why the collapsing of theoretical and observational *terms* simultaneously effected a collapse between observational terms and observational *experience,* and why the latter fell noiselessly under the aegis of theories, propositional contents and background knowledge along with its semantic counterpart. Yet this seems too quick a move. I am not alone in thinking that there has been an unfortunate sleight of hand here:

> The result of this conflation of language and experience is that any attempt to distinguish between observational and theoretical language, on the one hand, and observational language and experience, on the other, is caught in a vicious circle: because all language is saturated with theory, then observational language will always be theory-laden, (from Quine); and because observational language is always theory-laden, all observational experience will also be dependent on theory (from Hanson and Churchland). The circle is complete when we note that because all observational experience is theory-laden, then any language we use to describe that experience will also inexorably be imbued with theory. There is not much solace here for the apologist of theory-neutral observational experience, let alone theory-neutral observation language.[19]

---

[18] They go on to add: 'Another consideration leading to the same point is that what is verbally expressible about human sensory information falls far short of what we can discern differences between; for example, fine differences in shades of colour, or complex gestalts like facial appearances or expressions. That is why police identikit pictures are much more useful than the accompanying description ... ideas like these are doubtless what is behind the intuition that the sensory is just radically unlike the verbal.' C. Mortensen and G. Nerlich, *Aspects of Metaphysics*, pp. 1- 2.

[19] G. J. O'Brien, 'The Observation-Theory Distinction Revisited,' pp. 4-5.

Regardless of the historical reasons for the move, and whether or not the position admits of a vicious explanatory circle, the general malaise described here is close to the heart of contemporary philosophy and it needs to be remedied. As O'Brien notes, it is not just a problem of separating theory-ladenness from observational language, but language and theory-ladenness from observational experience. Paul Feyerabend's comments demonstrate a rather nasty instance of the affliction outlined:

> Experience arises *together* with theoretical assumptions and not before them, and an experience without theory is just as incomprehensible as is (allegedly) a theory without experience: eliminate part of the theoretical knowledge of a sensing subject and you have a person who is completely disorientated and incapable of carrying out the simplest action.[20]

There is clearly something wrong here for essentially simpler reasons: theories, concepts, language and their descriptive ilk have been irrevocably bound up as necessary requirements for sensing subjects, and the idea of any reasonable conception of a sensing subject is claimed to be quite 'incomprehensible' without such high-level mediations. However, would the removal of theoretical knowledge from a dog entail that the animal is entirely incapable of experiencing the world? Hardly. It seems easy to grant that dogs don't have *theories* about the world in any precise sense agreeable to inferential linguisticism; dogs do not (plausibly) make theoretically informational, nor linguistically propositional judgments. But it seems simply bizarre to suggest that they can't have contentful experiences because they have no such features. *Reductio ad absurdum.* This must mean that the inferentialist proposal needs to be substantially revised or reformed: contentful observational experience is importantly different to theories, concepts and language in some important sense. It is just that the important sense in which it is different seems unavailable on the terms of the inferentialist proposal.

It is clear what has happened here: the collapsing of the theory-dependence of observational terms to the theory-dependence of observational experience has simultaneously collapsed the quite legitimate separability between the various elements of high-level inference. As we saw earlier, however, propositional content could be understood independently of language as representational judgments. And, inference could be understood independently of the influence of sophisticated background knowledge. Here, however, the sense in which experience needs high-level features, has been confused with the necessity of such features for the intelligibility of *language*. This innocent 'carry over' has thus left contentful observational experience being *defined* by such features and no other. Experience has thus come to be seen in terms of both linguistic, propositional and theoretically informational judgments. It is this which has engaged us to consider the absurd situation in which some creatures who do not have language do not have experiences, or that blind people are deficient only in respect of not using a certain part of an observation language, or that the idea of a 'sensing subject' without theory is 'incomprehensible.'

An overly sophisticated account of experiential content is as much a mistake

---

[20] P. K. Feyerabend, 'Science without Experience,' op. cit., p. 168.

as using language as the sole arbiter of beliefs. The strategy best adopted is to take a levels-of-content approach and to treat the importance of high-level features in decreasing orders of magnitude from sophisticated to very primitive experiences. In relation to primitive experiences, instead of arguing that all experience is vitally underpinned by high-level considerations, one can argue that only some experiences are. Experience can have a sensational aspect; which, far from being 'bare and meaningless and irrelevant to knowledge'[21] is in some sense still crucial for it. There may be aspects of experiences which are informationally significant, regardless of the input of high-level inferential factors and this need not amount to reinforcing foundationalism (see Chapter 10 for this). Instead of following this sleight of hand mentioned, I shall be drawing on the suggestive remark made by Armstrong mentioned in Chapter 1 and developed in Chapter 2. Again, the aim is not to rule out the importance of inference at a sufficiently high-level, but instead to suggest that features of high-level embeddedness is not the only, nor prime, consideration.

Ultimately, we want not a dog being wagged by its tail, or a great Gippsland worm, but a picture in which both high-level theory and structured, low-level observational experiences feature as mutually reinforcing elements of a larger story. And this larger story must be the nature of mental content. Because such contents are importantly conscious and sensational, we will, inevitably, be broaching *property dualism*. I want to consider a form of property dualism on these grounds as still being a serious and workable option. It is claimed here there must be some kind of *felt* properties to certain sensational experiences because not all content can be fixed exclusively by high-level influences such as language, representational descriptive content and theories. Some of what will be said later will, therefore, be relevant to the 'qualia' issue in the philosophy of mind. Detailed consideration of such matters will be deferred until Part IV.

The causal, sensory and epistemic orders

Isolating a sleight of hand in the terms of the inferentialist proposal has displayed a confusion between high-level influences and low-level content. This confusion has lead to a seriously misleading characterisation of experience.

An important result of this is a loss of the distinction between the causal origins of experience and the sensory and epistemic outcomes that experiences bring. These distinctive features shall be called the *causal, sensory* and *epistemic orders*. The causal order is simply the stimulus inputs on the sense organs, the sensory order is the level at which experiences are sensed or felt, the epistemic order is the level at which experience can yield sophisticated reliable or unreliable knowledge. On the continuum view of content all these orders are central to capturing the nature of contentful experiences.

Each complex human experience participates in these orders to a greater or lesser extent. However, the low-level experience of evolutionarily primitive creatures may participate in only the causal (or causal and sensory) orders. It is a plausible point that while conceptually unsophisticated creatures participate in the causal order and by and large receive similar perceptual inputs to that of more sophisticated creatures it is nonetheless clear that how that information is

---

[21] H. I. Brown, op. cit., p. 88.

used is very different. Very sophisticated creatures use sensory information to build large-scale conceptual models of the universe; very unsophisticated creatures do not. (In the simplest case, such information only achieves reactive behavioural responses in such creatures.) The problem with accounts of experience and content which ignore such differences is that perceptual data is seen predominantly in terms of the construction of meaning and 'significance' in the acquisition of knowledge but not in other terms. Content is thus seen only in terms of its epistemic function, not in terms of its causal function or sensory function. The inferentialist proposal has tended to ignore the importance of all but the epistemic order.

Hanson's passage at the beginning of this chapter associates 'meaningful' seeing with the formation of sentences in describing the world and gaining knowledge; Brown's passage associates perception simply with epistemic significance; Churchland's and Feyerabend's words suggest that perceptual data are strongly associated with the structure of language and theories. It goes unstated here the extent to which experiences arise concurrently as *causes* and, particularly, as *sensations*.

In inferentialist treatments of content what is generally stressed is only *one* of the functions of perceptual data in an organism's interaction with the world; hence the preoccupation with language, belief networks and theories. But, there is, of course, an obvious *causal* role of perception too: the raw 'nerve impingings' as Quine might have it. It is not being suggested here that any of the inferentialist theorists that have been mentioned lose sight of this feature, only that, by adopting the inferentialist proposal, they are in danger of belittling or ignoring its importance.

Another more crucial consequence of an inferentialist treatment of content is that it ignores the sensory order altogether. At its most extreme, this attitude results in the view that because content does not play a sophisticated epistemic role in animal and infant cognition, it does not thereby play a role in the overall economy of their experiential states either. This move would be to ignore the point made by Armstrong that even though high-level epistemic notions like belief are inappropriately applied to such creatures, there is no reason to suppose that they are thereby *inferior* in some sense (Armstrong's continuum metaphor is apposite here). Descartes' views about animals are, of course, an extreme example of this tendency, but so are some of the views of some contemporary materialist theorists.

However, the sensory order has an important selective function and should be included in any account of experience and content. The distinction between the various orders of content (causal, sensory and epistemic) parallels the distinction made earlier between proximal stimulations (which are psychologically non-inferential), low-level sensations (qualitative and partially inferential) and descriptive content (strongly inferential).

There is a clear need for an alternative to the observational account and the inferentialist proposal. The observational account was deficient by ignoring the important point that experiences have to be organised in some sense involving inference. The inferentialist proposal, by contrast, seemed to take the importance of high-level factors to the point of overkill. These features are over-emphasised and stressed to the extent that intuitions snap: that there are no sensing subjects without theory; that the blind are deficient only in respect of an observation language; that animals are experientially *in vacuo*. As mentioned, the reason for such claims is possibly historical, involving the rationalist legacy of Kant and Descartes, and the move to conflate observational language with observational experience.

What we have seen in this chapter is the end result of this philosophical slip: the holism thesis applied to observational terms has come to help situate experiential content in terms captured by linguistic propositional and theoretically informational judgments. If what has been argued so far is plausible, then this move is misplaced and there may be more to experiential content than what the inferentialist account stipulates.

Conclusion

Two major claims have been made in this and the previous chapters:

1. It has been argued that the inferentialist proposal rests on a rather confused and misleading connection between the theory-ladenness of observational terms and the theory-ladenness of observational experience. The effect of this confusion has not been insubstantial, tying meanings and language up with experiential content. The counter-intuitive consequences of such a confusion were obvious, and arguments were presented against this view. It has also been argued (in Chapter 1) that the view has historical roots going back to early rationalism - at least to the views of Descartes and Kant. This influence has been instrumental in making content attributions only along sophisticated, 'high-level' criteria. In each case, these supports are of no real comfort for the inferentialist proposal even though they have been of major importance in keeping the inferentialist myth going.

2. The inferentialist proposal is not the only account in which high-level considerations are said to influence the content of experience. Another account is the continuum view, which holds a substantially weaker claim: that experiential content can be characterised by such high-level features only to varying degrees. The continuum theory makes up for both the deficiencies of the observational account and the excesses of the inferentialist proposal. More supports for adopting this approach are developed in the subsequent chapter where the relation between belief and experiential content is discussed in detail.

4 Experience and belief

> Whenever we talk about perceiving things in our environment or talk about perceiving features of things, we can also talk of acquiring knowledge of particular facts about these things.[1]

> Total ignorance is not a sufficient condition for total blindness.[2]

Epistemic and non-epistemic seeing

Introduction

The role of beliefs in the content of experience will now be discussed. I will attempt to do two things: (i) rule as inadequate an account of experience in terms of the belief content of representational judgements; and (ii) show that even the notion of a belief can be understood in graduationist terms. By giving a fairly precise account of the relationship between belief and experience, it will be argued that the most plausible way beliefs influence experiential content is in the manner the continuum account specifies.

Belief fixation and experience

Experiences amount to being mental states of some complex kind. This can clearly be understood in a number of ways. A continuum approach has been advanced in which the content of experiences can be said to be states fixed by a number of variously sophisticated and non-exclusive means. The usual approach to this issue, however, has been in terms of a choice between two rival accounts which disagree over one main feature which is said to be central to experiential states. The feature which divides the two views is the role of beliefs:

> The [rivalling] accounts may conveniently ... be labelled respectively as

---

[1] D. M. Armstrong, *Perception and the Physical World*, p. 108.
[2] F. I. Dretske, *Seeing and Knowing*, p. 17.

'epistemic' and 'non-epistemic'. The former attempts to analyse seeing (or perception generally) in terms of belief (or knowledge) or the acquisition of beliefs. According to it, an analysis of seeing things or events necessarily involves reference to believing-that, or to seeing-that, which, in turn is analysed, partially at least, in terms of believing-that. It is not held, generally, that seeing-that can occur without seeing things or events; but it is held that the former notion is the fundamental one. One, but not the only, impetus to developing this kind of theory is the wish to avoid ... the admission of items (sense-data, etc.) that ... are not physical or public items but are nevertheless 'perceived' or 'sensed' when we perceive physical things and events.

The opposing account holds that there is some basic seeing ... that is 'non-epistemic', i.e., does not necessarily involve acquisition of beliefs (or knowledge) and can be adequately analysed without reference to the concept of a belief at all. On this view, although someone who sees a thing or event may also in fact see-that something, and so acquire some belief, the notion of seeing-that must be analysed by reference to the more basic and non-epistemic notion, seeing.[3]

We saw in Chapter 1 that experiences are importantly connected to the notion of a belief. Beliefs were shown to be connected to 'high-level' abilities - to know and describe features of the world; specifically, to form various kinds of representational judgements. Given that experiences are always underdetermined by sensory arrays, background beliefs help sort out perceptual data in a meaningful form. In this chapter the 'epistemic' account of perception will be compared to Dretske's view which allegedly eschews the emphasis on beliefs altogether. Jackson's contribution to this issue will also be looked at in this context. The claim shall be that the epistemic and non-epistemic accounts capture features of certain *kinds* of experiences, and that it is better to combine their insights in graduationist terms rather than treat them as rivals. The notion of a belief in the 'high-level' representational sense - believing-*that* - receives some modification in the discussion that follows.

Epistemic seeing: Armstrong's case

The 'epistemic' view will be recalled as Armstrong's belief-based account, which was outlined briefly in Chapter 1. Armstrong has described the essentials of his 'epistemic' approach to perception as 'the acquiring of true or false *information.*'[4] For him, this information amounts to propositional states of a non-linguistic kind which are also belief states of some kinds, which may be either true or false. Armstrong's sense of 'proposition' has been defined in terms of representational judgements. Beliefs are obviously important in this context, for, as has been argued on behalf of the inferentialist proposal, experiences fix beliefs of certain kinds. The content of Sherlock Holmes's experience of the cigar-band and Jones's body, was epistemic in an important sense because Holmes could perceptually discriminate objects of knowledge: a

---

[3] F. N. Sibley, 'Analysing Seeing' in *Perception: A Philosophical Symposium*, pp. 81- 2.

[4] D. M. Armstrong, *A Materialist Theory of the Mind*, p. 224.

cigar-band, a dead body, objects in certain relationships, and so on. One could also mount a case, as Armstrong does, for saying that experiences have propositional features. The epistemic and propositional features are two of the important 'high-level' influences on experiences.

On Armstrong's account, experiences involve either beliefs about 'the *current* state of our body and environment'[5] or an inference from one's current belief and background knowledge: 'I acquire the belief that there is a certain muddy pattern of marks on the floor now, and this causes me to acquire the further belief that somebody came in with muddy boots last night.'[6] Information acquisition by means of belief content is information by means of possession of prior concepts: experiences-*that* something is the case always presupposes concepts of some sort, even if, on Armstrong's view, some concepts are 'subverbal' and 'perceptual' as would be the case with animal experiences.[7]

On the face of it, it would seem implausible to argue that all experiences are beliefs-*that* something is the case. Experiencing perceptual illusions (like the bent stick illusion) are cases where what is seen is not what is believed. However, Armstrong's theory offers an account of such experiences too. He argues that even if the content of an experience may not correlate with a belief that someone holds, it is nonetheless true that there is some informational content, some believing-*that*. A coin may look elliptical from a certain angle, for example, even when it is plainly believed to be circular. For Armstrong, this would be a case of a 'potential' belief which is later rejected in the context of background knowledge about the laws of perspective. For Armstrong, there is no question of complicated proto-mental properties like elliptical sense-data; there are only 'potential' beliefs 'which we have some tendency, but no more than some tendency, to accept.'[8] Experiential content, on his view, is then only properly of a representational nature, and the deliverance of sensory inputs is an important, but certainly less significant, part of this procedure of belief-fixation. The content of experience is not the input, but the *beliefs* derived thereby. A belief in something illusory is, for Armstrong, still a belief, albeit a 'potential' one. Armstrong's account will be considered again after an outline of the opposing position.

Non-epistemic seeing: Dretske's case

The second main account mentioned here, the 'non-epistemic' account, is formulated in reaction to such a view. Although there is some dispute about the interpretation of 'non-epistemic' in this context, this account is best exemplified by Dretske's work. Dretske rejects the move that identifies *seeing* something to *believing* that there is something which is seen. On his view, there is an important sense in which experiences are not believings. There are at least two reasons given for adopting this view. The first is that the relationship between believing and seeing is not symmetrical. Believing *that* something is a certain

---

[5] Ibid., p. 210.

[6] Loc. cit.

[7] See ibid., pp. 202 and 210; pp. 341-2. That he must hold this is a result of his rejection of the language-like account of the propositional content of beliefs.

[8] Ibid., p. 225.

way and not another does not guarantee that experiences which are *not* believings are *not* seeings:

> The fact that we normally do believe something about the things which we see in this way is irrelevant. The point I am driving is that our failure to believe these things would not, in itself, prevent us from seeing what we see in this way. The bewildered savage, transplanted suddenly from his native environment to a Manhattan subway station, can witness the arrival of the 3.45 express as clearly as the bored commuter. Ignorance of X does not impair one's vision of X; if it did, total ignorance would be largely irreparable.[9]

This kind of argument is not very convincing on its own. It certainly does not demonstrate that there are no beliefs or sets of beliefs in such a case. Armstrong, of course, can argue that even if the savage were ignorant of features like trains in his experience, he would still *believe* that there was a certain object in his experience moving towards him. As his experience has a certain projected representational content, it still involves beliefs in Armstrong's sense. (There is, after all, some*thing* that the savage sees.) However, this doesn't seem to be Dretske's point, despite the misleading example. What he seems to be suggesting is that there can be certain aspects of an experience which are not belief-like in Armstrong's sense. The point seems to be that whatever their importance, beliefs are not necessary and sufficient for features of experiences seeming a certain way.

Dretske describes his account as showing that 'there is a way of seeing that is devoid of positive belief content.' [10] By this he means that there is a way of seeing in which there is no entailment relation from '*S* seeing *D*' to *S believing* that there is (was) a *D* that he saw. What brings out Dretske's point most clearly is the fact that one can have seen the number of distinct letters on the previous page, without entailing that one *believed* anything specific about those letters:

> Now I think that the likelihood is that, if you did read the entire page, you saw hundreds of different letters... What, then, are the necessary consequences of these hundred or so different statements about what you saw? Does each one entail that you had a certain belief about the way that letter looked to you? During the time that it took you to read the page, did you acquire hundreds of distinct beliefs about the assorted letters you saw? Granted, each letter that you saw must have looked some way to you, in some sense, but does that mean that you had to believe this? Can you remember believing anything of the sort?[11]

Again, Armstrong could reject such an account on the basis that even in this circumstance one at least believes that one is seeing words on a page. So, Dretske does not rule out a connection between believing and seeing. However, does Dretske establish that believing is not *necessary and sufficient* for seeing?

---

[9] Dretske, op. cit., p. 8.
[10] Ibid., p. 12.
[11] Ibid., p. 11.

With clarifications, it can be shown that he does.

What needs to be clarified is the sense of 'belief' that Dretske is objecting to here. His use of 'belief' throughout *Seeing and Knowing* constantly refers to believing that one saw *something,* or that something seemed like *that*. In view of this, it would seem obvious that the focus of attack is belief content of the kind the 'epistemic' account specifies as being crucial to experiences. Dretske is reacting to a view of belief as representational judgement; as a belief - *that* something is the case. And a belief-*that* something is the case, in Armstrongian terms, amounts to having *representational* content. Dretske's claim is that some experiences can be devoid of a positive belief content of *this* kind. In this sense, of course, the above example shows that one does not necessarily believe (represent) anything about *each individual letter* on the page (one might not even *notice* each individual letter as one reads). There is thus no entailment relation between seeing and believing in this case. So, believing-*that* is not necessary and sufficient for all cases of seeing. As shall be shown later, however, an important extension of Dretske's work would be to take his arguments as applying only to *this* kind of 'high-level' representational belief, but not another kind of 'low-level' belief. This would effectively make his view a *partial* non-epistemic account in some sense, not a *fully* non-epistemic account. Indeed, this qualification makes his account a far more coherent position for other reasons. It will also require us to revise and broaden the terms of the dispute beyond that of the 'epistemic' and 'non-epistemic' accounts.

There may be a further, independent sense in which Dretske's claims are instructive. At a certain level, it might be that some features of experiences, while *informational,* are not captured by belief states at all. There may be a sense in which some experiences are devoid of not only 'positive' belief contents, but *any* belief content. Some experiences might involve *unnoticed seeings,* but such cases are far from the kinds of sophisticated experiences Dretske uses for his examples. Dretske seems to be suggesting that there is no necessary and sufficient connection between seeing and believing; his examples show that some experiences have features which *need not* be believed (not that they *are not* believed at all). Dretske's claim, then, is not that there can be no beliefs in perception, but that there need not be an *entailment* from perceiving to believing in the 'high-level' sense of believing: ' All I am suggesting ... is that the possession of no particular belief, or set of beliefs, constitutes a logically indispensable condition for the individual's seeing what he does.'[12] Elsewhere, he is clear about his aims:

> I have not said that S ... can see something without any beliefs; I have only said that no *particular* belief is essential to the seeing. He may have many beliefs, and it may be essential (especially in the case of human agents) that he have some beliefs in order to qualify for such 'mentalistic' predicates as 'sees so-and-so'. Nonetheless, of no one of those beliefs is it essential that he has it.[13]

For Dretske, possession of high-level representational beliefs are a *generally*

---

[12] Ibid., p. 13.
[13] Ibid., p 17. n. 2.

necessary condition of being a certain creature which sees, but they are not a *sufficient* condition. To this extent, the label 'non-epistemic' for Dretske's position is a misnomer. Dretske's position is only *non-epistemic* if one's conception of belief is of the kind that Armstrong uses to support his account of perception; it might be partially epistemic otherwise. As shall be suggested later, there might be a sense of belief in which no *particular* states, objects or events in the world are represented, but which still constitute beliefs of some very primitive kind, if only because one must be capable of attending to certain qualitative features of an experience, even if there is not a particular thing or state of affairs that one is attending *to*. Specifically, the whole question of the relation between belief and experience is a matter of emphasis: there may be a number of different levels in which beliefs are involved in experiences, ranging from Armstrong's representational sense to low-level 'look-beliefs', which have no representational content but which are still belief-like to some degree, and also 'unnoticed seeings' where it makes no sense to speak of them having belief content at all. Dretske's examples fall into the second category; Armstrong's examples fall into the first category. Certain other cases which shall be mentioned later fall into the third category.

Does ignorance about a given perceptual situation still imply 'a rudimentary ... elementary belief ... that something is appearing to us in such-and-such a way ... or that something looks some way to us[?]'[14] Dretske doesn't think so. Again, he fully rejects Armstrong's strict necessary and sufficient connection between representational judging and the having of experiences. He concludes from the example given earlier (about seeing letters on a page), that even though *seeing something in a certain way* does normally issue in a belief that there is something *that* one sees, it need not be 'a necessary consequence'[15] of all cases of seeing. Hence, some 'seeings', on his view, have features which are genuinely non-representational and are not belief-like in Armstrong's sense.

The second reason Dretske offers for his position brings out why this might be true. Although Dretske is sympathetic with the view that some degree of belief content bears on experiences, he does argue that there is no case at all for ascribing such contents to all experiencing creatures. The 'epistemic' account, in Dretske's view, *over-intellectualises* the issue in taking all perceptual experience to have sophisticated belief contents. I am very sympathetic to this kind of claim. Take the case of the experiences of unsophisticated creatures, such as insects. It seems hard to believe-*that* such creatures see (represent) particular things. Some simple invertebrates have sensory detectors which are responsive merely to patterns of lightness and darkness or certain temperature thresholds.[16] Their 'experiences' seem merely reactive, not instruments to convey propositional or representational belief content. Similarly, a treatment in terms of 'potential' beliefs does not capture such examples: such creatures don't believe anything (even 'potentially'); they just *see* (lightness and darkness) *in a certain way*. The belief-based account seems far too strong in such cases. This, as Dretske notes, is particularly apposite to the experiences of unsophisticated

---

[14] Ibid., p. 9.

[15] Loc. cit.

[16] P. A. Meglitsch, *Invertebrate Zoology*, p. 653. See also H. S. Jennings: *Contributions to the Study of the Behaviour of Lower Organisms, passim*, especially second paper, pp. 31-71.

creatures like animals and infants:

> I would agree ... that whenever it becomes true to say of an infant that it can now see its mother, or of a rat that it can see the lever, it also becomes true to say of the infant and the rat that they see the mother and the lever as something - the mother looks some way to the infant and the lever looks some way to the rat. Must the infant believe, however, that something is a dark figure on a light background ... or that something looks like a dark figure? What *must* our experimental rat believe about the lever which it sees? I, personally, have no idea what the infant or the rat believes, or whether they believe anything, but I do think that the sorts of beliefs described [on the 'epistemic' account] imply an unusual degree of sophistication on the part of the creatures to whom they are ascribed.[17]

It would seem from this example that there are some kinds of experiences which cannot be captured in representational terms at all. This is most marked in creatures which can't detect things of the objective world (only say, lightness and darkness) but it is also marked in ordinary human experiences. Rubbing one's eyes gives an experiential content of certain colours, yet it would be a tall order to give an account of such an experience as a belief-*that* something is the case, because the experience is neither represented in the world (like a cigar-band) nor is it in one's head exactly - nor is this content, in any strong sense, of *information* like Armstrong's sense of belief. There simply seems to be no projected feature about such experiences to allow them to be accounted for representationally or epistemically.

A congenial interpretation of Dretske's work might be as follows: Dretske's claims might legitimate the idea that some experiences have observational features structured at an extremely low level. For some creatures, it is less important to believe-*that* one is seeing something in some circumstances, than for something to *seem a certain way to them.* Just as there is no immediately plausible reason why an invertebrate needs to believe that something is before it, as opposed to having a certain illumination in its visual field, so a savage does not need to *believe* in any specific way he is seeing (representing) a Manhattan subway train for features of his visual field to seem a certain way. Indeed, there may be several levels of experience and content corresponding to different levels of cognitive input for various kinds of organisms. This is the line that shall be taken on this matter. A sophisticated organism like Sherlock Holmes or a savage may have a good deal of representational belief content in their experiences; an unsophisticated organism may have rather less. However, Holmes may also have a belief content about an experience, but not necessarily believe-*that* something is the case (e.g., he may not believe that there is a cigar-band near Jones's body even if he sees it, because he is not concentrating or *attending* to what he is seeing). But it might also be true that things *seem a certain way* for such creatures, regardless of those influences.

Something 'seeming a certain way' is a rather ambiguous phrase, and Dretske uses it continually. This is unfortunate, as it can be interpreted as a belief-laden notion; it could be taken to mean that something seen 'is (seems like) a train', or

---

[17] Dretske, op. cit., pp. 9-10.

'is (seems like) red' etc., and hence could be seen as supporting Armstrong's thesis. For this reason, perhaps, Dretske's views have been seen as no real alternative to claims of epistemic accounts like that offered by Armstrong. However, there is a more subtle way of looking at the relation between belief and experience which neither Dretske's nor Armstrong's account seems to capture. It will be assumed here that the phrase 'seems a certain way' suggests there are aspects *of even belief-ridden experiences* that have features which are not belief-like in Armstrong's sense. Therefore, there is no reason at all to suppose that *all* features of experiences need to be captured in terms of the content of beliefs as representational or propositional linguistic judgements. Being able to see *in a certain way* need 'not involve the acquired abilities to identify, recognise, name, describe and so on.'[18] Some experiences might not, in other words, involve 'high-level' features at all. But on the other hand, experiences might involve belief contents which are something rather less than fully representational.

Individuating beliefs

It is clear that there are certain problems associated with the view that it is only in circumstances of high-level inference from representational states that 'beliefs' obtain. For it is possible that beliefs about some features of experiences can be logically detached from beliefs about these features as objects of experience - and vice versa. That this can be done suggests that there is, in fact, no *intrinsic* tie between them. Consider Jackson's examples:

> I may, ... see [a] tomato without believing I see it - perhaps I think it is a wax dummy, or perhaps I see it without in any way noticing it. Second, suppose I both see the tomato and believe that I see it, must my belief that I see the tomato derive from believing I see a red shape? ... Suppose that I glance briefly into the kitchen and see a bowl of fruit and vegetables containing a tomato. And suppose I am then asked whether I saw a tomato and whether it was red or green (that is, was ripe or unripe). ... I might be able to answer the first query without being able to answer the second; that is, it is possible that I noticed seeing the tomato without noticing in any way the colour (which I must, of course, have seen). Hence, it is possible that I believe that I see the tomato without believing that I see a red shape (though I *am* seeing a red shape) .... Every leaf seen on my walk must look some colour and shape to me and must be seen as having some colour and shape by me at the time of seeing. But, just as I may see something without noticing it, without believing that I see it, so something might look some way to me (or be seen as ...) without my noticing this in any way. As I drove quickly through the village, perhaps I saw the third house on the left without noticing or believing that I did. If so, the house must have looked some way to me, but I may not have noticed what way that was.[19]

---

[18] G. J. Warnock, 'Seeing', in *Perceiving, Sensing and Knowing,* p. 65.
[19] F. Jackson, *Perception: A Representative Theory,* pp. 25-26.

Like Dretske, Jackson tries to point out a more subtle and complex relation between experience and belief. These examples show that the idea that there is a necessary and sufficient connection between belief and content is a fabricated and misleading view of the matter. Though there is often a very close relation between belief and content; there may be content without there necessarily being beliefs in Armstrong's sense. One might represent in one's experience-*that* that one sees a tomato, without representing its colour; one might 'see', in some sense, autumn leaves while on a walk without representing them as autumn leaves. In some cases an experience can be seen in terms of having a 'high-level' belief; in other cases it can't. The point is that the 'epistemic' account is not *always* true of experiences, so it is not the only way in which they can have content. Moreover, as Jackson points out, experiences might consist to some extent of *unnoticed seeings,* whereby experiences register certain features without those features actually being noticed, and hence, believed.

To be more specific, Jackson's examples show a number of things: they clearly show that an experience can have some kind of content, without there being any particular feature of the experience that is *represented* (the autumn leaves example). Representational judgements cannot then be a necessary and sufficient condition for experiential content. However, they also show that there might be an aspect of some experiences that has representational content but which does not capture *all* the features of the experience. For example, seeing a tomato without representing its colour shows that a representational content may be present without capturing certain other features seen. Furthermore, the examples show that seeing is not necessarily tied to believing in any general sense as there is a case for saying that one can recall having seen the third house on the left without necessarily believing that one saw it. So, experiences can involve representational beliefs, beliefs with content that is not represented, represented beliefs which do not capture certain seeings, and certain seeings which are not believed at all but which are seen. I'll return to this kind of complex, multi-level view of the relationship between belief and experience later and suggest that this kind of view of the relationship between beliefs and experiences accords well with the continuum account of content.

The points mentioned above highlight some important problems which must be successfully handled by the epistemic account:

Firstly, it must be explained why *all* experiences should be seen as underpinned by beliefs-*that* something is the case rather than in other terms. Some cases of experiential content do seem difficult to place in the category of being believings-that. As argued in Chapter 1, an experience of an assemblage of objects seen with one eye and then both eyes does seem to have a different experiential content, but the belief-*that* one is seeing certain objects in certain relationships remains unchanged. Such a case has representational content, but this feature just does not capture the difference in the experiences. Nor does Armstrong's rather odd notion of 'potential' beliefs seem to capture this difference in content.

Secondly, if we are to take Jackson's or Dretske's claims seriously, then the relationship between experience and belief is more complex than the 'epistemic' account assumes as beliefs of sorts can occur without those beliefs having representational features. For example, one might immediately believe something about leaves on one's walk without representing them as leaves. It is clear that any tight relation between experiences, representational content and beliefs is oversimplified. The 'epistemic' account seems to capture only certain sorts of experiential beliefs.

Thirdly, an account must be offered of cognitively unsophisticated animal and infant experiences, which do not seem to have the features that the epistemic account says they do. Belief, on Armstrong's view, involves informational content and, at the very least, representational concepts. But none of these things seems terribly central to unsophisticated animal and infant experiences, nor to very low-level experiences as had by humans (even though these things might have *some* place in a more inclusive account of belief and experience).

A response to the third problem has been given by Armstrong in another context, but it is hardly a way of legitimating the belief-based account of perception. As we have already seen in Chapter 1, Armstrong entertains the idea that belief content attributions might lie along a continuum, a graded scale, between organisms of various degrees of cognitive sophistication. This sort of consideration is suggestive in that it might be sensible to treat the nature of beliefs in terms of *degrees* of applicability, rather than in all-or-none terms.

But if beliefs are treated in these terms, it is hardly an argument for accepting the stronger thesis that *epistemic* features are fundamental features of experience in the required sense. That Armstrong reaches for such a metaphor would seem to indicate that he is trying to overcome the deficiencies in his inferentialist analysis. When considering unsophisticated animal and infant experiences, for example, it does seem more plausible to look at perception in terms which incorporate 'epistemic' features but which seriously limit the degree to which a belief-based view can give an account of perceptual content. A subtler account would take into account such considerations as low-level content, unnoticed seeings, experiences with some belief content but without representational content, and so on.

Combining the epistemic and non-epistemic views

A non-dichotomous treatment of beliefs

The case has been given for both the 'epistemic' and the 'non-epistemic' account of experiential content. The 'epistemic' account captures experiences or features of experience having a discernible representational content, which can be understood as believing-*that* something is the case. Sherlock Holmes, for example, *did* believe that there was a cigar-band near Jones's dead body. The 'non-epistemic' account, by contrast, captures experiential content which seems to have features of a less sophisticated kind: several objects viewed with one or both eyes open may have a distinctly different look, but the belief-*that* one is seeing certain objects in certain relationships may remain the same.[20] On this

---

[20] I say 'less sophisticated kind' for good reason. Armstrong could presumably argue that even in this case there are different belief contents. However, it becomes very *mysterious* what Armstrong means by 'beliefs' if he was to insist on this. Suppose one concentrates hard on believing that one is seeing a table with one eye, and then opens the other eye - it seems undeniable that some feature of the experience has changed even if the belief has not. What could 'different belief contents' mean in such a case? Surely the most plausible account is

view, such beliefs are not necessary and sufficient for content at all. Armstrong's account thus captures experiential content with high-level features; Dretske's non-epistemic account captures features of experiential content which have certain non-representational *looks*. There are clearly stock examples which offer reasons for accepting both views to some degree.

Is either approach here necessarily more plausible than the other? If not, there might be a case for claiming that the two views need to be combined somehow. A way of doing this might be to allow different levels of content to feature in perception, but to recognise that none of these levels fully defines or captures its complex nature. This view of experience might embrace levels at which some experiences are fixed by high-level beliefs; others which are fixed by low-level appearances which might be primed for the organism in any number of ways - either endogenously or via the presentation of certain properties to highly discriminating sense detectors which operate on selected environmental cues. This suggestion will be taken up in detail in Chapter 8. The point here is that there might be a case for claiming that some experiences have several kinds of experiential content simultaneously. If this could be said to be true, then experiential content is neither fundamentally 'belief-like' nor fundamentally 'non-epistemic.' The terms of the dispute in this sense are misleading. Experience might, instead, have a number of different features; features for which it *seems* and *looks* to the subject a certain way, and features for which it is *believed* by the subject *that* it is a certain way. And there might be a number of different possibilities in between these extremes.

That there might be different aspects of experiential states which have these respective features is plausible on all but an inferentialist's treatment of experiential belief content. But it is also clear that the traditional formulation of the dispute about belief and experience has not admitted of a multi-aspect view. In terms of offering an account of experiential content, the formulation of the 'epistemic'-'non-epistemic' options above has come to give an either/or relationship, not a combination of the two. It has come to mean this: if the content of experience is not importantly belief-ridden, then it must be *observationally* fixed non-inferentially in some sense; if it is not observational, it must always have a representational content such that it is believed to be a certain way and not another. Both Armstrong and Dretske clearly see this as a dichotomous relationship and, equally, see the rejection of their own account as leading to undesirable alternatives.

While Armstrong panics over the rejection of the belief-based account of perception ('[If] perceptual experience is to be distinct from the acquisition of beliefs about the environment, [then it will become] some relationship that the mind has to non-physical sensory items'),[21] Dretske expresses a similar fear for any rejection of the observational fixation account, suggesting that a consequence of this line of attack ends in perceptual relativism ('if there was no non-epistemic way of seeing objects and events ... one would be lead to suppose that people who possessed radically different beliefs ... did not, indeed could not, see the same things ... this is but a prelude to the view that we each

---

that, along with high-level beliefs, there are less sophisticated features of experiences too, and that these are both evident in the case considered.

[21] Armstrong, (1968), op. cit., p. 217.

have our *private* perceptual world.')[22] No intermediate position seems to be possible on such statements of the problem.

This situation need not have arisen. In the usual way the dispute is formulated, an experience might have *both* features on each of the views mentioned (see Sibley's quotation near the beginning of this chapter). But how the topic is actually explored and emphasised for either 'epistemic' or 'non-epistemic' views, one kind of feature is usually seen as more fundamental, and hence, explicable in those terms. If there is a sense in which the two views are compatible whilst isolating two legitimate and important aspects of experiential content, then it is clearly not brought out in traditional expressions of the problem such as those given above. For both Armstrong and Dretske, to adopt one view is to largely reject the importance of the other. Hence, the issue becomes a dispute, not an acknowledgment of the various different kinds of content that experience may have.

This can be seen from some of the responses of adherents of each of these views. For Armstrong, who is an advocate of the view that perceptual content is importantly belief-ridden and propositional, the 'information-flow' account of perception can 'explain the other idiom.'[23] By this he means that an account of perceptual content in terms of the imposition of beliefs can *explain away* the intuition that features of experiential content can be importantly non-epistemic. By contrast, Dretske on occasion claims that perception can be accounted for entirely in terms of what he calls 'seeing$_n$'[24] which, he and others claim, 'has no belief content,'[25] and which can be experienced without 'making [any] judgement whatever.'[26] From what has been mentioned before, it is unclear how this kind of conclusion can be drawn from Dretske's arguments which only show that beliefs are not necessary and sufficient for some perceivings, not that they are not needed at all. Also, it is not easy to see how any kind of conciliatory approach could be possible with such statements of the dispute. Both kinds of theorists claim that their view of experiential content is fundamental and, in practice, largely ignore the application of the other.

Despite the divisive nature of the epistemic-non-epistemic dispute, adherents of each of these rivalling views do acknowledge the importance of some kind of compatibilist position. We have already seen Armstrong's rejection of a propositional basis for the content of animal experiences, and the suggestion of the continuum metaphor instead. This showed that he was prepared to embrace only some features of the inferentialist proposal and not others. Elsewhere, he allows for the possibility of *low-level* experiences, or 'small perceptions' [27] which do not seem to involve belief states and are not, demonstrably, cases of 'seeing-that':

> At a certain instant the perception occurs ... But this state disappears so

---

[22] Dretske, op. cit., pp. 76-77.
[23] Armstrong, (1968), op. cit., p. 228.
[24] 'Non-epistemic perception' is discussed in Dretske passim.
[25] Ibid., p. 19.
[26] Warnock, op. cit., p. 52.
[27] Armstrong, (1968), op. cit., p. 232.

rapidly - the impression fades so fast - that we may well be reluctant to describe it as a state of belief. The state is gone before there is any possibility of a manifestation of belief. And if there is no possibility of manifestation how can we speak of belief?[28]

The sorts of things Armstrong had in mind are 'immediate' experiences of the kind which admit of no inference - experiences like the 'mere registration of colour or shape.'[29] Armstrong allows that such experiences amount to the registration of 'visual properties of things' and that, 'by an automatic and instantaneous inference', such properties are fixed into beliefs about the perception of physical objects. Yet Armstrong gives no precise account of what it is to register the 'visual properties of things.' Does he want to suggest that there are some visual experiences which are not belief-like, or that some beliefs are non-informational in his sense? Either position would amount to modifying Armstrong's strongly inferentialist position. His position on this is unclear. What is clear is that such comments are not entirely consistent with the belief content being the fundamental content of experiences. If there are 'visual properties of things' registered in perception, in addition to 'beliefs about physical objects,' then such experiences need an account of some sort too.

Similarly, Dretske has claimed that one need not be pushed in the direction of assimilating experiential content to features of the observational situation:

> One could, I suppose, continue to insist that I was believing something at the time about the things which I saw, but that I simply can no longer remember the fact. Or, alternatively one could insist ... that I did not really see anything.[30]

It is clear that even the enthusiasts of each position are rather ambiguous about the extent to which their views offer complete accounts of experiential content.

The opposing positions described here correspond, with some reservations, fairly closely to what has been termed the inferentialist proposal and the observational account. In this context, 'seeing-that' corresponds to aspects of experiences which can be captured in terms of features of high-level inference; whereas, just 'seeing,' or 'seeing₀ ' amounts to something very close to the perception of sense data, which is (supposedly) non-inferential, 'direct' and immune from a belief-based, or 'epistemic' analysis. Neither view wants to hold that the only content of perceptual experience is 'epistemic' or 'non-epistemic'. The point of the divergence in views is over whether 'seeing (with a direct object) or seeing-that ... is the primary or more fundamental notion.'[31] One view stresses high-level 'epistemic' features; the other view stresses

---

[28] Ibid., p. 233. As Sibley notes, Armstrong elsewhere considers the possibility of a third way by admitting 'the notion of perceptual experience as something quite distinct from the acquiring of beliefs about the environment' without admitting non-physical sensory items, but adds 'I have been unable to see how this can be done.' op. cit., p. 217. See also, Sibley, op. cit., p. 127.

[29] Armstrong, (1968), op. cit., p. 235.

[30] Dretske, op. cit., p. 11.

[31] Sibley, op. cit., p. 83.

features of the observational situation and largely rejects the emphasis on beliefs. The means by which such views arise was outlined in Chapter 1. In this chapter, I want to give reasons for attempting the strategy of combining the insights of both approaches.

Before this is attempted, the slight difference in emphasis between the expressions of the two positions should be spelt out clearly. On the 'epistemic'-'non-epistemic' statement of the dispute, the discrepancy between the two views hinges centrally on the relevance of *beliefs* to experiential content; where 'belief' means the exercise of judgmental and representational abilities - seeing-*that* something is the case.

However, it is possible to take a wider perspective on the nature of experiential content than simply concentrating on belief fixation. By using the terminology of the inferentialist proposal and observational account earlier, I aimed to capture some of the other equally important high-level features which are also part and parcel of this tradition. It was also possible to show these features were separable. On my view, the terminology of the 'inferentialist proposal' subsumes the 'epistemic' account: it admits of more than simply beliefs; it also admits of propositional content, theories, descriptive concepts and so on, and these notions are critically linked. As argued earlier, the inferentialist proposal is committed to more than the 'epistemic' account, and it has a longer tradition going back to the influence of early rationalism. It seems appropriate for these reasons to retain my terminology rather than Sibley's.

The use of 'epistemic' and 'non-epistemic' in place of the wider doctrines mentioned actually leads to a stalemate on the entire issue. It ties the content of experience far too closely to the content of beliefs. As has been stressed, the standard account of beliefs is closely associated with representational content, or seeing-*that*. However, this marks the boundaries of the dispute too clearly, and brings the issue down to a *choice:* one approach where a representational/belief content is more fundamental, the other where it is not. This has had the effect of ignoring other high-level and, particularly, low-level features of experiential content. On a continuum view of content, the boundaries of the dispute are less individuated than this, and it is misleading to speak in such oversimplified terms.

It seems plausible that though the content of an experience might be representational in some circumstances, it need not be in others. Take the previous examples. In the case of seeing an object (Jones's body) it was obvious what was represented. On an account such as Armstrong's, what is represented is also what is believed; so perception, in this case, is closely tied to the belief that a certain object (Jones's body) is before one. However, take the case of two walls believed to be painted the same colour of yellow. Even though it may be believed that walls painted a certain colour are before one, and this captures the representational content, it might not capture the sense in which one wall might seem a different hue because light is falling on one wall and not the other. In such a case, there is still a content to the experience which the representational, belief-based analysis does not capture. But now take the case of the visual scene perceived with one eye and then both eyes. It is clear that though what is represented has not changed, the different content of one's experience does not thereby become non-epistemic: one still *believes* that certain objects are before one in certain relationships. A rejection of the 'epistemic', belief-based account of Armstrong does not give way to a fully 'non-epistemic' account such as that attributed to Dretske.[32]

These examples show two things: first, the epistemic and non-epistemic accounts should not be seen as a *dichotomy*. Just because the epistemic account does not capture certain levels of experiential content does not mean that a non-epistemic account will. So a rejection of one view is not an affirmation of the other. Secondly, saying a certain experience is not belief-like is not to say that it is non-inferential. To an experience of two painted walls of different hues one brings a memory of the effect of light on visual scenes which contributes to how the scene looks (even if memory may not be a sufficient explanation for how the scene looks). So a case which seems difficult to account for in the terms of the epistemic account does not simultaneously rule out the input of other high-level features.

This is a critical issue if the terms of the dispute are merely over the question of whether perception is 'epistemic' or not. For clearly, if there are some contents of experience which cannot be captured in either epistemic or non-epistemic terms, and some which are belief-like but not representational, then the whole dichotomy - either 'epistemic' or 'non-epistemic' - begins to look superficial and misleading.

Even though one might press for a broader analysis of the issue, this need not rule out the substantial importance of both 'epistemic' and 'non-epistemic' influences. The problem is this: if the issue is too closely defined in terms of beliefs, particularly beliefs as defined in terms of a representational 'believing-*that*,' then either experience is belief-ridden in this way or it isn't. By contrast, if one's account of how high-level features of experience influence experiential content is broadened to include features other than beliefs, it is possible to argue that some high-level features are crucial at times when others are not. As already indicated, this latter option is supported.

Following from this point, a way out of this bind might be to take Armstrong's 'small perceptions' as being *kinds* of beliefs. Armstrong's account could be made to include two broadly distinct beliefs: a high-level, representational belief, and a 'look' belief. A 'look' belief would capture the sensational aspects of experiential content (the kind of experiential content which seems otherwise immune from Armstrong's analysis) rather than representational aspects of experiences. This approach would preserve the Armstrongian intuition that experiences are *belief states* of some kind. Armstrong already admits of 'potential' beliefs and 'subverbal' or 'perceptual' beliefs in the case of animals - perhaps there is a case for saying that there are also low-level sensational 'look' beliefs as well as high-level representational beliefs-*that*. This strategy would also support the claim that some high-level features are relevant when others are not, and hence, goes some way to supporting the terms of a continuum view of content. On this analysis, there are many different kinds of beliefs - not just representational beliefs - and all of them are relevant to the fixation of experiential content.

The trouble with this argument is that it dilutes the notion of belief to the point where it becomes doubtful whether we need to talk about *beliefs* at all - at least

---

[32] As mentioned earlier, Dretske's account is best understood as 'partially' epistemic. I'll return to this point.

beliefs in the representational sense which Armstrong wants. It makes the whole idea of a 'belief' in this context very mysterious. As we have seen, Armstrong's inferentialist treatment of experiences captures a strongly informational sense of belief, which specifies concepts and propositional and representational states. However, Armstrong's acknowledgment of 'small perceptions' and his reference to a graduationist ('continuum') view of content to keep the legitimacy of animal and infant beliefs are a substantial move away from this view. A final severing of the position would be an admission that some beliefs are not of this 'high-level' sort at all. Whether Armstrong would take this line or not is not clear. What is clear is that if he does embrace 'small perceptions' then Armstrong's overall position can then be criticised as being too 'high-level' in its treatment of beliefs as well as experiences; too zealous to embrace the terms of the inferentialist proposal and not to see that there may be other kinds of contents which his account cannot capture. Armstrong's account could also be criticised as being *reductionist:* in assimilating all experiential contents to be beliefs *of a certain sort.* [33]

The issue here centres on whether to call sensational features of experiences 'beliefs.' One way of understanding Armstrong's position in this respect would be like this. If he insisted on treating all experiential content in belief-based terms, then he could properly be said to be maintaining an 'epistemic'-type analysis of sorts though it is clear here that some beliefs are not captured by high-level content; if he did not, then it is unclear how features of some experiences could fit with his inferentialist views. The issue of whether 'look' beliefs are *bona fide* beliefs would thus amount to a mere semantic disagreement, not a way of resolving whether or not his view of experiential content is adequate. If Armstrong wants to take this approach and keep calling the sensational features of experiences 'beliefs', then he can do so, but it should be noted that the rest of his claims about beliefs being 'inferential, 'conceptual' and 'representational' etc, no longer apply to them. In which case Armstrong's view is no longer really an inferentialist view of substance, but a continuum account along the lines being proposed.

This way of understanding the problem has its advantages. What once was a point of serious disagreement between Armstrong's position and my own view - the issue of belief content - has become a way of affecting a reconciliation. Interpreted as occurring in *degrees* of sophistication, 'beliefs' are no longer a threat to a continuum approach to experiential content.

However, although Armstrong's account can be interpreted in this way, it is still clear that the issue about how beliefs influence experiential content is an issue not only of *degree* but also of *kind.* We can speak of some aspects of experiences being belief-like in the 'high-level' sense, and we can speak of some aspects of experiences being belief-like in some 'low-level' sense. But there is still a genuine sense in which the low-level beliefs are quite unlike the high-level beliefs. Specifically, the latter, but not the former, require representational content, concepts, etc. We shall shortly see how examples of

---

[33] Armstrong acknowledges this to a certain degree: 'My account may be called a reductive account because the concept of perception is shown to be a complex concept, definable in terms of such concepts as knowledge, belief and inclination to believe.' Armstrong, op. cit., (1961): p. 121.

'look'-beliefs are not only hard to fit into criteria acceptable to Armstrong's analysis, but also hard to conceptualise as *belief* states - such cases make the notion of a 'belief' in this context unacceptably dilute.

But there is the further point that a combinatory analysis will not capture Jackson's *unnoticed seeings*. As mentioned before, some seeings simply seem to go unnoticed, and hence, are not *believed* at all.[34] These features, too, seem to be genuine cases of contents which are unbelieved at the time of seeing. Such cases are quite unlike even the non-representational beliefs mentioned earlier in the context of Dretske's examples. These factors also need to be included in the analysis.

It seems then that there are two possible strategies here. The first is to combine the intuitions of both the epistemic and non-epistemic accounts. This would mean that perception can be characterised by beliefs, but beliefs of various levels of complexity. If one can interpret Armstrong as having 'low-level' beliefs as well as 'high-level' beliefs-*that,* and Dretske's view as being *partially* epistemic and holding that experiences simply cannot be characterised in a *necessary and sufficient* way by representational content, then there seems no great conflict between the two positions.

The second strategy would be to rule out the application of beliefs to the very low-level end of the continuum. This option allows differences in degree between 'high' and 'low-level' perceivings, to shade into differences in *kind* at the polarities. 'Unnoticed seeings' would thus not really be counted as beliefs at all, though they are, in some low-level sense, *informational*. The next section will clarify the options here.

Sibley's account

Sibley recognises this need to stress another kind of belief content corresponding to lower level experiences. He considers several possible interpretations of Armstrong's work, but interprets Armstrong's epistemic account as the 'acquiring of beliefs about the physical world' in the strongest possible sense - the *representational* sense. In S's acquiring a belief, 'S must possess the concepts involved in that belief ... the status concept of a physical thing or of a physical environment.'[35] But this seems to Sibley a mistake. Such a strong view of belief content would require Armstrong to re-interpret unconvincingly cases of experiences which do not seem to be amenable to such an analysis in belief-like terms, and also to disparage unsophisticated animal and infant experiences. Armstrong might accomplish this by 'denying that our perceptions are distinct from our beliefs.'[36] But, according to Sibley, this

---

[34] Not believed in the 'high-level' representational sense of belief, that is. There is considerable evidence of beliefs being registered in the case of subliminal perception, which is a kind of unnoticed seeing. I wouldn't deny that this kind of seeing goes on. However, it is debatable if *these* kinds of subliminal beliefs are high-level in the required sense; or, if they are, if the kind of perceiving in question consists of the same *degree* of unnoticing as Jackson's examples. The continuum account allows for variations in degrees of unnoticing as much as it allows for degrees of noticing.

[35] Sibley, op. cit., p 126.

[36] Ibid., p. 127

'smacks of *ad hoc* theory saving.'[37]

Sibley argues against the thrust of Dretske's views, though his reasons are rather different from mine. The suggestion in this chapter is that we can interpret Dretske's view as proposing that there are features of experiential content which are not informational or inferential in Armstrong's sense. We should interpret Dretske as arguing against the claim that beliefs in Armstrong's sense are necessary and sufficient for all experiences, only some of them. It has *not* been suggested that we take Dretske to mean that there are no beliefs in perception. Sibley, however, takes Dretske to be claiming that perception contains *no beliefs at all:*

> Some of [Dretske's] statements ... suggest the extreme position ('I personally, have no idea what the infant or the rat believes *or whether they believe anything,* ' p. 10, my italics). Moreover, in those passages where he offers his positive account of seeing$_n$ (p. 18 ff.), there is no suggestion that S must, in seeing D acquire some belief. And since this account of seeing$_n$ is offered, I believe, as a full, not a partial, positive account ... we may conclude, I think, that his positive account of seeing *is* totally non-epistemic.[38]

Sibley has a quick response to this kind of *fully* non-epistemic account. He argues that there is a sense in which *noticing* something, or *attending* to something, requires a minimal form of belief, so a fully non-epistemic account cannot possibly be true:

> We are prepared to say that someone in a brown study, or grief stricken, or engrossed in an argument, 'stared at something unseeing', 'looked right through it without seeing it', etc. ... [If] correct, and if such obviously attention-involving locutions ... are interchangeable with 'seeing', it surely cannot be denied that there does exist a use of 'see' that involves attention and hence belief-acquisition. (Just as I take it to be absurd to say that someone glimpsed or spotted or, in one sense, saw something without giving it, or its taking, any of his attention, so I take it as undeniable that someone could not have spotted or noticed or otherwise given attention to something without acquiring some belief or other, if only the belief that, e.g., something happened or seemed to ...).[39]

Sibley's point is that every experience, even unsophisticated ones, must involve attention focusing, and consequently, beliefs. According to him, if one doesn't focus on something, one doesn't *see* anything, and since attention focussing involves noticing, seeing involves believing. Such an argument is clearly apposite to the cases offered by Dretske considered earlier. There is a sense in which the infant, the rat and the savage all noticed something, so their experiences did involve beliefs. This is another reason for considering

---

[37] Ibid., p. 126.
[38] Ibid., p. 85.
[39] Ibid., p. 96.

Dretske's account, at best, a 'partial epistemic' view. We have already seen reasons for rejecting this kind of claim with some of the cases Jackson offered. As we saw, some experiences may involve *unnoticed seeings:* one might 'see', in some sense, the autumn leaves or the colour of the tomato, without *noticing* that one does, so not *all* kinds of seeings involve noticings. Or, again, one might see something 'in the corner of one's eye' (say, the scratches on the window pane) without noticing them and only be able to have one's attention drawn to such an experience if the scratches were actually removed. Sibley's account is unacceptable if he takes all seeing to involve noticing (and hence, believing).

But there is another reason why Sibley's account is unacceptable. It concerns his interpretation of Dretske as holding a *fully* non-epistemic account, and not a partially epistemic account. Unlike Sibley, I am reluctant to attribute this view to Dretske. It seems to me that Dretske's vacillations over whether beliefs can properly be attributed to all cases of 'seeings' can also be interpreted to be questioning the degree to which high-level beliefs can account for some kinds of experiences, *not* that there are some experiences which do not have a belief content at all. Such a view seems simply implausible on the basis of examples Dretske offers for his account, even if it may be plausible on the basis of some of the unnoticed seeings just mentioned.

There seems to be another likely interpretation of Dretske's work, however, which is defensible: Dretske's emphasis might be closer to my own - that some aspects of experiences have features that cannot be captured by Armstrong's analysis; that some beliefs are 'look' beliefs rather than 'inferential' beliefs. His original arguments, after all, were directed against the view that 'no *particular* belief, or set of beliefs constitutes a logically indispensable condition for the individual's seeing that he does see.'[40] He was attacking the view that all experiences involve '*positive* belief content,' not the view that experiences could not do without *any* belief content.[41] On the interpretation given here, Dretske might have been making a point of arguing that there need not be any particular and identifiable representational aspect to an experience, not that there are no 'look'-beliefs in experience. There is an important difference in emphasis here, yet Sibley does not see this difference and interprets Dretske as holding a *fully* non-epistemic account.

Sibley's approach tries to avoid the counterintuitive nature of both the fully 'epistemic' and the fully 'non-epistemic' view thus interpreted. It amounts to an attempt at a middle-of-the-road position between Armstrong and Dretske. His claim is that a 'weaker and non-specific belief view',[42] which he calls a 'broadly epistemic account',[43] will avoid the problems associated with Armstrong's 'specific epistemic account.' The thrust of the position is that some kind of 'rudimentary' belief mostly goes along with perception ('not an

---

[40] Dretske, op. cit., p. 13. Italics mine.

[41] 'Positive belief content' is defined in Dretske as an entailment relation between the activities of some sentient agent 'S ...' and S's having a *particular* belief. See ibid., Dretske, p. 5. As we have already seen, Dretske's claim is that no particular belief is necessary for experience, not that no beliefs at all are necessary.

[42] Sibley, op. cit., p. 127.

[43] Ibid., p. 84.

inhibited tendency [or potential] to believe')[44] and that this rudimentary believing is of a very low-level kind: minimally, of something which 'existed' or 'happened.'[45] This is particularly apposite, in Sibley's view, to the unsophisticated experiences of animals and infants:

> If [a belief acquisition account of seeing] is to be tenable, it must apply to all creatures who see, including infants. No doubt many concepts are acquired and used in seeing; but many are not required. This must eliminate the kind of view [such as] attributed to Armstrong. Since, however, on any epistemic account some concepts are required, the minimum that would suffice would seem to be the rudimentary 'something' and 'existing' or 'happening' ... The infant who, for the first time hears a noise or sees a flash and jumps and cries must be held to at least think that something happened.[46]

The upshot of this kind of analysis is that beliefs are necessarily involved in perception, but they are not the kinds of representational beliefs Armstrong avows. Sibley then claims that experiential content involves rudimentary belief-like features which do not even imply 'a realisation that [something] looks somehow to [a perceiver] at all.'[47] Sibley wants, in fact, to rule out of his analysis 'looks' as well as high-level beliefs as the fundamental features of experiential content. Because of his treatment of Dretske, 'looks' implies perceiving something non-epistemically. But Sibley wants to react against this view. He claims that *his* beliefs, unlike Armstrong's, do not have a special connection with 'external or physical occurrences' but unlike Dretske, they do not become totally non-epistemic 'looks' or *seeings-as.* They remain, nonetheless, 'beliefs' in some sense. The argument for a primitive belief which does not imply anything looking a certain way, on Sibley's view, is that some primitive experiences do not lead the perceiver to believe that there is something about his experience which is one way rather than another:

> The situation can occur in adult as well as in infant life, when for instance we know that something (*in fact* a slight change in the lighting) disturbed our concentration, that we cannot say whether it was a change of lighting, a slight sound, or what. Its being a matter of *looks,* i.e., of *vision* (and hence of light and colour etc.), need not be incorporated in the belief of the perceiver.[48]

The point to be made against his account is this: Sibley takes the epistemic/non-epistemic debate to be one of an exclusive dichotomy, not aspects of an inclusive account in which both kinds of accounts may feature. On his view, either experience is fully 'epistemic', in Armstrong's sense, or it is fully 'non-

---

[44] Ibid., p. 127.
[45] Ibid., p 128.
[46] Ibid., p. 130.
[47] Ibid., p. 129.
[48] Loc. cit.

epistemic' in (how he has interpreted) Dretske's sense. It is this interpretation that is behind Sibley's rejection of 'look'-like features of beliefs. He takes Armstrong (rightly) to be advocating a highly inferentially-driven account of experience, and he takes Dretske (wrongly, I think) to be advocating a totally non-epistemic view of experience. Sibley also sees the dispute in terms of an exclusive either/or dichotomy. So, the upshot of his criticism of Armstrong leaves him in a curious position. He does not wish to agree with Armstrong entirely, but likewise, his view of Dretske is that there are no beliefs at all in perceptual 'looks', so he cannot agree with him either. This requires him to fall back on beliefs, but beliefs *which have no look-like features*. This makes his notion of an experience with a 'rudimentary' belief very odd indeed:

> If my arguments are correct, S may see D without having any belief about how D looks to him, or even any realization [sic.] that it does *look* somehow to him at all. S need not have either the concept 'looks', or any predicate concepts, or the concept 'being like something', or that of 'having a quality', or of the 'is' of predication.[49]

We don't have to accept this conclusion. The interesting sense of a 'look' belief is not that it is any form of high-level cognising; nor is it entirely non-epistemic. (Sibley attributes the latter view to Dretske.) The reason for invoking 'look' beliefs is that some experiential contents seem to have sensational features, features which the 'epistemic' account of Armstrong simply does not capture. Sibley realises that a more primitive kind of belief is needed here. His 'weaker and non-specific belief-view'[50] is, at least, plausible. His intuition is that very primitive experiences such as 'that something happened' or 'that something exists' are experiences so *inchoate* that they cannot be captured in terms which are representational, propositional or inferential, yet they are legitimate features of experiential content. The claim is that the very notion of a belief itself needs to be understood as occurring in *degrees,* not in all-or-none terms. The problem is that Sibley has taken the terms of the 'epistemic'-'non-epistemic' debate as an exclusive dichotomy, not elements of a larger, more encompassing account in which beliefs of many kinds may feature. Sibley's mistake was not to see that this kind of account can be read into Dretske's analysis, and so he does not have to reject the application of 'looks' to low-level beliefs. On this continuum view of beliefs, of course, 'look' beliefs which capture sensational features are as much a part of the overall account of experience required as Armstrong's 'propositional' beliefs-*that*. Even Sibley's 'rudimentary' beliefs can be plotted on the same graph. Consequently, Sibley has no grounds on which to rule 'looks' out of his account of beliefs. He only needs to do this if he: (1) accepts that there is an exclusive dichotomy involved in the application of beliefs to experiences, and (2) assumes that Dretske's non-epistemic account implies there are no beliefs at all in perception. The suggestion given here is that we reject both of these assumptions.

If it does not make sense to rule out look-like features in the application of beliefs to experience, then perhaps it makes no sense to rule out *unnoticed*

---

[49] Ibid., pp 128-9
[50] Ibid., p. 127.

seeings as well. Perhaps the correct account of the relationship between such things will include them in the one belief-experience taxonomy. There might thus be a qualitative difference between very low-level look-beliefs (not really 'beliefs') and higher level beliefs which have look-like features and still higher level beliefs which can be captured in terms of representational content. Just as there are differences in degree in a continuum, so there are differences of kind at the polarities. In what follows, I shall undertake a rough characterisation of this belief-experience taxonomy.

'Look'- beliefs

Experiential content may involve 'look'-beliefs. These beliefs might be fixed by sensational features of perception, and as such they are distinct from beliefs which are fixed by 'high-level' representational and propositional features. Even so, it is clear that several kinds of 'look'-beliefs are possible:

(1) One kind of 'look'-belief may not *really* be believed because it is not noticed. This is at the very end of the continuum. Such a case can be later recalled as something that one saw but did not notice (e.g., the third house on the left). Recalling assists believing in this circumstance, but at the outset the experience simply captures certain unnoticed and unbelieved *looks.*

(2) Another kind of 'look'-belief may have no representational features at all, but it is believed in a very simple way. (It might just be a belief 'that something happened' or 'existed.') These kinds of belief have no discernible object content at all. Call this a 'Sibley Look-Belief.' An example might be the belief that something has happened to how a painted wall looks, but not being able to say what it is. (Say the light on the wall has suddenly shifted unnoticed - without one noticing either the shift or *that one was looking at a wall*).[51]

(3) Another kind of 'look' belief might be that 'something happened' or 'existed' and being able to say what it was about that experience that looks different. (Say one is able to say 'something about my experience looks lighter/darker now.') Call this a 'Partial Representational Look-Belief'. (This is to be distinguished from a belief *about the wall* that it has changed.) Some of Jackson's examples fit into this category. We may also believe that we saw something (some tomatoes) without noticing anything about them (i.e., whether they were ripe or unripe).

(4) Yet another kind of 'look'-belief might be that there is some aspect of one's experience of a painted wall that looks different. (Say that one is able to say that 'this experience of a painted wall looks different from the previous experience of the same wall.') Call this a 'Representational Look-Belief'.

The above kinds of beliefs are all about features or aspects of experience which have a certain look, yet they have an increasing degree of sophistication. (A Representational Look-Belief is close to an experience which is a belief-*that* there is a wall before one, but it captures more about the *look* of the wall than the representational/propositional content of 'wall').

The important thing to note is that, if true, this characterisation of content is a

---

[51] If this seems implausible, imagine driving along a road without being aware that one is driving along a road, and then 'something happens' which changes how things look, without being able to say what it was, *or, indeed, how the look is different.*

substantial move away from traditional conceptions of the relationship between belief and experience. Moreover, it seems that this characterisation supports the claims in this book. Several differentiating levels of sensational features of experience corresponding to several levels of beliefs is entirely consistent with what has been termed the continuum view of experiential content.

Conclusion

In this chapter, the relationship between beliefs and experiential content has been looked at in detail. Two conventional approaches were considered. The conclusion arrived at is that there are stronger reasons for holding a continuum account of the relationship between beliefs and experience than either of these more traditional views. I effected a reconciliation between these approaches along the lines the continuum theory specifies. This involved treating beliefs as having levels of sophistication corresponding to the levels of sophistication of experiential content. The upshot of the analysis of experience and beliefs is that although sensational features of experience might be beliefs this does not warrant a treatment along the lines of either an 'epistemic' or a 'non-epistemic' account.

Part Two
EXPERIENCE AND STRUCTURE

5 Sensational content

> The external senses have a double province; to make us feel, and to make us perceive [1]

Sensational content

Introduction

Reasons have been given in the previous chapters for thinking that there might be features of experiential content which cannot be accounted for in terms of the inferentialist proposal. The discussion so far has centred around the relationship between belief and experience, and language and experience. It has been pointed out how several philosophers have taken experiential content to be fully characterised in terms of 'high-level' influences. We have seen that this kind of characterisation of experience stems from a confused and misleading account of content. In this chapter two recent views which argue for an alternative account will be outlined. From this, it will be argued that there is more to content than the inferentialist proposal specifies. An examination of various views, ancient and contemporary, on the structure of mental content is then attempted in later chapters.

Aspects of experiences

In the terms of the inferentialist proposal, experiences necessarily involve the inference from 'high-level' features: background knowledge, concepts and theories. Experiences also have representational and propositional features on this account. We have already had reason to regard some of these claims as being oversimplified and even misguided. Chapter 2 raised the question of animal and infant experiences and the whole question of how evolutionary considerations might bear on the issue of experiential content. The distinction between descriptive and sensational features led to the case for 'concept' to be viewed in a manner which did not imply 'high-level' abilities. Chapter 3 continued this examination of the terms of the inferentialist proposal and

---

[1] T. Reid, *Essays on the Intellectual Powers of Man*, p. 17.

distinguished low-level content from its association with language, meaning and theories - with linguistic propositional and representationally informational judgements. The conflation of observational language and observational experience was examined and shown to be of doubtful support for the inferentialist proposal. Chapter 4 distinguished beliefs as representational judgements from what was called 'look' beliefs. The suggestion here was that experiential content need not be understood in representational terms as high-level beliefs, as the very notion of a 'belief' itself could be said to occur in *degrees* of sophistication. All of these points made it seem likely that the inferentialist proposal needed to be substantially revised.

What arises from the preceding discussion is that the relationship between experiential content and high-level influences is more complex than either the inferentialist proposal or the observational account assumed. There seems to be a number of different ways in which high-level features can be brought to bear on experience, and a number of ways in which a full and adequate characterisation of experiential content escapes such an analysis. Cases of experiences where the various high-level features can be individuated have already been given. (To take one example: propositional content can be separated from language.) The claim is that this indicates that no single high-level feature is *necessary* for contentful experiences. There may be good reason, therefore, for thinking that none of the high-level features are necessary and sufficient. High-level experiences might also have distinguishable low-level, sensational *aspects*. As the idea that all experiential content is necessarily underpinned by features of high-level inference, and the idea that experiential content is basically non-inferential do not seem promising alternatives, I feel entitled to explore other options.

Drawing upon Thomas Reid, Christopher Peacocke[2] usefully clarifies experiential content in terms of *sensations, perceptions* and *judgements*. This tripartite distinction has been echoed recently by Allan Millar in terms of *sensations, sensory experiences* and *propositional attitudes*. Both typologies have a similar basis and can be treated together. According to Millar, 'sensations include itches, tickles, feelings of numbness, and experiences generally.' These, he claims:

> ... are always conscious in the sense of being episodes in the current stream of consciousness, though the subject may not always be conscious *of* them in the sense of noticing them. We may forget a back pain because absorbed in some activity, but it should not be inferred from this that while forgotten about the pain was not a conscious state.[3]

By contrast, propositional attitudes ' are states like belief, desire, intention, and hope, in which the subject has an attitude to some proposition.' Sensory experiences, by contrast again, are 'akin to sensations in so far as they are always conscious occurrences [but they] can be described in ways which involve the ascription to them of propositional contents.'[4] According to Millar,

---

[2] Christopher Peacocke, *Sense and Content: Experience, Thought and its Relations*.

[3] Allan Millar, *Reasons and Experience*, p. 11.

[4] Ibid., pp. 10-11. 'We can say that it visually appears to someone that *p*, meaning by that to

while sensations are always conscious (but need not be noticed), propositional attitudes 'are not always episodes in current consciousness.'[5] However, while propositional attitudes are characteristically captured in terms of 'giving the content'[6] of the attitude in question, sensory experiences - like sensations - are best captured simply in terms of how they are felt or how they *seem* to the subject. Sensory experiences thus have characteristics common to both sensations and propositional attitudes. However, they are also distinct. Like sensations (but unlike propositional attitudes), they are always conscious, *albeit* not always noticed, and like propositional attitudes (but unlike sensations), they can sometimes be said to be *about* something. The benefits of this kind of experiential typology is discussed in what follows.

The category of 'sensations' in the above classification is fairly uncontroversial. For both Millar and Peacocke it is roughly equivalent to what was earlier called 'low-level' content. This is awareness at one end of the experiential continuum. Such content can arise at several levels on my account as *unnoticed* experience in various sensory modalities. (Unnoticed *seeings* of varying degrees of sophistication were considered in the previous chapter in relation to Jackson's work.) Characteristically, sensations are contentful without requiring inferential and representational input (at its most primitive, there is no object-content at all in experiencing such sensations - i.e., they amount to what was earlier called 'purely sensational content'). As we have seen, a kind of very low-level experience may be present to some degree in every experiential amalgam as 'impurely sensational content.'

The class of 'propositional attitudes' or 'judgements' is also fairly uncontroversial. For both Millar and Peacocke, these categories are strongly inferential, requiring the input of high-level content such as representational, conceptual and propositional elements. A judgement formulated in response to an experience, for instance, characteristically requires that the subject *believe* something about the experience in question. This belief is what is captured when a subject 'gives the content' of a propositional attitude. A certain sound, for example, might be judged (believed) to be the sound of rain falling. The attitude, in this case, represents the experience as an experience of a certain kind. (It is a belief-*that* in Armstrong's terms.)

However, it is clear that the content of a judgment can cause the content of an experience to be taken as an experience of another kind altogether. A person experiencing a certain sound that is believed to be rain, might judge later that a stereo has been left on, and the 'rain' sound then comes to be heard as applause. The attitude representing the sound as rain has been influenced by the attitude that the stereo has been left on. Propositional attitudes or judgements

---

describe how the person's experience represents the world as being without implying that the person believes or is even inclined to believe that *p* ... [W]hen we see things we see them under certain descriptions. Looking at a rose bush, for instance, you might see it as a rose-bush where this would imply that your visual experience would not be as it is but for its seeming to you that a rose bush is there ' ibid., pp. 11-12.

[5] Ibid., p. 11. 'At any given time some of our propositional attitudes are conscious and some are not. As I touch my coffee mug I form the conscious belief that the coffee in it is cold. A few moments ago my current belief that my son is at school, which I undoubtedly held then, was not conscious.' loc. cit.

[6] Ibid., p. 10.

can fix the representational content of an experience by bringing to bear different kinds of high-level information to the perceptual situation.[7]

By contrast to propositional attitudes, 'sensory experiences' or 'perceptions' can be characterised in sensational terms as well as representational terms. They cannot be classified properly either as sensations or as judgements. That this is so needs some explaining.

Like propositional attitudes or judgments, 'perceptions' (Peacocke's term) or 'sensory experiences' (Millar's term) have some representational content in *most* cases (in normal human experience). But in other circumstances they may not have such features. Nonetheless, there will always be some sensational content in an experience, conscious or otherwise. This flexibility and independence in content is what distinguishes perceptions from judgments or propositional attitudes.

Millar offers a reason for distinguishing these kinds of contents. He suggests that a judgement or a propositional attitude, strictly speaking, must satisfy two principles: a concept principle and an intrinsicality principle. But a sensory experience does not always satisfy these principles. Simply put, the concept principle states that 'if a concept is an ingredient of the mental state then the subject must grasp the concept.'[8] The intrinsicality principle states that 'if token mental states in a given category (belief, desire, or whatever) have different contents then they are of different state-types within that category.'[9] More simply, the intrinsicality principle states that 'the representational content of a state is intrinsic to that state ... two states which differ in representational content are different states.'[10] These claims will be qualified later in light of the continuum account. For the moment, it shall be assumed that each of the principles need to be satisfied in their present form.

Obviously the two principles are connected. It is surely not normally possible to represent a given state of affairs without having a concept with which to represent that state of affairs (so the intrinsicality principle requires that the concept principle be satisfied).[11] Yet, by parity, to have a concept as an ingredient in a mental state requires that one can identify experiences of certain

---

[7] Peacocke, op. cit., p. 6. This need not happen. Sometimes the representational content of an experience is independent of the content of a judgement. 'A man may be familiar with a perfect *trompe l'oeil* violin painted on a door, and be sure from his past experience that it is a *trompe l'oeil:* nevertheless his experience may continue to represent a violin as hanging on the door in front of him.' loc. cit. Peacocke notes that: 'The possibility of this kind of independence is one of the marks of the content of experience as opposed to the content of judgement.' loc. cit. I shall look at other cases where the content of a judgement can be separated from the content of experience below.

[8] Millar, op. cit., p. 20. 'If, for example, you believe that your pet cat is a Russian blue then you must grasp the concept of a Russian blue.' loc. cit.

[9] Ibid., p. 21. 'Thus if Kate's belief B is the belief that p and Fred's belief B' is the belief that $q,$ then B and B' are different beliefs in the sense that they are different belief-types.' loc. cit.

[10] A. Millar, 'What's in a Look?,' pp. 86.

[11] Peacocke affirms this point: '[I]t is in the nature of representational content that it cannot be built up from concepts unless the subject of the experience himself has those concepts: the representational content is the way the experience presents the world as being, and it can hardly present the world as being that way if the subject is incapable of appreciating what that way is.' op. cit., p. 7.

representational state-types (so the concept principle requires that the intrinsicality principle be satisfied).[12]

In the case of propositional attitudes or judgements (desires, beliefs and so on) both these principles are satisfied. (It seems hardly possible to desire/want/believe some *p* without having the concept *p*, and it hardly seems possible to have *p* as a concept without knowing what kind of thing *p* would represent.) But in the case of sensory experiences, these principles are not so easily satisfied. To take an example used previously: a perceptual judgement of a tomato both requires that I have the concept 'tomato' and also requires that the token experience I am having is a state-type intrinsic to a representational content of a certain kind (which someone else can share). However, both these conditions need not be satisfied. I can, for instance, experience a visual scene with a tomato in it without necessarily engaging the relevant concept (perhaps I am in a hurry or am being distracted at the time) and two people can share the same experience even if one possesses the concept and the other doesn't (but this will not mean that their experiences are thereby of a different representational state-type). This kind of content is what makes an experience a sensory experience or a perception, rather than a propositional attitude or a judgment.[13]

According to Peacocke, judgments ('propositional attitudes') involve 'past experience' and are inevitably inferential in content involving all the high-level influences mentioned in previous chapters. However, perceptions ('sensory experiences') can have both *non-representational* and *representational* aspects. The non-representational aspects are supposed to be 'independent'[14] of inference, but not entirely: the representational aspects capture the inferentialist's idea that there seems to be a representational or an *object content* to experience, while the non-representational aspect captures the idea that experiences can have observational features. Peacocke's two 'aspects' of perception then, are supposed to capture the intuitions of both the inferentialist proposal and the observational account: the *representative* aspect has a determinate content; the *non-representative* aspect has a *sensational* content. He explains:

---

[12] Peacocke seems to affirm this point too: '[T]he representational content concerns the world external to the experiencer, and as such is assessable as true or false ... this content is something intrinsic to the experience itself - any experience which does not represent to the subject the world being the way that this content specifies is phenomenologically different, an experience of a different type.' ibid., p. 9.

[13] Millar adopts the convention of calling an experience which fails to satisfy the above principles an *F- type* experience, and an experience which satisfies these principles to be an experience *such that it seems to the subject that an F is there*. The former is 'an experience of the type which an *F* would yield, that is, would produce under certain suitability and normality conditions.' The latter is an experience which, 'in the absence of countervailing considerations its subject would believe that an *F* is there.' op. cit., pp. 1- 2. The idea is that in some cases (like the ones just mentioned in relation to the tomato) an experience can be *F- type* without necessarily being an experience such that it seems to the subject that an *F* is there. (Being distracted or not having 'tomato' as a concept yields one sensory experience or perception, but not the corresponding propositional attitude or judgement.) Only in having *both* experiences according to Millar, can one yield an experience *of an F*. (loc cit.).

[14] C. Peacocke, op. cit., p. 5.

> Historically, the distinction between putative perceptual experience, and sensation has been the distinction between those experiences which do in themselves represent the environment of the experiencer as being a certain way, and those experiences which have no such representative content. A visual perceptual experience enjoyed by someone sitting at a desk may represent various writing implements and items of furniture having particular spatial relations to one another and to the experiencer, and as themselves having various qualities; a sensation of small, by contrast, may have no representative content of any kind ... Representational properties will be properties an experience has in virtue of features of its representational content; while sensational properties will be properties an experience has in virtue of some aspect - other than its representational content - of what it is like to have that experience.[15]

The representational content of a perceptual experience, Peacocke says, has to be given by a 'proposition or set of propositions'[16] which specifies the way the experience represents the world to be; for instance, the items of furniture or, in the case of Sherlock Holmes, the cigar-band, Jones's body and the relation of 'nearness' of the body to the cigar-band. The representational content of an experience seems properly classified under what was previously called descriptive content. The non-representational aspects are not usually specified in this manner, but are properties by virtue of an organism being capable of having sensations of certain sorts. This is equivalent to what was previously called 'impurely sensational' content. The distinction is: a representational content is the content of an experience which is specified in words by an application of descriptive concepts (say, about the presence of certain things in one's visual field, i.e., of the form x is $\emptyset$); a non-representative experience is specified in quite different terms, perhaps in terms of some element of experience which is simply sensed. Is there any reason to think that there is a basis for a distinction here? This needs to be established.

Representational content

Consider the following cases offered by Peacocke:

> (1) You are standing on a road which stretches from you in a straight line to the horizon. There are two trees at the roadside, one a hundred yards from you, the other two hundred. Your experience represents these objects as being of the same physical height ... Yet there is also some sense in which the nearer tree occupies more of your visual field than the more distant tree. This is as much a feature of your experience as is its representing the trees as being the same height ...We can label this problem, the 'problem of additional characterisation'...
> (2) Suppose you look at an array of furniture with one eye closed. Some of the pieces of furniture may be represented by your experience as being in front of others. Imagine now that you look at the same scene with both

---

[15] Ibid., pp. 5.
[16] Loc. cit.

eyes. The experience is different. It may be tempting to try to express this difference by saying that some chairs now appear to be in front of others, but this cannot suffice: for the monocular experience also represents certain objects as being in front of others...

(3) Consider an example in which a wire framework in the shape of a cube is viewed with one eye and is seen first with one of its faces in front, the face parallel to this face being seen as behind it, and is then suddenly seen, without any change in the cube or alteration of its position, with the former face now behind the other. The successive experiences have different representational contents. ... Yet there seems to be some additional level which the successive experiences fall under the same logical type.[17]

The above are not problems of perception as such, but problems for an entirely *representative* view of experience. If experiences are said to have only representative features, then the above are dilemmas, because they clearly illustrate that there are things about experiences which are not representational. The first example shows that a tree can occupy more of the visual field despite being represented as the same size as another; the second shows that something non-representative about the experience of the furniture can vary despite the representation of the furniture being 'held constant'[18] and the third shows that something can *look* the same, (i.e., 'non-representational similarities' can occur) despite the *variation* in what is represented.[19]

The first example, 'additional characterisation,' can occur in a number of situations even when experiencing one object on successive occasions. Sometimes this is known as the phenomenon of 'size constancy.' A distant object under certain viewing conditions, to take an example, can actually seem larger than the optically represented size on the basis of that perceived distance. However, one can usually operate satisfactorily in the world by ignoring such changes in apparent size.

This phenomenon has some explanation in the psychological literature. Objects normally become *smaller* when seen as being distant; however, when viewing conditions are disturbed by features such as atmospheric mist, apparent distance of an object can be exaggerated. (This occurs when viewing the moon: the presence of an horizon within the field of view causes the moon to appear

---

[17] Ibid., p. 12-16.

[18] Ibid., p 13. The point here is that the representation of the objects will not vary, but there is something qualitatively different about the experience. Peacocke notes that this phenomenon also occurs in aural experiences: 'A stereophonic recording of a wave breaking sounds quite different from a monoaural recording, even if one cannot locate aurally the direction of the components of the whole sound.' ibid., p. 14.

[19] The point is, there will be something that seems the same about the cube, despite the representational differences. Peacocke notes that the Duck/Rabbit example was not used here because 'the arrangement of lines on paper remains constant' (ibid., p. 17) in this case, and the similarity of the successive experiences could be attributed to the representation of these lines. The wire cube example shows no such representational stability: the frame of the cube is represented differently, but *something non-representational seems the same* which accounts for the switch.

larger there than it does at the zenith.)[20] When this happens, the brain compensates for the decrease in retinal image by correspondingly enlarging the distant object. This occasions a discrepancy between the true distance and the apparent distance, and the apparent perceptual dimensions of the object is thus distorted. So an object can be experienced as both larger than and smaller than it should be on the basis of its represented size.[21]

In underwater situations this size constancy effect is very pronounced. Even very familiar objects, such as a diver's hand can seem too big, or too close. It is unlikely, however, that such experiences can be explained entirely in terms of the brain's enlargement of the retinal image, as the experience of distant objects under unusual viewing conditions. Such objects as one's own hand seem too familiar as objects and could hardly be seen as so visually deceptive. Another explanation offered to account for this phenomenon is that there is a conflict between different perceptual modalities - in this case proprioception and vision - and what 'feels' to be at its correct distance, looks too near, or alternatively, what appears at its correct distance, is actually represented visually as being too large. The sensational content of 'small' or 'large', in this case, seems to bear no intrinsic relationship to the visually represented experience with which it is usually associated. Interestingly, divers adapt to this problem in ways which suggest that they attend to different aspects of the perceptual situation.[22] We shall shortly see another example in which discrepancies arising from different sensory modalities can yield similar ambiguous perceptual results. Such cases are suggestive in indicating how there can be more to an experience than how it is visually represented. Clearly, if there can be enlarged visual aspects to an experience despite its optically represented size, then there is plainly more to an experience than *simply* its projected representational features. In other words, Peacocke's point, that sensory experiences involve both kinds of features, seems to have some basis.

There are other more obvious ways of making the point. The 'problem of additional characterisation', for instance, does not arise only with *size* in the visual field. Peacocke notes that it can also arise in the case of visual *colour,* and aural *loudness.* Two walls of a room uniformly painted in terms of hue, brightness and saturation, might still look different in some non-representative fashion. And two car engines running equally loudly, might be represented as being indistinguishable in volume 'but again it seems undeniable that in some sense the nearer car sounds louder.'[23] These examples suggest again that some sensational content can be wrested from the representational aspects of one's experience. (How one *represents* the situation is only a part of one's experiential content in these cases.)

---

[20] My thanks to Roger McCart for pointing this out.

[21] See: H. E. Ross, *Perception and Behaviour in Strange Environments,* pp 54- 56. passim.

[22] 'Divers respond to the conflict in different ways, some perceiving mainly size-distortion, and others mainly distance-distortion. If the diver moves around under water, or handles objects, he begins to adapt to some aspect of the distortion. Some divers adapt to size and *counter adapt* (perceive increased distortion) to distance; others do the opposite; and a few manage to adapt to both size and distance, thus learning new size constancy rules which are appropriate to the underwater situation.' ibid., p. 57.

[23] Peacocke, op. cit., p. 13.

These examples are interesting, but it is not clear that they quite capture one major feature of experiential content. For one thing, the distinction Peacocke offers between representational and non-representational (sensational) experience should not be seen as being too rigid. There seems to be a clear case for saying that there are many *intermediate* cases here. There is a case for saying, for example, that some experiential contents might be neither exclusively sensational nor representational in content. A visual experience one may have upon initially waking up in the morning seems to have both kinds of features, but appears to be characteristically neither one nor the other. (The vague waking experience seems initially neither representational nor strictly sensational, like an unnoticed back pain.) It is unclear if such an experience should be said to have exclusively representational or non-representational aspects. This is not necessarily a problem with Peacocke's distinctions, it might just show that there may be various levels at which these features of perceptions might overlap. This would be consistent with the continuum account being advocated in which several degrees of content can occur jointly in single experiential amalgams. In any event, there are problems with a view which stresses that only *representational* features fully capture the nature of experiential content. Non-representational sensational content ('impurely sensational content') seems to occur in experiences too.

There are other cases which seem to go against the claim that only certain high-level features capture the content of experiences. One can, for instance, think of examples which separate representational content from sensational content, but retain substantial degrees of inference from background knowledge, concepts and theory. But, even here, there are aspects of the experience which remain unaccounted for. There is no sense in which the experience of music, for instance, is fully captured by its representational content. Though it may be inferential in some other (complex) sense, there is still something different about the experience of music that such inferential features do not capture: a solo drum player, for instance, produces music which sounds grouped in some way (it has certain representational features) but such features clearly don't exhaust the content of the experience, otherwise there would be no difference between a solo drummer and a drum machine (and no reason to prefer one over the other). Likewise, a subdominant chord resolves naturally to its tonic chord in a plagal cadence in a manner that seems to have other features beyond the (doubtless) cultural familiarities and preferences which give rise to such musical conventions.[24] What we can understand about such examples is that they exhibit features of experience which have a representational content and varying degrees of inference from background knowledge and theory, but which still have features that these aspects of experience cannot capture. Such features, moreover, amount to more than a mere mechanical stimulation of the sense organs: there is an experiential *content* to them which just does not seem to be representational or fully culturally informed (though it does seem to be structured in some sense).

---

[24] Peacocke suggests the example of hearing a chord as an augmented fourth rather than as a diminished fifth: 'Someone can have this experience without having the concept of an augmented fourth. His hearing it that way is necessarily linked to the resolutions of the chord that sound right to him.' ibid., p. 25 Such examples seem to be structured in some sense which does not seem to be fully representational or dependent on background concepts.

Such considerations as those given above lend some support to the idea that there might be features of experiences which escape the terms of the inferentialist proposal. And this, in turn, seems to lend support to the idea that there are sensory contents ('perceptions') as well as wholly judgement-informed experiences. The examples given above clearly suggest that neither the concept principle nor the intrinsicality principle captures *all* the important features of experiential content of interest in such cases.

Another example which lends more support for this claim is the phenomenon of visual grouping. Grouping is a pervasive representational and conceptual feature of experiences in most circumstances. One ordinarily brings to bear concepts of objects in normal human experience which help to sort out the various representational features of the visual scene before one. This is the intuition which makes the application of Millar's 'concept principle' and 'intrinsicality principle' seem so plausible in the context of experiences. Sherlock Holmes undoubtedly brought to bear concepts of objects, relations and events to sort out his visual scene. In the case of grouped experiences, the application of the concept principle also yields the application of the intrinsicality principle (because one applies concepts, one's experience yields certain grouped representational features). Holmes's experience thus exhibited a content that had projected certain representational state-types. Indeed, visual grouping is ordinarily so commonly tied to the concepts and representations that one brings to an experience, that one ordinarily 'sees' one's experience as a group of *objects*. Yet the case of visual grouping as necessarily involving 'high-level' concepts and representational content is obviously too simple a story, even if it might be true of normal human perception. For it is clear that in other circumstances one may not have a concept with which to group some scene and yet one's experience might be 'intrinsically grouped' in some fashion. The arrays below seem to involve no organisational concepts (beyond the concept of 'line') yet they are clearly seen in one way rather than any other:[25]

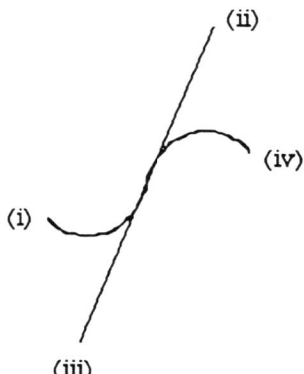

Figure 2 Ambiguous line groupings

---

[25] I. Rock, *Introduction to Perception*, p. 259. In the first array below (i) and (ii) and (iii) and (iv) are seen to be grouped; in the second array (ii) and (iii) are seen to be grouped.

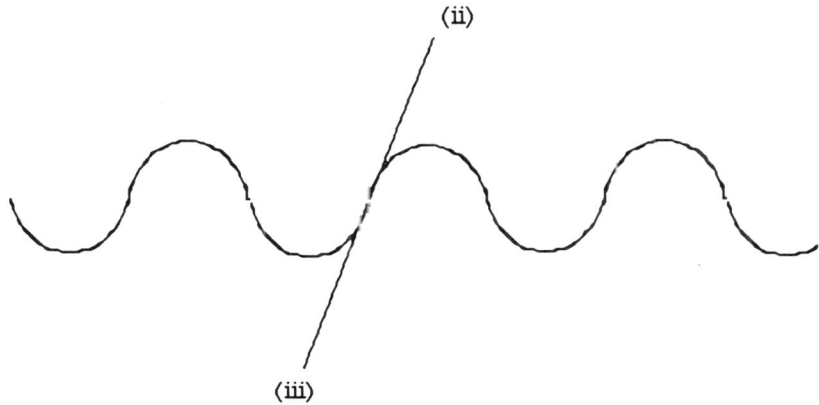

Figure 2 Ambiguous line groupings cont'd

This kind of case does not seem to require concepts in the very strong sense in which representational or propositional linguistic concepts are needed. But there does seem to be a structural way in which the various experiences are organised. Are we to call this pattern of organisation 'inferential' in the high-level sense or not?

It seems to be extending the notion of inference too far to answer this question in the affirmative; however, the experience does not seem to be altogether 'sensational' either. Again, like the music case, this experience seems to be structured, but not entirely representational; nor does it seem to involve the imposition of sophisticated concepts.

There are more interesting cases of grouped experiences than this. Peacocke suggests that the following array:

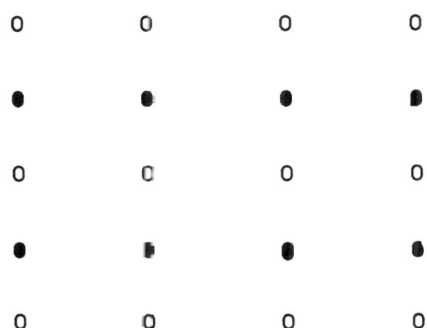

Figure 3 Ambiguous dot array

shows that experiences can be 'differently grouped in successive experiences [being] seen as either rows or columns'[26] i.e., as the following configurations:

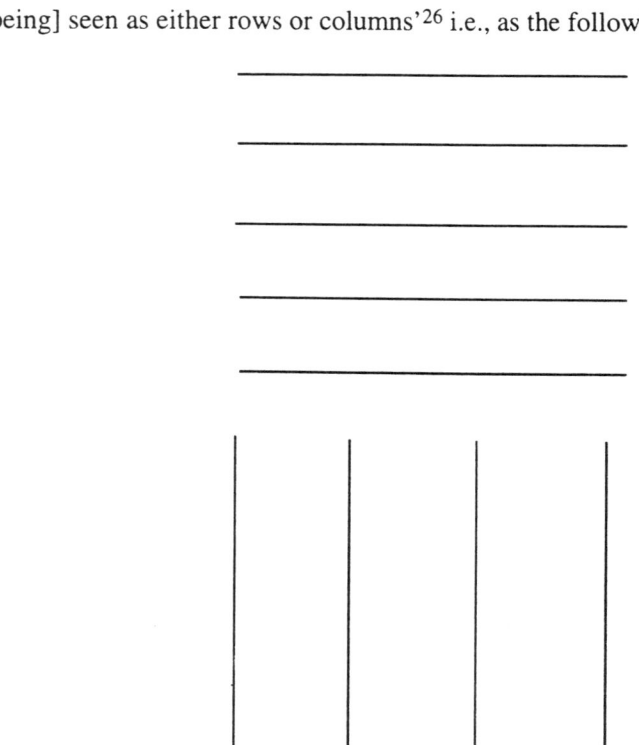

Figure 3 Ambiguous dot array cont'd

He also suggests that this phenomenon might demonstrate a problem with the idea that perceptions might have intrinsically sensational properties. This is because switches in aspect can be distinguished 'within the class of sensational properties of experience.'[27] (This, in turn, seems to suggest that there is nothing intrinsic to the experiences which makes them a sensational experience of one kind rather than another.) It shall later be suggested, however, that this is precisely what one should expect of such experiences if the continuum account is true. The case of intra-grouping aspect switches (such as that between rows and columns) is an instance of the various features of an experience being attended to at different times. And this is possible only if experience has the character of being a composite of various kinds of content simultaneously.

The point of the examples given above is simply to demonstrate that the application of concepts and representational content do not exhaust a specification of the nature of experiences. Both the concept principle and the

---

[26] Peacocke, op. cit., pp. 25-6.

[27] Ibid., p. 26. This example is taken from Rock, op. cit., who describes the original configuration as 'unstable and ambiguous.' (p. 257).

intrinsicality principle seem to be insufficient to capture the content of sensory experiences or perceptions, even if they might be adequate to capture the content of propositional attitudes or judgements. (This is the reason that both Peacocke and Millar see the need to postulate a further category which is neither proposition-like, nor sensation-like.) There seems to be a qualitative kind of sensational or perceptual content in the former kinds of experiences which simply cannot be captured in strictly 'high-level' terms. (Some of the above examples suggest that there is more to an experience than its intrinsic representational content; others suggest that the application of the concept principle is irrelevant to some grouped experiences.) These examples notwithstanding, it is nonetheless clear that philosophers have not been completely wrong to concentrate on high-level features when giving the content of experience. In each of the above examples the content of the experience does involve appeal to *some* inferential features. (In the case of the line groupings, it is simply the structural features of a 'line'; in the case of the resolving chords, it is the structured features of a culturally familiar musical progression.) The point is just that the extension of such inferential features as *necessary and sufficient* characteristics of experience generally seems to have been seriously over-emphasised.

The above considerations are important if they are true, and they do *seem* to be true. The considerations here should suggest that there is an inherent flexibility in the notion of experience being inferential or non-inferential, which neither the inferentialist proposal nor the observational account allows for. Some experiences, while not captured by inferential features, are certainly informed by them to some degree. This leaves neither the inferentialist proposal nor the observational account in a position to claim to be fully adequate accounts of experiential content, the above examples being instances in which experiences which are otherwise strongly inferential *yet still have content which cannot be captured in inferential terms.*

There are even stronger reasons for doubting the terms of the inferentialist proposal as a full and adequate account of experiential content. Peacocke notes that in 'the normal human experience ... visual field properties are associated with a representational content,' [28] but it is, in principle, possible to conceive of cases in which the sensational property and the representation of certain objects are present but where it is unclear to what extent there is a projection of these features onto the representational content of the world being experienced. Such cases offer examples of representational experiences without the normally projected state-type features. This is so in the case of congenitally blind people equipped with a tactile vision substitution system (TVSS), which registers the output of television cameras in terms of the motion of vibrating rods on the subject's back. These patients learn to transform vibro-tactor displays on their skins into 'visual' arrays, projected in space. But although a 'projection' of sorts occurs here, what kind of projection is it? According to the results of such a procedure, the subjects seem to undergo 'intrinsically spatial sensations ... which are not those of pressure or vibration, and which are reported to be quite unlike those of touch.' Furthermore, in some studies, the patients report that their spatial sensations seem to be centred around the lens of the camera, not

---

[28] Peacocke, op. cit., p. 14.

their backs, or objects in the world. Now, although this kind of experience may involve *some* kind of projection, it is clear that the projection need not be associated with representational content of objects in the world. The reports of subjects undergoing such 'experiences' are also very curious: As well as saying that these sensations appearing to come from the face of the camera not their backs, nor out in the world, they also suggest that the visual data seem to exist in two dimensional space with no depth. According to such subjects, the normal vocabulary of 'seeing' (presumably that vocabulary associated with representational content) is inappropriate for capturing the experiences.[29]

The evidence, of course, admits of several interpretations. What it might mean is that one can have experiences which are both unlike visual sensations and visual representations. The subject might not represent the content of his experience in any fully projected way like Sherlock Holmes does with the cigar-band, although it seems he/she is still consciously aware of certain (non-visual, non-tactile) representational features. This phenomenon is very odd, but we might think of reasons for this: it seems *prima facie* reasonable that in order for an organism to achieve success in modelling experiences in terms of their projected representational contents, a requirement is that such an organism undergo prior non-projected (or partially-projected) representational experiences in the first instance. (In a congenitally blind person these inchoate partially-projected experiences don't come via their usual route due to the defect in the visual system, though this route can, apparently, be short-circuited to produce the appropriate sensations in the absence of their [visual] representational correlates). What a blind person experiences when equipped with a TVSS are spatial sensations with only partly-projected features that his visual system would fully *represent* if his visual system were operating normally.[30]

The suggestion that one can have sensational features of spatial experiences, but not necessarily fully *projected* features of the same experience, is damaging for the inferentialist proposal. But the idea that such aspects of experience might be necessary *precursors* to fully projected, representational features seems plausible for evolutionary reasons. Briefly, it would seem that if inferential/non-inferential dimensions constitute a *continuum* and not an exclusive dichotomy, then some primitive kind of content must be available to very unsophisticated organisms simply to help them survive. As mentioned in Chapter 2, there might be selective advantages in having some kind of *sense* of spatiality without very complex representational content. One need not be able to *fully* project one's experience as a certain spatially located object in the world (though it is doubly advantageous if one can do both). All one has to have, in the simplest case, is a visual field experience of some vague spatial kind without *fully* projected features ('fully' in the sense of having the projected features associated with a given representational content). One need only the *sense* that something is fast

---

[29] Ibid., p. 15. See, for instance: G. Guarniero, 'Experience of Tactile Vision,' pp. 101-4; P. Bach-y-Rita et al, 'Vision Substitution by Tactile Image Projection,' pp. 963-4.

[30] A possible analogy to the case of the congenitally blind person's sense of space is the phenomenon of waking up in a strange place and 'not knowing where you are'. At the instant of waking one experiences certain spatial sensations of things being in certain vague relationships, but one's projection of them is not clear. (The table is in a vague direction within one's visual field etc.) As one becomes more conscious of the situation, of course, the projected spatial features become more dominating than the partly-projected spatial ones.

approaching, rather than representing that an object is fast approaching. One could even run a line similar to Dawkins here: if no eye, better a light sensitive patch than nothing. Similarly, of no projected state types, better a semi-projected sense of spatiality than nothing at all.[31]

Of course, like a very unsophisticated organism, the congenitally blind cannot represent objects spatially in any visual sense either. However, in such a case, it is better that an organism can feel, at least, some kind of representational aspects of experience, if it has no other more sophisticated abilities; but even if it did, given that one can project spatial features of objects *incorrectly,* it is also selectively useful to be able to *sense* spatiality without necessarily being able to fully project it. Sensing a visual field enlargement is useful selectively, since one may be *wrong* about exactly what one projects, and how one's projection is occupying visual space. How an experience is processed depends less on the actual *object* represented, than on the segregation of certain groups of stimuli which are then available for later more detailed processing.[32]

Another consideration here is the point that one might somehow register features of experiential content without necessarily *representing* those features at all. It is this kind of phenomenon that Millar has in mind when he considers what he calls an 'aspect' of experience. The example he has in mind arises most vividly in the case of colour perception:

> Sensational properties can be further illustrated with the help of the notion of an *aspect*. A uniformly red surface looked at from a particular point of view in particular conditions of light may present a richly variegated pattern of light and shade and hue. This pattern is a colour aspect and is as much an objective property of the surface as its colour which is uniformly red. Often, perhaps more often than not, we do not notice the colour aspects of the things we look at. That is one reason why it is difficult to paint and draw. But even if in looking at the red surface we failed to notice the variegated pattern it presents, there remains a sense in which our experience could be said to register the aspect. Even if we are not attending to the aspect in a way that would enable us to describe it, our experience would in normal circumstances have a phenomenal character which would be different if the aspect were different. A change in the position of the light source, for instance, would alter the aspect and this would normally produce a change in the phenomenal character of the experience. Registering the colour aspect in question is a sensational property. An experience can possess this property and yet not be *of a surface presenting this aspect in question*. One could obtain an experience of the latter sort by attending to the aspect with the artist's eye, but an

---

[31] Richard Dawkins, *The Blind Watchmaker,* passim, especially 'Making Tracks through Animal Space'.

[32] There is some evidence for the independent processing of subjective contour brightness and sharpness which suggests a limited application of 'higher-order' cognitive mechanisms. There is also some evidence for an expanded role in perceptual processing for so-called 'preattentive' vision (i.e. low-level stimulus grouping which does not depend on the identification and analysis of that stimulus). See: S. Siegel and S. Petry, 'Evidence for the Independent Processing of Subjective Contour Brightness and Sharpness,' p. 233-41. See also: M. Bravo and R. Blake, 'Preattentive Vision and Perceptual Groups,' pp. 515-22.

experience might register the aspect even if it did not result from such attention.³³

In this case, the experience of a coloured hue might not seem to be fixed onto the experience of the painted surface as such; it may seem, instead, to be a product of *attention*. (One may notice a painted surface, yet not the change in hue, even though one registers the hue and can attend to it when required.) The passage quoted from Sibley in Chapter 1 gave a case of scratches on a window. In this case, one might not be attending to the scratches, yet the scratches may still present themselves as blurry 'in the corner of one's eye'. There is a difference in these cases. The first example shows that an aspect may not be noticed and yet be present in one's experience (the colour hue); the second shows that an aspect might be noticed and yet not *projected* in one's experience (the window scratches). So, as well as there being unnoticed seeings, there can be unprojected noticings or low-level registerings. Such examples are problematic for a representational view of experiential content and the inferentialist proposal generally. They are a problem because such examples show that some features of experience are simply not captured by high-level influences.

There are more interesting cases of experiences with non-representational features. Beck offers a case of colour perception in which the features of a colour hue can be noticed to switch between aspects in successive experiences of the one projection. In Beck's example, the intersection of three sets of differently coloured circles is a combination of the colours of each circle in equal proportions. Yet when the circles are seen on various inclined planes, the intersecting colour can be seen only sometimes as a mixed colour and sometimes as an unmixed colour as seen through the overlain 'transparent' part of one circle.³⁴ In this example, it is also possible to notice only one aspect or the other; the other not being obvious until it is pointed out or concentrated on. Millar's claim above about often not noticing the colour aspects of the things we look at is clearly a pervasive feature of colour perception. It is attention that makes us notice certain colour features over others. But when one is attentive to changes in aspect one can also notice successive aspect shifts as Beck's example shows. The class of alternating sensational experiences in this case is clearly experienced as something quite different from the representational content of the experience as circles of certain non-uniform colours.

The case of intra-grouping aspect shifts mentioned earlier is no less mysterious than the aspect shifts in Beck's surface colour example. Such cases show that the content of an experience can oscillate between its various aspect features as a function of attention. And this is perfectly intelligible if the *complexity thesis* is true and experience is composed of various interposed (sensational, representational, etc.) elements as an experiential amalgam. In concentrating on an experience, one cannot normally notice all its various aspects. But over time, and by concentration, those various aspects can come to be the subject of one's attention (hence, the phenomenon of aspect-switches). Peacocke's problem earlier need not be a difficulty unless it is assumed that

---

33 A. Millar, 'What's in a Look?', op. cit., pp. 88-89.

34 See J. Beck, *Surface Colour Perception,* plate 1.

experiences have one or other sensational property and not several kinds of content simultaneously.

The phenomenon of *attention fixing* itself is troublesome for the inferentialist line. In perception, it is important to be able to *notice* something without representing it or knowing what that thing is - it is important for the visual system to *register* information without the necessary input of 'high-level' features. It is well known in the optical sciences that parts of the retina (in particular, the extreme edge) is very sensitive to low-level informational inputs such as movement, but not to highly complex, inferentially-mediated discriminations like objects. The very physiology of the eye, it seems, allows us to register low-level, selectively useful 'aspects' - of scenes, events, etc. - without being able to process that information intellectually. In Dretske's terms, it allows us, paradoxically, to 'notice them even before one sees them.'[35]

Several examples have been given where significant experiential content can be shown to issue in circumstances in which the representational content of an experience is either absent altogether or occurs in degrees. Representational features of experience clearly do not fully capture what has been called low-level 'aspects' of content. An experience can have certain representational features as well as having aspects which do not seem representational. An aspect may also be noticed or unnoticed without being projected. Aspect shifts can also occur in successive experiences of the same projected object. My conclusion about such cases is that they are a problem for the inferentialist proposal and, in fact, go some way to add to the plausibility of the continuum account. On this account it is plausible that there are such low-level sensational features of experiences as much as high-level features, and, given the complexity thesis, there *should* be such sensational features in every experiential amalgam.

Epistemic content

Another feature of the inferentialist proposal is the emphasis on background knowledge in experiential content. On this view, the content of one's knowledge necessarily filters one's experience. Sherlock Holmes brought to bear implicit knowledge of objects and events as well as information about Jones, his assailant's smoking habits, etc., in order to have the experience he did. Experiences are necessarily epistemic on this view.

However, while such claims are plausible for aspects of some experiences, they are not plausible for the experiences of conceptually unsophisticated organisms, nor even for experiences of a certain type. Again, the phenomenon of colour experience must be seen as a difficulty for this account. In this case, while it may be clear that one *represents* certain features of the world, one is very hard-pressed to see the relevance of the influence of 'high-level'

---

[35] F. I. Dretske, *Seeing and Knowing*, p. 15. Gregory remarks of the extreme edge of the retina: 'when stimulated by movement we experience nothing, but a reflex is initiated which rotates the eye to bring the moving object into central vision, so that the highly developed foveal region with its associated central neural network is brought into play for identifying the object. The edge of the retina is thus an early-warning device, used to rotate the eyes to aim the object-recognition part of the system on to objects likely to be friend or foe rather than neutral.' R. L. Gregory, *Eye and Brain: The Psychology of Seeing*, p. 91.

background knowledge. It would seem, in fact, that *despite* what one knew about colours, one cannot help but experience them in a certain way. 'Seeing' a colour amounts to perceiving contentful features which are independent of what colours actually *are*.

C.L. Hardin considers various illusions as being problematic for any broadly 'physicalist' account of the phenomenon of colour. The implications of this view are problematic for any inferentialist account of experiential content also. Colour, on the physicalist account, is a feature of wave-lengths of light hitting the retina and exciting photoreceptors, which, in turn, hyperpolarize and generate electrochemical signals in the surrounding cells. Colour perception is a purely physical process involving purely physical mechanisms. The process of absorbing the various frequencies of such lightwaves is supposed to account for the phenomenon of colour.[36] But 'Bidwell's Ghost' is a striking challenge to this view, as Hardin explains:

> Imagine the following experiment. Before you is a spinning disk, illuminated by an ordinary incandescent lamp. If most people are asked what color they see on the face of the disk, they will unhesitatingly reply that they see a bluish green. ...[T]his proves to be a trick of sorts. When the wheel is made to turn very slowly you see a half-black, half-white disk with a slot through which a red lamp flashes. You saw no red at all before, and you can discern no bluish green now... This particular afterimage phenomenon is called Bidwell's ghost...When you view Bidwell's ghost, it is always open to you to deny that you are seeing bluish green, on the grounds that after-images are not physical objects and only physical objects have colors. But it is then fair to ask you what color you do see. Red? Grey? No color at all? None of these answers is intuitively very appealing.[37]

It is not satisfactory to appeal here to the colour properties of spectral wavelengths of light either, as the anomalous cases can be multiplied. A projected 'pure' yellow light of (roughly) 577 nanometers is perceptually equivalent to the superimposition of a 'pure' green light of (roughly) 540 nanometers and a 'pure' red light of 670 nanometers. There is no trace of 577 *nm.* light in the superimposed light, though it *looks* exactly the same as its isolated equivalent.[38] A further example of a colour illusion is when a blue,

---

[36] For details, see C. L. Hardin, *Colour for Philosophers: Unweaving the Rainbow, passim.*

[37] C.L. Hardin, 'Colour and Illusion,' from *Mind and Cognition: A Reader, op. cit.,* p. 555.

[38] Perceptually equivalent yet physically inequivalent colour visual stimuli are known as *metamers*. The examples of this phenomenon are legion: the case of the colour white, for instance, which is a composite of wavelengths of all colours and seems to have no visible chromatic colours at all. And it can be demonstrated in the phenomenon of 'simultaneous contrast' that a physically identifiable colour when placed alongside other colours can induce the complementary colour in that region. The point here is that '.. any theory of colour that is to be of any interest, must go beyond a set of raw stipulations to the effect that such-and-such wavelengths are to count as red, and that so-and-so wavelengths are to be cyan, and so on ... At the very least, we can demand of a theory of colour that it satisfactorily represent what is going on when we see red and brown and white and black in ordinary life.' For multiple examples, see Hardin, ibid., pp. 556-8.

green or red light is projected onto a white surface. Such colours appear as such - i.e., as blue, green and red; however, when a yellow light is projected onto a white surface, it appears as *white* at the surface. This phenomenon is particularly puzzling, given that the physiology of colour vision supposedly involves the excitation combinations of only three types of cone cells which contain only red, blue and green pigments.[39] Such cases throw doubt upon the 'physicalist' account of such experiences. For, as Hardin notes: 'the physicalist who would reduce real colors to wavelengths of light should be able to pick out the *real* colors on the basis of physical considerations alone.'[40]

Physicalists have different approaches to this issue. Colour has been taken by some physicalists (e.g., Armstrong) as a complex environmental property. Other physicalists (e.g., Smart) have taken colour to be a secondary property which can be analysed reductively. The reductionist-type proposal has to meet the kinds of problems just mentioned. The other kind of proposal has to face the difficulty that the complex physical processes in question are highly disjunctive (and, hence, cannot easily be described) but, worse still, they don't seem to capture our ordinary conception of colours as we experience them. There really seem to be no other authentic possibilities to deal with this problem despite recent attempts to develop intermediate positions.[41] Marie McGinn argues that we cannot have our ordinary 'subjective' understanding and our physicalism too:

> Either colour is identical with some complex physical property of a surface (for example, its propensity to reflect light of a given wavelength), but the apparent connection between colour and the notion of an object's looking like this is lost. Or, colour is accounted for in terms of primary qualities on perceiving subjects, but at the cost of creating an intensional realm whose contents are conceived as subjective qualities beyond the scope of scientific investigation.[42]

Of course it doesn't follow that colour aspects are beyond the scope of scientific investigation at all. More argument needs to be offered for this to be a plausible claim. What does follow is that what one experiences appears to be different from what is *known* about the physical properties of such experiences. Knowing what a colour is, doesn't help one with cases of colour illusion. This is as much a problem for inferentialism as it is for physicalism. There appear to be features of colour perception which are qualitatively irreducible to how physics tell us a colour should behave in the case of superimposed wavelengths of light. 'Background knowledge' may capture Holmes's experience of Jones and the cigar-band, but it doesn't capture certain features of how colours *look*.

---

[39] For an account of the physiology of colour perception, see: S. L. Merbs and J. Nathans, 'Absorption Spectra of Human Cone Pigments,' pp. 433-435.

[40] Ibid., p. 557. Presumably, on the strength of such examples, the same conclusion should have to be reached on the so-called 'dispositional' account of colours. For a critique of such a view along the same lines, see: P.A. Boghossian and J.D. Velleman, 'Colour as a Secondary Quality', pp. 81-103. See also their 'Physicalist Theories of Colour'.

[41] See: K. R. Westphal, *Colour* ; C. McGinn, *The Subjective View*.

[42] M. McGinn, 'On Two Recent Accounts of Colour', pp. 316-324.

Nor can colours be captured by representational features. Take the case of the after-image produced by a camera flash-bulb. In such a case, the red spot precisely obscures the photographer being represented in the experience by the people being photographed, yet there is no question that the red spot is *located* in the experience as any represented feature: rather, the transitory colour appears to be a *sui generis* feature of the experience or an 'aspect' of the experience in my sense. The colour flash seems to be a partly qualitative, not an entirely representational, experience.

Colours have some quite peculiar features which militate against the idea that they can be captured in the terms of the inferentialist proposal. Katz isolates several distinguishable aspects of colour perception which he describes as the 'modes of appearance' of colours.[43] *Surface* colours, according to Katz, can be distinguished from *film* colours. Colours can also have *voluminousness* and *transparency*. So-called *mirrored* colours can also be distinguished from those which have *lustre;* and colours with *luminosity* can be perceptually discriminated from those which have *glow*. (I shall outline only some of these below. For further details see Katz.)

Any of the above features of colour experiences must be seen as problematic for the view of experiential content being criticised. This is so because not all the features mentioned can be captured in inferential terms. Katz shows that where some colours seem to be localised 'so precisely at an exactly definable distance'[44] (e.g., the colour of a piece of paper), other colours 'seem to be gauged only with some degree of uncertainty'[45] (e.g., viewing the colour of the sky through a hollow tube, or viewing a spectrometer where the location of a colour is judged to vary widely at distances between 50 - 80 cm). The first kind of colours seem to belong to an object or surface and hence are called 'surface' colours; these alone seem to have a representational content. The latter kind of colours, however, seem not to be so located and are known as 'film' colours. These colour appearances have other distinguishing features: the appearance of film colours also seems to have an essentially frontal plane orientation, whereas the surface colours 'may appear in all possible modes of orientation',[46] corresponding to the orientation of the object. Surface colours can also have a wrinkled or smooth texture, whereas film colours are always uniformly smooth. In the case of film colours, it also seems as though one can penetrate deeply into the colour. In the case of surface colours, however, the colour seems to present a barrier beyond which the eye cannot pass 'as though the colour ... offers resistance to the eye.'[47] Compare the blueness of the sky as a film colour and the orange of a pomegranate as a surface colour as examples which exhibit these characteristics. These features are not stable characteristics of colours. Katz notes that 'all possible intermediate stages are to be found between surface colours and film colours.'[48] It is also apparent that colours of

---

[43] D. Katz, *The World of Colour*, p. 7.
[44] Loc. cit.
[45] Loc. cit.
[46] Ibid., p. 71.
[47] Ibid., p. 8.
[48] Ibid., pp. 9-10.

the one kind can be made to have features of the other in some circumstances. Various influences can also be made on both surface and film colours which change their appearance. Seeing a colour through one eye, rather than both, results in surface colours appearing to recede; seeing a surface colour through a small aperture (e.g., a key hole) makes it seem like a film colour in having a frontal plane orientation. Looking at the orientation of a film colour (e.g., the blueness of the sky) can be influenced by the presence of surface colours in the same visual region when they stand in clear relief (they will often make the blue of the sky 'bend towards' the object).[49] However, when no surface colours are present, a film colour seems to lack spatial localisation (e.g., the subjective visual grey experienced when one's eyes are closed).

Some surface colours also seem to have volume which is quite distinct from the volume of an object. Ordinary objects have no volume in respect of their colour (even though the object itself has volume). However, the grey of a fog or the colour of a liquid may appear to have volume by seeming to occupy tri-dimensional space. According to Katz, a colour can have voluminousness only when it is transparent. The more dense a fog becomes (and correspondingly less transparent) the more it takes on the appearance of film colour. The volume filling surface colour of the fog is lost with an increase of opacity.[50] A colour, however, can be transparent without having voluminousness at all (a coloured perspex sheet does not seem to occupy tri-dimensional space like a moderately thick fog).

Such features of colours are variable in the extreme and seem to be quite different to the representational localisation of the particular surface colour of an object. Moreover, it is easy to ignore these features; it is easy to see the world simply as groupings of surface colours. This is so because we have largely adapted to attend to such colour aspects over others (we normally see colours in terms of coloured represented *objects*). There are, however, strong reasons for thinking that this is but one mode of appearance of colours among others. Presumably there is a case for claiming that this is the most survivally useful of all colour aspects (it is, after all, objects which are the source of many of our survival needs and avoidances); however, this should not go to rule out other colour appearances. The point here is that such features of colour experiences seem too complex to be captured in the simplistic terms of the inferentialist proposal.

Colour reductionism seems to be false, and so does a simple view of colours as being the surface properties of objects. Why should a reductionism of perceptual experiences to 'high-level' features (such as representational or epistemic content) be true? The suggestion here is that this issues from a skewed conception of the observation/theory distinction. This has led to an over-emphasis being placed on the importance of high-level input to experiential content. There seem to be good reasons, however, for taking a somewhat less extreme proposal seriously.

Some experiences have aspects like 'additional characterisation' over and

---

[49] Ibid., p. 73. 'In general, the more distinctly the surface colour acting upon it deviates from [the] orientation [of the film colour], the more the film deviates from the frontal-parallel position.' Loc. cit.

[50] Ibid., p. 21.

above what is represented in the experience; others are spatially represented in some sense, yet not fully projected; others still have content in a way which is not influenced by background knowledge and concepts. Colour experiences seem to have features which cannot be captured in entirely representational or epistemic terms. Besides this, there are reasons for supposing that some experiences, though involving inference, are not propositional and also cases where it is an over-rationalisation to speak of theory being involved. In view of this, it seems plausible that the various features of high-level inference do not influence experience *en bloc*. It is also plausible that they do not have the important focus that the inferentialist attributes to them. In the light of the examples given, Millar's concept principle and intrinsicality principle certainly do not capture some interesting features of experiential content. There are some features of experience which escape such characterisations.

Considerations like this may suggest that the tripartite characterisation of sensations, sensory experiences (perceptions) and propositional attitudes (judgements) is a more accurate way of describing experiential content. Generally speaking it is a better account. However, it is not the kind of characterisation being defended in this book. The claim is that an even more compelling proposal would allow for degrees of influence even *within* the various levels of experience. That is, there seems to be no logically compelling reason to stop at Peacocke's or Millar's three-way distinction between sensations, perceptions and judgments.

A number of considerations suggest an application of graduated categories even within these divisions. Firstly, the phenomenon of intra-grouping aspect switches (above), like the colour aspect switches, seems to indicate that within the class of sensational properties, distinguishable contents can be isolated (this not only demonstrates a fundamental role for attention in the fixation of experiential content, but also that certain structural grouping abilities require low-level inferential capacities). Secondly, the phenomenon of representational aspects and non-representational aspects within the class of sensory experiences alone seems to be too rigid: there is surely a case for saying that some experiences can be neither strictly representational nor non-representational in Peacocke's or Millar's sense (e.g., the vague waking experience, or the experience of a film colour). Finally, both the concept principle and the intrinsicality principle seem to be too blunt. What constitutes a 'concept' in the case of the line groupings given above? How does having the concept of Russian Blue capture an unnoticed (but registered) colour aspect? What constitutes an 'intrinsic' representational state-type in the case of experience via the tactile-vision simulator? A more plausible application of such categories would not be just to judgements or propositional attitudes, but to lower order, less sophisticated contents in various degrees of sophistication.

Such experiences seem to require more than just sensory inputs and rather less than high-level concepts, background knowledge and representational states. The typology of sensations, perceptions and judgements does not capture such considerations. Though the accounts offered by Peacocke and Millar constitute an improvement on the inferentialist proposal and the observational account, they still require some refinement.

What can we conclude from all this? Peacocke's view of the matter is this:

Those who say that sensation has almost no role to play in normal, mature human experience, or at least in normal human visual experience, commonly cite as their ground the fact that all visual experience have some representational content. If this is indeed a fact, it shows that no human visual experience is a pure sensation. But it does not follow that such experience does not have sensational properties. It is one thing to say that all mature visual experiences have representational content, another thing to say that no such experience has intrinsic properties (properties which help to specify what it is like to have the experience) explicable without reference to representational content. We can label those who dispute this view, and hold that all intrinsic properties of mature human visual experiences are possessed in virtue of their representational content, 'extreme perceptual theorists'.[51]

What are called 'intrinsic properties' here correspond fairly well to what has been called sensational aspects of experience (Peacocke also calls them 'sensational properties'). On the basis of the previous discussion, it would seem there *are* intrinsic properties. By implication, of course, the inferentialist proposal stands in need of serious revision.

Peacocke's claim suggests a way of transcending the traditional dichotomy of the inferentialist proposal and the observational account. He claims (rightly in my view) that even though straightforward, inferentially-informed perceptions ('mature visual experience') contain representational content, it *does not follow* that such experiences do not also have sensational properties. In other words, Peacocke admits the possibility that low-level content is always present even in straightforwardly 'high-level' perceptions.

Of course, being an 'extreme perceptual theorist' is another way of saying that experience needs a background of theories and concepts to embed the representational contents; it is another way of describing the terms of the inferentialist proposal. But, as Peacocke notes, this does not rule out a complexity thesis: that experience actually contains low-level content as well. He does not attempt to provide a reason for this, but a reason for this is provided in what follows.

Several reasons why the inferentialist proposal won't work

Beyond the problems already mentioned, there are several immediately plausible reasons why the inferentialist proposal is not adequate.

The first reason: for the fully inferentialist view to be true, experience must be loaded with high-level concepts which are epistemic in the required sense. Experiences must involve descriptive concepts drawn from background knowledge. (This, in essence, is Millar's 'concept principle': 'a concept can be an ingredient of the content of [the representational] state only if the subject possesses the concept. If a person believes that he caused embarrassment at the party the other night then the concept of embarrassment is an ingredient of the content of his belief.')[52] This sort of principle naturally translates into

---

[51] Peacocke, op. cit., p. 8.
[52] Millar, op. cit., (1985) p. 86.

experiential content on the terms of the inferentialist proposal and hence, experiential content is seen as representational and propositional etc. But it is fairly clear that the concept principle will not work.

As Millar notes, if this is true then it means that only if a person has a concept of a ϕ can they have an experience of a ϕ, and (importantly) if the concept differed, then so must the experience. But this is less than self-evident, as he explains:

> Tom, a keen gardener, is looking in the direction of a dahlia. Being in good order, he has a visual experience of a dahlia. Dick, his decadent flat-dwelling friend, lacks even a rudimentary knowledge of horticulture. He does not even know that dahlias are flowers, never mind that they grow from tubers, come in a variety of gorgeous bright colours and so on. In fact, Dick lacks the very concept of a dahlia ... if the hapless Dick were to look at the dahlia from Tom's point of view he *could not* have a visual experience of the same type as Tom's. His experience would differ from Tom's in respect of its representational content for the simple reason that for want of the right concept he is in no position to judge that there is a dahlia before him. The counterintuitive feature of this analysis is the implication that Dick's experience would have to differ *qua* experience from Tom's. No problem attaches to the fact that while Tom would be prompted to judge that there is a dahlia before him, Dick would not. The problem is to see why experiences which differ in this way would have to be different sorts of experiences.[53]

There are some things to be distinguished here. Millar seems wrong about one of them. Presumably Dick would *represent* the same thing in his experience that Tom does, even if he didn't know what that thing was (leaving aside chronic myopia etc.) In this sense the experience is the same. However, Millar is right to isolate the problem that, on the inferentialist proposal, Dick must have had a different experience from that of Tom in some sense because he lacked certain background knowledge. If descriptive concepts drawn from background knowledge are a necessary feature of the inferentialist proposal, then the experiences in question would have to be qualitatively different. But this doesn't seem intuitively right at all. Knowing what a dahlia is should not influence the experience one has in any *qualitative* way. One should be able to register something about an experience (besides its representational content) without knowing what that thing is. If not, knowledge can be conflated in a *necessary* way with experiential content, in the manner the inferentialist account stipulates. But this seems less than plausible for reasons already given. One can register an 'aspect' without 'noticing' or 'knowing' it; so in this sense we can say that Dick's experience is not different from Tom's. Millar calls the *necessary* conflation of knowledge with experience 'a consequence of the judgement theory,'[54] by which he means a view of experiential content which is heavily inferential. If a consequence of the inferentialist proposal is that experiences must differ qualitatively for want of high-level beliefs and concepts,

---

[53] Ibid., pp. 90-1.
[54] Loc. cit.

then this hardly rests well with what we take to be commonsensical about perception. What seems true about this case is that Dick has the same qualitative experience, but simply does not recognise a particular object in his experience as being a dahlia.

The second reason: for the inferentialist proposal to be true, there would have to be *no more* to the content of such experiences than the concepts drawn upon. But this too seems to be doubtful, since representational experiences, experiences *that,* always seem to be under-determined by other features. An experience of a tomato, for instance, is under-determined by the experience of a tomato-like thing or a fake tomato. The experience of *tomato-likeness* by the presence of shape and colour features, *under-determines* the presentation of the tomato, since one can experience such things without (actually) experiencing a tomato. This is a pervasive feature of experiences generally, if one looks hard enough.

> The idea we are examining is that visual experiences represent or present possible states of the world. Their contents are supposed to be built from concepts under which physical objects and scenes fall. The trouble is that where the concept of a ϕ is of this sort, there is always more to there being a ϕ before the subject than can be captured by an experience.[55]

This is precisely the reason that justifies Peacocke's comment above. The fact that there can be more to an experience than that which is represented or built from concepts is the reason why sensational content can escape the terms of the inferentialist proposal. However, it is not suggested that representational judgements, concepts etc., should be jettisoned from experiences altogether. The claim is just that we need to adopt an application of 'degrees of concept' to experience and say that there are also aspects of experiences which do not depend on the high-level influences drawn upon.

As mentioned in Chapter 2, the notion of a concept in this connection is an ambiguous one. There seem to be two legitimate senses of concept, and the inferentialist employs only one of them. Following Peacocke, it was suggested that 'concept' could be understood in terms of *mode of presentation of a property,* and there seemed to be two kinds of such modes: descriptive and sensational. From the emphasis placed on representational and propositional content, it is clear that the inferentialist holds that there are descriptive concepts, concepts which label and itemise certain represented objects of experience. However, there are also aspects of experience which seem simply sensational, not descriptive or representational. In the sense that experience needs concepts, my suggestion is that both kinds of concept are required. This would avoid the problem that there cannot be more to experience than the (descriptive) concept drawn upon.

The third reason: for the inferentialist proposal to be adequate, it must be true; but high-level features simply do not penetrate through experience in any *comprehensive* way at all. Just as what is represented is not the only feature of experiences, so too what is congruent with background theory does not necessarily exhaust what is *sensed.* The upshot is that Peacocke and Millar are

---

[55] Ibid., pp. 94-5.

right about needing at least a three-way categorisation of experience content. There at least needs to be a distinction between high-level judging, perception which is both judgement-informed *and* intrinsically sensational, and proximal stimulations (which are not 'experiences' in any sense, but patterns of causal stimulation at the sensory surfaces). Jerry Fodor has also reached this conclusion in another context, which will be considered in Chapter 8.

The fourth reason: this concerns the application of very high-level inferential features to animal and infant experience. Unsophisticated creatures have experiences which need not be fixed by the terms of the inferentialist proposal, particularly linguistic propositional judgements and descriptive/representational concepts. Such features seem irrelevant in these cases. On the other hand, experiential content needs to be fixed somehow, so it would seem that some kind of low-level sensory content is required here. That low-level contentful experiences occur in addition to inference, would seem to have an important evolutionary function: for it seems reasonable that observational sensations fix simple contentful experiences for all organisms in a biologically *direct* manner. The reason this might be true is obvious enough: by conscious observational experience, the etiological evolutionary lead is kept short, which would otherwise necessitate long, unwieldy and time-consuming inferences. Extinction often offends if credit is asked, so certain perceptual information has to exist in the form of a basic and uncomplicated *given* for those organisms for whom rapidity of message and survival is important. Ultimately, the argument for a continuum view on the relation between low-level observation and high-level inference must rely on this sort of evidence. And the argument would go something like this: for phylogenetic reasons, animals have (essentially) the same, though less well developed, conceptual equipment as us. They do not possess the facility to describe and, in particular, to propositionalise over their experiences, but they do have concepts of sorts, and they do *sense;* so sensing has content too, much more than the 'proximal stimulations' lead us to believe. This kind of non-verbal, contentful sensing would seem to be the main mode of belief fixation in animals and infants. For in their case, inferential abilities are sparingly developed if at all, and yet something has to be recognised just to make sense of how their movements are guided. The issue of animal experience will be dealt with in detail in Chapter 7.

Conclusion

A reconsideration of experience along the lines of the continuum account sees low-level content feature with high-level content along a graded, non-exclusive scale. Experiential content, may be an *amalgam* of several kinds of content. For the most part we can account for experiential content in these high-level terms; however, this is far from saying that inferentialism is correct. More needs to be considered than the elements of high-level inference. What also need to be considered are: (i) evolutionary principles (an account needs to be given of the experiences of unsophisticated creatures, and the fact that some content are selectively advantageous); (ii) the fact that the features of high-level inference can be separated and distinguished; and (iii) the possibility that the rationalist influence on philosophy has been far too strong, and has led to an over-emphasis of high-level features in our assessment of experiential content.

Peacocke's and Millars' views go some way toward suggesting that experiential content is more complicated than the inferentialist proposal says it is. These views are essentially in sympathy with my own. As we have seen in this chapter, there are aspects of experiential content that the inferentialist proposal simply does not capture.

6 Idealised and naturalised experience

> It is therefore just as necessary to make our concepts sensible, that is, to add the object to them in intuition, as to make our intuitions intelligible, that is, to bring them under concepts.[1]

Kant: experience idealised

Introduction

This chapter outlines the rationalist heritage central to the inferentialist proposal. Kant's metaphysic of experience will be assessed and compared with Lorenz's biological perspective on Kant's innovations. In Chapter 7, the question of low-level animal experience will be looked at in the light of the inferentialist proposal and the continuum view. In Chapter 8, Fodor's account of the mind as an informational system will be discussed. Fodor's account of the structure of mental content is suggestive of a multi-level view of perceptual processing and, with modifications, is an important support for the view that there are several non-exclusive degrees in which contentful properties may appear to experiencing organisms. In concluding this part, the causal role of low-level content is looked at in some detail.

Kant's metaphysic of experience

Kant has supplied a very influential view of the origins of experience, which could, in modern terminology, be called an information-theoretic account, involving the presentation of data, its organisation and its output. Kant's metaphysic was directed at how the objects of knowledge are possible, of course, but it is also a strong general claim about the nature of experience. Experience, to Kant, was a function of the material of sense unified by the

---

[1] I. Kant, *Critique of Pure Reason*, B75. p. 61. (In the following citations from Kant, A and B refer to the first and second editions of the *Critique* - 1781 and 1787, respectively.)

categories of reason.

On the orthodox interpretation, Kant's view was that experiences were the *organised matter of sensation*. What came in as input through the sense organs was a disorganised sensory material which was then sorted into intelligible bundles, and it was this sorting function which made experience possible.

This sorting was achieved by an 'inescapable duality'[2] of two departments or faculties of the mind, two mind-imposed structures - the *forms of intuition* and the *categories*. The former was a receptive faculty; the latter, an active one. The former shaped intuitions by means of structuring experience in space and time - objects were necessarily experienced *in* space and *in* time, and hence, both space and time were 'declared to be 'in us' [as] forms of our sensibility.'[3] This organisation of experience in space and time allowed sensible intuitions to be actively brought under the faculty which actively imposed what Kant called 'categories' on experience, which, as well as constituting generalised forms of space and time, also imposed other necessary features to objects such as cause, relation, permanence and so on.

There was a good reason for applying this bipartite division of the faculties to experiential content. On the one hand, experience required singular or particular instances of things to be present in perception - like certain objects in time and space (it is impossible, according to Kant to experience the world in any other way). On the other hand, experience required general concepts to recognise a particular object and classify it. To recognise a particular object, spatio-temporally located, required a *general* conception of space and time of which this particular experience was an instance. It would be impossible to be aware of a particular thing undergoing successive movements in time, for example, were it not for these general categories.[4]

The duality of function also went both ways: just as the material of sense being formed in space and time required general concepts to recognise them as such, so if such abilities are to be exercised, 'we must have material on which to exercise them; particular instances of general concepts must be encountered in experience.'[5] The two mind-imposed faculties were, thus, intimately connected. For Kant, knowledge was possible because the conditions of experience were possible, and what made experience possible were these categories of understanding and forms of sensible intuition.

The categories and forms of intuition were a function of the operation of the human mind (Kant did not care much for how animal experiences originated). As the faculties made experience possible, they were not derived from experience so they were said to be *a priori:* schemata of our minds which we imposed on reality like a grid to make sense of it. We obtained these categories just by being human. But the categories were stable structures - one could not change one's experience of some object in time, as a temporal object, because the experience of time itself was a mental fixture; a sensible intuition. Nor could one penetrate beyond how one's categories represented objects to actual objects, because such things were possible for us only as items of knowledge and

---

[2] P. F. Strawson, *The Bounds of Sense: An Essay on Kant's Critique of Pure Reason*, p. 20.
[3] Loc. cit.
[4] Loc. cit.
[5] Loc. cit.

because relation, space and causality, etc., made them possible. We could know about such things only through how experience was organised. This was legislated by the categories and the forms of intuition, so what objects were like *independent* of our experiences we could never venture to find out. However, we did know how experiences originated, so at least that was something. For Kant, the innovation of explaining experiential content was achieved at the inevitable and regrettable sacrifice of a realist account of empirical knowledge.

The capacity to have experiences is then a function of *two* cognitive faculties operating in unison; one which frames the chaotic 'manifold of intuition' (the 'imagination') and the other which applies general intellectual concepts upon it, by virtue of which it becomes an experience of a certain type (the 'understanding'). This is an important distinction, because it is one thing to have an 'awareness' of something indeterminate in space and time, and it is another thing to have knowledge of something determinate in space and time *as a* certain object. On Kant's account, the two faculties were supposed to explain both as requirements for experiential content. The important thing is that there is first the inchoate material coming into the sense organs as input and then there is the organisation of this input by the operation of the two kinds of framing apparatus.

There is much debate over what Kant meant by this 'material of sense,' and also the function of the 'forms' of intuition and the categories of the understanding, though there is little doubt that the latter were something like transcendental logical conditions for the possibility of experiences, which legislated unity to experiences prior to our having them. The categories gave sensory inputs the only means by which they could become items of empirical knowledge. As for the former, this is, I think, harder to determine.[6] In fact, there are a number of tensions in Kant's 'formalist' account of experience and its relation to the mind-imposed faculties which I would like to try to isolate in setting out the concerns of this chapter.

Everything would seem to be so clear-cut in Kant's famous analysis: he didn't want to 'sensualise' all concepts of the understanding by considering them 'empirical or abstracted concepts of reflection'[7] (as the empiricists did), but nor did he want to 'intellectualise appearances' (as the rationalists did). The two faculties *together* made experience possible, by 'filtering' in various ways the material of sensibility and 'imposing' intellectual categories upon it. The 'material' the faculties worked with was 'undifferentiated and indeterminate'[8] in itself; an inchoate material conveyed by the sense organs which 'affected', in some sense, the human process of representation. We have experiences not by representing them by such sensations, but representing *through* them by means of the faculties of imagination and understanding. Since *ex hypothesi* we cannot but work through the categories and forms of intuition, we cannot ever experience the material of sense in itself as anything determinate, and it cannot be an object of knowledge for us even though it provides the 'matter' of our

---

[6] Recent work has uncovered multiple ambiguities in Kant's notion of sensation. See L. Falkenstein, 'Kant's Account of Sensation,' pp. 63-88. And, by the same author, 'Kant's Account of Intuition' pp. 163-195.

[7] R. Pippin, *Kant's Theory of Form: An Essay on the Critique of Pure Reason*, p. 30.

[8] Loc. cit.

sensible intuition. The whole business prior to when the faculties get to work is rather like some sort of formless 'empty grasping.'[9] This sort of treatment of perceptual content, being strongly mind-dependent, makes it legitimate to call Kant a defender of what I have called the inferentialist proposal.

There are considerable tensions with this sort of metaphysical profile of experience, however, especially in regard to the relationship between the 'matter' of sensation, the forms of intuition and the categories. The question of the nature of this 'material' which supplies the stuff on which the forms of intuition and categories operate, for instance, is extremely puzzling. What, precisely, is the connection between this material and the forms and categories which make experience (and knowledge) possible? I am not asking here for a description of this matter, as in Kant's view it has no description beyond legitimating the 'formal' process of experiencing. But I am interested in why Kant thinks that this matter necessarily lacks any sort of contentful unity in itself.

The quick answer to this is that the categories and forms of intuition supply conditions for knowledge and experience and the senses supply the material on which the faculties operate, but this is clearly not an argument for why the matter of sensation has no contentful structure prior to such influences. This issue is important because it seems the orthodox view of Kant's theory is quite unclear on the relationship between the matter of sensation and the organisation of this matter at the integrative level of 'high-level' knowledge. Indeed, it might be suggested that this lack of clarity has ramifications for the work on the theory and concept neutrality of observational experience. It shall be argued in this chapter that even on Kant's account, there is some degree to which experiential content may escape the imposition of high-level structures and so Kant's metaphysic can be read as according with the central thrust of the continuum account.

Tensions in Kant's account

An argument for why the sensory component of Kant's analysis of experience has no inherent organisational structure can be expressed in the following way:

> Simply put, any claim for the representative function of sensation alone will flounder hopelessly on the question of *false representation.* Considered as a mode of knowledge, such purely sensory representation must be capable of turning out to be false ... If it is the *senses* which represent x to me, and if x was not in fact the object sensed, how am I to explain what happened? If the senses represent things in themselves unclearly, and it turns out that the object represented was not the object the senses purported to represent, I seem to be faced with the alternative of saying it represented what is not, or saying that in such cases that the senses do not represent at all. The first [negative entities] has never been satisfactorily explained, and it is not open to us to argue that the senses only represent when they represent truthfully. (Of course, if I claim that the senses represented obscurely, and that I misconstrued that

---

[9] Ibid., p. 35.

representation, Kant would claim that this concedes his whole point. He would claim that this admits that the senses do not represent but merely provide the material which the understanding must discriminate). The solution must be that the senses do not represent at all, but only contain the results of the affection by objects on our senses (appearances) and are construed as representing only when so interpreted by the spontaneity Kant calls the understanding.[10]

The claim here is that if we get knowledge from the material of sense, and that 'knowledge' turns out to be false (through a mirage, say) then we would be hard-pressed to explain what happened. We must in this case say either that we had knowledge of what is not the case (a negative thing) or that we did not receive knowledge from the senses at all, but only the substance for the 'judgement' that we made, in this case, erringly. Kant's response to why the material of sensation requires the input of the faculties of cognition is, basically, that if it was itself a source of knowledge, we could not make coherent sense of how it was possible to be *wrong* about our judgments.

As Pippin points out, this 'undetermined' nature of sensation in Kant's view is a radical thesis, 'denying at once central, although differently expressed, claims in Plato, Aristotle, Descartes, Locke and Hume.'[11] The long tradition of the 'passive intuition of sensible form'[12] is jettisoned by Kant in favour of a 'judgement' focused analysis, whereby 'sense' is a mute, malleable fabric furnishing the material of experience, though being in no sense an articulable or well-defined medium itself. Kant himself displays just how radical this thesis is when he tries to tease out the difference between the identical sensations involved in a true judgment and one in the context of 'dreaming':

> The appearance depends upon the senses, but the judgement upon the understanding ... The difference between truth and dreaming is not ascertained by the nature of the representations which are referred to objects (for they are the same in both cases) but by their connection according to those rules which determine the coherence of the representation in the concept of an object and by ascertaining whether they can subsist together in an object or not.[13]

So Kant seems to put all his weight upon the forms of the imagination and the categories of the understanding which supposedly determine the veracity and 'subsistence' of the material supplied in appearance. However, although this seems intelligible as a consequence of Kant's views, we still need an argument to the effect that the matter of sensation *requires* such formal constraints to make it necessary to be organised in this fashion. Drawing on Kant, Pippin notes:

> There is all the difference in the world between claiming that we do not seem to be able to make intelligible to ourselves a conception of

---

[10] Ibid., p. 30.
[11] Ibid., p. 35.
[12] Ibid., p. 35.
[13] I. Kant, *Prolegomena Gesammelte Schriften*, Vol. 4, p. 290.

experience wherein some item is not experienced under some description ('intuitions without concepts are blind') and claiming that the description *constitutes* the item's being experienced ('the combination of the manifold in general can never come to us through the senses'). The former is compatible with the description of the way sensibly apprehended unities are experienced (or described) within the conceptual scheme we have; the latter ties any experience of unity (or determinacy or complexity) much more closely to those describing capabilities. Thus the question to raise is why this use of the matter-form dichotomy; this claim that sensations comprise only the undifferentiated material of experience, and that all formal unity or determinacy is a result of taking up the manifold and unifying it?[14]

This is a good observation, and I wish to stress it for my own purposes. The point here is that there is both a *weak* and a *strong* theme running through Kant's metaphysic of experience in the relationship between the faculties of cognition and sensation. The orthodox interpretation of Kant's views is misleading insofar as it neglects to distinguish these very different themes. The weak theme, as indicated, is that intuitions without concepts are blind; the strong theme is that categorical synthesis is *necessary* for the possibility of experiencing anything at all. These themes are usually conflated in commentaries on Kant's work, though it is clear that they have quite different commitments: the former seems to suggest that it is *useful* for experience to be described and categorised; the latter suggests that experience of any kind cannot occur without it. This is, however, not just a consequence of how one interprets Kant's views: Pippin claims it is actually a point of confusion in how Kant himself understood his own theory. But it was not a confusion which applied to *both* the faculties of the mind; it essentially applied to one and not the other. The problem case, in particular, was the role of the categories of cognition to the material of sensation.

There is textual evidence to support the claim that Kant was very confused on this issue. Graham Bird has cited examples from Kant in which he shows that it is comparatively easy to demonstrate that space and time - as forms of intuition - can be necessarily related to the matter of experience,[15] but arguing to the same conclusion on the question of the influence of the categories, Kant's remarks produce 'either contradiction or incoherence.'[16] In some passages, Kant seems to want to say that the categories are *necessary* for sensation, otherwise 'nothing is possible as an object of experience,'[17] but elsewhere, he claims that 'objects may appear to us, without their being under the necessity of being related to the function of the understanding.'[18] Bird concludes by remarking: 'it seems that Kant is saying inconsistently that appearances both are, and are not

---

[14] Pippin, op. cit., 35-6.

[15] It is very hard to see how one could experience anything without that experience being 'in' space and time. See: G. Bird, *Kant's Theory of Knowledge*, p. 57. The relevant passage in Kant is B 121-123. (Bird uses the Kemp-Smith translation).

[16] Loc. cit.

[17] Loc. cit. The relevant passage in Kant is B 125-126.

[18] Ibid., p. 58; Kant, B 122-123.

necessarily related to the categories,' and hence: 'there is no impossibility in supposing that appearance might be given in intuition independently of [concepts of] the understanding.'[19]

How might this conflicting situation arise? The forms of intuition and the categories are both mind-imposed structures for Kant, yet one being an 'active' faculty is clearly a more sophisticated *intellectual* ability. It was the categories which applied Euclidean geometry, among other things, to experiential content. The other faculty seems clearly a less sophisticated ability, but nonetheless still a critical means by which one frames the material of sense. Kant's concern in the passage cited above is strictly with the categories, not the forms of intuition.

The function of the 'categories' is, of course, to label experiences under certain general concepts. Judging appearances thus involves appeal to certain propositional features and hence involves inference. Moreover, experiencing an instance of an object in time is, in a sense, *described* or 'judged' by this faculty in terms of successional events of the same type, and this presupposes that there is some general conception or background knowledge that the subject has of temporally and spatially ordered events. In terms that have been used before, what Kant calls the 'categories' harbours all the general 'high-level' features we have been considering in this book. But significantly, it would seem, from the previous passage cited, that Kant himself is at least *allowing* the possibility that some experiential contents do not require the input of such sophisticated high-level inferential mechanisms at all.

The doubts Kant seems to be entertaining here is over whether or not it is *logically* impossible to experience something in sensation without imposing such intellectual capacities. And he seems at least to be allowing the possibility that this is not logically *impossible* - i.e., that one *can* have experiences of sorts without such input. However, this interpretation of his claims clearly runs against the orthodox interpretation of Kant's famous metaphysic of experience outlined earlier.

This seems paradoxical: if it is possible that some level of experience is not informed by such intellectual (categorical) features at all, then this creates an internal tension between Kant's theory and the traditional interpretation of it. The usual story is that *both* the categories of cognition and the forms of intuition are necessary structural features for organising experience of any kind. But now it seems that while in places he insists that categorical synthesis is necessary, elsewhere he doesn't support a prejudice in favour of 'formal' organisation at the level of the understanding, only at the level of the imagination. It seems that though Kant thought that it was necessary to frame the material of sense in space and time, it was *not* necessary to impose categories on it. To say the least, this seems very un-Kantian.

When one considers this carefully, however, it does seem to hang together with the reasons given for the postulation of the faculties in the first place. The argument mentioned earlier that false *knowledge* cannot be given any plausible account if experience was not organised in both these ways seems, in fact, to be a shortfall from the grander claim that the matter supplied by sense must *necessarily* be informed by these faculties. As Kant seems to have noticed, there is no logical entailment from one claim to the other: one can still claim that

---

[19] Loc. cit.

knowledge requires categorical input, without claiming that all experiences do. All the 'intuitions without concepts' thesis guarantees is that experiences do not make much sense without being described and otherwise intellectually processed (such an experience could hardly be described as *knowledge*, if it wasn't); but as Kant seems well aware, this does not secure the *stronger* claim that there are no experiential contents at all *without* such 'high-level' intellectual concepts. Bird explains this point by examining Kant's remarks in relation to unsophisticated animal experiences:

> There is certainly something odd in envisaging a situation where appearances are presented but cannot be described, though it is not easy to pin down the kind of absurdity involved. It will not do to say *simply* that our habitual mode of identifying what we perceive involves the ordinary resources of description. For it is certainly possible to speak of creatures who are able to perceive, even when they have no such conventional devices ... To promote such an argument against Kant ... does not produce a good enough reason for denying Kant's claim that it is logically possible to perceive without being able to describe what is perceived ...The obvious way to resolve this paradox is to suppose that when Kant claims that appearances are necessarily related to categories, he is not denying that it is logically possible for them to be uncategorised. *The kind of necessity involved in the former claim is not, then, a logical necessity.*[20]

There is every reason why the relationship here should not be a 'logical' or necessary one. These reasons add to make Kant's metaphysic of experience (with qualifications mentioned) a far more plausible account than the usual version we know so well. The 'creatures' being referred to here might possibly be animals and infants - and, as have been claimed elsewhere - such creatures surely lack some of the conventional devices of 'high-level' description and categorisation in the sense Kant required, yet they do have experiences in some sense. Any suggestion to the contrary is simply to reinstate the rationalist legacy inherited from Descartes.

The usual version of Kant's theory of experience, of course, does not allow for such subtleties - animal and infant experience was not on Kant's epistemological agenda, so it naturally did not arise as a problem case. But it is clear they must be considered: if such creatures do possess any categorical input at all, it is certainly not the input of the level of sophistication that, according to Kant, the categories imbue *our* experiences with - Euclidean geometry and complex generalised concepts concerning space, time and relation. In this sense, experiences without concepts are certainly not blind. If they were so, animals would not be experiencing creatures. I shall be returning to this issue in the next chapter.

But there is another important point to note here. The doubt about the logical necessity of the categories in organising experience does not escape application to the forms of intuition either. For, just as it seems implausible that the entire edifice of *a priori* concepts should be brought to bear on all cases of experiential

---

[20] Ibid., pp. 58- 60. Italics mine.

content (given animal experiences), so it seems implausible to claim that other high-level features cannot be separated and distinguished, and have to apply *en bloc*. Given the separability of the various features of high-level input, for instance, it would seem that *not all* features of experiential content *necessarily* have to be framed in space and time.

What kinds of experiences would escape such features? We have already considered some cases. The Peacocke examples, for instance, must be seen as a problem for Kant's theory: while it might seem obvious that some experiences seem to have representational, spatial and temporal content, other 'aspects' of those experiences just seem to be *sensational* in some sense. It is not clear how Kant's forms of intuition doctrine, for instance, might capture sensational aspects of certain experiences such as the tree which seems to occupy more of the visual field even though it has certain fixed spatial and temporal features. The relevant experiential content in question seems to escape such an analysis. The extent to which both the categories and the forms of intuition are said to affect the material of sense, then, perhaps has been over-emphasised by traditional Kantian scholarship and even, in places, by Kant himself - there may not be a logical relationship between these various elements of mental content as much as a *highly likely* and *very common* relationship. And this qualification may apply as much to the high-level forms of the imagination as to the high-level categories of the understanding.

We are splitting hairs here, but it is necessary to split these hairs. The central point is that saying experiential content can be uncategorised, or somehow escape the forms of intuition, amounts to an 'odd' kind of experience is one thing; to reject this as impossible is quite another. If the claims that have been made in this book are in any way plausible, it does seem that experiential contents can have sensational aspects both with and without sophisticated 'high-level' input. So there are grounds for saying that there is not a *necessary* connection between experience and the faculties at all. Kant was right, it seems, to have the doubts he had; orthodox Kantian scholarship was wrong to ignore him.

This kind of interpretation of Kant is certainly possible if the terms of the inferentialist proposal can be weakened and some kind of continuum account of experience maintained instead. If so, then Kant's 'inferentialism' would no longer be a threat to the view that there are some experiential contents which do not depend on the input of inferential mechanisms. The revised view would end up holding that at *some levels,* experiential content depends on the input of fairly high-level background beliefs and concepts; at a very low level, experiential content does not require this input all. Between the extremes, there might be cases in which some categorical input is required, but not others, etc. All this has been rehearsed in earlier chapters, and have already seen how some aspects of content do not seem to be closely tied to high-level input. Now it seems we can revise Kant's metaphysic of experience to *agree* substantially with these considerations.

If we can take this claim seriously, then one could perhaps take the opposite line on the traditional view of Kant's relationship between the faculties and the material of sense. One could say here that it is not clear how the faculties could determine the appropriate formal organisation if one's experiential content had no structure *independent* of the imposition of the categories of reason and the forms of intuition. Rather than holding the usual stronger theme here, it might be argued that even though intuitions without concepts do not make much sense without categorical descriptions, this is no reason to say that concepts constitute the content of such intuitions. It would make more sense to say that some sort of 'pre-packaging' would seem to be the minimal requirement needed simply in order for the faculty of the understanding to carry out its representative function. Pippin again:

> It may be that we need to conceptualize a sensory manifold; but it seems equally the case that we must have some cognitive grasp of the manifold in order to know which concepts to apply. ... It seems open to assert that we only know which rules to apply in order to connect these representations because of something apprehended 'in the nature of representations.'[21]

This runs directly against the grain of Kant's analysis of experience and content. On the usual story, it was plausible to suppose that all the structure of experience was given by the interpretive cognitive elements and that non-interpreted sensations furnished the unstructured material for this. But then Kant's argument for why we need a distinction between sensory experience and knowledge to account for false experiences is a substantially *weaker* claim than the claim that false experiences are only possible if the content of sensation is entirely without structure itself. It may be that *most* of the content is supplied from the cognitive faculties and the forms of intuition, but at least some (an indeterminate amount) is present 'in the nature of representations.' Contentful aspects of experiences might thus escape the imposition of both the forms of intuition and the categories.

On such an analysis, false experiences would still be possible in the circumstance where *most* experiential content was supplied by the faculties, but some aspects of such content escape their influence. It may be that some structure or content is provided by sensation itself, *albeit* not a requisite amount to guarantee conceptual knowledge. It is suggested there may be a place for an organisation and structure at *both* the level of knowledge and concepts and, to some degree, the level of sensations. And if this is true, then the inferentialist claim that all experiential content depends on high-level organisation would be false.

There is another issue here concerning the extent to which sensation is organised by the categories and the forms of intuition. If the usual story about Kant is right, then it is more accurate to hold fast to the undifferentiated and content-less nature of such sensations. But then it is unclear how and why such material can *link* us with the world in the way that it does if it is contentless. If sensation *is* completely without organisation, then it is not obvious how and why there can be a certain inexorable relation between our sensations, our interpreting faculties and 'the world': specifically, how the latter is in some sense amenable to the parameters of the former. For we cannot, it must be conceded, frame experience in *any way whatsoever,* but only in certain determinate ways. How does this happen if the material of sense is formless?

---

[21] Pippin, op. cit., p. 39.

More specifically: why are *certain* ways favoured for organising appearances over others? Pippin asks the question in the following way:

> If Kant's claim is true, how do we then describe the fact that empirical knowledge about the external world seems to be directly guided by sensation, that our interpreting faculties are restrained in a way yet to be explained by some feature of our sensations that does seem directly connected with what we ultimately take to be a public, spatio-temporal world? If sensations do not provide any direct [i.e., organisational] link with such a world, what kind of link do they provide?[22]

This seems to be partly an empirical matter: the issue is how low-level perceptual processing mechanisms feed into the development of high-level knowledge. The central point for Kantian scholarship is that if the metaphysic of experience offered is heavily inferentialist, as it is usually taken to be, then it would seem that Kant is lacking an account of how the faculties frame the material of sense in the way that they do. Any suggestion that it is quite arbitrary how this happens would seem unsatisfactory, and any appeal to low-level content, which in some sense 'guides' the application of the faculties, would make it seem plausible that the account is rather less dependent on the imposition from high-level features than orthodox scholarship would have us believe.

Two major tensions, then, arise for Kant's view of experiential content: (i) Does the claim that the matter of sense does not provide grounds for knowledge *guarantee* that such sensation itself has no content at all (or is this a *non sequitur?*); and (ii) if sensation is itself without organisational form, how can the categories seem to be guided in their application? Simply asserting the orthodox view of Kant's theory in response to (i) is inadequate since, as we have seen, there are passages from Kant himself which indicate that he thought otherwise. Responding to (ii) in any way which does not allow some features of content to evade the imposition of the high-level faculties seems simply implausible in view of the examples of sensational content given in the last chapter.

Conflicting intuitions: the problem resolved

A recent paper on Kant's theory of intuition is apposite here. Lorne Falkenstein argues plausibly that Kant actually presented *two* quite different accounts of his 'sensible intuition' doctrine at different periods of his thought: one in terms of 'singular representation' and the other as 'immediate cognition.'[23] The former account best captures the view inherited from the scholastics, whereby the sense organs 'could be imprinted with the forms of external objects, in much the same way that wax is imprinted by a seal.'[24] Upon this 'singular representation'

---

[22] Ibid., p. 44.
[23] See L. Falkenstein, 'Kant's Account of Intuition,' op. cit., (1991). The references to Kant's two views of intuition are, respectively, A713-B741; Logic §6, and A19-B33. These, and the following citations are taken from the first and second original Hartknoch editions.
[24] Ibid., p. 170.

cognition acts to extract the discriminating features of objects. For Kant, however, it was a quick and decisive move from this to think of the one process as merely 'receptive' and the other 'facilitative.' On this view, 'sensory data are ...'coordinated by a natural law of the mind' (*Inaugural Diss.* §4) ... an *act* performed by the mind, not a datum *received* by it.'[25] This move is taken seriously to form the basis for a *second* account of intuition, where all reference to an impression *prior* to intellectualisation is lost, and intuition becomes just a 'blind grasping' with no form or content at all. Falkenstein calls this 'the blindness thesis'. The point is that in the one account there is some primal, pre-structured content to sensible intuition, in the other there is none.

Falkenstein gives persuasive problem-based reasons for the evolution of these views in Kant's thought, and so, helps us to see how the one view gives rise to the other. Hence, we are able to make sense of Kant's quite different claims about the manifold such as the following:

> Our cognition springs out of two fundamental sources of the mind. The first of these is that by which representations are sensed ... the second the capacity to cognize an object by means of these representations ... through the first an object is given to us; through the second this object is thought.[26]
>
> Sensitivity gives the mere material to thinking ... intellect disposes of this material and brings it under rules or concepts.[27]
>
> All our intuition is bound to a certain principle of form under which form alone can be something discerned by the mind immediately or as singular, and not merely conceived discursively through general concepts.[28]

One case clearly spells out the orthodox 'inferentialist' interpretation of Kant's views, the other something far less clear, seeming to suggest that there is at least a singular representation in sensation prior to its being conceptualised. The perception of the phenomenon of objects in time is a good example of how and why Kant arrived at this latter view. In the case of time, time itself cannot be defined as a wholly *intellectual* structure because temporality is perceived in singular, not general terms. The perception of time must be a case of 'singular' instances falling under 'general' concepts, so the 'perceiving' of things in time has a singular content in experience as well as a general, intellectual content. This feature of Kant's thought was outlined earlier when describing his general theory. Kant, it seems, wanted to keep this distinction, but also the idea that there was an extraordinary amount of high-level intellectual input involved in perception. Hence, the two views of the manifold. The point Falkenstein makes is that both of these views are *needed* when Kant's concerns are isolated. For, where some of Kant's remarks stress the necessity of intellectual input for an adequate conception of experience, other remarks stress that there are some

---

[25] Ibid., p. 173.
[26] I. Kant, op. cit., [A50-B74].
[27] I. Kant, op. cit., [Ak IX 36].
[28] I. Kant, *Inaugural Dissertation*, (1770) §10: Translated by Falkenstein.

aspects of experiences which are solely derived from some aspect of sensation itself:

> [Kant] argues that time and space are not known by intellect. From these points, the conclusion that space and time must be forms of the sensible world follows immediately. Since all our sensations are in fact arrayed in space and time, it follows that space and time must be orders of sensations, and since these orders are not infused by intellect they must be products of sense itself. But since these products of sense are not due to sensation, the matter of sense, it only remains that they pertain to a further, special element of sense, a form distinct both from sensed matter (sensation) and from all form invented by the intellect.[29]

This is, of course, an argument for why the forms of intuition have to be a distinct cognitive capacity from the categories, and necessarily of less sophistication than them. There must be an organisational form of space and time which is relatively *non-intellectual* on this reasoning. However, this is also an argument which sheds insight on a theme which is implicit in Kant's theory and which has not been brought out in the literature. For if the forms of intuition have to structure experience in a manner which is less sophisticated than the categories, and if the categories themselves are not logically *necessary* for all experiential content, it seems open to assert that what Kant is suggesting in his metaphysic of experience is something far more subtle than the usual inferentialist emphasis given to his work: he seems, indeed, to stand mid-way between embracing the inferentialist proposal and something much weaker; namely, that high-level factors influence experiential content by *degrees*.

There is a further complication to this. Paradoxically, Kant also held the 'blindness thesis' whereby sensations devoid of input from the intellect are without content. He argues elsewhere that sensation is 'blind', 'for us as good as nothing,'[30] which suggests that intellectual concepts are *necessary* to infuse content into sensations. These claims are clearly antagonistic. Something had to give way and, according to Falkenstein, it was a single, coherent conception of the sensory manifold:

> Kant claims that time must be an intuition because different times are only parts of one and the same time and because intuition is that representation which can only be given through a singular object. The argument apparently is that, because there is really only one time, it cannot be represented intellectually. But this argument comes to nothing given the blindness thesis. If blindness is correct, there can be no cognition of singular objects independently of intellectual synthesis. So, if time, or the different parts of time, are not intellectually represented, we cannot say anything about them; in particular, we cannot say anything about their singularity. But if they are intellectually represented, if we do have concepts of time or times, then these very concepts falsify Kant's claim that all our intellectual representations must, in principle, be general -

---

[29] Falkenstein, op. cit., p. 176.
[30] I. Kant, op. cit., [A90-B122].

either that, or Kant must admit that time is *not* singular.³¹

The two views of the sensory manifold lead to other absurdities: Falkenstein points out Kant's remark in his *Logic,* where he argues that 'where a savage sees a house in the distance the use of which he does not know, he has the same object before him as another who knows it is a dwelling furnished for people.' Leaving aside the imperialist connotations of the word 'savage', and the implausible point that a so-called 'savage' would *not* have a concept of a house (perhaps 'aeroplane' is a better example), there does seem to be a problem here. Because Kant also wants to claim that the savage's cognition of the house is 'mere intuition' while for the cognition of the civilised person it is 'intuition and concept at the same time.'³² There is an immediate problem of how this can be coherently sustained, given Kant's ambiguous view of the relationship between the interplay of the categories, the forms of intuition and the material of sensation. Falkenstein seems to suggest that it cannot be sustained without jettisoning the fully 'inferentialist' interpretation of Kant's thesis. This, at least, has some textual as well as argumentative support:

> The passage hints that it is possible to perceive something without synthesizing the array under concepts (we could hardly suppose that there would be a house-shaped hole in the savage's visual field because intuitions without concepts are blind). This implication is seconded by Kant's claim at B422n that an indeterminate empirical intuition is perception, and further reinforced by the ... passage (A320-B377) where he claims that intuition is a perception ... which not only relates immediately to an object, but is single.
> But if any of these claims were in fact true - if the savage's perception of what we recognise as a house were 'mere intuition' - then synthesis under the categories would not be necessary to effect a unity of apperception and thereby become conscious of anything manifold. Thus, a crucial premise of the Transcendental Deduction - the claim that all connection is an act of intellect (B129-30) and that a collection of matters can never be brought to consciousness insofar as it is merely presented through the senses, but only insofar as the matters are connected in a single thought (B132-3) - would fail. For the argument of the Transcendental Deduction to be correct, the savage must be supposed either to see nothing at all (which is implausible) or to synthesize the variety presented in intuition under some other concept (in which case perception is not 'mere intuition' but intuition rendered intelligible through intellectual processing).³³

I don't think this is wholly right. We need to consider the respective roles of the forms of intuition and the categories once again. Presumably, like the 'Tom and the Dahlia' case in Chapter 5, the savage would *represent* the same visual scene (the house) in space and time as the civilised person does, even if he did not have the concept of what it was he was looking at. Even if the blindness thesis

---

³¹ Falkenstein, op. cit., p. 182.
³² Ibid., [Ak IX 33].
³³ Ibid., p. 191.

were true, the savage could still represent the same perceptual data in space and time *even if* the intuition was not fully intellectually informed. (To suggest otherwise would be to confuse the various levels of high-level influence that I have argued are separable.) However, Falkenstein is right to point out that Kant is committed to saying that the forms of intuition are a distinct capacity from the categories of the intellect and that more needs to be considered than the imposition of 'the intellect'.

However, the point is germane for more reasons than this. If there is a genuine difference in sophistication between the function of the understanding and the imagination, it seems that Kant must be committed to *weakening* his view of the blindness thesis to something like the following: that the intellect is often *involved* in classifying and making experiences comprehensible; not that it is *necessary* for all aspects of experiences. Intuitions may be blind without concepts, but it doesn't mean they are empty. On this revised account, there are good reasons for admitting that the fixation of experiential content need not occur in all-or-none terms, but rather by degrees, and this seems to tally closely with my own continuum view, not the orthodox view attributed to Kant.

Falkenstein's point is not to dismiss entirely Kant's views on time, or the Transcendental Deduction for that matter. The point is rather that there is a serious problem with scholars' treatment of Kant. Part of the reason for this issues from his thoroughly ambiguous doctrine of sensory intuition: Kant seems to have wanted to say both that it depends on input from the intellect (in my terms, 'inferential' content), and that there is also a more primal aspect of contentful sensation which is *prior* to intellect. This also applies to the function of the imagination, since there are aspects of experience which even the imposition of space and time cannot capture, as we have seen. The problem is that the traditional scholarly treatment of Kant's position has, for one reason or another, affirmed the primacy of the categories and the forms of the imagination in the organisation of experiential content, and has not tried to uncover the limits of their influence. Orthodox scholarship has not recognised the subtleties, and has taken Kant to be a full-blooded *inferentialist*. However, this interpretation runs against both his marginal remarks, which suggest the contrary view, and his ambiguous conception of the relation between the material of sense and the faculties of cognition. I have tried to suggest that there is more to it than that. The nub of this issue, of course, extends beyond the problems with which Kant was most concerned to the nature of inference vs observationality generally. It extends beyond Kant and his categories to the whole issue of the bearing of inferential content on experiences. However, Falkenstein offers some interesting suggestions in relation to Kant's contribution: notably, to henceforth regard Kant's account of 'concepts' not as being a 'species of high-level intellect', but as 'no more than a subset of the representations delivered by intellect.'[34] In other words, to admit a number of levels of possible integrations of the content of sensible intuition. This might allow room for particularly low-level integrations which are quite unlike the kinds of high-level structures essential to the inferentialist view. In view of this, it is perhaps better to treat Kant not as an inferentialist, but as an early proponent of an information-theoretic account of perceptual content, where there are several distinguishable

---

[34] Ibid., p. 192.

levels of structure to experience. This approach allows for a contentful level which is not, strictly speaking, expressible or explicable in terms of 'concepts' in any recognised (high-level) sense. The view of Kant as an inferentialist must, on this view, be modified because of the ambiguities in the notion of 'intuition.' There is, it seems, more to intuition than inference. A more contemporary information-theoretic approach to perceptual content which runs along these lines will be presented and discussed in Chapter 8.

Falkenstein summarises this kind of analysis by saying, that 'preserving these claims requires recognising intuition as a *distinct* cognitive capacity from intellect'; [35] and that 'concepts are only one among the products of intellectual synthesis; there are also perceptions and images.'[36] One may wonder just how 'perceptions' and 'images' actually feature in this revised Kantian account. Without overdoing speculations here, it is suggested that Kant had perhaps more of a continuum account of experiential content than has hitherto been recognised.

This is not a book about Kant's ideas, but about experience and the degree to which it has low-level sensational features. The claim is that low-level experiences have some content other than that which is imposed on them by 'high-level' concepts, background knowledge and theory. The thrust of the foregoing section is that there are at least a number of inconsistencies in Kant's views of the structure of experience being *comprehensively* organised by the interpretive faculties of intuition and imagination.

Lorenz: experience naturalised

Experience and biology

Konrad Lorenz has furnished a way of resolving some of the problematic features of Kant's views on experience in evolutionary terms, by making the notion of the categories answerable to the strictures of evolutionary biology. His views are worth a slight digression to complete the section on Kant. Lorenz begins his study of Kant by asking a number of pertinent biology-related questions levelled at the notion of the *a priori* categories of cognition:

> Is not human reason with all its categories and forms of intuition something that has organically evolved within a continuous cause-effect relationship with the laws of the immediate nature just as has the human brain? Would not the laws of reason necessary for *a priori* thought be entirely different if they had undergone an entirely different historical mode of origin, and if consequently, we had been equipped with an entirely different kind of central nervous system? Is it at all probable that the laws of our cognitive apparatus should be disconnected from those of the real external world? Can an organ that has evolved in the process of continuous coping with the laws of nature have remained so uninfluenced that the theory of appearances can be pursued independently of the things-

---

[35] Ibid., p. 193.
[36] Loc. cit.

in-themselves as if the two were totally independent of each other?[37]

Lorenz adopts a scientist's view of the origins and structure of experience, and although sympathetic to some of Kant's views, he takes issue with him over the notion of the categories as *a priori* mechanisms. His complaint is not that the conceptual apparatus of thought organises experiential content (a feature of Kant's thought that he described as '[a] great and fundamentally new discovery')[38] but that the explanation of its importance in structuring experience does not involve considerations of the 'organic nature' of the apparatus, and 'does not pose the basic biological question concerning their species-preserving meaning.'[39] It seemed likely to him that the categories are 'not something immutably determined by factors extraneous to nature, but rather something that mirrored the natural laws in contact with which they had evolved in the closest reciprocal interaction.'[40] In other words, the *a priori* forms of cognition that Kant used to make sense of the experience of objects and our knowledge of them, were *evolving* structures and *natural* ones, just like dolphin fins. It occurred to Lorenz that the idea that experiences were cognitively formed somehow by the apparatus of the mind into items of knowledge, could somehow be presented and reconciled with evolutionary biology. This was important to do because, on Kant's view, the limits of possible experience by virtue of the form imposed by the categories were logically the same for both man and amoeba. In view of our knowledge of evolutionary processes, this seemed deeply implausible, and an 'unjustifiable anthropomorphism.'[41]

Lorenz's claim, by contrast, is that if one was to hold onto the idea of a 'forming' of experience at all, then what was capable of being experienced must vary in sophistication from organism to organism - otherwise one could not account for the role of inference and background knowledge in the experiences of humans, the apparent non-cognitive awarenesses in animals and babies, the tactile sensations had by plants, and so on. Removing the heavily rationalist emphasis on 'high-level' features of cognition could make the structure of experiential content a purely natural phenomenon, evolving according to the selective pressures on differentially sophisticated organisms. Lorenz's diagnosis, hence, is to 'naturalise' the concept of the forms of experience and make them a function, not of strictly intellectual *a priori* categories of the mind, but of the development and adaptation of organs of the body to real natural laws present in the world. To cope with these laws and to negotiate them through millions of years of evolution, the functioning organs themselves have been shaped organically to 'think' in certain forms. This hypothesis, in a sense, avoids Kant's idealist troubles with objects in the real world being inaccessible to a realist view of knowledge acquisition. For Lorenz, this is a position not worth entertaining.[42]

---

[37] K. Lorenz, 'Kant's Doctrine of the a priori in the light of Contemporary Biology,' p. 23.
[38] Ibid., p. 25.
[39] Loc. cit.
[40] Ibid., p. 24.
[41] Loc. cit.
[42] His comment is worth reproducing: 'Any person not sicklied o'er with the pale cast of

The point is that, in an 'organic' manner, 'our forms of intuition and categories are embodied in our evolved capacity to 'fit' to that which really exists in the manner in which our feet fit the floor or the fins of a fish fits the water.'[43] For Lorenz, then, the origins of experience are natural mechanisms shaping the evolving organism's capacity to respond to the world. Contentful experiences, like the functioning organ of a body, are a functional outcome of this adaptation.

There is a point to Lorenz's claims, and the point is this: to the extent that Kant's view of experiential content is a useful and informative one, it should be considered outside its traditional rationalist framework. The idea that the *a priori* categories are relevant to the fixation of experiential content can be plausible only if those categories are seen as occurring along the phylogenetic tree, and this means that they must be seen as having *variable* degrees of sophistication. This development of Kant's view of how the intellect mediates sensation then ensures two things: (1) that the experiences of unsophisticated organisms like animals and infants are not seen as necessarily *inferior* to the way in which human beings organise their experiences with high-level categories; and (2) that the idealist dichotomy between the mind-dependent structured world of *phenomena*, and the trans-empirical world of *noumena* could be transgressed on naturalist grounds. For Lorenz, but not Kant, our representations of the world through experience assure us that they correspond to that world - because of the dialectical interaction by which the two have simultaneously evolved. For Lorenz, the question of closeness of 'fit' and idealist scepticism simply does not arise. Nor does the need to conceive of elaborate transcendental arguments for the possibility of that real world.

Lorenz does not aim to rule out the idea of the imposition of 'high-level' categories in the formation of experiential content. His claim is that the cognitively informed experiences of humans - the forming of objects in space and time and so on - is a certain highly adapted evolutionary response to selective pressures. But so too, presumably, are what have been called the sensational or low-level 'aspects' of experience. Both are legitimate ways in which experiential content is organised.

Presumably, there would be an evolutionary justification for the distinction in the levels of sophistication: at a push, one could say that a sensational experience was a *lower-order* adaptation to stimulus and situations in the natural world where high-level features are not required, or where conceptually fixed experiences simply take too long. (cf. Fodor's claim about the 'etiological route' to beliefs 'being *shorter* in observation than in inference.')[44] Such an account might constitute an evolutionary justification for the relevance of both low-level sensational experiences and high-level, intellectually informed experience to survivalist strategies.

I differ from Lorenz in only one respect. To his plausible evaluation of Kant's metaphysic of experience, the further claim is added that in no sense are

---

philosophical thought, would regard it as utterly perverse to believe that everyday objects around us only become real through our experience of them.' K. Lorenz, *Behind the Mirror*, p. 14.

[43] K. Lorenz, op. cit., p. 24.

[44] J. A. Fodor, 'Observation Reconsidered,' p. 31

the levels of experiential content entirely distinct: if the terms of any account of such content are to be amenable to evolutionary biology, then it is plausible that experiential content can come in *degrees* of sophistication and can also occur jointly. What I have called 'aspects' of content can occur simultaneously along with representative, highly inferential content by virtue of both kinds of features having been selectively advantageous. We have seen several examples in previous chapters in which both high-level and low-level features do seem to be aspects of some experiences. We have also seen how this account may even be consistent with Kant's more marginal views. It only needs to be added that this kind of naturalist reading of the issue provides further support for the continuum account of content rather than any inferentialist view.

Conclusion

In this chapter, the continuum account was shown to be congruent with a certain reading of Kant's work, and to be consistent with the evolutionary emphasis of Lorenz's view of experiential content. The usual interpretation of Kant's theory can be modified to give a more plausible perspective on the relationship between high-level inference and low-level sensations. However, we still need an argument for taking sensory aspects of experience to be an evolutionary adaptation. The next section looks at the issue of animal experiences in this connection.

7 Animal experiences

> The common defect of those systems, which philosophers have employ'd to account for the actions of the mind, is that they suppose such a subtility and refinement of thought, as not only exceeds the capacity of mere animals, but even of children and the common people in our own species.[1]

Consciousness and concepts

Introduction

In the last chapter, Lorenz's naturalised account of experiential content was compared with an unorthodox reading of Kant's views. In this chapter, the issue of animal experiences will be confronted. It will be suggested that the continuum view of content is the best model with which to handle such cases. Various inferentialist views will be treated and rejected.

Animal consciousness

It has been maintained throughout this book that animal experiences constitute an important case for the view being suggested. The claim is that animal experiences consist largely of certain low-level sensory features which amount to concepts, but not concepts in any sophisticated, high-level *descriptive* sense. High-level features are not, generally speaking, relevant to animal experiences. But there are still sensory 'aspects' of low-level experiences to account for how animals fix appropriate sensory beliefs.

A claim such as this seems uncontentiously true, given what we know about animals in any philosophically unreflective sense. We feel confident, for instance, in attributing to animals beliefs about the experiences they undergo despite them being cognitively impoverished compared to us. We feel that they believe in some sense that they are experiencing features of their perceived environment, colours, shapes and so on. We also feel confident, to some degree, in attributing more sophisticated beliefs to complex animals about

---

[1] D. Hume, *A Treatise of Human Nature*, p. 177.

objects and events in the world. (Dogs being able to perceive their master, for instance). The inferentialist proposal, however, has a rather different view of animal experiences, coming, as it does, from the Cartesian and Kantian rationalist tradition. Such a tradition asserts that animals have no basis for contentful experiences because they have no high-level concepts and no propositional contents and, in particular, no language to express them. Such a position, as has already been pointed out, is a consequence, and a *reductio*, of the inferentialist proposal.

The kind of view in mind here has been characteristic of Descartes' work, but also a surprising number of contemporary theorists, who openly make claims like the following:

> I see no reason to attribute any of the mental states that involve intentionality [e.g., belief, thought, etc.] to the 'lower' animals [non-persons]. On the best available understanding of what is involved in intentional descriptions ... a fairly high-degree of rationality is a prerequisite.[2]

Such a position seems rather less than obvious, given what we often assume about animals. Therefore, the burden for supporting such a view clearly lies with those who defend it. The argument to this conclusion must amount to showing what is wrong with the suggestion made above regarding the 'philosophically unreflective' view of animal sensory consciousness. This generally has two elements: showing animals are not conscious of their sensations at all, and showing that animals do not have concepts of any kind. Each of these suggestions will be discussed below and both will be dismissed. The views of some of the modern-day adherents to this view will also be looked at and rejected.

Most arguments designed to show that animals are not conscious of their own experiential states make an assumption that begs the question in favour of the rationalist legacy; they often involve an *appeal* to an inferential background of thinking, concepts and other high-level cognitive capacities. One such argument is given in Radner and Radner's *Animal Consciousness:*

> If all thinking involved reflection on one's mental states, then any being that failed to think about its own thinking would fail to think at all; in other words, it would be mindless. In such a case, it would be fairly easy to argue that animals do not think. One would simply have to point out that they lacked the wherewithal to engage in introspection. Having no concepts of pain, anger and so on, they cannot be said to identify their own feelings and passions, and thus they cannot form the belief that they are, in this state rather than that. Moreover, having no concept of self,

---

[2] A. Townsend, 'Radical Vegetarians,' pp. 85-93. For similar Cartesian sentiments in this matter, see: S. Hampshire, *Thought and Action,* esp. p. 97. For a statement of Descartes' views and an attack on them, see J. Cottingham, 'A Brute to the Brutes?: Descartes' Treatment of Animals', pp. 551-559.

they cannot be said to know that they have mental states at all.³

This is not a complicated argument to disentangle. It is a valid argument and is of the following form (I shall supply a missing premise-P1):

P1: The content of all conscious mental states involves thinking
P2: All thinking involves reflection on the content of one's mental states (introspection)
P3: Introspection involves having concepts of pain, self, etc.
P4: Animals have no concepts of pain, self, etc., and, hence, cannot form beliefs that they are in conscious states
C: Animals do not think and thus are not conscious of their own states

The argument is, admittedly, conditional in the original; it has been expressed in its most positive form. Even so, it is difficult to see why anyone would take this argument seriously. It seems simply false to draw the conclusion that animals don't undergo any conscious states from the major premise that being conscious requires reflective 'thinking.' There are, for instance, some conscious states which do not require this ability even among organisms who can reflectively 'think': (A person may forget a backpain while engaged in some activity, for instance, but it should not be inferred that it was not a conscious state).⁴ So to assert premise (1) to get the argument going may be already to set off on the wrong path.

For the purposes of my account, the suspicious premises here are 1, 3 and 4; the suspicious premises for the Radners are 1 and 2. A rejection of all these premises in their present form will show that though the argument is valid, some of its premises are false, and so is the conclusion.

The Radners' interest in this argument is to deny the claim that 'all consciousness is self-consciousness.'⁵ This, they believe is the assumption that is in error, an assumption which is due to a confusion arising from the work of Descartes. Their point is that this confusion springs from views on the nature of consciousness which 'play two different roles in Descartes' theory of mind.'⁶ The details will not concern us here, but textual evidence they supply supports the idea that, according to Descartes, consciousness is both *synonymous* with experience, and also that it consists of that 'of which we are conscious'⁷ where thought has, *as its object,* consciousness. The claim is that this ambiguity is the reason that animal consciousness is often denied. If consciousness is taken in this *latter* sense, then animals may not be so endowed, as they may not be thinking (reflecting) beings.

I say 'may not be' here since it is clear that even if the claim about the importance of reflective thought is granted, it is not obvious that the argument would go through to the desired conclusion. Anyone who held this view would

---

³ M. and D. Radner, *Animal Consciousness*, pp. 34-5.
⁴ See C. Peacocke, *Sense and Content: Experience, Thought and its Relations*, pp. 12-15.
⁵ Radner and Radner, op. cit., p. 30.
⁶ Ibid., p. 23.
⁷ Loc. cit.

hardly have *established* that animals were not conscious from such premises, even if the premises were accurate. Nor would they have established that animals have no such reflective intellectual ability at all. However, this point will not be developed here. There are far better reasons to cast this kind of argument in doubt and, in doing so, provide reasons to consider the continuum account more seriously.

It has been suggested that experiential content might involve two broad kinds of features: high-level inferential, descriptive content and low-level, sensory content. It has also been shown how the terms of the inferentialist proposal draw exclusively upon high-level features largely from the attachment to the Cartesian/Kantian rationalist legacy it inherited. Such high-level features constituted criteria for separating the provinces of man and animal, as has been explained. The point to be made here is that the argument just mentioned explicitly endorses the inferentialist criterion for consciousness by asserting that consciousness requires a high degree of self-reflective 'thinking.'

This criterion is, of course, inherently unfair given the circumstances. No-one expects or claims that animals are conscious in this sophisticated deliberative, reflective sense. No-one would want to claim (sensibly) that even complex animals can perform the feats of conscious cognitive integration that Sherlock Holmes can perform; in this sense, animals are not conscious. But, to an important degree, the argument against animal mental states above endorses precisely this, and argues from the (relatively) uncontentious claim that as animals do not possess reflective awareness, to the *stronger* claim that animals are not conscious at all. But clearly, this stronger claim leads to a deeply counterintuitive conclusion. For the accurate and relevant sense in which animals might be conscious is that they are conscious of their sensations and their *perceived* environment. And this seems, on the face of it, absurd to deny. Fido will come when he is called; he chases cats; he avoids punishment. Such behaviour is surely reason enough to believe that Fido has some conscious contents of experience at some level, even if it is not captured by strongly high-level inferential abilities. The inferentialist stipulation to any other conclusion seems simply too strong.

The point here is that the argument above does not call these lower-level experiences into question; it *does not* demonstrate that animals are not conscious of their experiences as much as (at best) demonstrate that certain feats of high-level deliberations are not achieved by animals. The latter is an agreeable claim; the former is reached without argument, and is almost certainly false. Animals may still be conscious of important features of their *perceived* environment.

There are several issues here of course. For one thing, 'being conscious of features of one's perceived environment' is to be too vague; the sentence blurs too much. To develop this kind of claim would require spelling out that animals can, in fact, be conscious of several things about their environment: Dogs, for instance, we would uncritically assume, perceive spatial relationships between objects (they search behind objects for food etc.) They also have memory and can locate things temporally, hence they have some background knowledge, some memory of previous experiences and so on. They are also conscious of lightness and darkness, and have remarkable auditory and olfactory discriminatory abilities, etc. Some animals then perceive both complex and simple features. Of course, one cannot say the same thing about all animals.

The extent to which amoeba or sea-slugs or simple invertebrates experience their perceived environment is very unclear. Some less sophisticated creatures would seem to have some of these capacities but not others. Nonetheless, it is a principle of sufficient reason to assume that to the extent certain animals are similar anatomically and biologically to ourselves, they must, at least, share some of our abilities to consciously discern aspects of the perceived environment and *believe* something from such perceptions. This is mentioned because, oddly enough, the point is not obvious to some philosophers at all.

This brings me to the second point: the phylogenetic argument that was mentioned earlier should be brought out in the open. For it is possible for a latterday Cartesian to argue that animals are not even conscious in this non-reflective sense, and this does not rule out the hypothesis that they are mere mechanical automata responding to cues from the world in the way that a machine or computer would. Such a situation is, of course, a logical possibility, but it scarcely seems a plausible claim: especially since it is uncritically accepted that there is some kind of biological link (and lineage) between species with similar taxonomical features. It seems very unlikely that animals which do share the same neuroanatomical features would not share the same perceptual and discriminatory capacities to some degree. A world in which sufficiently similar and closely evolved organisms (e.g., chimpanzees and man) happen to be radically distinct in the ways in which they perceive the world would be a very odd world indeed. (This is so especially if we are asked to imagine one such organism to be a mere automaton with no perceptual abilities at all).[8]

For these reasons, it is false to assert that the criteria for evaluating the question of animal consciousness lies in the ability to reflect/introspect and perform sophisticated inferential operations. It is false to suggest, from this, that animals are not conscious of their perceived environment in some sense. One can still say that they are importantly conscious of their sensory and perceptual states, and this seems a fairly undeniable claim. Of course, in saying this one must be wary of the vagueness in this claim. Some (complex) animals can discern features of the perceived environment which do require some 'high-level' inferential, though perhaps not 'reflective' abilities (dogs perceiving spatial relationships, etc), but this need not be so for less sophisticated organisms. Still, the fact that *some* conscious experiences are by nature reflective, should not license the move to suggesting that non-reflective experiences are not conscious. Allowing some conscious experiences to be characteristically reflective does not mean all are. Some *p*'s are *q*'s should not license the move that non-*q*'s are non-*p*'s. Such a move doesn't fit with the evolutionary scheme of things and it simply takes for granted precisely what is in dispute.

The first premise is flawed for similar reasons as those outlined. If 'all mental experience is characterised by thinking', and 'thinking' here is taken to imply a high-level inferential capacity, then the premise is misapplied for animals. No-one should be suggesting that animals are necessarily *reflectively* conscious. If (1) is taken to cover *all* kinds of perceptual experience, then it is simply false, as

---

[8] Hume seemed to be aware that some kind of comparative analysis was required here: "'Tis from the resemblances of the external actions of animals to those we ourselves perform, that we judge their internal likewise to resemble ours.' op. cit., p. 176.

it has been argued in this book that one can have contentful experiences without necessarily concentrating or deliberating in any sense at all. (Aspects of a colour experience, for instance, might be registered without thinking or knowing about them at all.) This indicates that conscious experience at one level demonstrably does not involve 'thinking' (if, that is, we take 'thinking' to involve high-level inferential capacities). Premises like (1) will clearly not assist the argument under consideration.

Premises (3) and (4) hinge once again on the ambiguity of the word 'concept': specifically, the suggestion that concepts can be descriptive in character and sensational too. As Wittgenstein observed, 'pain' concepts are modes of presentation that we learn, in one way, by behavioural gestures and ostension, which we learn to label, describe and specify in terms of types: 'sharp' pains, 'dull' pains, etc. (How a pain is described, moreover, depends on broad *theories* about what *sort* of observed behaviour is appropriate to what sort of pain descriptions). But, if as I have been suggesting, it is reasonable to separate the notion of concept from only its descriptive or propositional linguistic mode of presentation, then concepts of pain might be said to be importantly *sensational* as well. This seems plausible on grounds we have considered already - that the descriptive mode seems to 'miss out' on something about the experience. As has been suggested in this book, it is one thing to conceptualise a pain under a certain description, and another to conceptualise it as a certain felt quality. What sort of 'pain' concept might an animal be said to have? Clearly not the descriptive or linguistic kind of concept, but almost certainly the sensational kind and, again, it seems absurd to deny this.

I conclude from this brief assessment of the argument that animals are not conscious at all, two simple points. Firstly, it is inherently unfair to claim the terms of the dispute here to be high-level inferential features, 'reflective' consciousness, etc. This is to beg the question that what is salient here is only that which characterises some features of *human* consciousness. Secondly, even if these are the terms of the dispute, it does not license the claim that animals are not conscious, since some kinds of (sensory) consciousness may not be captured in such terms.

Animal concepts

If the argument that animals are not conscious fails, it is still open to the upholder of the inferentialist proposal to assert that animals are perceptually deficient because of a lack of high-level concepts with which to fix representational and descriptive features of experience. Animal cognition cannot be characterised in such terms. Animals do not, for instance, believe, or otherwise conceptualise, that Jones's body is near the cigar-band. Since descriptive features of experience need to be fixed by concepts, this brings us naturally to the argument that animals might not actually have concepts (and hence, no experiences) at all. Again, like the claim that animals are not conscious, this claim too has many contemporary adherents.[9]

---

[9] See, in particular, P. T. Geach, *Mental Acts: Their Content and their Objects*. See also, N. Malcolm, *Thought and Knowledge*. Geach, for instance, argues that since animals lack concepts they cannot make judgements or have intentions (those requiring concepts).

There is a direct reason why a claim like this will not work. Concepts generally are clearly *non-uniform* in structure and content. There is no earthly reason why we should expect that concepts can only be considered in sophisticated anthropocentric terms, as reflective features of cognition which can be described and which involve inference from high-level background knowledge - features which animals clearly do not possess. It is this point that Routley has in mind when he argues:

> The notion of 'our concepts' or 'our conceptual scheme' (with the 'our' not too tightly specified, but perhaps excluding temporally or culturally remote humans) is something of a myth: concepts, discriminatory abilities, vary enormously among humans as among animals. (In a strict philosophical sense, which there is a point in inventing, and which many philosophers are prepared to accept, there is no *the* concept of a bone: such a unique concept supposes uniformity which does not occur). Furthermore, only a fairly low and undemanding level of discriminatory ability is required for the attribution of beliefs, as our dealings with humans help reveal. Fido certainly can meet these standards, he can distinguish bones, including the one in question: he has *a* concept of a *bone*. His concept may, like mine, lack the nuances of the archaeologists' concept; but it will include features such as those linked with taste and smell that mine and the archaeologists' lack, and it will almost certainly be richer than Baby Bunting's concept.[10]

For these reasons, it seems fatuous to argue, as many philosophers have done,[11] that only high-level concepts could fix beliefs and conscious experiences in animals. The 'fairly low and undemanding level of discriminatory ability' in terms of taste and smell that Routley refers to, in fact, does the job, and this is clearly a *sensory* capacity of sorts. And it is this 'discriminatory ability' that appears not to be inferential, but which is nonetheless conceptual, that interests me. For what is being suggested is that this is an important feature of contentful experiences too. Routley highlights the importance of this feature when he reveals the extent of conceptual variability between species:

> When it comes to conceptual poverty it is commonly humans that are poor in comparison with animals: animals can discriminate objects and types of objects in ways that elude humans (and often humans cannot be taught to make similar discriminations e.g., because they lack the appropriate sensory apparatus). Dogs generally have considerably better knowledge (information if you like) on much that concerns bones than humans e.g., the location of old bones, the many scents and shapes of bones, the immediate history of various bones and so on .... More to the point, dogs' ability to discriminate bones and their types considerably exceeds

---

[10] R. Routley, 'Alleged Problems in Attributing Belief and Intentionality to Animals,' p. 390.
[11] Notably: Davidson, Bishop, Stich and Descartes. See J. Bishop, 'More on Thought and Talk,' pp. 1-16. I discuss Davidson and Stich below.

that of humans in important respects. Consider, in particular, the different scents of bones. A layman may be able to distinguish a few dozen scents; a perfume expert would distinguish many more, perhaps in excess of thirty thousand (as with perfumes or perfumed bones); but a dog could distinguish *vastly* more again, in fact as many as there are physical things. This reveals two points of importance: a dog's conceptual *richness* in *certain* matters concerned with bones as compared with humans; and the variability in human conceptual apparatus.[12]

The issue needs refining here of course. Discriminatory abilities on my account, may simply be sensational for some creatures, though they may also be sub-descriptive and hence, low-level inferential for others. A dog is a fairly sophisticated creature compared to a rat or a sea-slug; it is likely that it could make *some* inferential discriminations, such as location of objects in certain relations. Such concepts then have partially sensory aspects and partially descriptive aspects. For other creatures the discriminatory ability may be merely sensory. This amalgam story does not run against the continuum account of concepts, of course, but reinforces it.

The variability in the human conceptual apparatus that Routley mentions is undeniable and obvious. Humans seem capable of low-level sensory discriminations like animals, but they are also capable of high-level descriptive conceptualisations (as archaeologist-type concepts of bones testify). In terms of conceptual variability, we clearly span the concept continuum to an awesome degree. But the point about variability of conceptual apparatuses should be extended to the variability in kinds of concepts here. This is not brought out in the above passages, though it is a reasonable implication of them. Variability in concepts is a function not just of different conceptual apparatuses but importantly different categories of concepts and the two points are clearly connected. The claim Routley makes is that there appear to be highly developed 'smell' concepts in dogs which are shared to some (moderate) degree by perfume experts, but not by the rest of us to whom the concept of a bone amounts to having only some kind of descriptive anatomical significance.[13] This, of course, is true. An interesting, though neglected, point here however is that there might be an important difference in the kinds of concepts that are relevant to perceptual cognition generally. Some concepts, it is suggested, capture descriptive and propositional content; others capture *sensational* content.

Concepts are best defined as modes of presentation of properties, and animals can presumably be presented with properties of various sorts as we can - specifically in the form of what has been called 'sensory' concepts. It might be in dispute whether they can reach the feats of high-level cognitive integration we do, but it should not be in dispute that they have concepts at all. This belies an association of 'concept' with only the high-level capacities that cognition serves and not the lower-level capacities. It is this association that leads to the latter-day Cartesian treatment of animal cognition (of which, more shortly). But this emphasis surely seems wrong. The issue, properly, seems to depend on the

---

[12] Routley, op. cit., p. 390.

[13] Of course this does not hold for all humans. Two-year-olds wouldn't have a concept of a bone in this descriptive sense either.

varied capabilities of organisms in receiving different sorts of information and the *manner* in which it is received. This is precisely what we want. For it seems fairly clear that the concepts animals have involve integration of experience at an importantly sensory level, not only through complicated high-level processes like inference.[14] This accounts for Fido's manifest abilities with (say) manipulating and discovering bones, while preserving the insight that animals, in some sense, are conceptually poor, and are not in possession of high-level concepts and theories.

Humans seem to function with a certain competence at a sensory level also (witness: the perfume expert), but we also function at a higher descriptive/epistemic level involving another quite sophisticated network of concepts, which integrate quite different information, as in the archaeologists' concept of a bone. This descriptive ability is not uniform, and degrees of competence among people and cultures are evident. (I, for instance, have no archaeological knowledge and cannot form the relevant concepts of 'bone', but my next-door neighbour, being fond of that sort of thing, might.) These latter concepts involve highly inferential appeals of relatively sophisticated access to background knowledge of chemistry, geology, anatomy and so on. Perhaps some human beings, senile and intellectually deficient, have something like a low-level sensory concept of a bone (for instance, smell and touch); perhaps others have a concept of a bone as being a certain shape and colour; perhaps others have an archaeologist's concept of bones. Perhaps, (plausibly) we lose conceptual integrative capacities with age and gain them with maturity. The point here is, though there might be a difference in sophistication and *kind* here between the two broad kinds of modes of presentation, there is no point in denying the efficacy of such different sorts of concepts obtained for different purposes utilising different mechanisms and being differently presented. The division in concept is at least a plausible suggestion, given what we know about the variability of our own concepts and the deficiency of high-level concepts in animals. We evidently need both. Thus there is no argument, unless on quite parochial grounds, for saying that animals *do not have concepts.* And all arguments which suggest so are not making this distinction.

These points are ignored by philosophers keen to claim that animals cannot have concepts at all. The way such philosophers argue this is usually by claiming that animals cannot have conceptual contents sufficient to fix attitudes like *beliefs*. And 'conceptual content,' again, means here high-level descriptive concepts, not sensory concepts. Correspondingly, 'beliefs' here means high-level epistemic beliefs. Stich, for instance, has an argument of this kind, an argument which specifies that attributions of belief depend on an already shared conceptual richness between relevant (human) parties:

(1) Our difficulty in specifying the contents of animals' beliefs derives not from an ignorance of animal psychology but rather from a basic feature of the way we go about assigning content to a subject's beliefs.
(2) We are *comfortable in attributing to a subject a belief with a content*

---

[14] On the continuum view, of course, the degree of inferential and sensory content depends on the sophistication of the organism in question. So some inferences may be involved in animals which are phylogenetically similar to us.

only if we can assume the subject to have a broad network of related beliefs that is largely isomorphic with our own.
(3) Where a subject does not share a very substantial part of our own network of beliefs we are no longer capable of attributing content to his beliefs in this area.[15]

Stich closely ties belief attribution to the kinds of beliefs that humans share among one another. Of course, human beliefs are mostly considered to be of the high-level propositional and descriptive variety. (Armstrong's example in Chapter 1, for instance, was of several people believing the proposition that the earth was flat). Clearly, if beliefs are understood in this sense, then animals do not have beliefs, and thus, we cannot assume that they are conceptual creatures because we cannot attribute beliefs like this to them.

We can attribute beliefs to animals, of course, so there is something intuitively wrong with this argument. The following resolution is suggested: just as we cannot doubt that animals have some sorts of concepts, we cannot doubt that animals have some sorts of beliefs. We normally have no doubts, for instance, in assigning the content of Fido's seeing his master with the food bowl equalling Fido's believing that he will soon be fed. Again, however, the issue needs dividing here. What this belief might not be is a sophisticated mechanism involving inductive reasoning (Fido thinks: 'I was fed at approx. 6.15 last night, so this behaviour means feeding time'). This is a 'high-level' inferential ability, involving access to background knowledge; something that we have agreed Fido may have only to a limited degree. But this does *not* mean that Fido doesn't have beliefs of any sort at all. Fido can have beliefs if the notion of 'belief' is weakened to include what has been called 'look'-beliefs.

Hence, fixing the terms of the argument by a tacit stipulation of a sophisticated notion of 'belief' in terms of conceptual contents of certain kinds has helped Stich gain territory, only if we admit that this is a reasonable assumption. It is precisely this assumption, that the *only* conceptual contents possible are of a sophisticated inferential nature, that we are rejecting with the continuum account. On my view, Fido (and other animals) can still have beliefs, if it makes sense to say that observational experiences can fix beliefs of a low-level sensory kind. And, as it seems quite plausible that Fido *does* have beliefs, and does *not* have high-level descriptive concepts, (but *does* have concepts of some kind), it seems that a very low-level of belief fixation in terms of *sensory* concepts is required here. There may, in other words, be more ways of attaching beliefs than only to high-level descriptive concepts; sensory *looks* may also fix kinds of beliefs. And they should, because in Fido's case or that of a sea-slug, there is clearly not much else to go on.

Obviously all this is complicated, but the point here is that the *most* someone could say about the conceptual poverty of animals is that animals do not have high-level inferential, cognitively penetrated concepts as we clearly do. But claiming that they have no concepts *at all,* and worse still, no concepts with which to fix states like belief, is not only counterintuitive, but an unreasonable view which avoids the complicated and problematic area of the nature and structure of concepts in the context of experiential content, and the obvious

---

[15] S. P. Stich, 'Do Animals have Beliefs?' p. 22.

degrees of animal intellectual/cognitive sophistication. Stich commits this error:

> [G]iven Fido's *conceptual* and *cognitive poverty* in matters concerned with bones, it is surely wrong to ascribe to him any belief about a *bone*. To clinch the point, we need only to reflect that we would certainly balk if the same belief were attributed to a human who was as irremediably ignorant about bones as we take Fido to be.[16]

There is no justification for this conclusion because the premise here can be questioned. Fido is clearly not conceptually ignorant in matters concerned with bones. He may be conceptually *poor* in certain respects if we take the ability to conceptualise to be an exclusively 'high-level' descriptive capacity. But *poor* doesn't mean conceptually *empty*. And imagining a person who has Fido's discriminatory capacities but no more, does not 'clinch the point' for Stich, because we could argue that such a person still has a belief about bones as well as Fido does; a belief admittedly, which is not at all sophisticated or congruent with a network of other descriptive beliefs, but a belief nonetheless. 'Clinching the point' for Stich here is no more than begging the question. Stich has failed to see that the nature of 'concepts' runs deeper than the kinds of concepts that humans are able to share with one another in a descriptively rich cognitive network. But this is plainly a *superficial* view of concepts. Perhaps conceptual content runs between species as well as between human individuals, and that there is some reason to claim that not all such contents are specifiable in terms of high-level considerations; some are importantly observational. Stich's view makes the inference criterion the starting point for his argument, and so, begs an important issue. It is suggested, therefore, that his argument will not work.[17]

But there is another important reason why Stich's argument will not work. He says that we are comfortable in attributing beliefs only when the 'attributees' share related beliefs which are isomorphic with our own. There is something wrong with this claim also. 'Isomorphism' with the sorts of things that *we* believe, as a criterion, is more than unjustifiably anthropocentric; it is also culturally totalitarian, for, if it were true, it would mean that other human beings could not be said to have beliefs. Referring to Stich's argument, Routley notes

---

[16] Ibid., pp. 18-19.

[17] I hasten to add that I am not opposed to *all* of his argument in this respect. Stich, like Churchland, articulates the view of *psychological holism:* that beliefs and concepts necessarily occur in networks or systems. This principle is harmless and probably true. It is plausible that animals too, have belief 'systems'. It is arguable, however, whether this claim itself gets Stich what he wants. For, as mentioned, he wants to rule out significant content attribution to animals on the basis that their 'network' is not as thoroughly 'integrated' and high-level as ours. This is clearly a *non sequitur*. For it is open to argue, as I do, that there are distinctions of a qualitative nature between the high and low level contents. It is plausible, indeed, to suppose that we have relatively isolated low level contents *in addition* to content of an inferential sort, and that this might occur as a system of content sub-systems. (This is, in fact, the burden of modularity theory which I shall discuss in Chapter 8.) It is not legitimate to claim that beliefs etc., *must* occur in the context of the high level networks only, and that each part must be inferentially accessible to each other part etc. See J. Glover, *The Philosophy and Psychology of Personal Identity,* for a statement of this kind of view.

that this is a ridiculous suggestion:

> The ascription of beliefs to animals, to members of other remote cultures, to various ancient and future peoples, is done commonly enough by the layman, without discomfort, without semantic propriety, and without the insinuation of substantial theoretical assumptions. It does seem a *reductio ad absurdum* of the common network view incorporated in (2) and (3), that temporally or culturally remote humans cannot be attributed beliefs with specifiable content.[18]

Davidson's argument for the same conclusion is also worth noting in this context. It is even more starkly 'inferentialist' than Stich's argument:

> (1) Only a language user can have a concept of belief;
> (2) Only a creature who has the concept of a belief can have beliefs.
> (C) Therefore, only a language user can have beliefs.[19]

This is simply intellectual foolishness. Both of these arguments have false conclusions, to say nothing of the premises. They clearly ask too much of concepts and beliefs, to say nothing of language, and thus lead to counterintuitive cases. Where Stich's position implies that other cultures do not have concepts or beliefs, Davidson's position rules out young children and mutes for similar reasons, as well as animals which clearly do seem to have the requisite conceptual content: Fido evidently believes that Ginger Puss is in the tree when he hears her miaow, despite not being able to string one word to another - and despite not having any 'high-level' inferentially-sophisticated background knowledge about trees and cats. For Stich and Davidson, inferential linguisticism rears its ugly head. The point here is this: the ability to use a language and the ability to access high-level descriptive concepts and other inferential features is not relevant to *all* forms of belief fixation; specifically, the low-level concept formation evidently achieved by animals. The problem here, especially in Davidson's case - but also in Stich's - is keeping the notion of belief too closely tied to high-level cognitive capacities like language.[20] There is no justification for this if there can be reasonably said to be lower level cognitive capacities which can fix beliefs by means of sensations. And, there

---

[18] Routley, op. cit., p. 392. Routley notes also that this view is in 'circularity trouble': 'For consider (2) as affording a necessary condition of a subject's having a belief with specific content. In order to attribute such a belief, we should have to know already that we can attribute such beliefs to the subject-which one cannot in general do without (epistemic) circularity. Insofar as the network view forces us toward solipsism, that too is a *reductio* of it.' Loc. cit.

[19] An extracted argument from D. Davidson, 'Thought and Talk' in S. Guttenplan (ed.), *Mind and Language,* pp. 22-23. See Routley, op. cit., p. 390

[20] Stich is less obvious with his interpretation of content isomorphism and makes no explicit tie with language. But note that, in relation to content attribution, he does use words like 'broad', 'largely', 'substantial', in the preceding argument, which gives away the emphasis on high-level inference.

seems to be reasonable common sense evidence that this is true.[21] The claim that 'high-level' inference is *necessary* for animal cognition is clearly too extreme. Like a besotted lover, inference goes even where plausibility does not ask him to follow, and reason enough has already been given to think that such features need not be required to fix *all* kinds of content.

The claim that animals are not conscious of their sensory states is false and the claim that they do not have concepts or beliefs is also false. Animals are certainly cognitively *poor* when compared with humans, but, as Routley says: 'cognitive poverty, of many sorts, is not material for the attribution of beliefs.'[22] 'Cognitively poor' should mean here *cognitively poor relative to us,* and to our high-level concepts; 'belief' should mean here a high-level epistemic notion. However, as has been argued, this is not the only kind of belief we have, and it is not the only kind of conceptual contents we can speak of. 'Cognitively poor' does not mean cognitively *empty,* and not all beliefs are epistemic in the sense required. Numerous common sense examples show that animals have concepts of sorts, and have low-level kinds of beliefs which fix them: the interesting and important issue here is the sense of the words 'sorts' and 'kinds'. The arguments in support of the view that high-level inferential factors are *necessary* for cognition in animals have failed to address this issue by obfuscating the distinctions here. But the resolution is simple: at the very least, animals have certain important sorts of *sensory* concepts, and such concepts clearly fix some sorts of important low-level sensory beliefs. Propositional beliefs and inferences of an epistemic kind are qualitatively distinct from this level, though both levels can be represented on a graded scale. Some sophisticated animals (e.g., dogs, dolphins and chimps) can even have some inferential features as well, though probably not of the propositional or linguistic kind - though one wouldn't want to rule anything out in such cases.

The claim that there is a graded scale here should not seem implausible. It is sanctioned from an evolutionary and phylogenetic perspective, though it also seems intuitively fair. Animals are not exceedingly different creatures from us, though they are clearly less sophisticated in fairly obvious ways. The nature of their mental content - their beliefs, their concepts, their experiential world - is likewise only different from ours by degrees. It seems appropriate, therefore, to allow degrees of cognitive sophistication rather than ruling one kind of creature as having these features and the others not. Plausibly, humans have very high-level beliefs and concepts and experiential content; animals have rather less than this in decreasing orders of magnitude. That 'higher' organisms can override such mechanisms of belief fixation with a high degree of cognitive inference merely expresses a degree of conceptual sophistication or competence; it does not rule out the possibility of low-level sensational concepts in animals. We can, in fact, endorse the very real differences in cognitive competence between animals and humans, and use them to cast doubt on the arguments, by showing that the notion of cognitive content naturally bifurcates into different sorts of concepts. The way of sharpening the dispute is to maintain a distinction

---

[21] See B. E. Rollins, *The Unheeded Cry: Animal Consciousness, Animal Pain and Science,* and D. Griffin, *The Question of Animal Awareness: The Evolutionary Continuity of Mental Experience.*

[22] Routley, op. cit., p. 389.

between the relevant types of concepts and the accessibility of largely sensory concepts to animals. This seems an appropriate solution. It is appropriate because we have already agreed that animals *do* have conscious sensory states. We would face a difficulty with this if we jointly upheld the argument that animals have no concepts at all; the reason being that a certain cognitive capacity seems a necessary and sufficient condition for any sensible attribution of conscious perceptions to animals at all. As Routley has noted:

> Likewise animal *perception* presupposes animal beliefs. Are we to say that the small birds saw the raptor overhead, but that none of them believed that another bird was overhead? Yet surely we are not expected to forego (the advantages of) ascriptions of perception to animals ... It is enough that (i) perception guarantees certain ... attitudes, and that (ii) these attitudes, under conditions sometimes satisfied by animals, guarantee beliefs. Both (i) and (ii) are readily satisfied. For that a sees xf (e.g., the raptor overhead) implies that a sees that xf (e.g., the raptor is overhead), so satisfying (i), and the latter normally guarantees that a believes that xf, so satisfying (ii).[23]

The above is, at least, a plausible argument, but note: just because perception needs concepts (like belief), it doesn't follow that perception or belief needs high-level inference. Animal beliefs and concepts might be informationally local and conceptually low-level. If this is plausible, then it seems reasonable to grant a further claim: given that the perceptual/discriminatory abilities of animals presuppose attitudes like beliefs, the reverse might be reasonably said to hold also. Attitude and belief formation would seem to require at least a minimal conscious perceptual/discriminatory ability for such attitudes to be fixed to certain states of affairs and events in the world. To believe anything about Ginger Puss' predicament in the tree, Fido would have to be consciously aware of some experience that he was having. The experience would have to be a *contentful* experience for Fido in some minimal sense. The important point here is that we have admitted that Fido does not have high-level descriptive concepts as we do, and we have admitted that Fido's experiences *do* presuppose contentful states like beliefs. It seems that the only way that we can grant both of these claims is to keep the idea that some contentful states are fixed into beliefs through being simply sensory and informationally low-level. The possibility of this is all that is needed in the foregoing section. The possibility of low-level contentful experiences in animals is enough both to avoid latter-day Cartesianism and to make a continuum view of content seem a very likely option.

Conclusion

Much of this chapter has been concerned with points that may seem fairly obvious. The case for animal experiences being at a number of interestingly distinct levels has been presented. On the view given here, there are aspects of experiences which are low-level and sensory (in the sense that they are required

---

[23] Ibid., p. 404.

to fix look-beliefs), and aspects of experiences which are inferential (which are required to integrate such low-level beliefs into full-blooded high-level theory). There are also a number of intermediate possibilities: sophisticated experiences which have low-level 'aspect'-like features, and so on. It has not been claimed that no inference goes on in contextful, low-level experiential states, only that high-level cognising is not necessarily part of that story. The continuum proposal asserts that there are all sorts of graded possibilities with respect to the cognitive penetration of sensation by inference, and the two elements are dialectically interposed, not antagonistic. It is suggested that several non-exclusive kinds of content fits better with evolutionary continuity and also with the ethological and developmental facts.

We have seen in this chapter how the legacy of the inferentialist proposal has resulted in views that ignore the common knowledge that animals are conscious of their perceived environment and have primitive concepts. At its most serious, views which rely on a more sophisticated account of content result in animals being seen as having no experiences at all. It has been argued that none of these views are credible.

8 Modularity and insularity

Perceptual analysis ... is not, truly speaking, a species of thought.[1]

Content modularity

Introduction

The focus in this chapter will be a recent contribution to perceptual psychology and how its view of the organism as an informationally complex group of subsystems can be adapted to support the continuum account being presented. This view will first be outlined and modified before turning to the issues of epiphenomenalism and evolutionary theory. The chapter concludes by arguing that low-level informational content should be understood as having a causal informational role in perception.

Modularity theory

Jerry Fodor has recently advanced an information-theoretic model of perceptual content. Like Kant's view, it is fundamentally concerned with the presentation, processing and output of data, though unlike the orthodox reading of Kant's position, it is not entirely 'high-level' in its approach. It is a view which highlights the difficulties with the inferentialist proposal and it goes some way towards resolving the question of whether experience is in some sense organised at a low level prior to high-level conceptual organisation. In this chapter, Fodor's modularity thesis (with recent modifications) will be outlined. What has been argued so far receives some support from Fodor's work in perceptual psychology.

Fodor's approach to the nature of experiential content is to treat the organism as being like a *computational machine*. In his view, what perception must do is to so represent the world as to make it accessible to thought.[2] This occurs by means of 'subsidiary systems' which operate to effect informational exchanges,

---

[1] J. A. Fodor, *Modularity of Mind*, p. 43.

[2] Ibid., p. 40.

by 'provid[ing] the central machine with information about the world; information expressed by mental symbols in whatever format cognitive processes demand of the representations that they apply to.'[3] Explaining how these subsidiary systems represent the world in order to make it accessible to thought is the aim of Fodor's modularity theory of the mind.

The account Fodor offers describes a 'trichotomous functional taxonomy'[4] to effect this process of representing the world in thought. *Transducers, input systems* and *central processors* constitute the machinery, each with a specific function. I shall briefly describe each in turn.

Transducers are described as 'analog systems' which function to map 'proximal stimulations onto more or less precisely covarying neural signals.' 'Proximal stimulations' here refer to strictly physical information impinging on the sense organs; 'covarying neural signals' self-evidently refers to the information such stimulations instigate in a neural form. Transduced neural messages covarying with proximal stimulations are mediated by input systems to deliver 'distal outputs'. These outputs are meant to represent, and characterise in a suitable vocabulary, the arrangements of things in the world; again, in a computational form that the machine can understand.[5] In being mediated by the input systems, the information is altered from its non-inferential form, as surface stimulations on the sense organs, to a meaningful inferential form within central processors. The input systems thus 'encode'[6] but do not translate the output of the transducers to the central processors which use and store these representations as data in a cognitive context. The informational schemata thus flows from the mapping of the stimulus (transducers), to encoding its products (input systems), to storing and retrieving it in the form of representational icons (central processors).

The distinction between the input mechanisms and the central processors is crucial to Fodor's taxonomy. In making the distinction, Fodor noted that it was one thing to process information and it was another thing to have it available as material for inference from one's 'background beliefs and set.'[7] Here he takes sides against much work done on the mechanisms of perception from Kant onwards. Perceptual analysis, typically, has appealed to background information, concepts, cognitive structures and the like, to make sense of how perception is possible from the input of proximal data, and this has been deemed necessary on the strength and persuasion of 'poverty of the stimulus' arguments.[8] Such arguments emphasise that sophisticated cognitive mechanisms must be available to filter experiential content, since perception was always underdetermined by sensory arrays. In earlier chapters it was discussed how assumptions like these give rise to an inferentialist theory of content.

Fodor generally agrees with this sort of evaluation of the inferential nature of perceptual processing, but also notes that, in some respects, perception itself is

---

[3] Loc. cit.
[4] Loc. cit.
[5] Loc. cit.
[6] Ibid., p. 42.
[7] Ibid., p. 43.
[8] J. A. Fodor, 'Precis of The Modularity of Mind', p. 2.

less like inferring and more like *reflexing*. If so, then this may be a basis for distinguishing mechanisms which effect a high-level inferential contribution to perceptual processing, from mechanisms which are reflex-like in character, and responsive locally to the transduced outputs of proximal stimulations (i.e., sensations). This may even offer a basis for explaining primitive experiences of animals (and cases of low-level content in humans) which do not, intuitively, seem to have much to do with high-level concepts, inference and background knowledge. The proposal is obviously central to our concerns in this book.

Fodor's claim is that there has been a confusion in applying the 'poverty of the stimulus' arguments to perceptual processing; specifically, a confusion as to what the arguments are supposed to demonstrate. What the arguments try to show is that it is reasonable to assume that perception needs inferences to sort out stimuli into coherent perceptual patterns. And a non-inferential basis for perception in terms of proximal stimulations cannot fulfil this, i.e., we cannot construct perceptual data from a concept-free input. But, it is unclear what the inferential story tells us exactly on closer inspection: does it mean, for instance, that perceptions are *wholly* inferentially mediated; or that this is mostly the case - perceptions *mostly* appeal to high-level inferences?

This difference is important, because as we saw in Kant's case, it was actually ambiguous what the mediation by the categories and forms of intuition was designed to show; the sensible manifold could have been the basis for some kind of intrinsic perceptual structure, albeit a structure insufficient to guarantee high-level conceptual knowledge. We also saw that there was a case for claiming that the 'top down' heavily inferential approach is not even fully argued for in Kant's writings, and is inconsistent with some of the more marginal claims in his writing. In view of the continuum theory being advanced, of course, this is a point of crucial interest: for if true, then it casts in doubt some of the strongly pro-inferentialist work from Kant onwards.

In the case of the Sherlock Holmes example, however, the value of the 'poverty of the stimulus' story seems clear cut, and makes sense of Holmes's abilities: we saw that he was able to extract from peripheral sensory clues a meaningful body of perceptual information about the dispositions of his suspects, their habits and the likely perpetrator of the crime, and that this was a function of the role of inference in perceptual processing. In this case, it seemed a straight forward case of the *penetration* of sensations by inference.

On the strength of what we have been considering so far, of course, this is all a bit quick: though it might follow that Holmes needed to form inferences to reach conclusions, it *does not* follow that *without* inference, concepts, etc., Holmes could make no meaningful perceptual discriminations at all. The conclusion that he could not just does not seem to follow from the 'poverty of the stimulus' arguments. The whole 'poverty' argument seems even less sound when animal experiences are considered: for since unsophisticated animals are said to have few inferential mechanisms at their disposal, then they must have no experiences. But as was argued in the last chapter, this does not seem plausible at all; certainly not in the face of the phylogenetic link between animals and ourselves. Rather than high-level factors constituting a dividing line between experiencing humans and non-experiencing animals, it seemed far more plausible to view the relationship as being a matter of degree, not kind.

The inferentialist proposal has been criticised in previous chapters on both of these grounds. A weaker view of the relation between experience and features of high-level inference has been presented instead. It is now suggested that Fodor's modularity theory provides some empirical as well as theoretical reasons for taking the continuum account seriously.

Consider the action of a reflex: say, my blinking when you attempt to poke me in the eye. This could not, by a long shot, be considered a perceptual response to stimuli, because this is not an integrated representation of proximal stimulus: it does not represent the action of poking in thought, as a perception must represent the world in thought. Indeed, it doesn't seem to represent anything; it is just a 'straight-through' unmediated connection of stimulus to reaction. Rather a lot of significant perceptual integrations actually seem something like this too, as Fodor observed; for example, the cases of face-recognition, object-recognition and the perception of speech-patterns, vocalisations and utterances. Such perceptions are domain specific, immediate and, seemingly *encapsulated* from inferential analysis in terms of background knowledge. Fodor's claim is that some level of perceptual processing has, in fact, properties rather like the properties that reflexes have.

On orthodox inferentialist views, such as Kant's, there is no distinction between cognitively penetrated (inferential) percepts, and so-called encapsulated ones. On the Kantian view, the categories and forms of intuition uniquely determine the percept on the basis of prior schemata structured 'in the mind.' For experience to be possible at all, the forms of intuition and categories have to organise the manifold of intuition. Intuitions without concepts are blind. A judgment may err (be 'false') through insufficient sensory input, but essentially perceptual processing must occur by means of the faculties. Fodor's point is that this sort of approach may explain how we experience anything at all given the underdetermination of proximal stimulation. However, on this view of perception, there is no flexibility to allow for the kinds of perceptual content that is insulated from background beliefs and concepts and which seems to *resist* background interpretation. Fodor's argument that this sort of non-inferential and encapsulated perceptual processing *does* occur rests mainly on his account of the Muller-Lyer illusion.

The Muller-Lyer illusion: cognitive encapsularity

The familiar Muller-Lyer illusion goes something like this: two lines of identical length are presented with arrowheads on each end pointing in and out respectively (see below, figure 4). Line (b) *looks* longer than the other owing to the figure being interpreted three dimensionally as a 'concave corner with its edge receding from the viewer.'[9] The other figure, (a), is perceived (again, three dimensionally) as projecting a convex corner, which appears to emerge toward the viewer, and thus, appears shorter. Despite appearances, the two lines in question are actually the same length. The discrepancy between the two projections in the illusion can be explained by a wealth of background information which constitutes 'a complex of assumptions about the relation between three-dimensional objects and their two-dimensional projections,'[10]

---

[9] J. A. Fodor, 'Observation Reconsidered,' p. 33.

[10] Ibid., pp. 33-4.

like those, for example, relating what we know about the edges of rooms, doorways, and so on. Adding credence to this 'top down' explanation is the plausible claim that some people (particularly those from other cultures) and children, are less susceptible to the illusion than those familiar with edges, corners and their perspectival relationships, presumably owing to a demonstrable lack of culturally attuned background beliefs.[11]

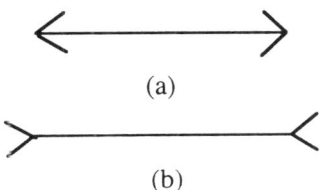

(a)

(b)

Figure 4 The Muller-Lyer illusion

Fodor's point about all of this is simply that if high-level influences penetrate perception *wholly,* then why is it not the case that the knowledge that the illusion *is an illusion* penetrate one's perception of it?

> The Muller-Lyer is a *familiar* illusion; the news has pretty well gotten around by now. So it's part of the 'background theory' of anybody who lives in this culture and is at all into pop psychology that displays like [this] are in fact misleading and that it always turns out, on measurement that the centre lines of the arrows are the same length. Query: *why isn't perception penetrated by THAT piece of background theory?* Why, in fact, doesn't *knowing* that the lines are the same length make it *look as though* the lines are the same length?[12]

According to Fodor, what the Muller-Lyer shows is not that perception is highly cognitive. Rather, it suggests just the reverse: that how the world looks

---

[11] See: W. H. R. Rivers, 'Observations on the Senses of the Todas', pp. 321-96. There is some dispute in the literature whether the differences here can be attributed to a difference in such 'carpentered environments' or whether it can be attributed to other factors such as retinal pigmentation or education, which may contribute to the effectiveness of the illusions. For a summary of the literature see: J. O. Robinson, *The Psychology of Visual Illusion.* See also: G. Jahoda, 'Retinal Pigmentation, Illusion Susceptibility and Space Perception', pp. 199-208. It would be sufficient for the 'top-down' view that most of the influence on the perception of such illusions come from such environments, even if it was not the only influence.

[12] Fodor (1984), op. cit., p. 34. Frank Jackson makes the same point (about the same illusion) in *Perception: A Representative Theory* in the context of 'refuting' the idea that 'when a "looks" statement is true, an appropriate belief statement is true.' (p. 38) The point here, of course, is that the high-level belief-based 'epistemic' account of perception is seriously misguided.

can be 'peculiarly unaffected by how one knows it to be.'

Cases like this can be multiplied to include the Ames room and the phi phenomenon illusions, and also to cases not involving vision. Fodor cites the phoneme restoration and the click displacement effects in speech as other examples. (In these cases, a subject can hear a recording of a word that has had a phoneme cut out and a 'click' put in its place. Despite being told about the alteration, a subject will still *hear* the entire word).[13] Fodor's conclusion about all this is, in an important sense, damaging to the case of 'top down' perceptual processing:

> The issue raised by the persistence of illusion is not, ... whether some inferences are 'more conceptual' than others ... [The] issue is: How rigid is the boundary between the information available to cognitive processes and the information available to perceptual ones? How much of what you know/believe/desire actually does affect the way that you see? The persistence of illusion suggests that the answer might be: at most, less than all of it.[14]

The accusation is that there is all the difference in the world between claiming that perceptual inferences from background knowledge are available to perceptual integration, and claiming that perception is cognitively *penetrated* by such inferences. Perceptual implasticities make the idea of cognitive penetration seems highly implausible.[15] For cognitive penetration to be true, it would have to imply 'the continuity of perception with cognition.'[16] But if Fodor's claims about perceptual illusion are reasonable, then it would seem that perceptual implasticities do imply a 'radical isolation of how things look from the effects of much of what one believes.'[17]

Fodor's diagnosis is that there are, on an increasing scale, three sorts of architectural arrangements in respect of the relations between cognition and perception: a case where *no* background information is available to perceptual integration; a case where *some but not all* background information is available; and a case where *everything one knows* is available to integration. The first seems implausible in view of the poverty of the stimulus arguments, and the third seems implausible in view of the Muller-Lyer illusion. Fodor's claim is that, on balance, the second seems the 'better bet.'[18] Certain contents are always *encapsulated* from knowledge and beliefs.

Within the limits of analogy, Kant's model is a useful comparison. Kant faced two options with respect to the categories and their influence on the content of experience: one was that they wholly determined (read: cognitively penetrated) the structure of the manifold of sense. The other option was that the

---

[13] Fodor, (1983) op. cit., p. 66.

[14] Fodor, (1985) op. cit., p. 2.

[15] Fodor, (1984) op. cit., p. 35. Fodor calls what I have called the inferentialist proposal, the 'cognitivist interpretation'.

[16] Fodor, (1985) op. cit., p. 3.

[17] Fodor, (1984) op. cit., p. 35.

[18] Fodor, (1985) op. cit., p. 3.

manifold of sense is somehow organised (read: is 'encapsulated') in some primitive manner, despite the imposition of the categories. It would seem that Fodor explicitly takes the second option, whereas it is unclear if Kant does. (Though if his views of the sensory manifold are as systematically ambiguous as has been pointed out, then it may well be that the orthodox view of Kant is misguided, and that he was actually sympathetic to the second option too).[19]

H. I. Brown has reached a similar *tertium quid* on the nature of our perceptions, and though the boundary he is drawing is unclear, he seems to be suggesting that there are certain important encapsulated *constraints* on perception. Referring to ambiguous perceptual illusions like the duck/rabbit and the face/vase illusions, and in response to the relativist objection that such stimuli can be 'perceived in any way at all', he writes:

> We can begin our response by noting that I have nowhere maintained that theories create their own data or that our theories *alone* determine what we perceive. Rather, the objects of perception are the results of contributions from *both* our theories *and* the action of the external world on our sense organs. Because of this dual source of our percepts objects can be seen in many different ways, but it does not follow that a given object can be seen in any way at all. Consider again the duck/rabbit. We have already seen that this figure can be seen as a duck, a rabbit, a set of lines or an area, and one might plausibly imagine its being seen as a piece of laboratory apparatus, a religious symbol, or some other animal by an observer with the appropriate experience. But try as I will, I cannot see this figure as my wife, the Washington monument or a herd of swine.... I do not maintain that theories impose structure on a *neutral* material. The dichotomy between the view of perception as the passive observation of objects which are whatever they appear to be and perceptions as the creation of perceptual objects out of nothing is by no means exhaustive. *A third possibility is that we shape our perceptions out of an already structured but still malleable material.* This perceptual material, whatever it might be, will serve to limit the class of possible constraints without dictating a unique percept.[20]

Of course, there are some important differences in the claims here. Fodor is suggesting that there are boundary conditions on what the perceptual apparatus can do computationally; Brown seems to be saying that *what is in the world* limits perceptual content. Clearly though, there are also some similarities here. Perceptual experience is a function of perceptual equipment interacting with the world as it impinges on our sense organs, and constraints can occur at the junction of both levels. The interesting issue is the exact nature of this relationship.

I want to draw attention here to the important distinction between the central processors and the input mechanisms in light of the foregoing. The point of the subsidiary systems is to provide information to a computational machine in a

---

[19] The *first* option that Fodor mentions, of course, is closed to all those persuaded by the poverty of the stimulus arguments.
[20] H. I. Brown, *Perception, Theory and Commitment*, p. 93. Italics mine.

form that it can understand, about the world in which it operates and engages in informational exchange. On any ordinary view of perceptual processing, a distinction is normally made between 'cognition' (employing high-level background beliefs and so on) and 'sensing' (which is responsive to the output of proximal stimulations). In Fodor's picture, this is amended with the introduction of a third 'mechanism.' Sensations, on his view, become 'responsive solely to the character of proximal stimulations and [are] non-inferential' while cognition is 'both inferential and responsive to the perceiver's background theories.'[21] Fodor's innovation is to 'split the difference'[22] between the sensory component which is non-inferential, and the cognitive component which is inferential, and to postulate a new mechanism which has both these characteristics. This mechanism Fodor calls a perceptual 'module':

> A module is, (inter alia) an informationally encapsulated computational system - an inference-making mechanism whose access to background information is constrained by general features of cognitive architecture, hence relatively rigidly and relatively permanently constrained. ... at least some information that is available to at least some cognitive processes is not available to the module.[23]

With its informationally encapsulated and relatively permanently constrained cognitive architecture, the 'module' allows perceptual integration to occur at a lower level than input from high-level beliefs, theories, background knowledge, etc. And it is this which is supposed to account for the fact that in some perceptual situations, what one sees is curiously unaffected by what one knows or believes.

There may appear to be some confusion in the above passage. Fodor is explicitly claiming that a module is an inference-making mechanism, whereas before he seemed to be embracing the *non-inferential* character of reflexes as a distinguishing feature of some kinds of perceptual integrations. The claim is, however, that a module is inferential only in respect of information confined within its own modular 'architecture,' and that this information is still permanently encapsulated from the high-level inferential deposits of background beliefs and concepts.

Empirical supports for modularity

I would like to turn now, briefly, to some of the empirical supports for the idea that perception is modular. We have seen that the visual effect of the Muller-Lyer illusion admits of an interpretation contrary to the usual explanation in terms of the penetration of culturally acquired background beliefs about common geometric patterns. The alternative view was that not all perceptual mechanisms are inferential and at some perceptual level, how certain information is received is *unaffected* by how things are believed or known to be, and this seemed to indicate a more primary processing level is available to

---

[21] Fodor, (1984) op. cit., p. 36
[22] Loc. cit.
[23] Fodor, (1985) op. cit., p. 3.

complex perceptual organisms. This is hardly a decisive argument on its own, and so Fodor provides us with a wealth of other cases. The interesting thing about them is that not only does visual perception seem like this, but there are examples which show that many other types of information processing, both auditory and tactile, also seem informationally encapsulated in his sense; in fact, low-level perceptual integrations of all kinds are modular.

A good example is the processing of speech sounds. Evidence by several theorists, including Liberman,[24] has suggested that the way subjects hear a signal greatly depends upon whether the signal is in the form of an utterance or not. This seems to indicate that the mechanisms of audition are, in an important sense, 'pre-tuned' to be responsive to certain types of meaningful acoustic contexts. If this is an adequate hypothesis, then it would seem to fit in rather well with the Chomskian view that natural language has certain unique and universal grammatical properties which are responsive to species-specific learning systems. It would jointly account for the ability of a language-speaking organism to learn language so rapidly. The phenomenon of speech 'tracking' or 'shadowing' is also relevant here: as Fodor reports, a significant number of people can repeat continuous speech with only one quarter of a second latency, and also understand what they are saying.[25] These findings seem to display that in order for certain highly efficient responses of utterance and speech recognition to be possible, the integrations must be unmediated by complicated cognitive processes and fairly local and direct in their application. Other examples include phoneme recognition, face recognition and the recognition of three-dimensional shapes, all of which suggest the same sort of reflex-like responses to certain sorts of stimuli.[26] These studies indicate that a special kind of perceptual mechanism is operational - domain-specific in its function and 'modular' in performing it.

How else might this sort of data be made informationally accessible, if not in a modular (encapsulated) fashion? Fodor sketches an alternative means which involves the employment of a 'similarity metric' and a conceptual 'prototype'.[27] The suggestion is that perceptual integration might happen by a matching of data against an inferential standard, and by assessing the degree of closeness or 'fit'. If this was the way in which perceptual integration of utterances or faces, etc. occurred, then it would mean that we could imagine 'a quite general computational system'[28] which was 'horizontal' in structure, i.e., it could cross perceptual domains, and assess facial data in the *same* manner in which it assessed speech vocalisations, colours or cows. In this case: 'The procedures for estimating the distance between input and a perceptual prototype should have pretty much the same computational structure wherever they are encountered.'[29]

---

[24] A. Liberman et al, 'The Perception of the Speech Code', pp. 431- 461.
[25] Fodor (1983) op. cit., p. 61. Source of reference, W. Marslen-Wilson. 'Speech Shadowing and Speech Perception'.
[26] Ibid., See Fodor (1983), passim.
[27] Ibid., p. 49.
[28] Loc. cit.
[29] Ibid., pp. 49-50.

If this is meant to be a rival to the modular hypothesis, then it is not a good one. For, considering how 'eccentric' a stimulus can be, it would be somewhat remarkable that such perceptual integrations could occur for such things at all, let alone with the speed that they do. A more likely possibility, the one that Fodor presents, is that some primitive modes of perceptual recognition are already 'tuned'[30] to 'special classes' of stimuli, and so operate in a relatively isolated fashion from inferential prototypes, to achieve recognition *fast*. This is not to say, of course, that *all* feats of integrative processing are performed in this 'modular', domain-specific way. A complicated activity, like playing the piano, demonstratively requires inferences from background beliefs and set, not only to make informed perceptual judgments about the object itself, but to work out what possibilities are open to one if one wanted to use it. Inferences from one's life history, memories of concerts, childhood music lessons, as well as knowledge of harmony, chordal relationships, etc., are relevant here. But if one's intention does not happen to be to play it, but to use it as a piece of furniture, then all such background beliefs about pianos can be abandoned. This is not so with face recognition, speech analysis, and perception of three-dimensional objects. It is not only that these sorts of perceptual integrations just seem positively impervious to background knowledge, beliefs and concepts; it simply seems that such things do not even *bear* on such lower level responses, and, as they do not, it scarcely seems an issue that they could be 'conceptualised' in any other way. Rather, what is most clear about such *ex hypothesi* modular tasks is that *we can't but* integrate them as we do:

> You can't help hearing an utterance of a sentence ... as an utterance of a sentence, and you can't help seeing a visual array as consisting of objects distributed in three-dimensional space. Similarly, *mutatis mutandis,* for the other perceptual modes: you can't, for instance, help feeling that what you run your fingers over is the surface of an object.[31]

The claim is not that *all* perceptual processes are modular, and thus informationally encapsulated. It is only that it is questionable that all perception involves the imposition of high-level inferential features and that the boundary between what is available to perceptual processes and what is available to cognitive processes is inferentially porous. If it was inferentially porous, then all perceptual processes would predictably involve a certain amount of high-level inference in the form of background beliefs and concepts, but as we have seen, the evidence just doesn't run this way. However, Fodor is far from claiming that *no* perceptual processes are inferential: the point is that *it depends on the level of processing in question.* Some (complex) processing certainly involves cognitive mechanisms, inference and so on, but some of the simplest cases of perceptual integration are not influenced by them at all. This is transparently clear in the case of the Muller-Lyer illusion, but it is also, if we believe Fodor, evident in utterance and speech sound recognition, tactile object integration and perhaps even the recognition of colour primitives. Perhaps, this also might be true of the kinds of perceptual integrations that unsophisticated

---

[30] Fodor, (1985) op. cit., p. 52.
[31] Ibid., p. 53.

animals perform: summarily, we might begin to believe that animal awareness is informationally local too.

Fodor has provided grounds for thinking that there may be some perceptual content which is not necessarily dependent on high-level features and this is tantamount to a rejection of the inferentialist proposal we are considering. However, there have been modifications of Fodor's view which need to be noted.

Content insularity

Cam's thesis

Philip Cam has suggested, like Fodor, that in constructing a perception from available sensory information, certain 'assumptions' are adopted by the perceptual mechanisms which may be false in the light of background knowledge.[32] One of the Muller-Lyer lines may look longer, for instance, despite our knowledge to the contrary. As to how this might happen, he offers three possible answers: (1) there is a lack of physical connections between high-level knowledge and the lower order mechanisms of perception; (2) the cognitive processes contained in high-level language ability outstrips the lower perceptual processes which have 'a relatively primitive competence'[33] (meaning: that they literally cannot communicate with each other); and (3) the two, cognition and perception, are physically linked and can communicate but sometimes, when 'highly conditioned', the assumptions that the perceptual mechanisms employ can 'override' this higher processing.

The first two explanations, he notes, are compatible with Fodor's account of the informational encapsulation of perceptual modules; stressing that, for both reasons, the architecture and the assumptions of the module are 'inaccessible' to penetration by intellect, and so, operate autonomously. But Cam's point is that the third option also is 'not without grounds to recommend it.'[34] The advantage of the third option, he believes, is that it fits better with the facts. His argument is that the cases that Fodor considers to substantiate the encapsulation of the modules (lines, faces and so on) are 'arguably all highly conditioned by experience. Rooms are nearly always rectangular (at least in our culture), faces protrude, solid shafts that appear to join do join and so forth.'[35] The point is that if the perceptual mechanisms are constantly confronted by such stimuli with no intervening 'counteracting cues' then 'homebased assumptions might do just as well as ignorance of intellectual knowledge to account for the effects.'[36] Thus, the perceptual modules may be operating autonomously *not* because they are totally constrained from high-level features, but because they have been *conditioned* to function in that way.

The perceptual integrations of ambiguous stimuli support his case. In the case

---

[32] Philip Cam, 'Insularity and the Persistence of Perceptual illusion', pp. 231-43.
[33] Ibid., p. 232.
[34] Ibid., p. 233.
[35] Loc. cit.
[36] Loc. cit.

of the duck-rabbit where alternative perceptual possibilities feature, there are no overriding perceptual preferences made by the input systems and either 'construction' will do - hence, one's perceptual integration of the stimulus (how it *looks*) can also oscillate easily between cognitive interpretations. This is not so with strongly constrained perceptual information. In cases where homebased processing has 'solidified', this becomes increasingly less possible. (This is why, perhaps, the sun always seems to rise and the earth never seems to sink, despite our knowledge to the contrary, or that we can't help feeling an object when we run our fingers over it.) In Cam's view, only this latter kind of content, strictly speaking, seems to be informationally encapsulated in Fodor's sense.

The point is that 'rather than having informational encapsulation in some cases and permeability in others and the attendant difficulties upon sorting out why this might be, perhaps we should posit a single principle to cover them all. The principle would be (roughly) that perceptual analysis will accept instruction to the extent that its own preferences are not clear and univocal.'[37] Cam's claim, *contra* Fodor, is that the assumptions that low-level modules employ in integrating sensory stimuli do not always suggest encapsulation, bull-headedness or recalcitrance from conceptual processing, but an *insularity* or narrow-mindedness. The modules first call 'on their own resources', and they tend to be guided by information or suggestions intruding from other 'authorities' 'only to the extent that decisions based upon their local information base leave open further or alternative possibilities.'[38]

Unlike Fodor, Cam allows the possibility that the low-level architectural arrangement of the module is not 'permanently constrained' from high-level influences, but, to some degree, open to it for use when conditioned tendencies do not influence it in other ways. This seems to be a plausible suggestion and it is supported by empirical work suggestive of a more flexible arrangement between the influences of higher and lower content structuring.[39]

Cam's analysis of perceptual mechanisms seems on the surface to support a more subtle account of content than Fodor's modular view. On Cam's account, the information that the low-level processing units possess is conditioned by experience, though not determined by it, due to the conduits of sensation being informationally poor. Instead, early and constant sensory irradiation of particular kinds is sufficient to form constraints which make up the organic 'home-based preferences' of the lower-order informational system. And these preferences amount to primitive conceptions of things 'looking longer' etc.

However, the *prima facie* advantages of an insularity account should not go

---

[37] Loc. cit.

[38] Ibid., p. 234.

[39] Loc. cit. This account is particularly plausible in view of cases of Muller-Lyer decrement, where the illusion has been shown to reduce in effectiveness not through prolonged exposure, but 'cognitive recalibration.' (D. J. Schiano and K. Jordan: 'Mueller-Lyer Decrement: Practice or Prolonged Exposure', pp. 307-316). Though the evidence is ambiguous here, it seems to tell against the views that attribute illusion decrease to features of neural fatigue. By contrast, what seems to be central is learning and practice in response to experience as much as to features of the processing system. This seems to indicate that there must be experiential permeability of modules rather than encapsulation.

toward ruling out the encapsularity view. Fodor's account also allows for such subtleties if read correctly. There is no principled reason why the encapsularity view could not be seen to encompass such cases of content which seem clearly less dependent on the constraints of information contained in the modular architecture. The differences between the views may be simply a matter of emphasis. Fodor stresses examples where low-level content does not seem to be influenced by background knowledge; Cam stresses cases which demonstrate that occasionally it does seem to be influenced in this way. However, in principle, Fodor's modularity view remains as flexible as Cam's insularity view. Content which seems to be 'narrow-minded' in Cam's sense may also be seen to be informationally encapsulated, providing that encapsulation is understood to occur in levels or degrees.

I shall not attempt to adjudicate between these views as this issue is not central to this book. Whether the modules are best described as encapsulated or insulated is of no concern to me here. The important thing is that there is some degree of isolation of perceptual content from the mechanisms of high-level inference. However one interprets the insularity/modularity distinction, the important thing is that inferential input is not *necessary* for all forms of perceptual content. Both Fodor's and Cam's views suggest that this is indeed the case.

Something important follows from all this. If content can be said to have some independence from high-level reasoning and it is granted that experiences can have sensational aspects (as argued earlier), it seems natural to conclude that these features of content might be modular-like in Fodor's or Cam's sense. The examples of sensational properties offered in Chapter 5 might be best understood in terms of informational features of experience at a very low-level. And these features might function is just the way Fodor and Cam suggest (being relatively constrained from high-level influences).

Earlier chapters have argued that animal and infant experience, must be understood as contentful in some sense. It also seems natural to conclude, from the material just discussed, that the kind of perceptual outputs in question are just those that may be central to the perceptual systems of unsophisticated organisms. Modular-like informational content of an impurely sensational nature may be the kind of experiences had by such primitive creatures (in various degrees of complexity). This point seems to fit with the arguments against the inferentialist proposal offered earlier, for, as previously discussed, there is no good reason to deny contentful experiences of some kind in organisms which are phylogenetically related to us. This claim could be strengthened by taking seriously the suggestion that the deliverances of perceptual mechanisms are largely subject to selective pressures and that experiential content of all kinds has a causal role in perception. If true, then the origins of modularity might suggest a view of content susceptible to the influence of evolutionary pressures on developing perceptual mechanisms. The kinds of contentful outputs processed by the modules could thus be seen as being causally responsive to selectively important features in an organism's environment.

To factor in evolution here requires that low-level contentful information be seen in terms of an evolving system, responsive to relevant features of the world that system was engaged in, and able to process naturally; in other words, what were observable properties for that processing system. Such processing would be similar to Lorenz's 'organs' of the body being able to 'think' in certain forms. On this view, the nature of content should certainly be a part of an evolution-primed biological account of organisms.

To take an evolutionary line here means that the content of the informational modules would be responsive to both input and high-level cognition (if available). It would also be inherently flexible and could occur among species in *degrees*. Some unsophisticated organisms might not have high-level processing at all, only modular units; others might have some but considerably less than humans, and so on. This would also allow for the possibility that low-level inferential content (sub-descriptive inferences) may be available to fairly sophisticated animals, like dogs and chimpanzees. The outline of an account of this kind was given in Chapters 1 and 2. It is now suggested that some kind of modularity view goes some way to supporting a continuum account of content.

On the continuum account, at each extreme of the continuum there are quite separate structures to our perceptual organisation of experience: a lower-order level which contains sensory information, which is local to perceptual domains of 'looks', and a high-level structure which is influenced to some degree by these home-based preferences. Each kind of content is important in selective terms for experiencing organisms (an argument will be advanced for this in the next section). It is suggested here that in fact the lower level of perceptual integration is a kind of low-level concept which is informationally primitive, and to an important degree, insulated from the high-level influences. The home-based preferences which have these characteristics have been called 'sensational concepts' to distinguish them from other kinds of higher-level conceptualisations.

That a modular view of content rests well with a Lorenzian account of the naturalistic and organic basis of perceptual structure is convenient for my purposes. It is far easier and certainly more parsimonious to view the organism as a processing system which operates in response not only to mechanisms of inference, but also to selective pressures at an important lower-order sensory level: to contentful colour aspects and other such fairly undemanding discriminatory features, which need not be tied to high-level concepts and background knowledge etc. Moreover, it also seems instructive to see such a low-level ability, as Lorenz did, as an ability which can vary among species and creatures depending on their perceptual evolutionary bias. These points go together uncompromisingly well:

> The notion of constrained faculties views humans less as all-purpose machines and more as biological organisms that have, through the course of evolution, developed specialised 'mental organs' that are used to deal with different aspects of their physical and mental worlds. Each organ imposes its own set of constraints on the types of knowledge structures it uses, such that we have different domains of cognition with different formal properties.[40]

---

[40] F. C. Keil, 'Mechanisms of Cognitive Development and the Structure of Knowledge', in *Mechanisms of Cognitive Development*, p. 94.

Such an analysis rests well with an account of the perceptual structure that conceptually unsophisticated animals actually seem to have. It seems quite in order to suppose that some unsophisticated animal and infant cognition, though bereft of high-level content in the manner specified by the inferentialist proposal, is fixed around certain lower order conscious observables that evolution facilitates. It is not unreasonable to suppose that some such informational constraints on concept acquisition are exceedingly primitive and are possessed by less differentiated organisms, and perhaps even constitute the sum total of their conceptual repertoire. In such cases, the matter of high-level inference is of little practical consequence in determining the content of their observational experience.

Fodor's claim that there is a 'third mechanism' between proximal stimulations and high-level cognition has given a further reason to reject the inferentialist proposal. Cam's modification of this view, along with evolutionary considerations, indicates that content is sometimes narrow-minded, not encapsulated. Both of these views are supported by empirical work suggesting that content is constrained to some degree from high-level influences.

Campbell claims that Fodor's modularity thesis actually 'underwrites the return of the requirement to save ... Appearances.'[41] But he also claims that this doesn't imply a return to Cartesian foundationalism:

> It marks no limit in breadth or depth of vision, beyond which speculation may not pass ... [but] place[s] the onus for explaining any incompatibility between theory and common sense on the theoretical, speculative side of the disagreement ... It is for the theory, not the observation, to yield.[42]

Such an interpretation of modularity theory would be generally sympathetic to the points made in this book. Primitive observational looks, which fix kinds of experiential content, might remain importantly distinct from high-level influences. It is theory, not observation, that needs to yield. Experiential content, in my view, must be understood to occur in *degrees* of sophistication, and to some degree at least, it need not involve high-level inferences.

As we have seen earlier, there are reasons for adopting a view of content which embraces several levels of informational complexity. Content, we saw, occurs along a continuum, from sensationally specified, to content which is highly inferentially specified. The former is immune to the higher level influences to a degree which is significant. A principle of parsimony applied in this context might be that one should not extend one's mechanisms of inference beyond their domain of utility. The inferentialist account clearly does this, and so is a seriously misleading picture of experience and content.

Phenomenological accessibility and epiphenomenalism

There is one important thing to add. It will be noted that the stress being placing on the *conscious* nature of low-level content does not mesh well with the essentially functionalist program behind Fodor's modularity theory. If Fodor is

---

[41] K. Campbell, 'Philosophy and Common Sense', p. 172.
[42] Loc. cit.

a major support in my characterisation of experiential content, it would seem that I am backing a loser, because Fodor's characterisation of the sub-systems central to perceptual mechanisms makes no reference to conscious accessibility, but, instead, only to the various computational levels at which information is processed. Fodor and consciousness are, it would seem, strange bedfellows.

However, it is not the case that Fodor altogether eschews considerations of conscious perceptual contents, even though it is certainly true that it is not a mainstay of his computational program. In an endnote to *The Modularity of Mind,* Fodor angles for 'phenomenological accessibility as a criterion of the output of the visual processes'[43] and states explicitly:

> It seems to me that we want a notion of perceptual process that makes the deliverances of perception available as the premises of conscious decision and inferences ... I want a vocabulary for the output of the visual processor which specifies stimulus properties that are phenomenologically accessible and that are, by preference, reasonably close to those stimulus properties that we pretheoretically suppose to be visible.[44]

And again:

> [T]he activity of modules determines what you would believe *about the appearances* if you were going just on the appearances. Less gnomically: modules offer hypotheses about the instantiation of observable properties of things.[45]

This just seems to be a convoluted way of saying that it is selectively useful for perceptual content to have conscious *felt* qualities. To suggest that our experience of colour hues or of enlargements of the visual field, for instance, must be 'phenomenologically accessible' in the way that we 'pretheoretically' take them in experience means, in plainer words: there is something *qualitatively* important about stimulus properties for the activity of perceptual processing. The dynamics of perception requires content to have *sensational* features. Indeed, it must be the overarching aim of any account of perceptual content and structure to offer an account of how some experiences can have such *felt* aspects. Felt experiences, of course, require some degree of conscious accessibility.

There are good reasons why experiences should have felt aspects, so Fodor should not need to conceal the point. The reason is entirely naturalist: there must be a way certain experiences feel or seem for the subject because sometimes, in the imposition of high-level inferences, we get our experiences wrong; we mistake sharp projectiles for balloons or feather dusters. A contentful visual field experience, such that something is getting closer, *even when we may know it isn't,* is helpful in sorting out what kinds of experiences we need to *concentrate* on; the ones, for instance, that may cause us trouble or injury. Such

---

[43] J. Fodor, (1983) op. cit., p. 136.

[44] Loc. cit. I would like to thank G. J. O'Brien for drawing my attention to this passage.

[45] Fodor (1984), op. cit., p. 41.

'phenomenal' features are made available as material for conscious decision and inferences. Such material is informationally contentful without being heavily inferential (though it may be inferentially informed to some degree). This probably has a lot to do with our evolutionary past. It would seem plausible that not all experiences can be captured by the nature of representational features, beliefs *that*, or 'high-level' knowledge imposition. Some contentful experiential features just have *looks*, and so are selectively useful as primitive, but necessary, processing units available to later, more discerning intellectual evaluation.

This kind of backdown from a healthy functionalist stance must be expected: it must be remembered, finally, that Fodor's psychological account is but one stratagem in the quest for an adequate account of experiential content; it may well be that the problem needs to be supplemented by other philosophical considerations, some of which have been considered here. As mentioned in the Introduction, there are several non-exclusive ways of treating the issue of experience and content. One of those is to look at the issue in terms of the mechanisms of perceptual psychology; another is to bring in evolutionary considerations. Many such influences may ultimately be necessary. An important aim of this book is to integrate such themes in an overall account. The upshot is that, Pickwickian or not, Fodor's 'phenomenological accessibility' criterion should be seen as an important feature of his theory, just as a contentful sensory manifold should be an important part of Kant's.

A similar kind of reasoning must be engaged, moreover, to avoid the objection that low-level insulated modules are epiphenomenally *irrelevant* to experiential content. This problem arises only if it becomes an issue as to how the low-level, phenomenal features - 'aspects' of experiences - feed into high-level perceptual processing. But it is clear what response must be given here. It must be that it is simply a contingent fact that evolution has *favoured* organisms that have evolved with sense organs having such phenomenal experiential features.[46] On evolutionary grounds the reason for this is clear enough: low-level, non-inferential content is not epistemically *idle* because it gives sophisticated organisms the informational basis for making conscious decisions about whether certain perceptual information is a threat or not, even in view of perceptual mistakes. It also helps us to process information in perceptual shorthand: noticing a certain 'look' helps us to work out where inferences are to apply. Cognitive development at this sensational level assures that the processing eventuates in low-level informational content which helps to filter perceptual wheat from chaff. Low-level 'look'-beliefs, in other words, act as the watchdog on unbridled and erroneous inference-making.

There have been positions which argue for a contrary view. Frank Jackson, for example, has argued that certain felt properties of mental states - experiential 'qualia' - are such that 'their possession or absence makes no difference to the physical world.'[47] This commits him to saying that the kinds of conscious low-

---

[46] This is not so for non-organic creatures, machines, robots, etc., which might develop 'high-level' inferential knowledge (scientific theories etc.) without such low-level features. Daniel Dennett, Hilary Putnam and Paul Feyerabend have made much of this point. I treat Feyerabend's views in the next chapter.

[47] F. Jackson, 'Epiphenomenal Qualia,' p. 473. Rpt. in *Mind and Content: A Reader*.

level outputs, which I have suggested are importantly efficacious aspects to experiential content, are actually causally *irrelevant* to the kinds of perceptual processing we make about that world. Such a claim would seem to be implausible in the face of evolutionary theory: evolution sanctions traits that are *conducive* to survival, not irrelevant; hence such qualitative properties must have some kind of causal importance in the evolutionary scheme of things.

However, Jackson's reasoning against this is as follows: just as a polar bear has evolved a thick coat, so it has evolved a heavy one. A thick coat is survivally advantageous because it insulates the animal from the cold; a heavy one is not survivally advantageous because it slows the animal down. But it does not follow from this that such an example refutes the idea that some traits can be causally impotent. Just because a trait can evolve which is not conducive to survival does not come in conflict with Darwinism. This is because the heavy coat, in this case, is an 'unavoidable concomitant' of having a warm coat, 'and the advantages for survival of having a warm coat outweighed the disadvantages of having a heavy one.' According to Jackson: '[t]he point is that all we can extract from Darwin's theory is that we should expect any evolved characteristics to be either conducive to survival *or* a by-product of one that is so conducive.'[48] Jackson's claim is that the appeal to Darwinism does not refute the epiphenomenalist's story about qualia, because such features can be in the *latter* category and not the former.

However, the whole evolutionary issue in the context being considered does render it highly unlikely that low-level sensational contents are 'epiphenomenally idle'. The kinds of experiences which are phenomenologically accessible as outputs of the visual modules, do not seem to be like the heaviness of a polar bear coat; they do not seem to be merely causally inert by-products of some other evolutionary selected feature. Sensational experiences do seem to qualify as features of experiences which *mostly* have a genuine causal role: they seem to occur as primitive informational content for certain organisms which can direct them to action. Sensing an enlargement of the visual field or a colour hue, does seem to be causally useful because such features can filter perceptual information fast (allowing rapid application for more detailed processing) and hence, they can localise the application of high-level inference. They also allow the organism to call upon essentially simple processed features, which are easily stored, to aid in remembering more complex features of objects.[49] So there do seem to be good reasons for thinking that contentful, low-level aspects of experiences are not epiphenomenal, even though they may be experientially *sui generis*.

The argument I intend to advance against epiphenomenalism was originally spelt out in detail by Popper in his defence of interactionist dualism. Its implications have most recently been outlined by Daniel Shaw in his paper

---

[48] Ibid., p. 474.

[49] Remembering how a house looks on the strength of comparing such experienced features with the aid of paint samples is a trivial example. Recall Mortensen's and Nerlich's 'identikit picture' as an example which is suggestive of a more serious causal role for low-level content. (In this case, remembering sensory features helps to trigger more informative details about a suspect which may result in accurate identification later. I will expand on these examples in what follows.)

'Natural Selection and Epiphenomenalism'. The argument hinges on two assumptions: firstly, that natural selection is the only known theory, at present, which can explain the emergence of purposeful processes in the world (specifically, the evolution of higher forms of life); secondly, that conscious experiences consist of mostly structured and organised features which provide higher organisms with an instrument for survival. Shaw expresses the essentials of Popper's argument like this:

> (1): The Darwinian theory of natural selection is the best theory we have for explaining the existence of what would otherwise be highly improbable states of orderly organization that exist in the organic world.
> (2): The theory implies that all (or nearly all) standard features of the members of a species of living organism that are of a kind that display or are capable of displaying a high degree of orderly systematic organization, must have gradually evolved and thereby have come into existence in virtue of the adaptive effects which such features have upon the organism's physical behaviour in relation to its physical environment...
> (3): The experiential aspects of human beings are capable of displaying, and frequently do display, exceedingly high levels of orderly systematic organization ... When a mathematician thinks through the steps of a complex proof, when a composer consciously thinks his way through the construction of a musical work, when anyone ... puts his mind to planning his days' activities, his monthly budget, or his tax returns, the experiential aspect of what takes place takes on what, from the explanatory point of view, is an exceedingly high level of systematic order.
> (4) Therefore Darwinian theory implies that conscious experiences must affect, or else are very likely to affect the physical side of human behaviour and, through behaviour, the physical aspect of our environment.
> (5) Therefore Darwinian theory implies that epiphenomenalism is false or else is very likely false.[50]

Shaw's point is simply that epiphenomenalism does not account for the systematic order common to experiential states and conscious processes generally, whereas an account which appeals to Darwinian principles does. Darwinist principles make it seem likely that any such set of ordered states must have been selectively useful (being able to 'affect the physical side of human behaviour') in order to have evolved at all (it would not be sufficient simply to have occurred as a concomitant feature of some other selected characteristic).

It follows that if the experiential aspects of human perception *are* systematic and ordered, it is highly likely that they have been (or are currently) causally efficacious, and hence, must have been subject to selective pressures. And if such states have a causal origin which, in turn, has effects on organisms, the

---

[50] D. Shaw, 'Natural Selection and Epiphenomenalism', in *Issues in Evolutionary Epistemology*, pp. 576-7; K. Popper and J. Eccles, *The Self and its Brain: An Argument for Interactionism*, pp. 73-4.

particulars of an epiphenomenalist account of content must be seriously wrong. Against the epiphenomenalist's story, the conscious processes which have an organisation and structure must have been valuable at some stage of evolution because they did (or continue to do) some actual causal work.

It does seem likely that low-level contentful experiential states are systematic and ordered in an important sense. When one is asked to remember the face of a person for the purposes of a police investigation the memory search that one undertakes involves recalling, in a quite specific way, the circumstances of meeting that person and the details of their appearance. Much of this routine ability requires a fairly high degree of inferential capacity to be requisite, but equally, much of it does not. One can instantly say, for instance, (without drawing explicitly upon background knowledge) if the hair colour of the suspect was the same or different from the colour of the coffee cup the police sergeant is holding. One can say quite precisely if the nose was *like* the one pictured or not. Such recollected features seem to be quite precise and organised and the stimulus that triggers them quite structured and specific. The benefits of having such informational mechanisms is that they aid us in rapid identification of certain perceptual features which require immediate processing and which can be easily stored and retrieved for later use (one may not be able to remember exactly when or where one saw the person in question, though one can easily recall if his hair colour was or wasn't like *that*). It is hard to see how such conscious sensory discriminations can be understood in entirely epiphenomenal terms. Information like this does not seem to be a by-product of some other selected feature - it does seem to have a distinct causal role.

Peculiar to this ability is that this informational content need not be explicitly available to the conscious inferential resources of the individual (one may fail to recall the nose or hair colour when merely questioned and not shown pictures), but it is nonetheless a feature of the agent's conscious recollections. One may even be unable to say in which respects the hair colour or nose is similar or different to the examples shown in the identikit pictures (one's only response might be a garbled: 'that's the one!'). A similar ability is also required in recalling colours with the aid of paint samples. Having the ability to make such unnoticed, sensational discriminations - which can be only later brought to explicit consciousness - is, of course, consistent with the continuum account being proposed. Much of police work relies on an individual's possessing this sort of an informational retrieval system as does work in interior design, restoration and decoration. The kind of sensory features recalled also require a perceptual matching of certain experienced features with others currently in sight often in a quite specific spatial or temporal order. Doubtlessly, other areas of human endeavour require the same kind of non-inferential or sub-descriptive inferential discrimination (recalling in an exam the order in which traffic lights appear, for instance). Sensational content of this structured and organised nature does seem to fit with Popper's Darwinian argument, and runs against Jackson's views. The kind of features important here do not seem to be causally impotent by-products, but experiential features which are structured and essential for basic survival. They are essential in the sense that organisms which are equipped with such non-inferential discriminatory mechanisms can best retain certain features of low-level content and apply it in new circumstances requiring instant identification.

There is also a plausible reason why *explicit* conscious discriminatory abilities might have evolved in complex organisms. This is in addition to the benefits of low-level processing which need not be explicitly conscious. The reason has to do with Popper's notion of open and closed behavioural programs in evolving biological systems. According to Popper, open programs evolve by natural selection due to the complex and irregularly changing environmental situations. Closed programs, by contrast, lay down the behaviour of the animal in great detail thereby precluding the possibility of taking advantage of survival-promoting opportunities. It is clear, according to Popper, which system is the better one for complex, perceptual processing organisms like primates. His view is that, by being equipped with open perceptual programs, an organism can more readily adapt to rapidly changing environmental circumstances. Being conscious of one's perceptual environment, at various levels of explicit awareness, is an important part of this survival advantage and, hence, constitutes part of an open system in Popper's sense.[51]

So there are several related reasons for thinking that low-level experiential content is causally useful: such features are structured and stimulus specific; they allow for rapid identification of certain perceptual features and they are also closely connected to the survivalist benefits of open behaviour programs. For the reasons mentioned, it seems likely that such content does have causal importance in an organism's overall processing potential. In the light of this, epiphenomenalism does not seem adequate as a *full* story about the nature of mental content. (Perhaps it might count as a *partial* story, but more on this below.)

The doctrine of epiphenomenalism actually contains a crucial ambiguity which needs to be noted in this connection. It concerns the sense of the 'idleness' of phenomenal properties. Daniel Dennett has argued that epiphenomenalism is a confused doctrine: on the one hand, it refers to a nonfunctional property or by-product, which 'while perfectly detectable, play[s] no enabling role, no designed role in the process of feeling and thinking.'[52] On the other hand, it is used by philosophers to mean '[an] effect but [which] itself has no effects in the physical world whatever.'[53] Dennett claims that the second philosophical meaning is too strong; it yields a concept of no utility whatsoever: 'Since x has no physical effects (according to this definition), no instrument can detect the presence of x directly or indirectly; the way the world goes is not modulated in the slightest by the presence or absence of x. How, then, could there ever be any empirical reason to assert the presence or absence of x?'[54] Dennett attributes the first doctrine to Huxley and the second to the writings of Broad, though he claims that only the second usage has gained philosophical currency. However, the two versions, he suggests, are as different in meaning as *murder* and *death*.[55]

While any claim about such sensational features being epiphenomenal in the strict philosophical sense is rejected (on the grounds that low-level content

---

[51] See Popper, ibid., pp. 252-3; also see Shaw, ibid., p. 580.
[52] D. C. Dennett, *Consciousness Explained*, p. 402.
[53] Loc. cit
[54] Loc. cit.
[55] Loc. cit.

mostly seems to have a causal informational role), it is possible that certain *features* of an experience may be epiphenomenal in the weaker sense. The argument against epiphenomenalism given above relies on the point that conscious awareness is *mostly* structured and specific (and hence is likely to have causal importance in the life of the organism). It does not rule out fragmentary awarenesses that, while detectable, seem to be haphazard and arbitrary in their origin and purpose (after-images etc.) This kind of content needs some account too, and it does seem that this is best understood as an accompanying feature of some cognitive state, not one that has been specifically selected for. However, it seems that in view of the points given above, along with my overall argument in this book, we need not embrace an epiphenomenal account of content just to account for these cases. It seems plausible that this *non-functional* sense of epiphenomenalism can actually be reconciled with an account of low-level content as having causal import. It can be reconciled with such an account if the continuum theory is true. The way to approach the issue is to say that certain *aspects* of low-level content may be epiphenomenal in this sense. The suggestion I would make, consistent with my overall continuum approach, is that while modular processing units offer low-level informational content which is *mostly* causally useful, it may also be true that some experiences have epiphenomenal aspects (with non-functional effects) when they are not *focussed on* or *attended to* by the organism in question. When certain low-level content is an *unnoticed seeing,* such content may fail to have any functionally causal role. However, since such experiences *mostly* have a causal role, it means that epiphenomenalism is *for us* an inappropriate theory of mental content.

Calling Dennett's two senses of 'epiphenomenal', epiphenomenal$_H$ and epiphenomenal$_B$ (after Huxley and Broad), I suggest the following kinds of instances are possible as aspects of a sensational experience (the instances below exhibit increasing degrees from being causally functional to being epiphenomenal):

(i) An experience of a low-level kind (say, a colour hue) has a causal (non-epiphenomenal) role when it is noticed or stored in the memory (and remembered later), and which activates some further high-level processing about that experience (that it is an experience of a ripe tomato or is the same colour as a paint sample, for example).

(ii) A low-level registering of a colour hue *has had* an epiphenomenal$_H$ aspect when, *after the experience,* the subject may notice something about the experience (say, that the hue in question differs slightly compared with the hue of a neighbouring colour), but which, *at the time of the experience,* does not cause the subject to respond in any way to this information (he does not immediately notice the colour of a ripe tomato, for example, but can recall registering a difference in colour later when asked).

(iii) A low-level registering of a colour hue *has had* an epiphenomenal$_H$ aspect if, *at the time of the experience* it is unnoticed, but later, when asked, can be remembered by the subject to be 'somehow different' in some inspecific way from other regions of the experience, but which, *at the time of the experience,* does not cause the subject to respond in any way to this information. An example might be when features of a room have changed (a skylight has been added) but being unable to pin-point the change.

(iv) A low-level registering of a colour hue is strictly epiphenomenal*H* if it is not noticed and not recalled, and cannot be retrieved as being experienced at all. (A lower animal or insect might have *purely sensational* epiphenomenal experiences in this sense.)

An experience cannot have epiphenomenal*B* aspects, on my account, since such an aspect cannot, by definition, have any physical effect on a subject at all.

Note that since most *human* experiences are cases of (i); and (ii) and (iii) are features which may later go on to be causally efficacious when focussed on and remembered, it seems appropriate to reject epiphenomenalism as a theory of mental content. For us, as experiencing creatures, low-level content can be stored, remembered and focussed on and can thereby bring about certain effects. This kind of approach to the problem is consistent with my overall view, because the account of content being supported can have several kinds of features simultaneously (the complexity thesis); it has not been suggested that there can only be one kind of content (either highly structured or not). A view of content which is capable of possessing non-functional aspects is quite *typical* of experience, according to the continuum account. However, this should not go to suggest that epiphenomenalism is an accurate account of mentality altogether. To suggest that experience has non-functional aspects is not to say that experience is non-functional *simpliciter* (by parity, to say that valve amplifiers seem to be able to function without transistors should not lead one to conclude that transistor amplifiers should be able to do so too).[56]

A final issue here is the evolutionary story best suited to my account of experience and content. The claim here has been that low-level features are selected for various reasons and that while aspects of mental content might be epiphenomenal, the role of low-level experience is, typically, causally informational. However, the possibility that organisms *might* have evolved *entirely* with epiphenomenal experiential content in the non-functional sense can not be ruled out. This preserves the intuition Jackson raises above (it might have been the case that, like a polar bear's heavy coat, qualitative features of content may have been epiphenomenal). As mentioned elsewhere, it is also possible that organisms might have evolved experiencing no low-level phenomenal properties at all.

However, this is the wrong way of looking at the matter. Low-level qualitative properties do exist and do provide informational content. Evolution is also a 'best fit' matter; it is not a process which is necessarily well-designed for adaptation or originating ideal survivalist strategies.[57] Whether a causally informational role for low-level content is the best adaptive possibility available for complex organisms, or whether aspects of content which are epiphenomenal might have played a larger role, is not at issue here. It only needs to be remembered that low-level content is, for us, typically, causally effective, and this is the way which content features in normal human experience. This is the perceptual world we *do* seem to inhabit. The fact that some aspects of experience seem to be epiphenomenal in the sense that they have non-functional characteristics need not indicate that low-level content itself is without causal import.

---

[56] D. Shaw, op. cit., p. 582.
[57] See: S. J. Gould, *The Panda's Thumb*, passim.

Conclusion

The preceding four chapters were concerned with an account of mental content. It was first argued that experiences have content which cannot be captured in inferential terms. Kant's account of the mediation of content by intellect was then discussed. It was shown that there is a sense in which an already organised or structured basis of sensation is consonant with his views. It was also argued that Fodor's arguments against the poverty of the stimulus idea are essentially correct: that sensations are informationally poor does not mean that they do not supply a means to interpretation at all. All of these points support my contention that the structure of mental content need not be seen exclusively in inferentialist terms. Both historical and contemporary accounts of the nature of mentality seem to support a more subtle account.

It was suggested that any account of experience needs to be combined with a more realistic view of the low-level experiences of animals and other unsophisticated creatures. The inferentialist proposal ignores these considerations and arrives at absurd conclusions in this context. Contrary positions suggest that there are other ways of considering this matter. The evolutionary approach of Lorenz claims that experiential content is facilitated by adaptation, as much as other features of the body, and hence low-level content seems to have a selective purpose. The issue of epiphenomenalism was also discussed in this connection and low-level content was claimed to have a genuine causal role. It was submitted that only a continuum account of content can include all the above considerations.

Part Three
EXPERIENCE AND SCIENCE

9 Experience without Feyerabend

Conceiving a science without experience is an effective way of ... moving on to a more comprehensive and more satisfactory kind of philosophy.[1]

A science without experience?

Introduction

It has been argued that the inferentialist proposal is deficient in several ways and that an adequate understanding of such issues must see a number of levels of structure applied to experiential content - one accessible to inferential input; the other consisting of content selectively structured around the detection of low-level sensory features. The continuum view also allows that there can be various sub-levels in between these extremes. The arguments against the inferentialist proposal so far have been rather general in nature. This chapter narrows the focus to criticise a specific kind of inferentialism in the philosophy of science.

Experience in the philosophy of science

Experience, as a category, is usually considered to feature as an important factor in outlining an adequate philosophy of science. However, there is much dispute about how this should be conceived. Specifically, there is a great debate about the exact relation between experience (given in 'observation'), the theoretical superstructure which may underpin such observations, and how a language of observations is to be given 'meaning'. We can take 'observational terms' to be such things as colour and shape words, and 'theoretical terms' to be 'electron', 'mass,' 'is a quark' etc. The question that arises here is ostensibly semantic: science employs both sorts of terms, but, problematically, the origins of their

---

[1] P. K. Feyerabend, 'Science Without Experience', in Collected Works, *Realism, Rationalism and Scientific Method,* Vol. 1, p. 135.

meanings seem very different. The first sort of term seems to be *observationally based,* whilst the second seems to be *inferentially based.* The broader debate about this issue, however, has come to centre on whether 'scientific theories and other general assumptions are nothing but convenient means for the systematization of the data of experience'[2] or whether 'experience *arises together* with our theoretical assumptions.'[3] The first option, broadly speaking, is generally taken to be *positivist* in spirit (what we observe and describe with our 'O-terms' is *given* in experience); the second, which has arisen in response to the first, is a fairly recent consequence of the move to *conflate* observational and theoretical terms, and to make the origin of their meaning come from the one and the same theoretical (and hence, *inferential*) source. The two relevant options here were outlined when discussing the historical origins of the inferentialist proposal in Part I of this book.

Much discussion has gone on over the issue of incommensurability which has been part and parcel of this debate. Such details will not be ventured into here. Instead, the differences between the two claims will be outlined and brought to bear on the issue of the content of observational experience. The central point for this purpose is that there are two approaches to the question of the relation of observation to theory. One supposedly amounting to a positivist account, stressing the importance of experience to the meaning of observational terms; the other amounting to an account which sees observational experience, as expressed in observational reports, as *originating in theories.* This chapter will reject the basis of the *second* account which seeks to make 'observational experience' simply a contrivance of *descriptions* or theoretical structures. It will be argued that this view presupposes a sense of experience which it cannot explain in such terms and, although the resultant position is not positivist, it is not entirely experience-free either. Ultimately, it can be argued that this approach can be traced to the conflation between observational terms and observational experience outlined in Chapter 3.

In what follows, the central concern will be Paul Feyerabend's rejection of the category of experience in the philosophy of science. Feyerabend's attacks are launched at the doctrine of positivism which he takes all experience-based accounts to assume. He offers compelling arguments to reject positivism and outlines grounds for a 'science without experience.' The claim here is that a rejection of positivism does not require a rejection of the importance of low-level experiential content, so Feyerabend's attacks are seriously misplaced. In arguing this, it shall simultaneously be argued that there is good sense in the claim that the *meaning* of observational terms is *not* given in experience. This chapter attempts this task, but not without changing the relationship between 'experience' and 'positivism' slightly in the process.

Positivism: what it is; how to be rid of it

In 'An Attempt at a Realistic Interpretation of Experience',[4] P. K. Feyerabend sets about eliminating the positivist notion that the *meaning* of an observational

---

[2] Ibid., p. 20. 'An Attempt at a Realistic Interpretation of Experience'.

[3] Ibid., p. 133.

[4] Ibid., p. 17.

term can be given somehow in experience. His analysis has a number of lines of attack. His main claim seems to be that the interpretation of an observational sentence such as 'I see red' is not logically *determined* by a given observational situation, even though this situation may evoke the acceptance or rejection of a sentence. Implicit in his approach is that while 'experience' as a category is normally said to be *given* by such circumstances, it actually arises out of our theoretical assumptions which crucially underpin our observational language.

In this important sense, Feyerabend is a clear advocate of what has been termed the inferentialist proposal. He claims that a child 'possesses means of interpretation even before he has experienced his first sensation.'[5] Since this theoretical approach, in Feyerabend's view, amounts to a rejection of the observational situation as a basis for experience (and offers instead its theory dependence), we shall have to look in detail at the supports for this claim. It shall be argued that this claim is wrong.

Philosophers have long argued that the observation-theory distinction could not be sustained; a factor which opened the way for a 'theory laden' conception of observation language. Feyerabend is also a strong advocate of this view, and uses it to launch his attack upon the 'positivist' conception of experience. The positivist view of experience is that content is best described in terms of what is 'given' in observation; it is this which is the basis for our observation language. (Later, it shall be questioned whether all positions which strongly emphasise experience as a fundamental category need, perforce, to be seen as 'positivist'.) First, the arguments against positivism as Feyerabend presents them.

The arguments against positivism

Feyerabend first takes the positivist conception to be an expression of what he calls a 'stability thesis': the commitment to the view that *'interpretations ... do not depend upon the status of theoretical knowledge.'*[6] He takes both instrumentalism and positivism as being expressions of this thesis: instrumentalism, because it takes theories to be 'tools for the prediction of events of a certain kind' and, at the same time, *denies* that these theories actually *describe* anything; and positivism, because it holds that *experience,* not theories, yields the structure of our interpretations given to our theoretical language, and in which our network of observation sentences are contained. The commitment to a stability thesis, particularly of a positivist kind, Feyerabend feels, is the ruin of any realistic characterisation of experience.

His argument goes as follows: a positivist conception, such as the one outlined, has *ontological consequences,* and some of these consequences may turn out to be false *even though we can't determine them as such.* His point is that if we use such an experience-based language, even just in communication, we already cannot but commit ourselves ontologically to certain general states of affairs, and we cannot assess them as being anything other than *true* on the basis of the language schema and metaphysic we are presupposing. He explains:

---

[5] Ibid., p. 133.
[6] Ibid., p. 20.

> [W]e make assertions not only by *formulating* ... a *sentence* (or a theory) and asserting that it is true, but also by *using a language* as a means of communication. Thus, when using natural numbers for counting objects ... we assume ... (1) that these objects are discrete entities which can always be arranged in a series, and (2) that the result of our counting is independent of the order in which we proceed ... However plausible these two assumptions may be, there is no *a priori* reason why they should be true.[7]

This may seem a strange turn, but Feyerabend continues:

> [I]t follows, (1) that those ontological consequences cannot have emerged as a result of empirical research (for if this were the case, the stability thesis would have been violated at some time in the past); (2) nor would it ever be possible to show by empirical research that they are incorrect (for if this were the case the stability thesis would have been violated at some time in the future). Hence, ... we arrive at the result that *every positivistic observation language is based upon a metaphysical ontology*.[8]

Feyerabend's argument here is that the positivist commits a flagrant case of *petitio principii*. Taking on credit a positivist model, which assumes the language of beliefs to be 'stable' constructs arising directly in response to experiential data, means that the observation language cannot possibly be *determined* as an adequate or *justified* language, without the metaphysic (the 'interpretation') which such a language describes being assumed *true,* and this is clearly a case of begging the question. The problem here is that the positivist *assumes* the stability thesis to start with, and so, cannot be in a position to justify their own language independent of the metaphysic of positivism. Pointing out that positivism begs the question naturally goes a good way to getting rid of it.

However, there are at least two recourses to justify such a positivist basis for meaning in language which Feyerabend notes: (i) the interpretation of the language can be defined and justified by its characteristics in use (the so-called *principle of pragmatic meaning);* and (ii) it can be justified by its 'given' in experience (the *principle of phenomenological meaning).* But Feyerabend ultimately wants to say that *neither* of these options works for the positivist. We shall see how he rejects these proposals and how the conclusion Feyerabend arrives at is sound in some sense, though strikingly inconclusive in another. Feyerabend may be right about the positivist failings on the question of how observational terms get their meaning, but this does not mean that 'experience arises together with theoretical assumptions and not before them.' Feyerabend's analysis commits the standard inferentialist overkill regarding the dependence of experiential content on features of high-level inference. And so, in an important sense, his claims for a 'science without experience' will not go through. More on this later.

---

[7] Loc. cit.
[8] Ibid., p. 21.

Positivist responses and Feyerabend's reply

Let's take first: the *principle of pragmatic meaning*. Feyerabend argues that if one claims that the conditions under which a language is *asserted* (i.e., the practical situation of the utterance) are important, then we would need to show why it is that any *particular* conditions of assertability are both sufficient and necessary for the meaning of the utterance over and above other similar conditions. Any reliance on practical conditions would seem to be arbitrary. In comparing the human being with a physical instrument in terms of the ability to receive data, Feyerabend says:

> [T]he fact that in certain situations it consistently reacts in a well defined way does not allow us to infer (logically) what those reactions mean: first, because the existence of a certain observational ability ... is compatible with the most diverse interpretations of the things observed; and secondly, because no set of observations is even sufficient for us to infer (logically) any one of the interpretations (problem of induction). ... the fact that in a certain situation he (consistently) produces a certain noise, does not allow us to infer what this noise means.[9]

These would seem to be unnecessarily sceptical arguments. The practical conditions of assertability *seem* to be relevant to utterance meaning. But the burden of avoiding the argument by saying how they are clearly rests upon the proponent of the positivist account. If one cannot give a *precise* account of the practical situation of making a certain utterance in relation to any number of sets of observations, then it hardly gives any strength to the assertion that the meaning of our expressions are 'given' in such a way, and it is simply playing one's own hand to suggest otherwise.

Feyerabend is not using 'pragmatic' here to designate some kind of Wittgensteinian position on language in terms of meaning being garnered from typical use situations or 'language games'. Feyerabend actually gives qualified support for this sort of picture of language in some of his other writings.[10] Meanings of terms are not, in Feyerabend's view, separate from the practice of using them. The point of the *principle of pragmatic meaning* that Feyerabend attacks is the claim that the meaning of a particular term is *only* determined by the person's tendency to produce it in connection with certain experiences. This is a much *narrower* notion of 'pragmatic' situations than adumbrated by Wittgenstein, and more closely ties meaning to experience. S. G. Couvalis explains this difference in the following manner:

> Consider the following case: whenever a person X observes what we call a meteor he utters the expression A. A speaker of our language in the same circumstances says 'a meteor'. According to the upholders of the principle of pragmatic meaning, A and 'meteor' (or 'a meteor') would mean much the same. But a Wittgensteinian would need to know much

---

[9] Ibid., p. 22.
[10] Notably 'Wittgenstein's Philosophical Investigations,' Revised and Rpt. in P. K. Feyerabend, *Philosophical Papers*, Vol. 2, pp. 99-130.

more about the utterance of A by X. Suppose X's tone is consistently reverential or fearful when he utters A; this might indicate that A means some kind of supernatural being or phenomenon rather than 'a meteor.'[11]

The point is that on the one version of the pragmatics of meaning the whole social group and cultural context is involved (the 'language game'), while on the other, the situational presence of certain experiences are (allegedly) sufficient. And, as has been outlined, Feyerabend's response to this is that the principle of pragmatic meaning does not get us past first base in justifying this principle.

The other way of justifying such an interpretation of observation language is the *principle of phenomenological meaning*. This argument is more important for our purposes, and Feyerabend spells out this strategy clearly:

> The principle of phenomenological meaning assumes that ... in order to explain to a person what 'red' means one need only to create circumstances in which red is experienced. ... [T]he meaning of an observational term is determined by what is 'immediately given' at the moment of the acceptance of any observational sentence containing that term.[12]

In this approach, 'positivist' in the true sense, we are to imagine the 'properties of things ... and their relations being 'read off' the experiences without any difficulty being felt.'[13] That is, the acceptance (or rejection) of the description of these things are uniquely determined by the observational situation. The view here sees some level of interpretation being given non-inferentially; specifically, the *meaning* of observational terms is determined by the observational situation. 'Descriptions of the observational situation' seems to mean for Feyerabend something like: 'constitutes the justification for the *holding of a certain statement* about a state of affairs'. This will be an important point of difference later, because the importance of experience as a category in the philosophy of science, can be held *without* the joint claim about determinations of meanings or descriptions.

Feyerabend attacks the principle of phenomenological meaning with force. The whole idea, he rightly declares, amounts to a *reductio ad absurdum*. In order for an observer of a phenomenon to determine whether or not an experience 'fits' (adequately) an observation sentence which describes it, he would need to 'attend to' not only the experience and the sentence *but also the relation between them* - and, in order to determine whether *this* was adequate, he would need to experience *further* relations between the two terms to ensure their adequacy. An infinite regress would be the inevitable result.

Feyerabend concludes that in such circumstances, 'the conditions of adequate report which we are considering at this moment are such that no observer will

---

[11] S. G. Couvalis, *Feyerabend's Critique of Foundationalism*, p. 4.
[12] Feyerabend, Vol. 1, op. cit., p. 25.
[13] Loc. cit.

ever be able to say anything.'[14] This is clearly a 'patently absurd'[15] position. And he points out that it would mean also that we would have to be parochial about what experiences we *select* as our 'proper' ground for the meaning of our utterances, and what experiences we selectively omit from such considerations. Any number of 'attendant' experiences can be said to be built into the relations of phenomenological adequacy; it is simply insupportable to suggest that one can rule out as insignificant some over others without grounds for doing so. And it is no good simply to appeal to the 'brute fact' of some experiences over others, for this accomplishes little. Echoing strains of Wittgenstein, Feyerabend says:

> It is no good repeating, 'but I *experience* p', for the question discussed is not what is experienced, but whether what is experienced is *described* adequately. And we have shown that this question cannot be answered by appealing to the relation of phenomenological adequacy.[16]

The issue here is *how* the relation of phenomenological adequacy can account for the *descriptions* of a sentence in reference to an experience. If a regress in the etiological circumstances of experiences and observational terms can be shown as a consequence of this sort of foundationalism, then a proponent of the principle of phenomenological meaning cannot, at least, appeal to *that*. But are there other options open? As Couvalis notes,[17] a relation of phenomenological adequacy between sentence 'S' and experience 'P' may be given an account in terms of *intentions*. 'S' describes 'P' would then be a matter of explaining how a speaker (or hearer) *gets the intention,* when 'S' is uttered in response to 'P'. But again, either the intention must be seen to be phenomenologically adequate to the term (and hence, regress), or the intention must simply be possessed somehow by the relevant parties when 'S' is uttered. But even if an intention could be possessed in this manner, how would it help? Surely the whole point of the principle of phenomenological meaning is to account for how meaning describes phenomenological situations (experiences)? Language users must be sure of this descriptive relation and the adequacy of the term used. If not, then there is no basis for saying that the meaning of an observational term is (logically) given by experiential circumstances. Couvalis concludes by asserting:

> 'S' describes 'P' as an observational term, implies that there must be some experience of which this 'describes' is a phenomenologically adequate description. But: ... we are not aware of any such experiences when we think that some term describes something. All we are aware of that is relevant is that term and the thing that it denotes. There is thus no empirical evidence of the existence of such experiences [*sic.*] This means that 'describes' cannot be an observational term and 'S' describes 'P'

---

[14] Ibid., p. 26.
[15] Loc. cit.
[16] Loc. cit.
[17] Couvalis op. cit., p. 6.

cannot be an observational sentence.[18]

The point here, of course, is that if it can be shown that experiences cannot give the meaning of observational terms, then it becomes doubtful whether experiences actually *contribute* anything at all to a subject's using a sentence to describe some experience. Of interest are only the observational term used and the thing it denotes. And if this is the case, then it becomes clear that a relation of phenomenological adequacy does not secure the interpretation of observational terms and for such an account we need to look elsewhere.

Another related way in which Feyerabend or his defenders could have laboured the point here would be to point out that the principle of phenomenological meaning is actually *circular* in its implication: in order to give an account of some phenomenon *p* in our experience (say, the colour red), we would need to use the word 'red' (and the concept 'red'). But then no account for the experience of the colour red could be given, because we needed the word 'red' to describe it. This brings out the point that Feyerabend wants to make: for with both the principle of pragmatic meaning and the principle of phenomenological meaning shown to be deficient, the claim is that, for an adequate account of the meaning of observational terms, we must turn to the imposition of 'high-level' theories and concepts. Alan Chalmers has highlighted this move in outlining a problem with the inductivist theory of knowledge:

> From all the perceptual experiences of an observer arising from the sense of sight, a certain set of them (those corresponding to the perceptual experiences arising from sightings of red objects) will have something in common. The observer, by inspection of the set, is somehow able to discern the common element in these perceptions, and come to understand this common element as redness. In this way, the concept 'red' is arrived at through observation. This account contains a serious flaw. It assumes that from all the infinity of perceptual experiences undergone by an observer, the set of perceptual experiences arising from the viewing of red things is somehow available for inspection. But that set does not select itself. What is the criterion according to which some perceptual experiences are included in the set and others excluded? The criterion, of course, is that only perceptions of *red* objects are included in the set. The account presupposes the very concept, redness, the acquisition of which it is meant to explain. It is not an adequate defence of the inductivist position to point out that parents and teachers select a set of red objects when teaching children to understand the concept 'red', for we are interested in *how the concept first acquired its meaning*. The claim that the concept 'red' is delivered from experience and from nothing else is false.[19]

Both of these objections hinge upon the same point: we cannot give an account of the meaning of experiential terms such as 'red' without presupposing the meaning of the high-level concept and hence a relation with what it is supposed

---

[18] Ibid., pp. 7-8.
[19] A.H. Chalmers, *What is this Thing Called Science?* pp. 29-30. Italics mine.

to 'match' when we use it. Feyerabend's point would then follow that the positivist assertion of the stability thesis is false. For him, 'positivism sooner or later leads to subjectivism.'[20] But, on reasoning such as he has given, observational terms *do* depend on the status of theoretical knowledge, and (following Couvalis's point) all that we actually seem to be aware of that is relevant in an observational situation is the term used and the thing denoted, not the experience. It is such considerations which lead Feyerabend to say: 'Phenomena [experiences] cannot determine meaning, although the fact that we have adopted a certain interpretation may (psychologically) determine the phenomena.'[21] It also leads him to consider the possibility that a 'natural science without sensory elements ... is neither absurd nor contradictory.'[22]

The overkill of the inferentialist's argument

> It must be possible to imagine a natural science without sensory elements, and ... indicate how such a science is going to work.[23]

There seems to be a great danger of concluding too much here about the consequences of Feyerabend's argument. This would be easy to do because Feyerabend is systematically *ambiguous* on the matter of what his rejection of the above arguments is supposed to demonstrate. Is all we are aware of in an 'observational situation' the term and the thing the term denotes or represents? Can we therefore have a 'science without experience'? Maybe not: maybe we also have observational experiences with certain sensational properties which do not themselves denote or represent, and such 'sensory elements' may be important in the way *we* do science. As pointed out in Chapter 5, Christopher Peacocke, among others, has argued convincingly that there is more to experiential contents than its 'representational content.' The latter is expressed in terms denoting the specifications of the 'observational situation' of objects and their representational features in the world; the sensational properties, he claims, cannot be so specified. On Peacocke's view, there are certain non-representational, 'sensational' properties of experiences, such as when a tree visually represented as the same physical height as another tree in the observational situation nonetheless seems to take up more of the visual field in some interesting qualitative, but non-representational sense. Something well worth considering here is that such low-level contents, though less important to doing science than the contents that can be captured representationally or propositionally, may yet feature in ordinary, everyday scientific activity. In short, Feyerabend's claim that we can have a science without sensory elements may be false.

The point here is this: one *might* agree wholeheartedly that whatever the relation between observational terms and observational experiences, it is a relation which does *not* fix meanings or high-level descriptions. As Feyerabend argues, it may be merely a *pragmatic* matter what sentences are asserted in

---

[20] Feyerabend, Vol. 1, op. cit., p. 35.
[21] Ibid., p. 27.
[22] Ibid., p. 132.
[23] Ibid., p. 132.

certain circumstances.[24] But though experiences might not fix meanings, does this warrant the seemingly *stronger* claim that 'we are not aware of any such experiences' etc., when we are using observational terms (or even when we are not: for instance, infants and animals)? Couvalis, for one, comes *very close* to saying in the above passage that because the principle of phenomenological meaning does not guarantee a descriptive link between meanings and experiences, that therefore *no sense* can be made of the notion of observational experiences in or outside the context of asserting and describing or responding to a certain representative situation. As shall be shown below, Feyerabend also seems to say this. But this claim should be seriously reconsidered. It is my contention that where *in places* Feyerabend seems to be arguing simply (and importantly) that experiences are not adequate to fulfilling a contentful role in the determination of the meaning of observational *terms* (instead, theoretical *descriptions* of observational experiences in theories *are* adequate to this role, in Feyerabend's view), he *also* seems to be arguing in places that there is no room in such a context for contentful observational experiences which are not themselves theory dependent. Hence, remarks of this kind, in his preface and elsewhere, seem to be either slips between these alternatives, or a positive equivocation of the latter, more radical, claim:

> [O]bservations (observational terms) are not merely theory *laden,* (the position of Hanson, Hesse and others), but *fully theoretical* (observation statements have no 'observational core').[25]

> The only difference between a blind person and a seeing person consists in the fact that the first one uses a different part of the theory (or some of the consequences of the theory) as his observation language.[26]

> Experience *arises together* with theoretical assumptions and *not* before them, and that an experience without theories is just as incomprehensible as (allegedly) a theory without experience: eliminate part of the theoretical knowledge of a sensing subject and you have a person who is completely disorientated, incapable of carrying out the simplest action.[27]

From such comments it is clear that there are two agendas here. The claim that experiences arise together with theories and have no observational core, and the assertion that the blind are deficient only in respect of using a different part of a theory, are quite different claims from the attack on the positivist account of

---

[24] Feyerabend's 'pragmatic' analysis of endorsing languages is the view that 'appropriate situations' (s) are presented to classes of human beings (C) in a circumstance such that certain atomic sentences (a) of a set (A) will necessitate the event 'such that every C when presented with a in s will run through a series of states and operations which terminates either in the acceptance of a or in its rejection by the C chosen.' Thus, we can that a subject has the ability to distinguish between situations when it can produce a specific reaction r whenever s is present, and does not produce r when s is absent. Feyerabend, op. cit., pp. 18-19.

[25] Ibid., p. x.

[26] Ibid., p. 33.

[27] Ibid., p. 133.

how observational terms get their meanings. It seems that Feyerabend might be guilty of confusing two issues: the issue of the inferential nature of observational language and the issue of the inferential nature of observational *experience*. Feyerabend seems to be implicitly committed to the latter while being explicitly committed to the former.

This sort of slippery slope from the theory dependence of observational terms to the theory dependence of observational experience has a long history. Such passages as those given above make Feyerabend a defender of the inferentialist proposal. Such claims can also be seen to feature, innocently, in the claims of Hanson, Sellars and Churchland, among others. But the implications of this sleight of hand are profound. One may well wonder at the consequences the above claims might have for animals and infants and *their* experiences. If one assumes the common sense view that such creatures have no theories, then it is hard to know what to make of the suggestion, for it does not seems plausible that a theoryless dog lacks experiences of some primitive kind because it is theoryless. The counterintuitive consequences of any commitment to an inferentialist account of content for animal experiences were discussed in Chapter 7.

To rebel against such a view seems natural: one could insist, in contrast to the muddle of the first quotation, that there is quite a firm distinction between 'observational *terms*' and 'observations' (one, properly, has a *semantic* content, the other need not - not all aspects of experiential content, in other words, are propositional linguistic). A distinction can thus be made between inferential *descriptions* of observations as opposed to non-inferential experiences of certain low-level sensations. (Animals and infants would thus, on this view, be experiencing organisms despite being theoretically *in vacuo*.) Similarly, one could insist, in contrast to the second quotation, that there is more to the experience of a sighted person than that of a blind person which does not have anything to do with theories and meanings (something instead which has a good deal to do with sensory, non-representational features like that of what has been called non-inferential 'aspects' of experiential content, such as the primitive experiences of colours, visual field enlargements, and so on). And similarly for the third quotation. A dog which *ex hypothesi* has no theories or descriptions would thus not be 'disorientated' etc., *because* it lacked these hypostatised features. Throughout this book, the case has been presented for a distinction between the high-level aspects of content and low-level (non-descriptive and non-representational) aspects.

But there is a more direct point here. One could hold a number of things in response to Feyerabend's replies to the threat of positivism, because there are essentially two issues being articulated: one revolving around *meanings* (and their determinations) and one revolving around *experiences*. Feyerabend *assumes* that 'the observational situation determines (causally) the acceptance or rejection of a sentence'[28] as being an entirely physical/pragmatic event, and such observations are always subject to the additional act of theoretical interpretation and thereby, given meaning. But, as these are unargued assumptions,[29] one is, at least, open to assert the contrary view: that

---

[28] Ibid., p. 19.
[29] See 'An Attempt at a Realistic Interpretation of Experience.' op. cit.

Feyerabend's emphasis on high-level interpretation is too inferentialist to be a fully accurate account of experiences, and that something in the initial 'observational situation' itself in fact provides some primitive level of organisation (*albeit* an organisation which is *non-semantic*). If anything like what has been suggested regarding the sensory content of experience is true, then it would seem that this could constitute a case against Feyerabend. One might claim, in other words, that Feyerabend's treatment of the issues of experience and theoretical interpretation *jointly* is an arbitrary and misleading view, and that asserting the one need not imply the other. There still might be a sense in which a level of content view, along the lines of the continuum theory, may make more sense as a response to both positivism and the inferentialist proposal. This is the line that will be taken later on.

If one could hold this, then one could simultaneously agree with Feyerabend, and reject any positivist account which tries to give an account of the meaning of observational terms (call it: 'Feyerabend's *overt* thesis'), while *also* holding that there is an important sense in which experiences are *non-theoretical and descriptions and meanings do not fully capture their content* (and so reject the import of what I shall call 'Feyerabend's *covert* thesis'). It is, after all, not obvious that Feyerabend is *confining* his remarks to the former overt claim, even though it would appear that they can be held separately and we can affirm the one and not the other.

This confusion may arise from an error in what positivism is supposed to mean as a philosophical doctrine, and what the observational-theoretical distinction in philosophy is supposed to achieve. Feyerabend clearly thinks that the latter is all about different aspects of *language,* and how language is given meaning in the context of science, and the relevance of the notions of prediction and explanation.[30] But clearly, the T-O distinction is also *primarily* about the differences between the *ontological* categories of observational experiences and scientific theories, though the distinction slides very easily between these two concerns. It is suggested here that, like the inferentialist proposal generally, Feyerabend is guilty of *conflating* these two issues.

As for positivism, although this may traditionally be said to be a philosophical position which attempted to derive everything from a foundation of experience (as mentioned, Feyerabend thinks that positivism 'sooner or later leads to subjectivism'), it does not seem to me that holding that experience is a central and important category means that *one thereby accepts the idea that experiences fix the meanings of observational terms, or that this important sense of experience is itself foundational.* One could, in other words, *agree* that the sensational contents of certain non-inferential, low-level experiences do not give the meaning of theoretical terms, and thus *agree* with Feyerabend's *overt* thesis and his rejection of the principles of pragmatic and phenomenological meaning, while also holding that there are contents which are associated with the sensational aspect of such experiences, which are actually not descriptive (like that of a language), and thus *disagree* with Feyerabend's *covert* thesis. And one

---

[30] The introductory remarks to 'An Attempt at a Realistic Interpretation of Experience' is enough to demonstrate this: 'Within science a rough distinction is drawn between theory and observation. This distinction can best be explained by formulating the conditions which a language must satisfy in order to be acceptable as a means of describing the results of observation and experiment.' ibid., pp. 17-18.

could hold all this and still not be a positivist.

In such a case, it would be debatable if one were adhering to any form of known positivism; though if it was a variation of positivism, it is demonstrably not the form that Feyerabend attacks. Feyerabend's arguments merely touch the view that positivism fixes the meaning of observational terms. All his arguments seem to have shown is that phenomenological situations do not determine *meaning*. However, there may be a way of agreeing with this claim and still keeping a sense in which experience is an important category in both the fixation of perceptual content and the practice of science (at least in the way *we* do it).[31] And one might be able to do this without being a 'positivist' in the sense Feyerabend is attacking the doctrine. Perhaps the issue at stake here might be a mere semantic point about what we mean by 'positivism', but it is possible that this revised form is not a form of positivism at all.

Thus, there are two discernible and distinguishable claims that arise out of Feyerabend's attack on positivism: (1) sensational experiences do not give the meaning of observational *terms;* and (2) such experiences do not have any 'observational core', but are instead, *fully theoretical*. The latter claim, is a broader notion, and as an *inferentialist* response would certainly be congruent with Feyerabend's later relativist views on the philosophy of science, but it also fits in with his remarks in 'Science without Experience' where he asserts that: 'sensation can be eliminated from the process of understanding' (in particular, natural science)[32] and - more explicitly - his hopeful claim: 'It must be possible to imagine a natural science without sensory elements.'[33]

Such remarks seem to indicate that Feyerabend thinks not only that it is possible to do science without using experience (because observational data do not fix interpretations) but also that science should be conceived *without* sensory elements at all - i.e., sensations do not *exist* outside of the interpretations (the meanings) that are given in theoretical situations. This latter claim is clearly inferentialist in the sense that used here, and is much more radical than the former (anti-positivist) claim.

But the covert thesis rests uneasily in an important sense here, as, for the most part, Feyerabend only seems to be arguing for the former, *weaker* claim. What *is* Feyerabend's position? It is this subtle ambiguity that will concern us later, for I want to affirm the *lesser* claim and *deny* the stronger claim; so we will need to find out exactly where Feyerabend stands in order to decide whether to jettison his general approach. As we shall see, with appropriate modifications, we will not have to. But with such modifications, we will once again be forced to turn from the inferentialist proposal Feyerabend seems to be

---

[31] It may not be an important feature in a society of extra-terrestrials who 'do' science but who are not constructed just as we are, with our sense organs, etc.

[32] He imagines a situation in which a computer without experience could assess the results of empirical measurements: 'To start with [experience] does not need to enter the process of *test:* we can put a theory into a computer, provide the computer with suitable instruments directed by him (her, it) so that the relevant measurements are made which return to the computer, leading there to an evaluation of the theory. The computer can give a simple yes-no response from which a scientist may learn whether or not a theory has been confirmed without having in any way participated in the test (i.e. without having been subjected to some relevant experience).' Ibid., Vol. 1, pp. 132-4.

[33] Loc. cit.

adopting, to a more subtle and elaborated account along the lines of the continuum account.

Forcing Feyerabend out in the open

Some speculation: the rejection of the principle of pragmatic meaning and the principle of phenomenological meaning has more significance than might initially be thought, if one looks at the import of Feyerabend's general theoretical strategy developed in *Against Method* and elsewhere. In fact, their rejection would seem to bottom out rather easily into the well-known and radical consequences which Feyerabend takes to be characteristic of the scientific enterprise. For if we can't make sense of the interpretation of our theoretical languages as being determined by either experience or the practical conditions of their assertability (and if we have no other obvious alternatives), then it seems that we have no good reason to think that such interpretations *can* be given good account. They become, as a result, little more than our 'prejudices' which influence our 'general ideas about things and their properties.'[34] On Feyerabend's well known *relativist* views, the *whole of science* which relies on such theoretic terms, becomes a manifestly political exercise: an institution devoted to dogmatically enforcing beliefs prejudicial to one interested party or another. There is no *objective* component to what science describes; it is all a matter of the political success of theories and the rhetorical skill of their adherents, and *any* theory (regardless of how absurd it is) will do the trick if it is promulgated with enough flair and charisma to captivate the masses. Moreover, if we take on board with this, the view that theoretical interpretations of observation languages do not, in effect, *persist* for very long and the historical observation that one theoretical interpretation can, and often does, effectively replace another, we might be inclined to reverse the order of dependence here, and see theoretical considerations being of more importance than experiences garnered from our observation reports. Instead of seeing theoretical developments as coming from experience, we might see experiences as coming from the inferential basis of interpretative theories. This is, it seems to me, the quintessential line running through most of Feyerabend's works.

Needless to say, this sort of argument shows a dramatic shift from the overt thesis to the implied covert thesis, and close corroboration of this is needed in order to attribute this view to Feyerabend. Feyerabend's position may be more subtle than this; the views mentioned here may even constitute different stages of his thought. But it is a move which is not unwarranted in his case, and it is behind some of his marginal comments in 'Toward a Realistic Interpretation of Experience' such as his approving citation of Bohr's remarks: 'no content can be grasped without form'[35]; and 'any experience makes its appearance within the framework of our customary points of view and forms of perception.'[36] And his claim (against Bohr) that 'the invention of new conceptual schemes

---

[34] Ibid., p. 29.

[35] In: P. A. Schilpp (ed) *Albert Einstein, Philosopher-Scientist*, p. 240, cited in Feyerabend, ibid., p. 22.

[36] Neils Bohr, *Atomic Theory and the Description of Nature*, p.1; Cited in Feyerabend, Loc. cit.

need not be psychologically impossible' and 'abstract pictures of the world (metaphysical or otherwise) may be turned into alternative interpretations.'[37] These points, Feyerabend believes, are *demonstrated* by the rejection he makes of the principle of pragmatic meaning, and rest well with his strong relativist views argued elsewhere.

Reading these passages along with the claim made earlier - that natural science should be conceived without sensory elements (only interpretations) - it is clear what Feyerabend's overall vision is: it seems that we are justified in saying that the most consistent way to interpret Feyerabend's view is in terms of the covert thesis: experiences (and science specifically) has no observational core and is, instead, fully theoretical. So, although Feyerabend's *covert* thesis is demonstrably different from his *overt* thesis, we can take him to be holding the stronger *covert* claim. If we took him to be making the weaker claim only, then we would have the matter of consistency with earlier works as an issue, and the throw-away remarks mentioned would have to be read in an entirely different way. Not much hangs on these expository points, however, so no attempt shall be made to justify them. It shall simply be assumed that Feyerabend's articulation of the stability thesis, that positivists (allegedly) hold, *should* read: *experiences* do not depend on the status of theoretical knowledge, as it is this more radical view that is on balance more consistent with his views. (And Feyerabend's view, of course is that this thesis should be rejected). This issue will be returned to after a discussion of the (original) 'overt' thesis: that interpretation *does* depend on the status of theoretical knowledge.

Further arguments for the overt thesis: mediating situations

Feyerabend asks us to consider a very basic case of where experience is seen to be fundamental to the interpretation of theoretical terms. He uses the example of 'everyday language' within scientific practices. On the positivist view of the language of such experiences, we should see such common-speak (say, about chairs and tables), as 'fairly insensitive towards changes in theoretical "superstructure."'[38] But thinking more clearly about it, Feyerabend argues, it is not at all obvious that there *is* anything theoretically 'insensitive' about even such a 'basic' and well-entrenched observation language:

> [T]erms which at some time were regarded as observational elements of 'everyday language' (such as the term 'devil') are no longer regarded as such. Other terms, such as 'potential', 'velocity', etc., have been included in the observational part of everyday language, and may have assumed a new use. ... [This] may well be due to the fact that the people using these particular sections are not interested in science and do not know its results; after all, theories as such cannot influence linguistic habits. What can influence those habits is the *adoption* of theories by certain people.[39]

---

[37] Feyerabend, ibid., p. 24.
[38] Ibid., pp. 30-1.
[39] Ibid., p. 31.

So, 'everyday language' and its perceived 'stability' may be a case of a community failing to adopt a new theoretical standard, but instead, remaining 'fixated' at an old one which may, for all practical purposes, be good enough for the job. By strength of reasoning, the well-entrenched common 'experiences' we have, might, as a consequence, be simply a case of laziness in adopting theoretical attitudes. The implication in Feyerabend's work is that 'experiences' might cut about as much ice as some ontologically redundant theoretical term in an archaic language, which has garnered its meaning from practical situations and common contexts and which still works well enough to prompt its occasional use. Neither are necessary or particularly interesting; they are just 'there', as it were, in the system.

This implication of Feyerabend's work has considerable similarity with the inferential impetus behind the eliminative materialism of Paul Churchland and, with necessary caution, the views of Wilfred Sellars, as will be seen in later chapters. It is suggested, of course, that both positions are, to an important degree, misguided in emphasis. High-level considerations do not, on my view, determine all experiential features of interest.

Another line of attack Feyerabend makes upon experience within the context of the philosophy of science and, particularly, the justification of the meaning of theoretical terms, is in his article 'On the Interpretation of Scientific Theories.'[40] Here he turns to the problem of 'mediating situations' and the various attempts to dodge the issue. 'Mediating situations' refer to such things as the physiological state of organisms when making perceptual judgements; their moods or states of health, drunkenness and so on, and other factors 'causally independent' from a given relation of an observer with an observed object, such as lighting conditions and obstacles. These things are important in his analysis of how meanings are given to languages, as the situations do not fit into any clear characterisation of how theoretical terms get their meaning from observational situations. Hence, they provide more ammunition for Feyerabend against the positivist threat. Feyerabend considers the influence of the mediating situations involved in observing bright dots through a telescope as a problem for the positivist account:

> [T]he mediating situation consists in the optical properties of the planets, the properties of the light which is reflected by them, the properties of the atmosphere of the earth ... telescopes and so on. ... the interpretation of sentences containing the terms to be explicated will depend upon the interpretation of other sentences referring to the states of affairs which are in no causal relation whatever to the state of affairs referred to by the former. For example, the interpretation ('the meaning') of 'the mass of the sun' will partly depend upon the interpretation of 'refractive index of the atmosphere of the earth'.[41]

The problem here is this: it is difficult to see how a positivist account, which admits only a basis of observational experience in the interpretation of theoretical terms, can avoid saying that these essentially causally independent

---

[40] Ibid., Ch. 3, pp. 37- 43.
[41] Ibid., p. 38.

situations, like 'the refractive index of the atmosphere of the earth', are involved crucially in the 'meaning' of a simple observation claim such as 'planet x is in such and such position'. (Less obliquely, more dramatically: how a T-statement about the curdling of milk in a churner can avoid having, as part of its meaning, something about the earth's rotation, etc.) Positivists, it seems, cannot *rule out* anything which is causally unconnected as having something to do with the meaning of such a term, and if they can't rule out anything, it fails as a position to make a distinction between what is semantically *relevant* and what is semantically *irrelevant* to the meaning of T-terms. Positivism, of the type Feyerabend is criticising, will have to get this consequence out of its way, if it is to get anywhere. The question is: how can the positivist give an account of the meaning of theoretical terms by experience, and avoid the bearing of causally unconnected mediating situations on them? (We can see, incidentally, the reason for Feyerabend's preference for a backdrop of *theory* here: the suggestion is that mediating situations would be selectively omitted from a *descriptive* account of how the appropriate terms get their meaning by the endorsing of the appropriate aspects of background theoretical assumptions, whereas, such situations would be a substantial *encumbrance* on the positivist account).

Feyerabend discusses three attempts at avoiding this consequence: (1) denying that mediating situations exist, (2) eliminating mediating situations, and (3) 'devising semantical rules which make the interpretation of the theoretical terms dependent on the interpretation of the observational terms only.'[42] The first two 'solutions' are disreputable and Feyerabend rightly rejects them. On the first he says that, 'it completely disregards the existential character of general scientific theories'[43] by which he presumably means that such mediating conditions are crucial to the development and the nature of scientific theories. The second he rules out on grounds that we have already seen: to *eliminate* mediating situations is to tie theoretical terms directly to observation terms, which sets up a regress of further mediating through the problem of trying to justify the terms observationally. His rejection of the third is more subtle. The third method amounts to trying to get the meaning of theoretical terms *from* the meaning of observation terms which include (as the O-terms come from 'observation') the multifarious mediating relations. But this raises the same problem again: namely, how can we account for a *difference* between what is semantically relevant to theoretical terms and what isn't? Feyerabend's argument turns on the predicate 'Ax' on which he says:

> [W]e may safely assume that 'Ax' means something different in 'If a colourblind man inspects x and sees grey, then Ax' and in 'If a man with perfect coloursight inspects x and sees grey, then Ax', and yet the method discussed at the present moment does not allow us to explain this difference by pointing to a difference in the observational terms employed.[44]

---

[42] Ibid., p. 39.
[43] Ibid., p. 38.
[44] Ibid., p. 39.

How then do we account for the difference in the interpretation of such terms without *dropping* the principle that they do not possess a meaning independent from experience?[45] If such terms do *not* possess a meaning independent from experience, we need an account which explains why there is a *difference* here, and if they *do* possess a meaning independent from experience, then *a fortiori* they are not derived from experience. And perhaps experience, after all, is actually derived from theoretical inference in the manner the inferentialist account specifies.

Problems for Feyerabend's account

Positivism and the continuum account

We would be playing into Feyerabend's rich, clever and complicated argument here to assume too much at this point and make the jump that he asks of us. The move from the rejection of positivist approaches of how terms *get their meanings* to the assimilation of experience to theoretical content *is* a jump in reasoning, and it seems likely that there are, as already mentioned, two issues here: (i) the issue of how terms get their meanings; and (ii) the issue of whether experiential content is entirely inferentially specified by high-level theory. These issues are conflated in Feyerabend's argument, and need to be teased apart.

But to grant what is surely a legitimate manoeuvre here: it *is* hard to see how an account which is strictly positivist and observationally based could furnish an account of the subtle distinction in the semantics of theoretical terms - the burgeoning weight of mediating conditions seems to see to that. But just because, for reasons that he mentions, observations are complicated, and positivists cannot rule out what is semantically relevant and irrelevant to the language, it surely does not *follow* that experience cannot provide us with some limits to what theoretical creations are possible, or that experience *comes from* a theoretical background. This clearly seems too swift a move to make. Does Feyerabend in fact make this move? Admittedly not in such explicit terms, but he comes dangerously close to saying precisely this. In the final analysis, it must be attributed to his views, if not his pen. In *Science in a Free Society,* he talks about 'how often the world changes because of a change in theory.'[46] This view seems the more consistent with his position stated elsewhere. It shall be assumed hereafter that this is in fact his position, and that this radical view issues from uncritically accepting the confusions of the inferentialist account of experience mentioned in the earlier parts of this book.

There is a major problem which arises when these claims are disentangled. Feyerabend can't have them together, and the differences between them are crucial. Moreover, there are good reasons simply not to accept the stronger claim. As stated throughout this book, but in Chapters 5 and 8 particularly, there is an important sense in which aspects of experiential content are not captured by high-level influences at all. As has been pointed out in an earlier chapter, J. A. Fodor and Philip Cam have convincingly argued for some degree

---

[45] Loc. cit.
[46] P. K. Feyerabend, *Science in a Free Society,* p. 70.

of isolation of observational experiences from mechanisms of inference, theories, concepts and so on. If this modular hypothesis is in any way reasonable, and if one is to assume that animal and infant experiences constitute importantly lower-order informational *givens,* then Feyerabend's arguments clearly would not apply to such cases. Indeed, the questions Feyerabend raises do not even *bear* on them. For what both the evidence and common-sense suggest in such cases is that the content of such experiences is importantly insulated from high-level theory, propositional content and concepts. The case for low-level aspects of experiential content has been presented throughout this book. If the argument is valid, then Feyerabend's claim that 'experience arises together with theoretical assumptions and not before them' clearly needs to be modified. The modification would amount to being something like: *some* experiential content arises together with theoretical assumptions; other 'aspects' of experience do not, though they may be concurrent with them. This might be, nonetheless, enough of a modification to the original claim to strip the inferentialist emphasis from Feyerabend's account.

But let us evaluate this situation again. Feyerabend is surely right about one thing: a project which is committed to the 'stability thesis' (that interpretations do not depend upon theoretical knowledge in any way, shape or form) cannot give an account of *itself* (i.e., its own language) without assuming that what its own language describes is *true.* And if the language *is* stable and well-connected with observation (and if neither the pragmatics of discourse (the *principle of pragmatic meaning*) nor the 'brute' nature of sensations (the *principle of phenomenological meaning*) can rescue any justification of meaning for it) then it stands and falls on its own merits. Historically, at least, positivism in its most general form has been seen to have very little merit at all.

The position is that the meaning of *terms* cannot be given in experience, as positivists say they can, and by implication the *stability thesis* is false. But we can avoid the implication of all these arguments and objections by simply dropping the requirement that *experience fixes meanings* (and we can subscribe to Feyerabend's *overt* thesis, but not the *covert* thesis). We can take what has been called *sensational* experiences (low-level content) to have no (or little) descriptive, semantic or representational basis, but to have some degree of sensational content which theory ladenness does not capture. This move would preserve both Feyerabend's attack on the positivist account of how observational terms get their meaning, and the argument for low-level insulated aspects of experiential content which is crucial to the continuum theory. Once again, however, we would be aiming not to legitimate one kind of view of the importance of experience, but dispensing with the whole positivist/inferentialist dichotomy.

To raise the points of difference here again: it has been said that something important may be left from the attacks on positivism, if one simply holds that experience at the sensation level is importantly non-inferential, even though this may not be enough to guarantee the meaning of expressions in language. There may even be a legitimate *continuum* in the way in which observational experiences are penetrated by theories and higher-level concepts. At the extremes of the low-level sensational aspects of experiential content there may be no such interference, while at the higher inferential level we may speak of a descriptive, representational content, and there may be all sorts of complex graduations in between. The situation is plausibly not as simple as a fully inferentialist account such as Feyerabend's makes out. The continuum theory allows for much more in the way of degrees of influence in this regard.

To give credit where due, Feyerabend may be right in asserting that experiential content is importantly descriptive/theoretical at this *second* level mentioned. But how does the full dichotomy rest with Feyerabend's analysis? This is unclear because Feyerabend seems systematically ambiguous as to what his argument was supposed to demonstrate. There is a good deal of textual evidence for this claim. For instance, Feyerabend himself seems unwilling at times to take his own strongly inferentialist claims too seriously. He says that: 'sensations can be eliminated from the process of understanding (though they may continue to accompany it, just as a headache may accompany deep thought).' And he makes the rather muted remark that: 'natural science without experience is *conceivable* ' which suggests that is all it may be. And also, he claims: 'I am not asserting that the natural sciences as we know them ... could be freed from sensation entirely ... the point is made that sensations are not *necessary* for the business of science and that they occur for practical reasons only'.[47] But at other times he is clear about the implications of the covert thesis and enthusiastically supports it. He tells us that experience enters science at three points: of test, assimilation of results of test, and understanding of theories.[48] At each of these points, according to Feyerabend, experience, though sufficient, is not necessary for science to occur (a computer with a suitable theoretical basis and instruments could make the appropriate judgements about data in respect of certain theoretical input). And even in a small child in the act of interpreting stimuli, he tells us, we can 'imagine that this interpretative apparatus acts without being accompanied by sensations (as do reflexes and all well-learned movements such as typing).'[49] The upshot in these cases is that experiences are not *necessary* because they do not contribute to our *understanding*, and as they do not contribute to our understanding, *ceteris paribus,* they have no non-theoretical (and hence, no useful) content.[50]

There are several issues here: if Feyerabend is claiming that we need not experience things in order to *apply* theories, he is right, but the point seems trivial: theories can be applied (conceivably) by a computer as he suggests, as it were, 'passively'. But as we have stipulated the requirements here *ex hypothesi,* we have not gained much territory. We have certainly not

---

[47] Feyerabend, Vol 1, op. cit., p. 133-135.

[48] Ibid., p. 132.

[49] Ibid., p. 133.

[50] Fodor has recently agreed with the view that there can be a 'science without experience', but argues that this does not, in effect, compromise his 'cognitive encapsularity' claim. See his: 'The Dogma that didn't Bark (A Fragment of a Naturalized Epistemology)'. For Fodor, the data that constrains science 'doesn't have to be perceptual' (ibid., p. 219). 'Providing support for making observations is just one tactic among many that scientists can use to achieve cognitive management' loc. cit. This is a reasonable claim in itself: scientists can obtain useful information in all sorts of (non-perceptual) ways. But this kind of claim is a far cry from the covert thesis of Feyerabend for whom 'experiences arise together with theoretical assumptions and not before them.' If one annexes the idea of a science without experience to this sort of view, it is clear Feyerabend is aiming not to explore the different ways of achieving 'cognitive management,' but to suggest that perceptual information is *redundant.*

demonstrated that the world is like this. (An imagined world, in which moral values were excluded from moral action, is not a *demonstration* that the world is devoid of such values). The stronger claim is whether a person without theoretical knowledge can be *conceived of as having experiences*. In one of his clearest statements of what I have called his *covert* thesis, Feyerabend tells us that this is 'incomprehensible':

> [E]xperience arrives *together with* theoretical assumptions, *not* before them, and that an experience without theories is just as incomprehensible as is (allegedly) a theory without experience: eliminate part of the theoretical knowledge and of a sensing subject and you have a person who is completely disorientated, incapable of carrying out the simplest action. Eliminate further knowledge and his sensory world (his 'observation language') will start disintegrating; even colours and other simple sensations will disappear until he is in a stage even more primitive than a small child.[51]

This is plainly begging some big questions. If we remove the analysis from persons, and apply it to animals, it seems patently false. We do not ordinarily think of dogs as having 'theoretical assumptions' or an 'observation language.' (Though one would need, of course, to distinguish what sense of content - propositional linguistic, theoretically informational, etc. - is being claimed here). Yet it seems philosophical foolishness, and a legacy of the rationalist tradition, to suppose that they are somehow experientially *deficient* because of this (this would be to ignore Armstrong's important point about the continuum mentioned in Chapter 1). The claim is, in any case, certainly not a demonstration of the asymmetrical nature of the dependencies which he avows. Feyerabend has no case for claiming that the hapless child from whom theories are being deviously removed is an unfortunate in possession of a crumbling sphere of sense. Indeed, it is hard to see how this can be maintained beyond mere assertion. And it is important for Feyerabend to argue for this strongly, for, if what has been suggested here can be maintained (*viz.*, about experience at one level being importantly low-level and having a pre-theoretical structure or content - relatively independent from features of high-level inference; and other levels having some degrees of representational, propositional content, etc.), then it would seem that one could easily hold the opposite thesis equally fervently: that it was simply a fact of selection that organisms evolved to experience the world sensationally and non-inferentially prior to their ability to acquire high-level theoretical knowledge. On this *rival* view of content, selection enabled organisms to discriminate low-level phenomenological similarities and differences, etc., which are immune from theory, simply by virtue of being organic, biologically and evolutionarily primed creatures.[52]

---

[51] Feyerabend, Vol. 1, op. cit., p. 133.
[52] Nowhere have I claimed this is a *necessary* condition of having experiences. Feyerabend, Dennett and Putnam are probably right insofar as conscious experiences are not necessary for carrying out actions. The world might (logically) have been occupied by unconscious automata, operating with far more dexterity and skill than we do. But I think that Fodor's claim that some philosophical worries are merely 'baroque' applies to such cases. The fact that

This point has been stressed before in another context. Here, it can only be gestured the general direction in which the analysis should go. When arguing against the objection that low-level sensational features might be epistemically idle and epiphenomenally irrelevant, the point was made that conscious experiential states do have an important selective utility: the reason an organism has 'felt' aspects of their experiences - looks and seemings - is to achieve a number of important tasks. (1) They help to *personalise* the experience; to localise it to an experiential centre from which action can be appropriately directed (the experience of pain is obviously one such case). (2) They are also useful for *directing* oneself to action - driving a car when something happens (say to the engine) enables consciousness to causally activate a new set of mechanical procedures, which direct one to make appropriate alterations and adjustments to one's 'programmed' pattern of behaviour (slowing down, stopping, etc). (3) Finally, the possibility of being inferentially misguided about the content of the experiences we project and identify gives rise to the need for another (selectively sanctioned) way of discriminating between stimuli that could be dangerous or harmful stimuli.

The value of, and the problems associated with, such a proposal cannot be investigated here. However, a simple point can be made. Feyerabend's assertion that, without theory, a 'sensing subject' would not be able to make any sense out of its environmental cues at all is at best, unsupported; at worst, it runs contrary to views which hold that not all observable features of interest are determined by the inferential end of the experiential continuum. There is clearly more than one story that can be told here. With such thought experiments, Feyerabend thus not only begs the question in his own favour, he ignores the possibility that a more subtle account relating experience and content might in fact be true. This is clearly an inadequate basis on which to support an inferentialist account of experience within the philosophy of science.

Moreover, the examples offered in support of the covert thesis hardly provide unambiguous supports for his views. What sense, for example, are we to make of Feyerabend's neonate who does not possess a 'stable perceptual world' but (apparently) 'passes through perceptual stages which are only loosely connected with each other.'[53] Feyerabend tells us that these stages 'embody all the theoretical knowledge achieved at the time,' but he does not explain how they do, without introducing the possibility of the child experiencing something, and even that can be taken two ways. In saying that the child 'reacts correctly to signals, interprets them correctly' *as experiences,* he is introducing the very low-level content - the experience- his covert thesis is suggesting we operate without. The very act of passing through various discriminatory stages suggests that infants might already be able to make some contentful sense of their surroundings - lack of high-level inference notwithstanding. Feyerabend asserts that 'the means of interpretation'[54] in the sense of a *theoretical* base, does the

---

philosophy has to deal with is that the world does, at minimum, have at least one species of conscious creature that we can be sure about, perhaps more. It would be a development of the view that I have given to trace the influence of Descartes' inferentialist treatment of animals as non-sentient creatures to the present day functionalist's conception of man in the same vein.

[53] Feyerabend, Vol. 1, op. cit., p. 133.

[54] Loc. cit.

job here, but it is certainly not clear how it does, if by 'means of interpretation' he means some kind of 'high-level' capacity. Since the example admits of contrary interpretations, one could easily and equally claim that being able to react correctly to signals and interpret them correctly, at least in terms of low-level similarities and differences in one's experience, is a *precondition* of being able to theorise anything about them at all (at least in the organic world we live in). And, as we have seen, there seems to be an important sense that certain already pre-interpreted sensational givens are 'modularised' from such influences - and colours seem to be one such case - so this is not necessarily a good example for Feyerabend's thesis. It is not obvious to me that a person could fail to be aware of some aspect of his senses in the scenario that Feyerabend provides for us. And it is important for Feyerabend to show this unambiguously if his claim is to succeed. For if the person is aware of his diminution of faculties (acutely or not) in the very primitive manner in which we may be aware of look-beliefs (*viz.*, as registrations of low-level information which fall short of being fully-fledged beliefs), then there is *some* sense in which that person's experiences are *not* dependent upon theoretical knowledge. It is suggested here that the example that Feyerabend raises may not, after all, support his case, and may actually constitute ammunition for an opposing view.

In the scenario outlined, we are asked to imagine the sensations of the theoryless person as having the characteristics of an observation *language,* but if 'aspects' of sensations can be contentful without that content being language-like, then the person might not be *totally* 'disorientated' and still have experiences in some important sense. This would seem to be the case with theoryless animals, which, on Feyerabend's view, would have to be incompetent in their motor-tasks because they do not have theories, though it is not obvious how this could be true. (Of course, if one assumes at the outset that all experiential content is propositional linguistic etc., then removal of this would occasion an inability of the person to understand a language, and much else besides. But this is merely begging the question that the only kind of content is of this character, which is what is in question.) The upshot here is that if Feyerabend cannot provide us with a good reason for thinking that the person did not have this access to some aspect of his own sensations while they shrank from him as his theories were being removed, he would be admitting what he is trying to reject [55] In view of such ambiguities, there might be a better way of looking at the relation between experience and high-level interpretation.

Positivism and low-level content

The theoretical-observational distinction, like the analytic-synthetic distinction, is a malleable one; it serves theorists with a number of possibilities, depending upon their initial persuasions. Feyerabend wants to run the theoretical and observational *terms* together and thence claim that the limits of our experience

---

[55] Of course, this is not to say that a person can't be made 'incapable' by the removal of part of the brain by surgery: what Feyerabend needs to support his case, however, is an instance of where the removal of *theories* in a person causes this response. As we shall similarly see with Churchland's inferentialist analysis, the onus is on Feyerabend to prove his point here, and the case in question does not allow him to do this.

are the limits of the theoretical language with which we are capable of describing or expressing such experiences. As he says, 'experience *arises together* with theoretical assumptions and not before them.'[56] (In the passage just quoted, the elimination of the knowledge of theoretical terms amounted to the elimination of not just observation terms, but the whole 'sensory world.') From this point, however, it is a short move to considering the possibility of a science without experience at all and the logical consequences of such a situation (the dependence of sensations on an inferential background). Feyerabend does not, however, consider the possibility of a *non sequitur* here. Clearly, the argument requires more support to make it stronger if it is to be maintained at all. For it doesn't seem to me to follow from the collapsing of the observational and theoretical terms and the theory dependence of observation doctrine, that the 'experienced world' is thus limited by them. Maybe there is a case for thinking that, in Feyerabend (and in the inferential proposal generally) the T-O distinction is run together *too* much and that there is a crucial sense in which not all experiences are theory dependent after all, even though we may claim, along with Feyerabend, that positivism does not hold up to his criticisms. It is suggested that these claims can be held jointly with no friction. If this can be done, then Feyerabend's *overt* thesis is entirely compatible with the continuum account, given necessary revisions.

Feyerabend assumes, in the *covert* thesis, that his critique of positivism is a critique of all experience-based approaches, because he tacitly assumes that all such approaches take on board the (revised) *stability thesis* - the idea that *experiences* do not depend upon theoretical knowledge. The suggestion being made is that this does not follow. It certainly does not follow from a rejection of the (original) *stability thesis* (*interpretations* do not depend on the status of theoretical knowledge) and positivism, that one also rejects experience as a fundamental category - even if one rejects the positivists' *version* of it. The sense in which experience is an important category here might just be more oblique: it might be a low-level primordial category. Positivism, in any case, holds an *empirical hypothesis:* that experience is a true source and foundation (testing ground) of knowledge.[57] Theoretical terms are either extensionally reducible, intensionally reducible or definable in such terms.[58] And it holds, hence, that interpretations of experience do not depend upon theoretical terms. If this is what positivism means, then Feyerabend has mounted an adequate criticism of it. Most theorists, including Feyerabend, take there to be entailment relations between such claims, but there is no reason to suppose that they cannot be held separately, and for that matter, no reason that one cannot hold that the category of 'experience' is crucial in other ways than those mentioned; for instance, without any entailment to foundationalism. What 'positivism' means or does not mean is actually open-ended.

Feyerabend attacks these conventional definitions *en bloc,* and he is probably right to do so in the case of positivism in the traditional sense. But there is the lingering question of whether we *need* to hold them together; for if we do not, then there is a case for being suspicious of whether Feyerabend actually gives

---

[56] P.K. Feyerabend, Vol. 1, op. cit., p. 133.
[57] Ibid., p. 132.
[58] Ibid., p. 37.

us a 'science without experience' and whether he, in fact, succeeds in his claim that experience comes from theories. Conflating all experience-based approaches with the stability thesis has given Feyerabend the focus for his attack; what is suggested here is that his enemy need not be so conspicuous as this. Indeed he may have no enemy at all, if we can support some sense of low-level contentful experience *without* ascribing to positivism. It may even be possible to hold *both* that experience is fundamental in the sense that it is prior to high-level interpretation (not all interpretations are theory dependent, but nor is experience necessarily the 'testing ground')[59] *and that* theoretical terms are crucial to knowledge. My claim is that Feyerabend has not rejected another possibility: that experiences come individuated and pre-interpreted as low-level sensational contents, and are subsequently re-interpreted in the light of our current theoretical knowledge at another (higher) level of processing. If one assumes the continuum account that has been presented in this book, these may be two *quite separate* senses in which 'experience' is important. In the one sense, experience is a low-level informational given to which categories like 'meaning', 'inference' and 'theory' do not apply in any attenuated sense; in the other, it is a category penetrated through and through by such mechanisms. But Feyerabend does not make this distinction, so all 'experience-based' programs are thus *positivist.* However, like Sellars, Churchland and others, I claim that Feyerabend has tried to throw the baby out with the bathwater, and that we need to get it back.[60]

We can go some way towards mounting a defence of this claim by returning to the problem of mediating terms, and trying to answer Feyerabend's difficulty: how to account for the difference in the interpretation of theoretical terms without dropping the principle that theoretical terms do not possess an independent meaning. We can suggest a response to this difficulty in a similar way to Feyerabend, that by abandoning the stability thesis and asserting that the theoretical terms 'Ax', in both scenarios, do possess an independent meaning, whilst hitching to this a *caveat:* that in rejecting the proposal that interpretations do not depend on the status of theoretical knowledge, we do not thereby assert that they *depend fully* upon theoretical knowledge, and that we allow that theoretical terms possess an independent meaning without thereby allowing them a *transempirical* status. Allowing the latter is suggestive of relativism. For if meanings had *nothing to do whatever* with certain experiences, (only inference) then the cascade of Feyerabend's relativism would flow.[61] But we

---

[59] Ibid., p. 132.

[60] Drawing on Campbell (1985) and Fodor (1984; 1988), Mortensen and Nerlich describe this low level sensory information as 'the honest check on high-level theory' because 'its causes are (mostly) outside the central control of our postulational mechanisms.' They also claim (plausibly) that: 'In holding that concepts are thoroughly sensory and that the explanation of experience is a primary role of correct theory, one is not saying either that theoretical concepts are 'analysable' into non-verbal propositional attitudes [inferentialism] or that experience can never be overthrown by theory [positivism].' C. Mortensen and G. Nerlich, *Aspects of Metaphysics.* (The interpolations are mine.)

[61] It would flow if one leaves aside cases of internalism without relativism as adumbrated by Putnam, or an otherwise fully theoretical account along the lines of Hesse in *The Structure of Scientific Inference.* The point here is only a matter of textual consistency: Feyerabend is led to relativism in throwing out the [experiential] baby with the [positivist] bathwater.

must also hold likewise, that the meaning of such terms is 'not dependent upon observation and nothing else'[62], for this would be to raise the positivist spectre. If we avoid the extremes, we come to another possibility: that experience, at one level, provides the structured possibility of observation, and that the role of theories, at another level, is to fit this content within pre-existing inferential patterns of meaning (theoretical knowledge).

By 'structured possibility of observation', I am not putting forward a new principle of phenomenological adequacy, that experience fixes meanings. It is not being claimed that this provides us with the interpretation of observational and theoretical terms, but just that observation does not come *entirely free* of interpretation: i.e., it does not come non-interpreted, only *pre-interpreted*. Applying 'red' to a red experience is possible only if red is *phenomenologically individuated* and distinct from other colours as a sensational experience of some informationally contentful kind. (By contrast, in arguing *against* the principle of phenomenological adequacy, Feyerabend argued that it did not *provide* experiential terms with an interpretation (meaning); Feyerabend may be *right* here. In making these revisions, we can then say that theoretical terms differ in their interpretation, not by matching adequately 'phenomenologically' nor by being trans-empirical (theoretical), but by being interpreted (respectively) with or without the input of certain low-level contentful sensations (certain 'looks'): thus, a blind person saying 'Ax' and a coloursight person saying 'Ax', then, differ in the intuitively plausible respect that the latter person, but not the former, is equipped *inter alia* with certain *sensational experiences* by which his theoretical interpretations are informed. But *what this does not need to mean* is that high-level semantic interpretation is *given by experience*. That is, one can carve the observation-theory threshold a little closer to *experience* than to theory without being accused of being a positivist. And, for the reasons mentioned earlier regarding the overkill of the inferentialist proposal, this seems at least a reasonable approach to the issue. In this version, a dog could still have contentful observational experiences without having to *say, theorise* or *infer* anything. And a blind man would be different from his sighted counterpart in a *qualitative* sense, without simply being possessed of 'a different part of [a] theory.'[63]

Moreover, what sensations *informing* inference might mean is that in the kind of world we live in (and for the kind of evolved beings we are), certain qualitative features of experience must be assumed in order for theory to be *applied*. And a blind person could not, strictly speaking, apply colour theory (except in some metaphorical sense) because of this deficit. The heart of the matter is that, though sensations are not necessary for the interpretation of theories and the semantics of observational *terms,* it is not the case that arguments for the inferentialist account explain such experiences away by a heavy-handed emphasis on theory-dependence. A blind man could certainly use colour theory,[64] but in the actual world we live in, there is still a considerable difference in terms of the 'richness' such a theory has for him, compared to a colour-sighted person (for the one, the colour has certain low-level 'look'-like

---

[62] Feyerabend, Vol 1, op. cit., p. 39.
[63] Ibid., p. 33.
[64] In a logically *possible* world perhaps even the sighted could only use colour theory too.

aspects; for the other it does not). And although this difference is not entirely in the proximal stimulations received, it is not entirely and exclusively in the theory that each has either, because such non-semantic content is needed (in an important sense peculiar to our evolution-primed world) to account for the respective richness of the respective semantic contents.[65] Such an analysis, of course, presupposes that experiential content is seen as occurring at a number of distinct levels of greater and lesser degrees of sophistication, but this is the view I hope to have established for serious consideration by the end of this book.

If this seems unsatisfactory, then we should consider Feyerabend's alternative. For it seems that Feyerabend is in no better position than the positivist view he was attacking. Feyerabend's view is that theoretical terms which characterise such experiences as colours actually get their content, (as well as their meaning), not from experience, but from the fact that we have adopted a certain interpretation of a *theory:*

> Thesis I: the interpretation of an observation language is determined by the theories which we use to explain what we observe, and it changes as soon as those theories change.[66]

It would seem that we haven't progressed very far from the pitfalls of positivism and the *stability thesis* here if the covert claim is supposed to run parallel to the overt claim. For, in taking on board the idea that theories provide the determinations of all *contents,* as well as of all meanings (*overt* thesis) and that the contents of observational experiences are likewise hitched to such interpretations, (*covert* thesis), Feyerabend *assumes the model (the metaphysic) of which he stands in defence.* In other words, one cannot give an *independent* justification of such a proposal without *assuming* the very interpretations which, he says, supposedly stand for experience. The initial argument against the positivist given earlier was that this could not be answered outside the ontology of positivism itself. However, it would seem that this complaint could go just as well for Feyerabend's own argument. *Query:* how are such inferences justified outside the claims of the *inferentialist* account? If Feyerabend's justification is that his approach is the *only* approach to the positivist alternative considered, then this claim is *false,* because another has been suggested in this book: contentful low-level experiences and meaningful inferences may be justified by quite separate criteria, and, in fact, may constitute quite distinguishable aspects of experiential content occurring along a non-exclusive continuum.

Of course, I am doing exactly the same thing here: assuming the model I am defending; not offering an *independent* justification for what has been taken as pre-structured low-level experience and its non-inferentiality at certain levels on the content continuum. And here, perhaps, it becomes a matter of which model is preferred. But the problem here is not one of justifying languages and interpretation, as it is for Feyerabend. Feyerabend's aim is to refute the claim

---

[65] This is not to say that a blind man could not have the semantic content independently. It just means that without the 'aspect' features, the meaning will be rather less contentful than that of an ordinary persons for whom the denotation of the sentences *look* a certain way.

[66] Feyerabend, Vol. 1, op. cit., p. 31.

that the interpreted meaning of a term is given in experience, and his analysis leans on not only the flaws of the empirical hypothesis, which he takes all experience-based accounts to assume, but also (jointly) the doctrine of the theory dependence of observation. For observations to depend upon theories, as Feyerabend seems to claim, it seems we need to give an account of the meanings of the terms of these theories, if we are to give an account of what these theories *assert* (what experiences are possible). In this way, Feyerabend is committed to having to justify the interpretation of such languages, as is the positivist. The difference between them is that one holds that as experience comes from theories, so does the 'meaning' of experience also come from theories; the other holds that theories come from experiences, *but gives no adequate account of how terms of those theories get their meaning*. This is the weakness that Feyerabend attacks. But again: the terms of his attack commit him to having to justify the meaning of observational terms *in his own (inferentialist) account*. My proposal is in no such bind, for throughout this book limits have been placed on the theory dependence of observation. It is suggested that high-level features such as theory influence experiential content occur by degrees, and that there are very primitive levels where inference does not apply. The position defended, therefore, can claim that high-level interpretation goes on at a level which is different *by degrees* to the level at which an organism (such as an animal or infant) can have certain contentful experiences. The problem of justifying the use of observational terms thus does not arise on the continuum account.

Of course, this sort of argument is plausible only on the assumption that the continuum theory is plausible: that there are several distinguishable senses of experiential content, and that only one kind of content is, strictly speaking, high-level and semantic/theoretical; another kind of content has aspects which are not. Not much is gained from this argument if it has not been demonstrated that the thesis is worth considering on other grounds. But, as shown, none of Feyerabend's arguments are in any way *deciders* for the fully inferentialist line on experiential content, so there are still some reasons to hold other, contrary, views.

Conclusion

Feyerabend's account of experience was designed to legitimate (in his words): 'the big step forward when the Aristotelian idea of the reliability of our everyday experience was given up and was replaced with an empiricism of a more subtle kind ... and [later] by rearranging our observational world in conformance with theoretical assumptions.'[67] What has been presented in this chapter is an empiricism of a subtler kind again. On my view, Feyerabend may be able to have an empiricism without positivism, but it may not mean that he can thereby have a science without experience.

With the theory dependence of observation doctrine rendered suspect, we are no longer committed to the assumptions of Feyerabend's thesis, *viz.*, to give an account of the *meaning* of terms designating experience. There is no requirement, as the continuum view claims that nothing of interest follows from

---

[67] Ibid., p. 134.

the meanings of experiential terms *vis-á-vis* low-level experiential content. The problem is thus, not one of justifying *languages,* but to give an account of experience, which it is suggested, comes already *with* low-level sensational content, i.e., pre-interpreted to some extent. My point in this chapter is simply to suggest that Feyerabend runs too far with the ball in his rejection of positivism. Outlawing positivism is not the same thing as outlawing experience.

Part Four
EXPERIENCE AND MIND

10 Sellars's myth

> The phrase 'the given' as a piece of professional-epistemological-shoptalk carries a substantial theoretical commitment, and one can deny that there are 'data' or that anything is, in this sense, given without flying in the face of reason.[1]

Outlining Sellars's thesis

Introduction

This part of the book will be in three chapters, two of them dealing with important arguments in support of the inferentialist proposal. In this chapter, Wilfred Sellars's rejection of the sense-data theory of perception will be assessed. It will be argued that his inferentialist views are of no consequence for the alternative view developed in this book. Chapter 11 will look at an attempt to eliminate low-level content by way of criticising the theory of 'folk psychology' while also assessing the claim that perception is 'plastic' and suggestive to high-level influences. Chapter 12 will look at the viability of property dualism in the context of the alternative account proposed.

Sense-data and low-level awarenesses

A major contribution to the issue of whether experiential content is influenced by high-level considerations is the theory of sense-data, a theory designed to legitimate objects of appearance. This view, which had support from the philosophers Russell and Price, among others, was in opposition to the view that objects were directly perceived. One did not experience objects directly, as the objects of one's experience could be non-veridical (such as when 'seeing' a stick as bent when it was partially submerged in water). These particulars constituted perceptual information non-inferentially acquired and known ('givens') which were essential to any perceptual act. (In veridical perception, the datum and the object happened to coincide).

---

[1] Wilfred Sellars, 'Empiricism and the Philosophy of Mind', *Science Perception and Reality*, p. 127.

Important distinctions have already been made in respect of low-level and fully inferential content. The central claim was that low-level experience is something distinct from perceptual judgements involving an inferential background of high-level features. As it stands, such a claim may seem similar to the views of philosophers sympathetic to the theory of sense-data. However, I want here to distinguish the continuum theory from the sense-data view to which it seems a close cousin. In this chapter, I shall outline where the continuum account stands on the complex question of perceptual 'givens'.

Sellars claims that all 'givens' (like sense-data) cannot be non-inferential particulars, as the sense datum theorists suggest. Rather, they must be subsumed and classified under independent concepts which are acquired by high-level concept formation, involving learning and background knowledge. In Sellars's view, the experience expressed by the proposition 'The stick seems bent' must take the form *x seems ø,* where ø is a concept of some sort, and to say that *x seems ø* (to make such a perceptual judgement) we must have acquired this knowledge inferentially. According to Sellars's, the idea of a non-inferentially known sense datum is a 'myth'. The point to be disagreed with here is the extrapolation from this rejection of sense-data to *all* non-inferential 'givens' in experience. It shall be claimed instead that some givens actually escape his argument.

While I agree with Sellars that a non-inferentially known sense datum is an absurdity, it shall be argued that not all 'givens' are equivalent to the idea of a 'sense datum'. Another sort of given could be a low-level awareness or - what I have called - a sensational 'aspect' of content. This, typically, could be *acquired* non-inferentially without being *known* non-inferentially in any 'high-level' sense (it may be known in some sense, yet not as propositional knowledge). The assumption that Sellars makes is that all givens, to be known, have to be subsumed under independent concepts of the propositional form *x is ø;* but it is not clear why all experiential awarenesses need to be so subsumed. An ability to be aware of sensational features of experiences may constitute an experiential given, even without the requirement of subsumption under particular high-level concepts which capture certain descriptively specifiable features. My claim shall be that Sellars has actually confused a number of issues in his argument: he has conflated the notion of sense-data with all experiential givens; he has mistakenly applied high-level epistemic features as characteristics of the given in general; and he has assumed an overtly propositional linguistic view of knowledge acquisition. Further, he has tacitly assumed a dichotomous treatment of the inferential/non-inferential distinction. All these points are misapplied in the case of low-level content.

Thus, I shall argue that Sellars's refutation of the notion of a sense-datum is misapplied for *some* forms of the given. The exclusive pairs: 'inferential-non-inferential' and 'epistemic-non-epistemic' applied to sensational givens, or 'aspects' of experiential content, is something of a category mistake because although an experiential aspect might be non-inferentially acquired it need not be non-inferentially known, and such an awareness can be informationally epistemic in some sense without necessarily being heavily inferential. The categories inferential/non-inferential are misleading in the sense that they suggest that content is either in one or other category (epistemic and inferential or non-epistemic and non-inferential). However, consistent with the continuum account, low-level awarenesses can be informational without being propositional linguistic (hence, there is room for non-propositional knowledge which is not fully inferential); and an awareness can have inferential aspects without being fully epistemic in any high-level sense (hence, there is room for informational content which involves some inferential connections but which is not necessarily known as such). Sellars has committed the mistake of being too simplistic in the application of such categories, and so there is still a sense in which content can be 'given' without falling prey to his arguments.

Two strategies on sense-data

Sellars claims that there are two important strategies that one can take once one has admitted the category of sense-data as a view on the nature of experiential content. One can say either that the sense datum of an object constitutes an adequate enough account of what our experience of an object consists in, and hence, an analysis of experience becomes an *analysis* of the nature of sense-data; or, one can claim that the central requirement for an account of experience is that the sense datum is a component of any relation between subject and object, and that this relation is *unanalysable*.

Sellars submits that the first tendency is a mistake of a piece with the naturalistic fallacy[2] but he also claims that both positions have a seriously flawed basis in the reasoning behind them, namely, that the givenness of ϕ is 'a fact which presupposes no learning, no forming of associations, no setting up of stimulus-response connections.'[3] By this sort of stipulation, Sellars has in mind the necessary inferential connections that must go along with the sensing of sense-data. However, it shall be claimed in this chapter that Sellars's arguments against sense-data do not rule out an important sense in which experience is 'given'.

Sense-data and unanalysability

The general response made *against* the idea that a sense datum does or should presuppose concept formation, stimulus-response connections, and the like, is an *a priori* one: the sensing of sense contents is supposed to be something akin to being conscious. It is not a faculty which is cultivated or formed under social conditions in response to goal-directed needs. The sensing of something being red, say, or the sensing of a pain, is fundamentally a *deliverance* not an *acquisition:* even if 'the ability to know that a person is now at a certain time, feeling a pain, is acquired and does presuppose a (complicated) process of concept formation,'[4] the very idea that one can *be* in pain or see red does not. Having to undergo training to 'see red' or to 'have a pain' seems as absurd as having to undergo an educational process to be a featherless biped.

This is not a good argument in anyone's book and Sellars rightly rejects it. For one thing, it begs the question in favour of the *unanalysability* of sense contents: precisely what is at issue. Even a sense datum theorist needs to

---

[2] Ibid., p. 131.

[3] Loc cit.

[4] Loc. cit.

explain why sense-data are unanalysable in terms of their being primitive or non-inferential (otherwise there would be no plausible grounds on which to admit them). Also, as Sellars notes, if we were to take the strategy that sense-data are unacquired, then we would be clearly precluded from offering an analysis of the proposition that x senses a sense content, which *presupposes* acquired abilities. That is, we must take as *a priori* too, that one *can make such claims* as that one is sensing a sense content. But any claim about any state of affairs, in Sellars's view, is of the form *x is ø,* which involves subsumption under high-level propositional content, and hence, inference. If sense datum theorists want to claim that one is sensing sense-data, it means that they are already presupposing acquired high-level concepts. To say that sense contents are unacquired in spite of this would mean that we cannot even claim that we *know* that any sense content we allegedly sense is the way that it appears to us. We cannot do this because we have already assumed that the knowledge of such things is unacquired; and if unacquired, then strictly speaking they are not known, because they cannot be subsumed under concepts like *x is ø*. But the ability to *say x is ø* is, according to Sellars, already constitutive of concepts, learning and inference, and so must be all forms of the given. The initial argument against the idea of non-inferentially known sense-data is, then, that the view commits a clear pragmatic contradiction. This argument requires expansion.

The problem of 'givenness'

The problem of the 'givenness' of experience, whether it be cast in terms of sense-data or not, is a problem of what exactly is supposed to be given, and what epistemic weight we are to allow it to have. We have seen on Sellars's view that the two possibilities for this doctrine are that our epistemic and experiential claims about the world can be analysed in terms of 'the given' or, more broadly, that the framework of givenness constitutes an inextricable part of the relation in experiential acts. The next step Sellars takes is to show that in either of these forms 'the given' collapses into a choice between either the failure of sense-data to provide a logical basis for the existence of knowledge, or sense-data as 'particularised items of experience'. The argument runs as follows: Any account of sense-data comes against the act-particular dichotomy - if sense-data are incorporated in a relation between subject and object, one can easily give an account of *knowledge* in such terms. An epistemic situation would occur when the act of sensing the features of an object and the object itself happen to coincide. This assumes that the act, in this case, includes the fact that the object is there, and that it is the object under consideration, and so on. On the other hand, if sense-data can only be properly described as *particular* sensations, i.e., an expanse of colour, a particular shape, a particular sound, etc., it is not clear how we can get full-blooded knowledge from such input. It seems that keeping the notion that sense-data can be analysed in terms of features of particulars *qua* particulars, proscribes having knowledge that the event occurred. The options appear to be:

> (a) It is *particulars* which are sensed. Sensing is not knowing. The existence of sense-data does not *logically* imply the existence of

knowledge, or
(b) Sensing *is* a form of knowing. It is *facts* rather than *particulars* which are sensed.[5]

Sellars says of this that:

> [T]he fact that a sense content was sensed would be a *non-epistemic* fact about the sense content. Yet it would be hasty to conclude that this alternative precludes *any* logical connection between the sensing of sense contents and the possession of non-inferential knowledge. For even if the sensing of sense contents did not logically imply the existence of non-inferential knowledge, the converse might well be true ... even though the sensing of a red sense content were not itself a cognitive fact and did not imply the possession of non-inferential knowledge. [T]he second alternative [implies the] existence of non-inferential knowledge for the simple reason that it would *be* this knowledge. But, once again, it would be the facts rather than particulars which are sensed.[6]

There may be some confusion about the terms here. Non-inferential knowledge is, in Sellarsian terms, direct knowledge of matters of fact of the form x *is* ϕ; inferential knowledge is knowledge obtained indirectly from other sources (e.g., background knowledge) of the form x *because* ϕ. 'Particulars' and 'facts' refer, respectively, to unique primitives to which knowledge is analysable (colours, expanses of light, shapes), but which are not themselves knowledge, while facts are acts of knowledge which cannot be so analysed ('The current British Monarch has been a Queen since 1953').

The point here is that if one believes that non-inferential particulars are sensed, then this is a *non-epistemic fact* which is unique and to which knowledge can and must be analysed (the sense-data theory). But knowledge of facts (inferential or non-inferential) on this view is not logically implied by the non-epistemic fact of particulars being sensed (even though, asymmetrically, the non-inferential knowledge of matters of fact may imply that particulars were sensed). Sellars's claim is that if one believes that sensing is a *sensing of facts,* then although knowledge can be derived from this view (it *is* knowledge) there would be no room for particulars, whereas, if one believes that sensing is a *sensing of particulars,* there is no logical entailment towards knowledge (inferential or non-inferential). The options appear to be mutually exclusive. But clearly, Sellars argues, one must have knowledge *if only to say that one knows one non-inferentially senses particulars,* so particulars cannot be non-epistemic; knowledge must be involved somehow. The task of Sellars is to show that for this reason the account of sense-data leads ultimately to a rejection of the notion that something is sensed. Moreover, rejecting sense-data, in Sellars's view, is supposed to go some way to rejecting 'the entire framework of givenness.'[7]

Sellars's point is that there is a serious confusion in the options among sense-data theorists, with the result that they often 'seek to have [their] cake and eat

---

[5] Ibid., p. 129.
[6] Loc. cit.
[7] Ibid., p. 128.

it,'[8] often opting for a philosophically jumbled account of sensing as *both* particular and act. This is probably a legitimate criticism of the sense-data account. However, the extent to which this raises a difficulty for givenness in general (the arguments against sense-data apply to a particular form of 'the given') is the extent to which one takes on board Sellars's point that one can regard any experience as being a datum, only insofar that this implies that we, thereby, know some fact about it (namely, that it is a datum of a certain propositionally and descriptively specifiable sort). It shall later be indicated that this is an implausible assumption - for the reason that certain 'givens' may be insulated and inaccessible to complete penetration by high-level conceptual knowledge, and do not face the requirement of being non-inferentially known in this way, even if they may be non-inferentially acquired. If, however, one admits this point, in the case of sense-data being given, then it follows clearly that there is an implication relation between the notions of something's being a sense datum and our having some sort of knowledge of it. And, as Sellars makes clear, leaning too heavily on one or other feature of sense-data as particular, or sense-data in the epistemic act of sensing, means that one 'sever[s] the logical connection' between them.[9]

Of course, there is normally meant to be some sort of logical connection between sensing sense contents and having knowledge on the sense datum account. However, to be an adequate account of knowledge in any full sense, the notion of 'givens' must bridge the particular-knowledge gap just mentioned. But sensings are usually understood as *foundational* givens and hence are *non-epistemic* on the usual story. The argument thus poses a problem for the sense-data theory. The point is that the sense-data theorist is caught both ways when it comes to the relationship between sensing and knowing: if they take this relationship to be unanalysable, then they break the supposed logical connection between them (sensings are thereby seen as non-epistemic particulars and knowings are seen as epistemic facts). On the other hand, if they choose to analyse sensings in terms of knowings, then sensings turn out (at best) to be *non-inferential* knowings and hence, they break the connection once more - full-blooded knowledge must once again be seen as distinct from sensings. We are thus left to wonder how sensings can possibly lead to or constitute full-blooded knowledge, if 'knowings' are facts and 'sensings' are particulars.

Clearly there must be more to sensing than the sense-data theorist allows. Because sensing particulars does not guarantee the sensing of facts, it is quite unclear how perception is supposed to yield acquired inferential abilities like propositional knowledge, learning, concept formation and so on. Sellars's suggestion, following from this argument, is that we abandon the notion of non-inferential givens entirely.

Sellars's view is that '*x* senses a sense content ... presupposes acquired abilities'[10] even if only to give an account of it as such. If we did not have any acquired abilities of learning, high-level concept formation, background knowledge, etc., it is hard to see how we could even *say* that x senses a sense content. It is from this basis that Sellars attempts to offer a rejection not only of

---

[8] Ibid., p. 129.
[9] Ibid., p. 130.
[10] Ibid., p. 131.

the category of sense-data in epistemology, but also all possible forms of 'the given.'

The rest of Sellars's argument follows from the assumption that experience presupposes acquired abilities. Much of the argument in response will be drawing upon the idea that it is consistent to suppose that we can have a sense content in some low-level sense, without thereby being able to capture the content of such an experience in terms of learning, knowledge, descriptive concepts, etc., despite Sellars's claim that these things are presupposed in every instance of the given. My claim is that low-level experience may still be contentful and yet not be captured in such terms. Thus, even though I shall be agreeing to some extent with his rejection of the myth of sense-data, I shall disagree with his claims about the 'given'. The point in this section has been that, according to Sellars, the notion of sense-data is a muddle of two ideas: data as particulars which are not known, and data as items of knowledge which are not sensed non-inferentially.

How sense-data sever the logical connection between sensing and knowing

The upshot for Sellars is that the 'Classical Sense Datum' theories face an inconsistent triad if they choose to sever the connection between knowledge and having sense contents. The alleged triad, and Sellars's comments, follow:

> A. *x senses red sense content s* entails *x non-inferentially knows that s is red.*
> B. The ability to sense contents is unacquired.
> C. The ability to know facts of the form *x is φ* is acquired.
> A and B together entail not-C; B and C entail not-A; A and C entail not-B. [W]hich one of them will [the sense datum theorist] choose to abandon?
> (1) He can abandon A, in which case the sensing of sense contents becomes a non-cognitive fact ... which may be ... a *logically* necessary condition, of non-inferential knowledge, but a fact ... which cannot *constitute* this knowledge.
> (2) He can abandon B, [which cuts off] the concept of a sense datum from ... ordinary talk about sensations, feelings, after-images, tickles and itches, etc.
> (3) But to abandon C is to do violence to the predominantly nominalist proclivities of the empiricist tradition.[11]

This is all endorsement of the same critical point. The important part is found in premise A: namely, that one is committed to the view that the sensing of sense contents implies the knowledge of such a content *in so far as it is a sense content*, and that abandoning this apparently leads to the view of sense as a 'non-cognitive fact.' (It is a non-cognitive fact because it is *known*, allegedly, non-inferentially.) The consequence is that full-blooded knowledge can never be constituted on this non-cognitive basis, and that one must uphold this premise as one must uphold the rest. Hence, the inconsistent triad.

Sellars's point is simply that none of the above options are available to the

---

[11] Ibid., p. 132.

sense-data theorist. The only remotely plausible way of escaping the inconsistent triad is to abandon premise A. But this leads to the undesirable conclusion that robs the sense-data theorist of one his central reasons for employing the notion of non-inferential givens in the first place - viz., to account for the foundation of knowledge. And, as Sellars stresses, since sense-data are *particulars* they cannot do that job - what is needed in accounting for knowledge is an account of *facts*. (And, importantly, for Sellars the sense of 'knowledge' that is of interest here is that which is captured by the propositional linguistic and representational features of an experience):

> For what is *known*, even in non-inferential knowledge, is *facts* rather than particulars, items of the form *something's being thus-and-so* or *something's standing in a certain relation to something else*. ... [T]he sensing of sense contents *cannot* constitute knowledge, inferential *or* non-inferential; ... [so] what light does the concept of sense datum throw on the 'foundations of empirical knowledge'?[12]

What is explicit here is that Sellars takes 'knowledge' to be constituted by high-level criteria. On this view, no sense can be made of the notion of particulars constituting knowledge since, by definition, particulars do not aid in the recognition of the propositional linguistic or representational content of an experience. (Particulars, like 'bent' sense-data, cannot stand in relation to other objects and cannot have a tokened form in one's language like a bent stick can.) And, Sellars reasons, since such a characterisation is required for an understanding of cognitive facts, there is forever an unbridgeable gulf between 'sensing' and 'knowing' on the terms of the sense-data theory.

This treatment of premise A does not altogether fit with the passage quoted earlier.[13] For previously, we saw that Sellars claimed that though a red sense content (say) were not itself a cognitive fact, it might still imply a connection between such a content and knowledge of sorts, if only because the 'converse' relation may hold: i.e., the knowledge of a certain physical object being red may logically imply the non-inferential sensing of a red sense content. This is, in Sellars's view, a consequence of the sense datum position: even though particulars being sensed does not imply knowledge, it would, he says, 'be hasty to conclude' the impossibility of the 'converse relation' from knowledge to the non-inferential sensing of sense contents.[14]

There seems to be a tension between these two claims. Sellars seems clearly aware that the 'converse relation' can guarantee knowledge in some sense, but it does not seem to influence his conviction that aims at upholding that one cannot abandon premise A without severing the knowledge and sensing of sense contents relation. But surely there is room here to abandon A and install the converse relation in its place. It does seem plausible that even if sensing sense contents does not itself constitute knowledge, 'aspects' of such experiencings may still feature as an important part of content in some low-level, yet informational sense. And it might be this low-level information that guarantees

---

[12] Ibid., p. 128-9.
[13] n. 6.
[14] Sellars, op. cit., p 129. I shall later exploit this asymmetry.

that one does sense something and that some content is thereby given non-inferentially.

This would be possible, for instance, if the either/or requirement of inference/non-inference - epistemic/non-epistemic were dropped and a graduationist thesis were put in its place. A graduationist view would suggest that the whole idea of knowledge in the context of experience should be seen in terms of varying degrees of informational content available to perceptual systems. Some of the content might be best described in terms of propositional linguistic knowledge and some might be best captured in representational terms or simply in sensational terms (i.e., as low-level informational awarenesses). Some content (recalling the complexity thesis) might need to be captured utilising a number of different levels of specification. Thus, the converse relation between sensing and knowing (that Sellars mentions as a possible option above) might well hold in the sense that the awareness experienced when undergoing sensational aspects might yield content which, though informational, is not propositional knowledge (and hence, is not a 'cognitive fact' in Sellars sense). But this content might still be epistemic content of some low-level informational kind (though *not* high-level propositional kind). Hence, a low-level non-propositional knowledge of sorts may guarantee that a certain sense content is given non-inferentially. By this means, the problem of the inconsistent triad would be overcome: premise A could be interpreted in terms of the converse relation Sellars mentions. On this interpretation, the sensing of sense contents certainly does not constitute high-level knowledge, however certain low-level seeings are still epistemically informational and thus guarantee that something contentful is actually sensed. This would, of course, mean that the kind of content acquired would not be sophisticated propositional knowledge. But it may be enough to secure a kind of non-foundational 'given'. Abandoning sense-data need not mean that one thereby abandons low-level content.

The upshot of the claims above is that they avoid Sellars's argument that the given is either a particular and hence not known (in the high-level sense of 'known'), or inferentially known (and hence, not 'given'). On this view, the non-propositional information received might guarantee that something is given which is so low-level that it does not constitute the epistemic knowledge that Sellars says is heavily inferential.

There is an advantage to this way of thinking. On this possible rival view, non-inferential sense contents of an informational nature might well feed into the knowledge of facts to some degree, though not themselves amounting to either knowledge or facts in any high-level propositional sense. Yet this content might still be present in what would normally be full-blown epistemic judgements. (This recalls the continuum thesis and the asymmetry thesis - at one level there is low-level content, at the other high-level content and while one level might contain the other, this inclusion need not be symmetrical). So Sellars might be *right* in his claim that low-level givens cannot constitute knowledge, yet *wrong* in thinking that because they cannot they must therefore be non-epistemic (hence, 'particulars' in his sense). Of course he may still be right in thinking that the sense-data theory cannot overcome his objections. Further, this sort of view might fit well with what is being considered recently as an important new direction in cognitive science - a move away from a highly language-driven account of informational content to include informational content of a non-propositional kind.[15] It would also fit in well with modularity theory since the kind of content in question seems to be informationally local and - to some degree - distinct from high-level cognitive processes.

The point for now is that Sellars seems to assume in the above argument that knowledge is exclusively an ability to make propositional linguistic or representational judgements (as we shall see, his sense of cognition is the ability to endorse *statements* to the effect that 'something is thus and so'). However, it should be clear from the points raised in this book that there is a sense in which perception involves a number of different levels of cognitive organisation. This would be possible, for instance, if it were admitted that there are several levels of differentially sophisticated content available to perceiving organisms - a possibility on the continuum view of experiential content, but not on any other. Sellars does not consider this possibility however, and since abandoning premise A leads only to perception as a 'non-cognitive fact' (and since he does not really consider the other propositions [B&C] as being any sort of option) he proposes a diagnosis of the dilemma:

> It [seems that] sense datum [are] a mongrel resulting from a cross breeding of two ideas: (1) The idea that there are ... sensations of red ... which can occur ... without any prior process of learning or concept formation; and without which it would *in some sense* be impossible to see, for example, that the facing surface of a physical object is red ... (2) The idea that there are ... non-inferential knowings that certain items are [red which] are the necessary conditions of empirical knowledge.[16]

The 'mongrel' is an endorsement of the two elements: sense as particulars and sense as the 'fact' of knowing itself. The rest of Sellars's argument is an attack upon the very idea that there is anything of substance in any joint claim which would legitimise an explanation of experiential content in terms of sense datum *without the use of prior concepts*. This, to Sellars, is the rotten core of the Myth.

The Central Claim

Before turning to further exposition of the argument we should return again to proposition A: *x senses red sense content s entails x non-inferentially knows that s is red*. For Sellars, holding this is not just a logical entailment needed to guarantee knowledge (to be rejected only on pain of making sensing 'non-cognitive'), but it is also a matter of being consistent: rejecting it would mean that one would be 'precluded from offering an analysis of *x senses a sense content* ' itself.[17] This may not seem all that clear. The argument for this is that if the entailment relation between sensing and knowing is 'severed' and if we deny the proposition that *x senses red sense content s entails that x non-*

---

[15] See: W. Bechtel and A. Abrahamsen, 'Beyond the Exclusively Propositional Era', *Epistemology and Cognition*, pp. 121-151.
[16] Sellars, op. cit., p. 132.
[17] Ibid., p. 131.

inferentially knows that s is red, then we are denying that *x senses red sense content s* is *acquired* knowledge. And since *x senses a red sense content* presupposes acquired abilities just in being able to articulate such a statement (so the argument runs), we cannot even sensibly *give an account of x senses a red sense content s* if we drop premise A. Result, an impasse: we cannot legitimise by argument the notion of an unacquired sense content as we are denying the grounds by which we give an analysis of that sense content. Hence, Sellars argues:

> It follows that he could analyse *x senses red sense content s* as *x non-inferentially knows that s is red* only if he [admits] that the ability to have such non-inferential knowledge as that, for example, a red sense content is red, is itself unacquired. [However] most empirically minded philosophers are strongly inclined to think that all classificatory consciousness, all knowledge *that something is thus and so,* or in logicians' jargon, all subsumption of particulars under universals, involves learning, concept formation, even the use of symbols.[18]

Sellars betrays his biases here, and no clear reason is given at this point, for accepting the 'strong inclinations' of 'empirically minded philosophers' over the inclinations of any other sort of philosophers. It is also clear, if it were not earlier, that Sellars's inclinations regarding knowledge, concepts, learning and so on are exclusively 'high-level' in my sense, with a tendency to (symbolic) inferential linguisticism (Note the emphasis here on 'classificatory consciousness'). What he seems to mean by capturing the content of an experience is to capture the propositional linguistic content and perhaps the representational content also (the phrase 'something is thus and so' is ambiguous in this regard). As we shall see later, he certainly thinks that content is, in some critical sense, propositional (i.e., language-like). In any case, it is obvious here that he places himself firmly in the tradition of thought that espouses the view that sensations (in whatever sense they are referred to) are comprehensively penetrated by such background theoretical considerations, high-level concept formation, language and the like. But his ensuing discussion is supposed to demonstrate a reason for this position. It will be claimed later that, in contrast to Sellars, it is *not the case* that being non-inferentially known is a logical entailment for all 'givens', and so some givens may yet still escape his argument.

Codes, languages and propositional contents

The next step in the argument is to introduce the notion of a linguistic code to account for the persistence of sense datum 'talk'. The claim here is that a code has no logical grammar of its own, but can act as a mnemonic device which serves to remind us of the part certain sentences play among other sentences in our language. If this can be upheld, then sense datum talk becomes just the operation of such a code within our language, and no claim can be made for it to designate anything experientially significant. The sort of thing which Sellars has

---

[18] Loc. cit.

in mind here is something like this: the sense datum code is imagined to receive its logical grammar from its relation with the sense datum language it is designed to prompt; its function being not logical, but *instantiational.*

Consider a traffic light code. Three signals (or 'flags') instantiate two states of the traffic: a state of rest (red flag) and a state of motion (green flag). (The amber/red combination functions as a transition signal between the one and the other). It would be a mistake to suppose that there was a *logical* relation between the signals and the motion or stasis they give rise to, or even the 'datum' they supposedly generate in observers. The proposition: *Red traffic lights present red sense-data* does not *logically* entail any sort of sense datum or any particular state of the traffic. What it *does* entail is that certain *other* sentences are logically valid inferences from it. A sentence like this is a flag code for a more specific sentence such as *The traffic light looks red to someone,* from which it follows that *Something looks red to somebody* etc. These can be linked (eventually) to other conventional sentences such as *Red traffic lights mean that traffic should stop or remain stationary,* from which whole syllogisms could be formed which direct appropriate action. But this is at the level of *sentences* which one can form from such propositions. The proposition *Red traffic lights present red sense-data,* however, is a look-alike sentence, not a real one, as it has no logic of its own, only a logic which is 'parasitical'[19] on the sentences which do, such as the ones indicated above. *Red traffic lights present red sense-data* has a logic insofar as it is similar in form to: *Red things are of a certain colour,* which has a logic linking it to such sentences as *Certain colours are red,* from which certain logical incongruities and inclusive relations can be illustrated, such as in jointly holding *Certain colours are red* and *Certain colours are not red,* both of which are subsets of *Some things are coloured* etc. The trouble with the original assertion, Sellars implies, is that it is itself alogical; it can only point to certain sentences which do not refer to a sense datum and which are already specific sentences embedded within a logical framework. One can only articulate *Red traffic lights present red sense-data* if, by it, one means *The traffic light looks red to x,* or some such sentence. On its *own,* it is not a sentence, but a code, a means of instantiating another sentence. The point of all these considerations is close to Sellars's lips:

> [S]ense-datum talk neither *clarifies* nor *explains* facts of the form *x looks ø to s* or *x is ø.* ... One would [instead] be constantly tempted ... to treat sense-datum flags as ... sentences in a *theory,* and ... as a *language* which gets its use by co-ordinating sense-datum sentences with sentences in ordinary perception talk, *as molecule talk gets its use by co-ordinating sentences about populations of molecules with talk about the pressure of gases on the walls of their containers.*[20]

The upshot of all this is that sentences which exhibit experience-talk about sense-data can be shown to be the 'grammatical analogies'[21] of genuine sentences, which expose the real relations between subjects and objects and

---

[19] Ibid., p. 135.
[20] Ibid., p. 137-8.
[21] Ibid., p. 142.

which clarify and explain this relation in a manner consonant with science, without employing the difficult category of 'sense-data.' The relation between sense-data talk and its 'demythologized' alternative will be something like the relation between a logical sentence and its *code*. The aim of Sellars is to show that nothing is gained, in fact, by explaining one's experience in terms of sense-data, if it can be shown that how things *look to be* amounts to how things really *are*.

Sellars's argument for this is made with the above considerations in mind and also by making what he calls 'a simple and fundamental point': namely, that 'the sense of 'red' in which things *look* red is, on the face of it, the same as that in which things *are* red.'[22] The point is, in claiming that an experience *looks* to be of a certain sort, we are, in effect, claiming more than how our experiences appear to us; we are also stating an assertion and endorsing the assertion for its propositional content. The notion of truth-conditional semantics is apposite here in explaining this. Sellars is suggesting that in any claim about the contents of our experiences we, in effect, plot the degree of statement endorsement on a graph of *veridicality:* we assess, in some sense, the degree of endorsement required in some given instance in which we are to make a certain claim about the experiences we are undergoing. Thus, 'x is red', 'x *looks* red', 'x *merely looks* red' ('it *looks as though* x is red') and 'x *looks* red to me now' all express differently weighted endorsements as to their truth content ('x is red' is stronger than 'x *merely looks* red', etc). This sets out an important distinction for Sellars, between what would otherwise be type-cast as simply expressing or describing an experience, against a sentence which does more than describe or report an experience, but also gives and (to varying degrees) withholds what we endorse as the propositional content of a sentence. Moreover, the propositional content, as the examples are supposed to demonstrate, is not any mysterious semantic notion, but simply the thing or circumstances which would make a sentence *true*.

Sellars's scenario of the shopkeeper selling coloured neckties is instructive here. The imagined case is that 'John' (the shopkeeper) has never looked at an object in 'other than standard conditions'[23] until he suddenly has to cope with the installation of the electric light in his shop. For John, the neckties in his shop look to have different colours under electrical lighting than they did when he saw them in daylight. John eventually responds to this change in his experiences by learning to stifle reports about how the neckties look in the new conditions, and introducing a fact-stating language of how they *are* as opposed to the reporting language of how they *look*. (It is supposed that he is simultaneously instructed in matters pertaining to the effect of electrical light on the neckties).

The propositional content endorsement idea is meant to clarify and explain this phenomenon. Until John was able to conclude from inferring *why* neckties were coloured as they were under the new conditions, he was only able to say how his neckties looked. Through a number of factors (the installation of the light, the linguistic pressure exerted by others more adept in responding to the change of conditions, and by repeated exposure) he was later able to obtain a

---

[22] Ibid., p. 141.
[23] Ibid., p. 142.

view of how the new environment made the colour change in a way which was independent of the way they looked to him and how he believed them to look: the new response would amount to John passing from a view of how a thing looks to him in his experience, to a less 'difficult' and less contentious view of what makes certain sentences about the colour of neckties true. His language, and the degree to which he endorsed the truth commitment of his sentences, would reflect this: he would fully endorse the contents of his expressions about the neckties under electric light as being of a certain colour, and be reluctant to endorse those expressions of how they look under these conditions; he would have learnt a new fact about the content of his experience talk, by moving from talking of how things look to him to a view of how things are *by understanding the circumstances which make the sentences true*. The important thing to note is that this propositional content is bound up with our ability to give an account of what we say; it is, in other words, immersed in our 'logical space of reasons.'[24]

> [T]he concept of *looking green*, ... presupposes the concept of *being green*, and that the latter concept involves the ability to tell what colours objects have by looking at them - which, in turn, involves knowing in what circumstances to place an object if one wishes to ascertain its colours by looking at it ... *which* conditions are standard for a given mode of perception is ... specified by a list of conditions which exhibit the vagueness and open texture of ordinary discourse.[25]

The claim is that we need to have a conception of what sentences it is appropriate to endorse in given circumstances before we can attest to the propositional content of a claim about our experiences. And such sentences, insofar as they have circumstances under which they are true, are already linked with the logical framework of a barrage of other claims which entail more such claims in a similar way as we saw 'Red things are a certain colour' entailed 'Certain colours are not red' etc.

It is important to see the strength and radical nature of this suggestion. For it is, in fact, closely connected with the further suggestion that the net *difference* between the propositional content of a claim and what the claim expresses is zero. There is, according to Sellars, nothing 'residual'[26] in stating a claim, endorsing the propositional content as if the circumstances it expresses were true, and stating another sentence in similar conditions. Thus, if I say 'I see that x, over there, is red' or 'It looks to me that x, over there, is red' or 'It looks to one as though there were a red object there', *the same propositional content* ('x is red') is endorsed by varying amounts. Moreover, the speaker of such utterances must be committed to the propositional content because *it is what would make each sentence true*. If logically committed to this content and some endorsement of it, the question becomes whether anything is 'left over' in this procedure to warrant the title of *being an experience*. Sellars's opinion on this is, in one sense, clear and unambiguous, though it will later be suggested that

---

[24] Ibid., p. 169.
[25] Ibid., pp. 146-7.
[26] Ibid., p. 151.

he leaves a very important option open.

> [The idea of a red sense-datum] runs up against the objection that the redness physical objects *look* to have is the same as the redness physical objects actually *do* have, ... [W]hen it is claimed that 'obviously' physical objects cannot *look* red to one unless one is experiencing something that *is* red, is it not presumed that the redness which the *something* has is the redness which the physical objects *looks to have?* [27]

This is a clear attempt at refuting the sense datum theory. The options, as Sellars sees them, are that one must either access a high-level concept of something which *is* red, or something which is not the same as the actual object, though it consists in having the same properties. This seems a plausible analysis of the situation; and, as he says, it is hard to get very far with the second option. For it seems incredible how a putative entity which is not the same as the entity, but which 'obviously' shares its qualities, could possibly *add* to any analysis of the propositional content of a statement about an actual object. The point is also rhetorical: couldn't we just turn the analysis a little to avoid the redundancy and say that a *look* is just a case of a *seeing that*, if the propositional content of the claim were true? If so, this way of looking at things has major ramifications for the whole logic of private experiential episodes. Hence, Sellars's previously quoted remark (Chapter 2) that instead of having a concept of something because we have noticed that thing, to have the ability to notice a thing is 'already to have the concept of that sort of thing and cannot account for it.'[28]

If endorsing the propositional content of a claim about the world is cognitively linked to such a range of assertions we might make, something important follows: it would seem that one must *begin,* not end, with a general high-level cognitive ability. Experiences *depend* on having conceptual contents such as that of a triangle under certain descriptively and representationally specifiable conditions. If this is so, then the mystery of sensing sense contents might be a case of 'knowing one's way around' one's codes or descriptions, and being able to (properly) assert them. Any reification of what such *codes* describe would indeed be a 'myth'. And since we can never characterise in an *intrinsic* way what is meant by such situations as 'Red traffic lights signal red sense-data', but only by what is logically a definite description (i.e., as the kind of entity which is commonly endorsed in such situations), then we could scarcely seem to be any better off if we instead maintained such talk 'as notational convenience, a code, for the language in which we speak of how things look and what there looks to be.'[29] Since we are no better off in reifying it, it seems false economy in doing so.

At the heart of it all this lies a thesis of *psychological nominalism.* Awarenesses, to Sellars, are not *sui generis* aspects of experience, nor are they the critical feature of mental acts. Rather, he is explicit about affirming his position as:

---

[27] Ibid., pp. 149-50.
[28] Ibid., p. 175-6.
[29] Ibid., p. 175.

> [T]he denial of the claim, characteristic of the realist tradition, that a 'perception' or 'awareness' ... is the root mental ingredient of mental acts and dispositions.[30]

And again:

> [A] view of the general type ... according to which *all* awarenesses of *sorts, resemblances, facts,* etc., in short, all awarenesses of abstract entities - indeed, all awareness even of particulars - is a linguistic affair.[31]

Moreover, as the facts which pertain to so-called 'givens' in experiences have to be *presupposed* on his account, (and if these facts are built-in to the logic of what sentences it is appropriate to endorse), it seems but a redundancy to suppose that awarenesses themselves are needed at all. The crucial thing seems to be one's ability to use language: the syntax of asserting claims about things is what is important, not how things appear for us in order to assert anything about them. The latter, in fact, presupposes already that certain appearings are equivalent to the common propositional content which would make such assertions true.[32]

Sellars is clear about how this notion of a propositional content is to be understood. It is not to be treated in terms which suggest that there is any content in an experience which exists outside the circumstances in which the propositional content is being endorsed. What we nominally call 'an experience', on Sellars's view, is just a circumstance under which we assert things. What we tend to assume beyond this is that there is something over-and-above this asserting which warrants the title 'being an experience'. But, according to Sellars, holding this amounts to little more than a requirement for verbal satisfaction:

> The notorious 'ing-ed' ambiguity of 'experience' must be kept in mind ...because the fact that *x, over there, looks red to Jones* would be a *seeing*, on Jones's part, *that x, over there is red,* if its propositional content were true, ... Certainly, the fact that something looks red to me can itself be *experienced*. But it is not itself an experiencing. ... This would give us a *predicate* by which to describe and report the experience, but we should ... be only verbally better off than if we could only refer to this kind of experience as *the kind which* could be described as the common descriptive component of a *seeing* and a qualitative or existential *looking*.[33]

---

[30] W. Sellars, 'Empiricism and Abstract Entities', *The Philosophy of Rudolph Carnap*, p. 445.
[31] W. Sellars, 'Empiricism and the Philosophy of Mind', op. cit., p. 160.
[32] Sellars remarks: '*seeing that something is thus and so* [is] an *achievement*, and ... sees [is] an *achievement word*. I prefer to call it a "so it is" or a "just so" word, for the root idea is that of *truth*. To characterize S's experience as a *seeing* is, in a suitably broad sense ... to apply the semantical concept of truth to that experience.' ibid., p. 145.
[33] Ibid., p. 154.

It should be noted at this point that Sellars does admit what was earlier (in Chapter 3) called the *causal order* in perception. He is explicit in affirming that perception involves a causal (physical) process.[34] Thus, in the passage above he allows 'an experience' to occur in the sense that the perceiving organism is bombarded with proximal stimuli. What he calls the 'common descriptive component' here is something similar to the representational sense of 'propositional content' that (supposedly) captures the experiential situation (we shall soon see Sellars collapse this distinction).

Although Sellars admits the causal order in experiential claims, he does not admit the *sensory order,* only an *epistemic order* (he admits the order which makes 'noticing' *statements* true, not the order which explains how noticings can have *felt* aspects). In the argument he presents, of course, what actually makes the propositional content of a sentence true is *learning;* specifically, learning the conditions that bring about the endorsement of a claim about the world (recall John learning the conditions under which neckties are said to have a certain colour). Learning and language, of course, are heavily inferential.

In this view of perception, the claim is that there is simply no room for sense-data to do any informational work. Since such objects of perception do no informational work they are therefore not necessary for content. And, since they are not necessary for content (and since they seem to be problematic for other reasons), there seems no good reason to admit such features. For Sellars, then, since no sense can be made of the notion of sense-data, no sense can be made of givenness in general. Givenness in general must be rejected since all givens presuppose that something is sensed non-inferentially.[35] Thus, the whole notion of a 'given' in experience is an incoherent one. According to Sellars, the focus in understanding perception should thus be on the *language* of experience, not the content that is, allegedly, 'given'. This sort of position is clearly inferentialism with a meat axe.

Sellars brings this out in an example of three assertions where the common propositional content is the same and their endorsements are different. The three assertions are: (a) *seeing that x, over there, is red;* (b) *it looks to one that x, over there, is red;* and, (c) *its looks to one as though there was a red object over there.* These expressions, he claims, differ primarily in that: (a) involves an endorsement of the idea that *x over there is red,* whereas in (b) this idea is only partially endorsed, and in (c) not at all. He then refers to *x over there is red,* as the *common propositional content* of these three assertions. He also suggests that we call any 'residue' of these experiences (i.e., that which is left over from any endorsement of the propositional content) the *descriptive content.*

A problem then arises as to how the three experiences which are suggested by those sentences could be identical. Can the propositional and the descriptive

---

34 '[T]he qualities of sense are a dimension of natural process which occurs only in connection with complex physical processes which ... become the complex system of particles which, in the current scientific image, *is* the central nervous system.' 'Philosophy and the Scientific Image of Man', in SP&R, ibid., p. 37.

35 Sellars is explicit about extending his argument to *all* forms of the given: 'many who today attack "the whole idea of givenness" - and they are an increasing number - are really only attacking sense data. ... If, however, I begin my argument with an attack on sense-datum theories, it is only as a first step in a general critique of the entire framework of givenness.' op. cit., pp. 127-8.

content of the experiences be identical, or not? If there is anything in 'givenness' talk at all, then the experiences must be identical, if the common propositional content is the same because, on Sellars's view, we specify the descriptive content indirectly by implying that *if the common propositional content were true, and if the subject knew that the circumstances were normal,* then all these three situations would be cases of *seeing* that x, over there, is red. But the question is whether there is anything intrinsic about the character of the *experiences* that could make them identical. Sellars is inclined to reject this idea outright:

> Thus, the very nature of 'looks talk' is such as to raise questions to which it gives no answer: What is the *intrinsic* character of the common descriptive content of these three experiences?[36]

Sellars's point is that it is difficult to see how the situations can have a common descriptive content because, whereas in (a) the perceiver must be in the presence of a real object; in (b) the object need not be red; and in (c) there need not be an object at all.

The claim is that the common descriptive content collapses ultimately into their respective (linguistic) propositional contents (how we characterise experiential *claims*). According to Sellars, there is no important sense in which the representational content of an experience is to be distinguished from such a characterisation. What would seem to be a basis for distinguishing between different senses of 'proposition' in relation to experience thus does not arise on Sellars's account. (Sellars does not consider it appropriate to suspect other 'residual' content might escape his treatment - but more on this below.)

We could take issue with this on grounds we have considered in previous chapters. The characterisation of what remains in an experiential situation after the propositional content is removed as *descriptive* content seems to favour an inferential analysis - precisely that which we may care to dispute (Sellars's conception of 'proposition' is my sense of 'propositional linguistic' judgment; his conception of 'descriptive content' is my 'representational' judgment.) As a first point, it is not obvious why any interesting sense in which there might be residual content in an experience needs be 'descriptive' in these terms. To call such content in these terms seems to require that the content should capture the representational features of the three experiences in some way which can be communicated *linguistically,* but this seems to be a tall order for low-level content such as I have been considering (it seems plausible that there can be an intrinsic content to the three experiences *despite* their not capturing representational/descriptive features). If what has been suggested is anything like the situation, then qualitative sensational aspects of experiential content are precisely not characterised by such features at all. In short, an interesting sense in which contentful experiences are 'given' might still arise in such circumstances. Sellars's argument that the only content of importance here is propositional is thus not a knock-down support for his own view; indeed, it seems to beg the question in favour of his own view (there may be 'residual' content which escapes both a propositional *and* a descriptive characterisation).

---

[36] Ibid., p. 151-52.

It is also unclear that identical propositional contents need entail an *identity* with respect to the residual content Sellars mentions. A case was considered in Chapter 5 in which subjects were said to have qualitatively different experiences if the propositional/descriptive concepts were different, and qualitatively identical experiences if the concepts were the same. Sellars seems to be committed to this too. Since, however, this seemed less than self-evident earlier, the connection between Sellars's descriptive and propositional content seems spurious. In the terms used before, Tom might have the same qualitative aspect of his experience as that of Dick, even if his experience were not filtered by the relevant propositional features.

Empirical studies seem to bear out precisely this point. If propositional linguistic features were *identical* to the residual content (and if language determines perception as psychological nominalism suggests) then one would expect that the experience would be different if the language was different. But this doesn't seem to be true at all. The language of Dani Indians divides the colour spectrum into only two categories: 'light' and 'dark'. However, in an experiment in which the Dani and a control group were asked to match colour chips, no differences in ability were detected between the two groups.[37]

So it seems that even if propositional contents are the same, there is no logical entailment that, along other dimensions, experiences need be identical, and vice versa. Aspects of experiences may differ or may not differ independent of propositional content. But just because there is no entailment here, this need not mean there is no 'additional content' to speak of; only that there is content which not captured in terms which are *descriptive* (or representational; or propositional linguistic). Thus, it is hardly surprising that Sellars's 'residual' content neither explains, in a descriptive way, the differences between each perceptual situation. For one thing such content may not itself be captured by descriptive, representational content; for another, it may not be logically connected with propositional, inferential content in the manner Sellars assumes it is. Such assumptions have already been criticised earlier in this book.

For Sellars, however, the argument above is a good rhetorical move. For there to be anything intrinsic about such contents, it would either have to endorse the common propositional content, (thus, affirming his thesis), or it would have to be explained how it is that the content can be the same when the endorsed situations differ greatly. With this point taken, the beast would seem to be dead. Nothing can be 'given' beyond what it is proper to assert, and what it is proper to assert is actually how things really are. There may, however, be rather less in this argument than first appears.

Criticising Sellars's thesis

Robinson on Sellars

Sellars's argument is ingenious and compelling. Still, some sense of 'the given'

---

[37] See E. R. Heider and D. C. Oliver, 'The Structure of the Color Space in Naming and Memory for Two Languages'. See also, Selby Hunt, 'A Realist Theory of Empirical Testing: Resolving the Theory-Ladenness/Objectivity Debate', pp. 150-151.

which is not tied to propositional contents (and which is not a merely causal process) may still live despite the criticisms. In this section and beyond, Sellars's interesting and challenging position will be criticised by first turning to an evaluation of his arguments by William Robinson.[38] I think Robinson is right in claiming that while Sellars's arguments are an effective rejection of certain *views* of the given, it is not an effective challenge argument against the given *as such*. I shall later offer a brief review of his counter arguments and endorse what are the salient points. For now, an evaluation of the extension of Sellars's arguments to the Given in general.

Robinson describes Sellars's critique of the given, as offering us 'a series of overlapping dilemmas':[39] whether the given can be said to be analysable or unanalysable, whether it is particulars which are given or knowledge itself, and whether it can be analysed in terms of epistemic criteria or non-epistemic criteria. The claim, for Robinson, is whether or not the dilemmas continue to hold for the notion of *givenness in general* or only for the sensing of 'sense-data'. Sellars assumes that attacking one species of the given is a 'first step' in a general critique of the 'entire framework'.[40] Robinson is concerned with arguing that there is an inequivalence in rejecting sense-data and rejecting what he calls (appropriately enough) 'primordial awareness', which he claims, 'might be entitled to be called a "given."'[41] We shall have to see later if this claim is justified.

The first set of dilemmas, as we have seen, concerns how 'givenness' is to be defined. There are two options: either (a) the givenness of sense contents is defined in terms of non-inferential knowledge of sense contents; or (b) the givenness of sense contents is 'a basic or primitive concept of the sense-datum framework'.[42] (a) is refuted by Sellars on the basis that sensing would have, on this account, to *be* knowledge; the other option (b) leads to a further dichotomy: (c) that sensing is a 'unique and unanalysable act'[43] or (d) sensing is analysable. The options of (b) and (c) conjoined are refuted by Sellars on the grounds that they 'sever' the sensing sense contents implies non-inferential knowledge relation. If that were true, Sellars argues, then we could never *have* knowledge (though he does stipulate the possibility of a 'converse' relation).

The conjunction of (b) and (d) meets further options: either (e) sensing is analysable in non-epistemic terms, or (f) analysable in epistemic terms. The conjoining of (b), (d) and (e) is refuted by Sellars on the grounds that if it were analysable in such terms it would make as much sense to speak of sense-contents as *unveridical* as veridical.[44] ('Epistemic facts cannot be analysed without remainder into non-epistemic facts.'[45]) And the options (b), (d), (f)

---

[38] William S. Robinson, 'The Legend of The Given' in *Action, Knowledge and Reality: Critical Studies in Honor of Wilfred Sellars*.
[39] Ibid., p. 85.
[40] Sellars, E&PM op. cit., p. 128.
[41] Robinson, op. cit., p. 84.
[42] Sellars, E&PM op. cit., p. 130.
[43] Loc. cit.
[44] Ibid., p. 134.
[45] Robinson, op. cit., p. 86.

conjoined lead to an inconsistent triad: one cannot give up any of its premises without ruling out sense as unable to give an account of knowledge. (Though it has already been remarked that this is inconsistent only on the assumption that the sensing of sense contents *entails* that it is non-inferentially known, and not 'the converse', that knowledge entails the sensing of sense contents). On all this, Robinson says:

> We have remarked that in this [Sellars'] discussion what is sensed is given. We are not, of course, at all entitled to the converse assertion. Yet if we regard the points we have been reviewing as applying to givenness in general and not only to sensing, it is not obvious at all that they do not continue to hold, and for the same reasons. If (c) is untenable for the reasons given, then so is (c'), 'Something's being given is a unique and unanalysable occurrence'. Likewise, if givenness is epistemic and epistemic facts cannot be analysed without remainder into non-epistemic facts, then (e') 'givenness is analysable into non-epistemic terms' is no better off than (e). Similar conditions hold for (f') 'givenness is analysable in epistemic terms'. Let us suppose that Sellars would accept our generalised version of his argument against sense-datum theories as a correct outline of his strategy against the given in general. Then, the rejection of the given depends on the rejection of (a), (c'), (e') and (f'). Conversely, if as I believe, Sellars has not shown the given to be a myth, it must be because he has not succeeded in rejecting one of these four claims.[46]

As mentioned earlier, Sellars does take his arguments against the sense-data view as arguments against the given in general. Thus, there is no real problem with an extension of his views to all forms of the given.

Robinson wants to suggest that the suspect claim in Sellars's argument is the rejection of (e'): that givenness is analysable in non-epistemic terms. He wants to suggest that his 'primordial awareness' sense of the given *can* be so analysed. I would like to follow through with Robinson's position, as it tallies, to some degree, with my own. It will be remembered that the acceptance of the inconsistency of holding that the given is both a basic and particular event and analysable in non-epistemic terms turns on the acceptance of premise A of the triad: that we *know* in some non-inferential sense that (say) *x is red*. If this is so, then we can't deny this without making sensing 'non-cognitive'; if we affirm it, then we subscribe to an inconsistent triad. It will also be remembered that although Sellars claims that particulars can never constitute knowledge, because they are *ex hypothesi* non-epistemic in nature, there *is* the possibility of the 'converse relation' guaranteeing knowledge in such a case ('the seeing that a certain physical object is red might logically imply sensing a red sense content.')[47] These were the two doubts expressed earlier.

Sellars's arguments about sensing sense contents can, it seems, be generalised to apply to the framework of the given. I shall summarise it as I understand it would go: if givens are *particulars* then they cannot constitute

---

[46] Ibid., pp. 86-7.
[47] Sellars, E&PM, op. cit., p. 129.

knowledge (they must be *non-epistemic* facts). But particulars cannot just be analysed in non-epistemic terms because it has to be shown why the *fact* of the particular given simultaneously endorses the propositional content of what would make a statement about it true. To do this, it must be *non-inferentially* known in some way. But with non-inferentiality of the given assumed, it seems we would have to face the inconsistency of not being able to give an account of the *statement* which verifies the given being non-inferential, because we cannot do that without acceding to the ability that (supposedly non-inferential) facts of the form x is ϕ are acquired *inferentially*, by learning, concept formation and the use of symbols. And if we admit this, then it is no longer non-inferentially known.

The questions that need to be asked, and on which this all turns, are, then:

¥: *whether the given cannot fail to be analysed non-epistemically to keep the myth and that this view must eventually be rejected.*

¶: *whether the given cannot fail to be seen as non-inferentially known to preserve the myth, but that this too must eventually be rejected.*

If both of these can be rejected the given might not be a myth. Another question is whether what is left would be worth keeping. I shall argue that it is.

Low-level content again

The concept of the 'the given' for Sellars is required in order to account for two traditional ideas: the idea that 'empirical knowledge rests on a 'foundation' of non-inferential knowledge of matters of fact',[48] and the idea that what is 'common' to all instances of givenness is 'the awareness of certain sorts ... of primordial non-problematic feature[s] of "immediate experience"'.[49] As noted in Chapter 1, these are largely *separate* issues. The first idea is the traditional doctrine of foundationalism; the second is the idea that certain appearances are 'read off' what is perceived, in some non-problematic sense, when having experiences without the necessary influence of high-level features. It was argued in the earlier chapter that the plausible claim that experiences are fixed by the observational situation, in some sense, need not be conflated with the foundationalist doctrine. This is an important point in this connection since to all this, Robinson adds a definition of what 'primordial' might mean here, to which, he stipulates, the notion of *independence* is crucial:

> An awareness is primordial if and only if there are no necessary conditions for its occurrence except:
> (i) conditions which follow analytically from the concept of an awareness of sorts.
> (ii) having a sensation or image; and
> (iii) conditions which are also necessary conditions for having sensations or images. (Thus, for example, an awareness could be counted as primordial even if it were believed that a necessary condition of it were the existence of a self, provided that such a condition was also regarded

---

[48] Ibid., p. 128.
[49] Ibid., p. 157.

as necessary for sensations or images).[50]

What is being claimed here for low-level awarenesses is clearly to be distinguished from foundationalism. It is not being claimed that such awarenesses are the basis of empirical knowledge; nor is it claimed that awarenesses are incorrigible. What is being claimed is that there are contents which have no necessary conditions for their occurrence beyond their being experienced at some low-level: it has not been stressed, for instance, that high-level features are involved in the experience in any necessary and sufficient way.

This definition also marks a difference between low-level content and the concept of sense-data. For where the notion of sense datum has traditionally been understood as *objects of immediate knowledge* (we have just seen Sellars's arguments against this idea) nothing like this is explicitly assumed, or follows from, Robinson's notion of a primordial awareness.

Granted this definition, a question can be asked: can it be said that Sellars argues *from* the claim that the given entails x has non-inferential knowledge to the claim that primordial awarenesses *also* entails that x has non-inferential knowledge? The question is important because primordial awareness might be entitled to be called a given, and if this can be run past Sellars's argument and survive intact, then Sellars's argument will not work for *all* instances of the given. Robinson claims that though there is no direct discussion of primordial awarenesses being different from 'the given' in its sense-data form, an argument for the non-inferentiality of primordial awarenesses can actually be constructed out of 'Sellarsian principles'[51] on which an attack on Sellars's position can be made. The reconstruction argument hinges on the point that all primordial awarenesses, if admitted at all, must for Sellars be linguistically *classificatory* (i.e., subsumed under descriptive concepts) in a form in which it would be proper to *assert* such things as 'this is f' (x is ϕ). This seems a reasonable claim from a Sellarsian point of view. After all, for Sellars, an unclassified awareness is not an awareness *of* anything, and hence is scarcely intelligible in such terms. A primordial awareness of sorts must be classificatory for Sellars, and being classificatory, must be non-inferentially known.[52]

If this point seems weak, then one should consider the role of concepts in Sellarsian terms. Although the notion of a concept is far from clear, the important and characteristic thing about them for Sellars is their role in guaranteeing experiential exclusivity and independence. Concepts enable distinctions to be made between one experiential situation and another. The important thing from Sellars's point of view seems to be that concepts provide a means of distinguishing experiences which have similar common propositional contents (recall the three experiences earlier). Since endorsing the propositional content of a sentence in an experience requires an individual to distinguish cases where it is appropriate to endorse certain situations and not others, it seems plausible that an individual be pre-possessed of the relevant and irrelevant

---

[50] Robinson, op. cit., p. 85.
[51] Ibid., p. 88.
[52] We saw Sellars mention this 'classificatory' requirement in the context of claiming that the sensing of sense contents presupposes acquired abilities (See n. 18.)

criteria (I take it that this is what is behind Sellars's remark (given in Chapter 2), that: 'to notice [a] sort of thing is already to have a concept of that sort of thing and cannot account for it.') Thus, only if an individual could conceptually distinguish between *its looking to one as though there was a red object over there* from *seeing that x is red,* could he be prepared to distinguish one state from the other, and be prepared to endorse one statement and not the other in view of the experiential circumstances.

Given this, it can be asserted non-controversially that: (i) every state can be associated with only one property, and (ii) no two properties can be associated with the same state.[53] In Chapter 2, 'concept' was defined as the mode of presentation of a property, and one of these 'modes' we considered to be *descriptive* (i.e., propositional) in content. It was also clear that *only* this mode possessed the above features. The point was also made, in the context of the continuum theory, that there are multiple levels of such concepts, some of which do not possess these features.

A crucial point here, however, is that Sellars starts out with a rather different assumption: namely, that all concepts are *descriptively classificatory*. In the context of this (and given the extension of Sellars's arguments against sense-data to all forms of the given), if one *did* assume that having a primordial awareness of sorts involved, and *only* involved, the use of descriptive concepts, (i.e., being classified or subsumed under them), then one can argue legitimately that:

> x has primordial classificatory consciousness entails x makes primordial use of a concept;
> x makes primordial use of a concept entails x immediately subsumes something under a concept;
> x immediately subsumes something under a concept entails x has non-inferential knowledge;
> therefore: x has primordial classificatory consciousness entails x has non-inferential knowledge.[54]

And the rest of Sellars arguments would follow from this point (that this view severs the relationship between sensing and knowing; that it presupposes acquired abilities etc.)

This might seem to be argument by stipulation; that all primordial awarenesses are classificatory in this descriptive way. And indeed I want to suggest that this is not the *only* way that the content of a primordial awareness can be thought of. But the point here is that it is hard to know what to make of a concept in Sellarsian terms, given what we have already seen of his inferentialist account, if it is not, in some way, classificatory in a linguistic sense - as a 'something that is thus and so'. And, if concepts are to be defined in this simple manner, then they can certainly support some sense of non-inferential knowledge, if only because to be able to classify and subsume something under a concept is to access something non-inferentially. Robinson's argument that Sellars actually *supports* this reasoning is that he 'never tries to

---

[53] Robinson, op. cit., p. 90.
[54] Ibid., pp. 89-90.

drive a wedge between *belief* based on immediate experience and *knowledge* based on immediate experience.'[55] The point here is that since Sellars does not, at any time, question that subsuming some sense-datum under a concept entails having non-inferential knowledge about it, it is a tacit admission that the same goes for any state at all. This very point will be a bone of contention later.

For Sellars, then, having primordial classificatory consciousness entails subsumption under a concept, and the same goes for 'primordial awarenesses', if there be such things. Primordial awareness equates with having non-inferential, classificatory knowledge on this account. The question now becomes whether the *use* of such a low-level concept entails a concept's *independence*. This is important, because if it can be shown that an awareness can be a primordial but not an *independently* subsumed classificatory concept, then we might be able to get past Sellars's argument. By an independently subsumed concept, I have in mind an *x is ø* kind of relation, a relation which captures propositional content. As we have seen, most high-level epistemic/descriptive concepts are of this kind, and are the mainstay of the inferentialist's program. Sellars, of course, explicitly employs this kind of classificatory consciousness requirement in his argument against 'all forms of the given'.

But this is where Robinson thinks that Sellars comes unstuck, for Robinson is inclined to think that the use of a concept does not necessarily imply a concept's independence. Particularly, he thinks nothing of the sort is implied by the use of a primordial concept. Certainly, if this implication is admitted, however, and if the foregoing can be said to be a reasonable re-writing of what Sellars would have to say, if low-level awarenesses were equal to sense-data, it would seem to follow through to the desired conclusion that primordial awarenesses were likewise non-inferentially known, and the rest of Sellars's argument would follow. But maybe there is a case for claiming that *not all awarenesses are independently classificatory concepts in Sellars's sense*. In other words, perhaps not all concepts are *propositional*.

An argument for this could be constructed along the following lines: from the premise that an awareness is conceptually low-level, it does not follow *necessarily* that an awareness is an *independent* concept, and being independently classifiable is surely a condition of knowing a concept non-inferentially. This seems to leave room for a sense in which some 'givens' are not epistemically subsumed in a similar manner to most other concepts (i.e., non-inferentially), and if epistemic non-inferentiality cannot be claimed for such concepts, then they would seem to slip through the net of Sellars's argument. Robinson explains:

> Does the fact that a use of a concept is primordial entail that that concept is independent? I am not sure. For I do not know how to rule out the possibility that a necessary condition of having a sensation or image of one sort is being able to have a sensation or images of other sorts. ... For example, it might be that anything that could be said to have sensations of red must also be capable of having a sensation of black. If so, and if we

---

[55] Ibid., p. 91. This is precisely the wedge I am driving. I am saying that there are observational beliefs which are contentful in a non-descriptive (sensational) way.

have primordial awarenesses of sorts simply by having sensations and images, then a necessary condition of a primordial use of a concept red would be the ability to make primordial use of the concept black; thus the concept red in such a case would not be independent.[56]

It is clear just what Sellars would wish to say to this. He would want to say that concepts like 'red' and 'black' are tied to their propositional contents; conditions which make them true, and also our endorsements of them. And he would also hold that we possess a highly sophisticated system of concepts about standard conditions of observations, normal observers, etc., which condition what sentences we need to hold in given circumstances. But the *endorsing* of propositional contents amounts to *subsuming* them independently; what we are after, in the example considered, are cases where concepts are not independently subsumed. We are after cases of where simply being aware in some primitive manner is in some sense prior or concurrent to the subsumption and use of high-level independent concepts, and not vice versa. By analogy:

> If I count the books on my shelf, I may say, as I point, 'One, two, three...' These words reflect a state of mind corresponding to the properties 'first book counted by me on this occasion, second book counted by me on this occasion,' etc. But I have not *subsumed* these books under concepts corresponding to these properties. Nor, indeed, *could* I have correctly done so until I had counted them. Even if I had said, 'This is the first book, this is the second book...', this would only look like subsumption but would actually be counting. Of course, my counting does provide a ground for subsumption by myself or another, of these books under such concepts as 'first book counted by me on this occasion.' But this is not to say that the original counting is itself a case of subsuming.[57]

Robinson has an important case to put here. Sellars has not considered the sorts of 'givens', the sorts of low-level perceptual contents which are quite different from givens which are independently-captured and linguistically-endorsed. He has, rather, assumed that all givens *which have any epistemic/informational significance at all* (like the particular case of sense-data) involve concepts which are subsumed linguistically and so, classified independently.[58] But reflection shows that this is implausible: in being aware of aspects of experience in some low-level sense, we can distinguish such features as 'red', 'black', etc., simply as patterns of qualitative similarity and difference; indeed, without this very low-level awareness, this discriminating ability, all subsumed concepts would tend to merge, be undifferentiated and homologous. (Try conceiving of 'red' in a classificatory way - as 'something which is thus and so' - without first noting

---

[56] Ibid., p. 93.

[57] Ibid., p. 103.

[58] It is important to add the rider about epistemic significance. As mentioned earlier, Sellars allows *proximal givens* (physical nerve impingings) to occur in perceptual situations. But the causal order is non-inferential *par excellence* and is non-epistemic in every sense of the word. It thus has no bearing on the current argument.

some red aspect or other, for example. It does not seem necessary that such an experience be *propositionally* distinguishable from other colours - i.e., 'red' from 'blue', etc. However, it does seem important that there be some non-propositional, qualitative features that are detectable - i.e., *this* experience differs from *that* one etc.) The survival advantages of having such informational features at one's disposal has been pointed out in previous chapters.

Such low-level content does not seem to be subsumed under concepts in Sellars's sense. It is this very basic and *primitive* level of awareness, an 'aspect' of experiential content, that has been outlined the preceding chapters. This kind of content is informational *without necessarily being epistemically high-level.*

Of course, given the *complexity thesis,* an experience can be epistemic in Sellars's sense while *also* having low-level informational features. It is not being suggested here that there must be only one kind of content or the other (though in the case of very unsophisticated creatures there is less likely to be propositional linguistic content). I am saying that it is also at this low-level that important informational features are available. It is this low-level content that allows a high-level representational judgement with propositional linguistic content to have features which escape a fully high-level characterisation of the content of that experience (recall Millar's example of experiencing a painted wall - an experience which has features which escape the imposition of both the 'concept' and 'intrinsicality' principle). The point here is simply that not all informationally salient features of an experience are 'epistemic' in Sellars's sense. There are clearly contents which cannot be captured in his terms.

There are empirical grounds for supposing that there might be informational features which are perceptually more primitive than contents which are captured propositionally. In recent studies on mental imagery, it has been noted that subjects can orientate pictures and letters and spatially order items in response to carefully worded questions. Given the speed in reaction time in which subjects respond to these questions, it has been argued that there must be a short-term quasi-pictorial image representation ability available as part of one's cognitive repertoire. It has been suggested that this ability features along with a more long-term representation which is more or less propositional in format, and that this short-term depictive visual image acts as a buffer on which some crucial, yet non-propositional information is processed. On this kind of view of cognitive processing, knowledge is understood to be represented uniformly, though available as 'different representation formats'[59] appropriate to different types of information. The details of such work cannot be summarised here. I have argued the case for a modular theory of content in Chapter 8, and suggest that interesting links can probably be made with the empirical work here. It seems plausible that perceptual modularity and the idea of representation formats along different informational levels might go to support a single view of content. In any case, it is clear from this kind of speculative data that Sellars's emphasis on the relevance of propositional knowledge to the fixation of content is somewhat overstated. If there are pictorial buffers which deliver

---

[59] See, for example, S.M. Kosslyn, *Image and Mind;* Bechtel and Abrahamsen, op. cit., p. 131. See also: L. A. Cooper and R. N. Shepard, 'Chronometric Studies of the Rotation of Mental Images', in W. G. Chase, (ed) *Visual Information Processing.*

informationally useful features, then clearly not all content is subsumed independently under descriptive concepts.

If we can sensibly maintain that there are good reasons for rejecting Sellars's assumption about descriptively subsumed concepts, then there might be a way of avoiding the criticism Sellars makes about 'all forms of the given'. If this can be done then some 'givens' may be seen not as features of 'subsumed' concepts in Sellars's sense. We may be able to think of sensational givens as being characterised by entirely different categories of concepts or different representational formats, and that while it may be sensible to speak of high-level content in terms which are propositional linguistic and theoretically informational etc., this might not be a way of capturing other kinds of content. Sellars's categories, it is suggested, are too simplistic in their application to 'givens' which are informationally low-level.

The easiest way of appreciating this point is by utilising examples which have been considered in previous chapters. The notion of a 'look'-belief, for instance, is a case in which a content might be experienced without necessarily being noticed. Another instance, is the case of a experience where certain features are noticed and others are not (seeing a tomato without registering its colour, for example; seeing the third house on the left etc.) Another case might be when informational content is only later recalled with the aid of appropriate cuing stimulus (recalling a colour with the aid of paint samples, for example). The point here is that if Sellars's central argument against all forms of the given rely on their being epistemically subsumed under concepts such that 'something is thus and so', these cases will not be captured by his analysis. For in the case of these low-level 'givens', there may be content albeit not enough to guarantee that they are subsumed independently. The important point about these examples is that while they may not be instantly recognised to be 'thus and so', they may still be informational: an experience would not have the content it does have without such low-level features. Another important point about them is that the low-level content of the experience may not be 'known' in any high-level sense (one might not be able to say precisely what the colour looks like) yet one may be able to 'pick out' the colour with the aid of a paint sample (equally, one may not - one might not be able to tell whether the tomato one experienced was ripe or not). That there can be varying levels of epistemic availability of such contents is, of course, central to the continuum account.

If the above is true, we can thus make the following criticisms of Sellars's argument: in my terms, it is implausible to take on credit the premise A, *x senses red sense content s, entails x non-inferentially knows that s is red,* and by an order of generality extrapolate to all instances of the given. For if it is meant to be a *general* truth about awarenesses, all 'givens' (i.e., not just sense-data) that to be non-inferential, they must be known as such, then it certainly needs further argument: for, unlike sense-data, a low-level awareness, or a sensational 'aspect' of a colour experience, for example, is not independently subsumed under concepts which are accessible to inferential knowledge. Rather, they involve very different kinds of content, distinct from the independent availability and use of other epistemically specifiable concepts, and this seems to be not a case of high-level knowledge as much as a distinct 'aspect'-like feature of such content, which, while epistemically informational to some degree, is not necessarily independently subsumable. (Similar claims could be made for the kind of content while experiencing the Muller-Lyer illusion - such content is not 'epistemic' in any high-level propositional sense, yet it is certainly informational.)

The following point is demonstrated by the appeal to Robinson: just as not all concepts are subsumed and independently capable of classification, *not all concepts are non-inferentially known*, and low-level awarenesses would seem to be a case in point. Low-level awarenesses are not cases like Sellars discusses, because not all concepts are independently subsumptive; some concepts amount to sensational features of subsumed concepts (such as when the ability to have a primordial concept like 'is longer than', or 'occupies more of the visual field' might fix epistemic concepts of particular objects occupying space). That is, we can *consistently* hold that we can be aware of certain low-level contents *without* claiming that our awareness is, itself, a case of descriptive and subsumed non-inferential knowledge. In Chapter 5 it was argued that low-level experiences are, precisely, *not* characterised by being epistemic in this propositional sense, because knowledge about what an experience should be like can be effectively divorced from how something looks.

The upshot of this analysis is that Sellars's inferentialist argument does not work for all instances of the given, for we can circumvent the objection that we are subscribing to an inconsistent triad by dropping premise A and, in fact, claiming that the awareness which is necessary for us to have inferential and non-inferential knowledge may be an aspect of experiential content (though not in any epistemic sense relating to knowledge, concept formation and the use of symbols). Similarly, we can reassess the idea that from the proposition that particulars can never yield knowledge, that 'the given' can never do so, in the following terms: we can say that the 'converse relation', regarding particulars and knowledge is, in fact, true to a certain extent. The *seeing* that a certain physical object is red *does* imply the sensing of a red sense content, insofar as we need to be primordially aware of low-level colour 'aspects', for instance, to provide the grounds for the subsumption and deployment of 'high-level' colour concepts. But as we have admitted that such high-level concepts about sensing are to be distinguished from an ability to be aware of content which is informationally low-level, we can avoid the slide back to sensing having to be some kind of *non-epistemic fact* in order to keep the sensing and knowing from the severing knife.

We can instead say this: the low-level sense of 'the given' is a distinct *way* of having knowledge; it is neither a non-epistemic *fact* nor a non-inferentially known one, and though it may be acquired non-inferentially through the process of receiving sensory inputs, it need not be claimed that it is *known* as such by subsuming such an awareness under independent epistemic/descriptive concepts of the form x is ϕ. We cannot do that with low-level contents because they are *simply not in the same category* as epistemic contents, and are non-subsumable. So Sellars's argument does not work with them.

The point is that 'looks', 'appearances' - low-level 'aspects' of experiences - can be cognitively and epistemically bankrupt to some degree, but yet still 'given'. It is just that the Sellarsian requirement that all 'givens' are impotent unless subsumed under high-level background knowledge does not apply to them. This is an issue only if one takes on board Sellars's polarised conception of the inference/non-inference debate. By contrast, if one assumes something like the continuum view regarding experience and content, then this kind of suggestion about *levels* of inference/non-inference does, in fact, make some kind of evolutionary and perceptual sense. Sellars's arguments against the given do not work on content which is informationally low-level.

If low-level content does not amount to being knowledge in Sellars's sense, then what kind of information do they provide? Provisionally, sensational experiences amount to a *kind* of knowing, *albeit* not related to concepts-of-knowledge as much as to low-level concepts-of-awareness. That is, we can 'know', in some (very primitive, non-propositional) qualitative sense, that we are aware of colour hues and the length of the lines in the Muller-Lyer illusion, without saying that this awareness is fully 'epistemic' in character - that is, epistemic in Sellars's sense. (Indeed, that such an awareness is not epistemic in some propositional or theoretically informational sense is precisely what is *demonstrated* by such experiences as the Muller-Lyer illusion).[60] We can, however, 'know' in some sufficiently attenuated sense here in the very same way as we can have a sufficiently attenuated 'belief' awareness (in my terms, a 'look'-belief). Such awarenesses can, of course, occur in degrees and some may involve sub-descriptive, sensory inferences in sufficiently complex animals, in addition to having these sensational aspects.[61]

But, that there can be content which has both low-level and high-level aspects does not go to rule out the point that low-level content is quite different in character from the descriptively classificatory concepts that may be concurrent with them. The kind of information that low-level givens yield amounts to being *quasi-epistemic* (or 'proto-epistemic', i.e., epistemic at a very low-level). This kind of graduationist view of knowledge can be rejected only if one already presupposes a high-level account of epistemology as Sellars's account does. The arguments and evidence adduced in this book run against such a view.

That this conclusion must be reached in the case of knowledge seems to corroborate our intuitions about animals and pre-linguistic children too: for Fido's informational repertoire is not epistemic in the high-level sense that Sellars seems to require, even though it does seem to be qualitatively *experiential*. And similarly, *mutatis mutandis,* with infants. (The counterintuitive nature of Sellars's emphasis on language being the *bearer* of content was outlined in Chapter 1.) The tendency to suggest that all content has to be informationally high-level to be any kind of content at all is the exaggerated claim of the inferentialist proposal.

None of the points mentioned above are relevant to the particular case of sense-data. The sense-data theory of perception requires more of an account of low-level content than has been claimed for experiential 'aspects'. Such a view

---

[60] If it *were* epistemic in character there would be a problem, because in this case the information would conflict with the rest of our knowledge about the lines precisely because the information doesn't square with what we *see*.

[61] In the case of the Muller-Lyer, of course, there is also a difference of degree between this kind of perception and a 'look'-belief: In the case of a perceptual judgement involving concepts like 'lines' these experiences seem higher up the continuum than those aspect-like experiences lower down. The Muller-Lyer experience is thus sub-descriptively informational. But, it also seems true to say that the kind of experience in the Muller-Lyer case is *closer* to a 'look'-belief than epistemically-permeated experiences of the Sherlock Holmes variety.

requires low-level content to be epistemically incorrigible and foundational - to be *objects* of knowledge in some sense. Sellars has mounted an important attack on this view. But just as not all contentful experiences are captured by propositional linguistic content and not all senses of 'know' have to be epistemically high-level, so not all 'givens' have to be understood in Sellars's terms. If what has been argued in previous chapters is accurate, it is also the case that it is inherently misleading to think of the relationship between experience and inferential features in exclusive terms: there might be a sense in which content can be understood to occur at a number of levels. This is what has been maintained with the continuum account.

If all this is true, then we can reject both ¥ and ¶ on the grounds that the arguments Sellars offers do not commit us to either, if we can sensibly obviate the impetus behind them: *viz.*, that rejecting an account of sense-data goes most of the way towards getting rid of all forms of the given. The claim: Sellars may have expunged the notion of sense-data from philosophy; he has not done so for all forms of 'the given', for *some* givens simply escape the terms of his inferentialist analysis. Sellars's own 'myth' has been to assume that, for the purposes of his argument, all forms of the given are equivalent. I hope to have shown this is not true, for his argument does not work on some of them.

Conclusion

> What's in a Look? If that is a question about visual experience pure and simple, the answer is. 'more, no doubt, than meets the eye, but a lot less than some folks think.'[62]

Sellars's arguments against sense-data do not apply to the category of 'the given' as such. There is a sense in which something's being given in experience as a sensational feature of content, an 'aspect' of experience, may not be non-inferentially *known* in Sellars's sense even if it may be non-inferentially acquired. Also, because not all concepts are subsumed and independently classified as propositional knowledge, not all 'givens' are high-level epistemic. Thus: ¥ and ¶ do not apply as characteristics of 'givens' in general.

My claim in this chapter is that low-level 'aspects' of experience clearly do not commit us to the sense-data theory: for such contents can be contentful without being items of high-level knowledge. The view that experience has qualitative low-level aspects is not, simultaneously, a claim about sense-data. So, although there may be less to a 'look' than the sense-data theorists suggest, there is still more that meets the eye than simple nerve impingings. Indeed, if one takes on board the continuum account of content, then there must be more to 'looks' than simple nerve impingings, since experiential contents are subject to evolutionary considerations, in greater and lesser degrees, which help to harness perceptual information for differentially sophisticated organisms. There are central evolutionary reasons why observation has to be disjoined from high-level content and there are phylogenetic reasons why some organisms have less to a 'look' than others. The discussion of low-level experiential content in the context of the philosophy of mind will be developed in the following chapter.

---

[62] A.H. Millar, 'What's in a Look?', p. 97.

11 Experience eliminated?

> If we have come this far, must the journey end here? Manifestly not ... the long awakening is potentially endless. The human spirit will continue its breathtaking adventure of self-reconstruction, ... But only if we try hard to see new opportunities and only if we work hard at leaving old frameworks behind.[1]

Experience and folk psychology

Introduction

In this chapter a stark and extreme inferentialist view will be examined - the eliminative materialism of Paul Churchland. If true, Churchland's account casts doubt on the claims being presented regarding the importance of low-level content to experiencing organisms. It will be suggested, however, that none of the arguments Churchland raises necessarily support an eliminativist view and that a continuum view of content is not ruled out by his account.

'A brave new world': Churchland's program

The position that Churchland adopts is the familiar one of eliminative materialism. The thrust of eliminative materialism is that one's ontology of mind, mental states, feelings, desires, beliefs - above all, sensational experiences - form part of a common-sense 'folk psychology'; a theoretical position which can effectively be replaced by a more empirically useful, more accurate materialist theory, which derives from the findings of neurophysiology and the science of brain chemistry.

The eliminativist program that Churchland advocates rests specifically on an antecedent theory of inter-theoretic relations in science. Eliminativists claim that what is said to be a sensational content of experience forms part of a redundant theory of our time, just like luminiferous aether and phlogiston were redundant theoretical notions at earlier times. The quest is the elimination of any folk theoretical notion of a sensory content. Eliminating such a theory, in

---

[1] P. M. Churchland, 'Perceptual Plasticity and Theoretical Neutrality', pp. 186-187.

Churchland's view, amounts to nothing short of a major reconstruction of our conception of ourselves. We are to imagine that to be awakened as to the sensational content of experience is to see such content as ultimately theory-embedded and transformable, and so, in principle, theoretically redundant. What will result from adopting this perspective is the elimination of folk psychological concepts and attitudes from common parlance.

There is some support for Churchland's views about theory change and inter-theoretic replacement. History has shown that theories, previously held in high esteem, can be replaced, superseded or altered radically in the course of scientific development. Thomas Kuhn's views on paradigm shifts place emphasis not on the static character of working theories, but on the revolutionary nature of the whole of scientific progress. Kuhn suggested that it is the very nature of theories to be transitory. On his view, theoretical speculation begins with a phase of pre-scientific speculation and moves toward what he called 'normal science' (harbouring a viable and operable research program) to finally, a crisis-situation where it clashes with another rival theory, and where one or other of the rivalling theories is eliminated in favour of its successor theory. This dynamic revolutionary process, to Kuhn, was the very essence of how theories behave. Moreover, theoretical change also changed the way in which we *saw* the world; not metaphorically, but literally: a medieval scientist working with one theory, and a contemporary scientist working with another, literally *worked in different worlds.*[2] Kuhn likened theories to perceptual *gestalts*. The efficacy of a theory in terms of telling us something about evidence, experimental results and observations was something akin to the interpretations inhering in the perception of a multiply ambiguous figure: it was possible to 'switch' from the story told by one theory to the story told by another radically different theory, not by changing the nature of the evidence or supplying different observations, but by switching the theoretical assumptions by scientific revolution. This idea, that theories undergo evolutionary transitions, supplant one another and constitute perceptual 'worlds' or 'paradigms' for the scientists who hold them, influenced Churchland greatly.[3] Some explicit claims from Churchland serve to illustrate this influence:

> [T]he question of ... perceptual judgements can be seen to turn ultimately on the question of the virtues of the theory in whose terms the responses are made. [O]ne's perceptual judgements [should] be made ... within the terms of the best available world theory .... Interpretation functions ... derive from or reflect our current understanding of the world, ... and on occasion, they must be changed, sometimes radically, as our understanding of the world grows and changes. Theories bite the dust, ontologies sink into oblivion.[4]

---

[2] 'Nevertheless, paradigm changes do cause scientists to see the world of their research-engagement differently. Insofar as their only recourse to that world is through what they say and do, we may want to say that after a revolution scientists are responding to a different world.' T. Kuhn, *The Structure of Scientific Revolutions,* p. 111, vide p. 118.

[3] For Kuhn's claims about paradigms being like visual gestalts see ibid., pp. 111-112.

[4] P. Churchland, *Scientific Realism and the Plasticity of Mind,* pp. 37-39.

There are many issues here: theories as perceptual gestalts, incommensurability, the revolutionary nature of scientific progress. The central point is that Churchland is partly influenced by the underpinnings of the Kuhnian philosophy of science and the idea of theory replacement. Churchland's 'interpretation functions' can be read with no great loss as Kuhn's 'paradigms' as far as the main point of the passages here is concerned. Of course, there is an important sense in which Churchland is imbued with the spirit of Feyerabend's early work also, and others. However, it is reasonable to assume that Churchland's views have, as a foundation, the structure of scientific revolutions largely in the way Kuhn presented it.[5]

This Kuhnian view of theoretical replacement would seem to be a paradoxical foundation for Churchland. For he ultimately wants to show not only that neurophysiology can *replace* folk psychology, but also that neurophysiology is, in some sense, the *correct* or *true* theory about such matters. This suggests a certain amount of tension with the Kuhnian view of theoretical replacement, where theoretical change is seen as a fundamentally *revolutionary* business with no special reverence for particular theories. (Kuhn's views are standardly considered to be relativist for this reason.) Perhaps this is not a troublesome charge for Churchland, because all he needs to hold is that the theory he is advocating is a *better* theory than that of folk psychology, not a *true* theory. However, it certainly seems at some points that Churchland wants to hold the stronger claim, which is quite inconsistent with the usual Kuhnian view of theoretical replacement. Churchland wants to say not only that the folk psychological way we interpret the world is deficient in comparison to the neurophysiological way because the former is faulty and misguided and the latter is not, but also that there is some sense in which we can speak of one view, one set of interpretation functions, actually being *right:*

> We may be the unwitting victims of an inappropriate set of interpretation functions. It is an empirical question whether we are; it is an empirical question which is the *right* set of functions; and it is the job of science, broadly conceived, to try to tell us what they are.[6]

For Churchland, the 'right' set of functions consists of the emerging details of neuroscience; the wrong set of functions consists of the folk-psychological nature of sensory experiences. Furthermore, it is *replacement* that is at issue in the case of folk psychology and microphysics, not *reduction*. Reduction, for the eliminativist, is not enough: his view is that folk psychology is 'simply too

---

[5] See also, P. S. Churchland's very Kuhnian remarks about the overthrow of the 'early intellectual ecology' of contemporary science. P. S. Churchland, 'Consciousness: The Transmutation of a Concept', p. 80.

[6] Churchland, (1979) op. cit., p. 39. Kuhn did, of course, retract the relativist implications of his own account in later papers and does not deny that some theories are right and others are wrong (see the *Postscript*). It is, however, of some doubt the extent to which he succeeded in reconciling his earlier and later views. (I am not suggesting that this is a flaw in Churchland's views, only that this tension creates a certain amount of conflict with the Kuhnian idea of revolutionary theory change.)

confused and inaccurate to win survival through intertheoretic reduction.'[7] However, Churchland assumes a great deal in accepting the Kuhnian picture of theoretical transformation. It is not obvious that Kuhn is correct in the details about the revolutionary nature of paradigm shifts. It is still less obvious that the elimination of our folk psychology in favour of neurophysiology is one of them. I will return to this issue.

The case for eliminativism

By elimination, the language of our folk psychology, our common-sense phenomenal predicates, is systematically exchanged for detailed physical reports in Churchland's view. He offers a number of examples of the sort of exchanges that he has in mind. In such a proposed program of theoretical replacement, we would no longer make such reports as 'X is red'. We would instead make a report like: 'X selectively reflects EM waves at 0.63×10^{-6}m'. Likewise, instead of saying: 'Y is warm', we would say 'Y has a mean molecular KE of 6.5×10^{-21}Kgm^2/s^2'. In such a theoretically 'awakened' society, people would talk of large amplitude atmospheric compression waves instead of loud noises; relative concentrations of hydrogen atoms instead of the sour taste of a lemon. The transformation of the detailed descriptions of microphysics from the vague and non-specific descriptions from folk psychology - especially the content of one's experiential states - would become an important educational inculcation not simply within philosophy and physics departments, but throughout entire societies and communities: the very composite intellectual fabric of people at large will be radically altered. As he says, 'the magnitude of the conceptual revolution suggested here should not be minimised: it would be enormous.'[8]

According to the eliminativist, these sorts of reports are not just held *concurrently* with our belief states about how things appear to us in sensations such as 'hot', 'red', 'loud' and so on, but that such reports can actually do away with such states and even this way of talking. Eliminativism is just that: the *abolition* of this common-speak. The project, as he sees it, is to change the semantics of observational predicates by constructing a 'framework of intuition to compete with (and I hope to supplant) the crude intuitions supplied by common sense.'[9]

How can Churchland know this sort of eliminativism to be a live option? The proposal that our epistemology and language need to be changed, as well as our view of folk psychological states, seems a dogmatic and indefensible claim. However, Churchland's point is that the language that specifies qualitative sensational states in experience simply does not *refer*, and hence should not be used. Such states are part of a redundant folk ontology. Churchland thus moves from the claim that qualitative sensational states are redundant, to the claim that

---

[7] P. M. Churchland, *Matter and Consciousness*, p. 61.

[8] Churchland, (1984) op. cit., p. 45. Hence, Churchland's claim that these perceptually reconstructed beings would no longer, for example, listen to the pounding surf, but instead listen to 'atmospheric compression waves being produced as the coherent energy of the ocean waves is audibly redistributed in the chaotic turbulence of the shallows.' Churchland, (1979) op. cit., pp. 29-30.

[9] Ibid., p. 8.

the corresponding language is featureless and eliminable. This does not seem an acceptable move in many ways. Taken as a broadly instructive program, this attitude would seem to put one's metaphysic (in this case one's theoretical paradigm) logically prior to one's epistemology. This claim, read in a very strong way, must be seen as relativist: if Churchland can do it on his theoretical paradigm, anyone can in principle do the same. The implications of a revolutionary overthrow of one theoretical paradigm by another might easily collapse into the characteristic relativist developments that Feyerabend made with Kuhn's views.[10]

This would seem to be an unacceptable consequence even for Churchland. If Churchland's only defence for this claim is the assertion that the epistemology of folk psychology deserves replacement by a more detailed and accurate neurophysiological epistemology, it would seem that this defence is open to anyone with a metaphysical axe to grind; so that epistemology becomes, on this view, the *slave* of metaphysics and not its *arbiter*. However, Churchland does provide more justification for this radical position.

Churchland's infrared cousins: argument from transposed modalities

Churchland's main argument for his eliminative views takes the form of a fable: We are invited to conceive of a race of alien beings indistinguishable from ourselves in almost every particular. We are to imagine that these beings are unusual in respect of their being unable to make colour discriminations about commonly perceived objects in the way that we do, due to their being constructed physiologically in a different way. Their handicap, however, has been compensated. These beings can, instead, make middle-range temperature discriminations *visually*.

For example, where we say of an object that it is 'hot', they say that it appears 'white' or '*looks* white' to them and, where we say that an object is 'cold', they say that it '*looks* black' to them, and so on; the basic difference being that temperatures are something *visual* to such creatures with 'white' and 'black' forming the extremes of temperature, with all graduations of grey in between. We are, of course, all equally linguistically competent and, except in the small matter that these people have no use for colour words, our languages are identical. The only substantial difference between us is that whereas these beings lack a visual sense for colour sensations and a tactile sense for temperature sensations, we possess these and lack the opposite.

What this thought experiment shows is that it is logically possible that a group of such beings could learn an alternative set of predicate expressions ('looks white' etc.) which they take to match with their world. But, what we have admitted is that *how the world appears to them to be in experience* has got nothing to do with the acquisition of expressions a being or beings may utter in reference to it. We cannot hold that *how things appear* is the crucial factor in the acquisition of our observational predicates, because it would mean that we

---

[10] Keith Campbell claims that on Churchland's view, if 'appearances which are out of harmony with theory can be discarded or ignored ... then we are ... doomed to move, rudderless, from one incommensurable theory to another as Feyerabend's philosophy would imply.' K. Campbell, 'Philosophy and Common Sense', p. 173.

would be in conflict with how *we* experience how things are, and how it may be logically possible to experience how things are. The thought experiment is cleverly designed for us to consider a situation in which 'looks red' and 'looks warm' are connected, *with no basis for the preference of one expression over the other.*

If this situation can be envisaged as at least a logical possibility, it has the following consequence, according to Churchland. It makes it difficult for us to claim that there is anything crucial in the observational situation above and beyond the inculcation of certain (logically possible) ways of speaking and referring in such a situation. And if this is so, then there is no observational basis for asserting that our expression in this context is more descriptively adequate than that of the aliens. It means, in other words, that we would have to justify why *our* colour terms are more appropriate to how things appear than their temperature terms, and this would not be easy to do. It would mean, certainly, that we were being 'insupportably parochial' toward certain visual sensations and judgements (our own) as against others.

For instance, if we succumb to a sensation-guided translation of observational terms, we must insist that *their* terms, 'cold', 'warm' and 'hot' really mean *black, grey and white* respectively, rather than *cold, warm and hot*. We would have to count as false substantially all of their beliefs about such predicates and their observational judgements about the world they experience. It would mean being biased toward our own set of beliefs and biased against theirs when their belief set 'has every virtue we can claim for our own habits of judgements in matters visual.'[11]

He does, of course, have a point here. If we were to hold to a sensation-based foundation of the meaning of *our* observational predicates, we would have to reject the ways in which such beings have amassed the use of *their* temperature terms, along with the appropriate nature of the terms themselves, and to translate their terms into ours. However, in learning such terms, the beings would have also gained a set of general beliefs about temperature, in much the same way as we have gained a set of beliefs about colour, and these would be hard to reject on pain of stating what to them (and us) seem either absurdities or falsehoods. It would, for example, be very hard to be convincing when we try to interpret what these people are saying in terms of colours and not temperatures when they say things like: 'snow is black' or 'molten lava is white', because interpreted in this way, these utterances are simply false to us. Equally though, the situation would be the same for them when they try to interpret our vocables and to suggest that what we mean by colour ascriptions are really temperature ascriptions. Taken like this, we would be faced with the absurdity that Negroes (for example) are 'colder' than Caucasians, or that 'My love is a tepid rose' etc. Clearly, if these sorts of things are to be avoided, (and they have to be to preserve the possibility of any sensible discussion at all) then we have to acknowledge that their observational terms have equal footing to ours in this respect, and that we should translate their perceptual reports as expressing beliefs about perceived *temperatures* rather than colours, and vice versa.

The point is that the meaning of such terms would have to be *given in*

---

[11] Churchland, (1979) op. cit., p. 10.

experience in quite a different manner for them from us, and that there would be no credible way of making a heterophonic translation without ruling out one such type of description. And, if there is no undogmatic, non-parochial way of deciding the point here, then there would seem to be an equal chance that *our* sensation-guided translation was as systematically false as theirs. Indeed, we must: 'be prepared to have the very same joke made of our own beliefs and visual capabilities with respect to black, grey and white ... we must insist that at least one of these two sets of beliefs is systematically false. But *which?* '[12]

The heart of the matter is that Churchland, like Sellars, wants us to do away with the idea that our language, our beliefs and our concept of ourselves is in any way based on how things appear to us; and more generally, that they have anything to do with what we observe, experience and 'feel'. If, as a matter of fact, colour perceptions can be correlated with (visual) temperature perception, then temperature perception is as good a perceptual basis for colours as is visual colour perception.[13] Hence, Churchland concludes, there is no basis for a preference for one over another and, therefore, no basis for our experience of temperature being more true to how things are in comparison with *their* experience. The only honourable way of making sense of the possibility of such a contrived case as this (short of a parochial interpretation) is to preserve the legitimacy of *homophonic* translation. Our respective sensory modalities are both responding to the same stimulus (temperature) and the only difference between us is that we have a very different means of detecting this feature.[14]

There are a number of closely entwined themes in this conclusion which shall be teased apart later. The point should be made that, behind it all, Churchland is claiming ultimately that there is nothing more to experience than learning an appropriate set or stock of terms in a language which is inferentially present prior to any perceptual act. He is not confining his remarks simply to the meaning of observational predicates.

Churchland's calorified cousins: argument from the irrelevance of sensory information

Churchland has a second important thought experiment to support his case. We are to imagine in this instance 'an isolated society of humans whose physiology this time differs in no way from our own.'[15] The only distinguishing feature between us and them is in the terms of language used in relation to heated bodies. Their view is that objects contain a substance called *caloric* which explains how objects can be hot or cold, liquid, gaseous or solid. For these people, caloric is held in material bodies, in varying amounts, rather in the way water is held in sponges. ... These people claim to *perceive* or observe, by

---

[12] Loc. cit.

[13] This possibility is not altogether fiction: Peacocke notes that 'Certain snakes have pit organs sensitive to infrared radiation, and information from these is built up into a map of the snakes infrared environment.' C. Peacocke, *Sense and Content: Experience, Thought and their Relations,* op. cit., p. 90. See: E. Newman and P. Hartline, 'The Infrared "Vision" of Snakes', pp. 98-107.

[14] Churchland, (1979) op. cit., pp. 11-12.

[15] Ibid., p. 16.

feeling, and on occasion by looking, that material bodies contain caloric fluid at various pressures.'[16]

The fiction is not altogether unfamiliar. The example is chosen because it illustrates how we actually thought of the property of a heated body prior to our present conception in terms of mean molecular kinetic energy. It is, as Churchland informs us, 'a slightly tarted up version of the now defunct theory of heat.'[17] The example will be familiar for another reason: it illustrates how observers can hold *false* views about the nature of the physical world (can make spurious 'observation judgements')[18] with respect to observable phenomena, and have uncritical confidence in their beliefs, and the rational acceptability of the content of their language expressing such beliefs. But, the important point for Churchland is this: to try to convince such people that the situation with regard to heated bodies was otherwise than what they suspected, or worse, that their theory about caloric was systematically false, would meet severe resistance *even though there was no such thing as caloric.*

Even though the caloric theory is false, we should try to appreciate its power. As Churchland points out, their conception of things is fairly powerful - much more so than our own feeble (common-sense) conception of 'hot' and 'cold'. They will notice and explain common phenomena which would otherwise be quite mystifying: 'To one who conceives of these "temperatures" as unequal pressures in two connected fluid reservoirs, an exchange of fluid until equilibrium is reached is the inevitable result.' Caloric theory may be false but it has great intuitive explanatory power. Moreover, because of its explanatory power, experience will tend to encourage and entrench the caloric model.[19]

The fable is very instructive according to Churchland. It demonstrates how *intransigent* theories about common sense observables can be, and how such theories might 'misexploit' sensory information. It also demonstrates, secondarily, how inappropriate *reduction* is here between the rival caloric and corpuscular/kinetic views (the former is reducible to the latter '*very* grossly if at all.') But the main theme here is that the fable is not isolated to such cases. In fact, *our* current theoretical ontology with respect to judgements about sensations - our experiences - might be, similarly, a case of theoretical mismanagement. As we saw in the case of the infrared cousins, the meaning of common observation terms like 'hot' and 'cold' is determined by the cluster of beliefs and assumptions in which they figure. The meaning of theoretical terms is grasped by way of an appreciation of the theory (the set of statements) which introduces them. 'From a purely semantic point of view then, our common observational framework for temperature is indistinguishable from a theoretical framework.'[20] By implication, our theoretical framework about sensations may be wrong too.

Enter the impetus for eliminative materialism. Sensory *qualia* are simply *irrelevant* to the acceptance or rejection of an observational framework; what is important is the *theory* in which such sensations figure. Bodily sensations, on

---

[16] Ibid., pp. 16-17.
[17] Ibid., p. 17.
[18] Ibid., p. 18.
[19] Ibid., pp. 17-20.
[20] Ibid., pp. 21-22.

this view, are customarily responded to in terms of singular judgments or statements; such statements are prompted by networks of beliefs informed by common sense. But *pace* the calorified cousins, common sense can be *wrong* about the detailed nature of such impingings, and *pace* the infrared cousins, the detailed content of such impingings constitutes the *product* of semantic and epistemic conceptualisation and not the *data* for it. Meaningful experiential content is fixed through belief sets and linguistic descriptions, not sensations. The claim is that the common sense framework, with respect to observational parameters like that of temperature and colour, has the character of a *theory,* and that there is every reason to think that such a theory can be systematically false. And as there is no discernible difference distinguishing the cases Churchland invents and our own, it strongly suggests that the conceptual foundation of our common sense folk psychology is similarly flawed.

The argument for this is not simply by means of elaborate analogies. Churchland discusses examples of common sense homilies regarding the heated properties of objects to make the point, and then tells us that 'the conception of heat that they represent is empirically incoherent.'[21] These examples involve cases like the claim that a heated body, if warmer than a second body, and if this body is warmer than a third, will necessarily mean that the first body is warmer than the third. But, as Churchland notes, such a distributivity rule can be seen to generate 'multiple inconsistencies',[22] depending on the substances being heated (e.g., wood, iron and water) and the criterion used to determine this rule as correct. Such cases do not suggest that sensations are central to making adequate and meaningful observation judgements.

Elsewhere, Churchland evaluates figure-ground perceptual illusions and arrives at a startling conclusion: subjects responding to the familiar Necker Cube, Duck/Rabbit, Old/Young Woman, Vase/Faces cases will produce remarkably 'plastic' responses, he tells us, and are able to voluntarily 'flip back and forth at will between the two or more alternatives, by changing one's assumptions about the nature of the object or about the conditions of viewing.'[23] This goes also for subjects equipped with inverting lenses, which effectively reorientate the perceptual field along the dimensions of 'up' and 'down'.[24] The claim here is that perceptual content is neither endogenously specified, nor in any way incontrovertible: if a radical reorientation of one's perceptual images can be achieved in less than a week (or immediately in the case of ambiguous perceptual figures) through learning, recoordination and adjustment, it begins to show that 'perception is very plastic and very penetrable indeed.'[25] In all these cases discussed, Churchland claims they indicate one important fact: that the central feature in perceptual discriminations is a *cognitive background* to experience. The crucial thing is *not* that perceivers are aware of certain contentful experiences, but that one has an inferential perceptual

---

[21] Ibid., p. 23.

[22] Ibid., p. 24.

[23] Churchland, op. cit., (1988): p 172. To take the Necker Cube: not only can it be seen in its standard rear/front orientations, but also as a hexagonal shape.

[24] See, H. Kottenhoff, 'Situational and Personal Influences on Space Perception with Experimental Spectacles', pp. 79-97.

[25] Churchland (1988) op. cit., p. 175.

framework which is suggestible by manipulation of the network of beliefs underpinning such a framework, in exactly the same way as the fictional human beings that Churchland imagines. The upshot is that the contentful nature of our common sensory experience is neither as fundamental nor as important as often supposed, and actually amounts to no more than a deeply faulty and misguided theory about ourselves, which, though having stood the test of time, should ultimately be abandoned. We, with our experiences, are in essentially the same position as the perceivers of caloric. Our observation predicates cannot be defended by a simple appeal to the 'manifest deliverances of sense' and thus, therefore, 'our conception of the world may [also] be myopic, confused or even just plain wrong.'[26]

Evaluating eliminativism

The argument in detail

It is important to note at this point that there are several important issues here, and they are systematically confused by inferential theorists. The first issue is that the meaning of observational *terms* is obtained through an inferential background of theory; in other words, terms are always theory-laden: the content of meaningful observational/perceptual *statements* must be grasped only through such an inferential background. Such familiar claims have been made explicitly by Churchland in some of the quotations preceding with the emphasis on 'perceptual judgements' 'meaningful observational terms' and so forth.

Another quite separate issue, however, is that the complex of one's theoretical background is completely revisable in content (the argument for this rests on the plausibility of the thought-experiments regarding alternative epistemologies and the assumption that Kuhnian type replicability - not reduction - furnishes an adequate account of theoretical and conceptual progress). The impetus for this view, for Churchland, is eliminative materialism.

Yet another theme, again influenced mainly by Kuhn, is that perceptual awareness itself is a conceptual matter: that the structured basis of perceptual content is a feature of the inferential background one brings to an observational situation. The argument for this is again, the plausibility of the perceptual world of the infrared and the caloric cases, and also the evident *plasticity* of perception under the suggestibility of background assumptions regarding the perceptual situation. Like Kuhn, Churchland thinks that perceptions are gestalt-like when one undergoes paradigm shifts.

A final (implicit) theme here is the view that bodily sensations prompt *descriptions* in linguistic terms and that such judgements are isomorphically equivalent in content to the sensations that prompt them, which are otherwise causally irrelevant in perceptual situations. This latter point is highly Sellarsian, and amounts to the view that there is nothing residual in the procedure of asserting a claim about a perceptual situation (say, *x is red*) and endorsing the content for its truth value. This claim was treated at some length in the last

---

[26] Churchland (1979) op. cit., pp. 24-25.

chapter. From the preceding discussion, this will also be seen as a fairly self-evident aspect of Churchland's views. This influence would seem to be behind the claim that features of experience *qua* sensory order should drop out of any analysis of experience and content, and consideration should instead be given to the nature of the theoretical *description* of that experience (which may be misguided and eliminable).

The various claims above can be summarised and shown to be connected in the very rough-hewn argument given below (I am indebited to a paper by G.J. O'Brien here).[27]
1. The semantic content of observational terms and descriptions in a natural language presupposes background theories. (*Theory dependence of observation language thesis - Attributable to Feyerabend.*)
2. Beyond the causal stimulus, the endorsement of the propositional/semantic content of an observational statement in any perceptual situation exhausts the significance of that situation. (*Sellars's thesis - Psychological Nominalism*)
3. Perceptual awareness is *plastic* and suggestible by learning new concepts. Hence, it is largely a conceptual matter how perceptions influence us. (*The Plasticity of Perception thesis*)
4. Perceptual awareness, therefore, is importantly a linguistic and conceptual affair: perception involves cognitive manipulations of a linguistically mediated conceptual framework, which exhaust the significance of the perceptual situation. *Perceptual awareness is theory dependent.* (Amalgam of 1, 2 and 3).
5. All theories have a limited lifetime and their content is replaceable in the Kuhnian manner (*Churchland's thesis.*)
6. We possess no immutable theoretical frameworks. Even the *perceptual content* of the theory of folk psychology will (eventually) be replaced by microphysics. (From 4 and 5)
7. *Intermediate Conclusion:* There is no non-theoretical content to perceptual experience; and no content which is ineliminable or non-revisable. (From 1-6)
8. *Conclusion:* Eliminative Materialism is true. (From 1-7)

This is not a tight argument, and it is not easy to express it in a more favourable way. Nonetheless, it is an influential argument, and has the desired overall effect for Churchland, by demonstrating that folk psychology generally, and experiential content specifically, are seriously flawed and inherently replaceable. It is clear, however, that the argument is too quick to be convincing. All of these claims can be treated separately and require different supports; it is not adequate to claim them to be more or less mutually supporting.

One can, for instance, hold that the meaning of terms and descriptions in a language are given via one's overarching theoretical views without being an eliminative materialist (Sellars holds to a form of constructivism, but not necessarily eliminativism: compare his 'manifest' and 'scientific' images). And, presumably, one can, in principle, hold that linguistic descriptions exhaust the content of a perceptual *statement* (Sellars's thesis) and yet not swallow full blown constructivism. One could also, conceivably, hold most of the above premises while criticising the plasticity of perception. (It seems logically possible to be a constructivist/eliminativist without holding that perception is

---

[27] G. J. O'Brien, 'Eliminative Materialism and Psychological Self-Knowledge', pp 50-51.

plastic).

But, the thing that interests me here is that one might hold both that observational *terms* are theory dependent, and also the view that folk psychology is severely limited in explanatory content, without holding that contentful observational experiences are theory dependent, or that they are eliminable. Indeed, there are good reasons for endorsing precisely this view. In other words, the contents of sensory information may be downright misleading, but this is a far cry from saying that there is no discernible content to speak of. There may still be aspects of experiential content, in my sense, which do not depend on the imposition of high-level theorising. It will be pointed out later that none of Churchland's arguments rule out this alternative interpretation of his argument.

Churchland, however, thinks that these premises go together and can be supported jointly. The arguments above are designed to bring out the overwhelming attitude of eliminative materialism: that the ontology, language and beliefs of folk psychology are inherently flawed and deserving replacement. And, a particular and important feature being replaced is the qualitative features of experiential content.

Assessing the argument

A number of things can be brought out of this argument when the case of the fictional beings is reconsidered. Churchland certainly claims that the *words* that the beings use in reference to their experiences are strongly theory dependent. 'Red', 'warm' and 'caloric' etc., are terms which presuppose a theoretical background. For the infrared beings, a colour term must be understood homophonically via a network of terms describing *visual* temperature discrimination. For the caloric community, common temperature terms must be understood as referring to the state of a non-existent substance. The meaning of the words used by both kinds of fictional beings is thus not connected to the features of the world they describe (for we experience the very same world). It is connected homophonically to the theory that is presupposed by the use of those words. Churchland affirms this point about the theoretical nature of meaning in these terms:

> The impossibility of ... heterophonic translation ... is just the impossibility of the thesis that the meaning of the common observation terms ... is given in sensation.[28]

> The meaning of a term ... is not determined by the intrinsic quality of whatever sensations happen to prompt its observational use, but by the network of assumptions/beliefs/principles in which it figures.[29]

It is clear from this that terms *get their meaning* from one's theoretical background and not from observations/sensations. For Churchland, sensations occur only insofar as experiencing beings are subject to a *causal order* (proximal

---

[28] Churchland op. cit., (1979): p. 11.
[29] Ibid., p 15.

stimulations), but such stimulations do not provide meanings or interpretations. According to Churchland, the role of the senses *qua* proximal stimulations, is merely to activate the conceptual framework that has been brought to the perceptual situation by the perceiver.[30] However, while this claim itself seems harmless enough, Churchland does seem to be advocating something stronger than this in his rejection of folk psychology; namely, that our existential commitments as to sensations as a *sensory order* also amount to just a theoretical set among others. The move here, note, is precisely an instance of the sleight of hand implicit in the inferentialist proposal of the meaning and theory dependence of observational terms, to the similarly embedded nature of observational experience which was mentioned in Chapter 3 and witnessed again in Feyerabend's and Sellars's work (Chapters 9 and 10). By taking on board all of the assumptions mentioned earlier, Churchland can easily make the quick and easy step from claims about the epistemic irrelevance of proximal stimulations to the meaning of observational *terms* (above) to claims such as the following concerning the plasticity of perception:

> In recent centuries, most humans have learned to perceive speech not just auditorily but visually: we have learned to read. Some have learned to perceive speech by touch: they read Braille. And some of us have learned not just to hear music, but to see it: we have learned to sight read musical notation. Now neither the eyes nor the fingers were evolved for the instantaneous perception of those complex structures ... but their acquired mastery here indicates the highly sophisticated ... capacities that learning can produce in them. And if these capacities, why not others?[31]

Here Churchland is not referring simply to the causal order which shapes our perceptual capacities. Nerve impingings do not change and develop or become transformed in any way. What he is referring to here is the transformation of experience *qua* sensory order. The kind of perceptual capacities he takes to be transformable are the kinds of contents that qualia theorists take to be central to any account of experience and content: sounds, colours, and so on - qualitative, contentful states. For Churchland, how we understand such sensations can be changed by adopting a new way of interpreting impinging data. Of course, the theoretical framework which he assumes will generate the non-standard perceptual capacities of most interest (and accuracy) is the one garnered from the emerging theory of microphysics. Thus, we should eventually 'see' sensations in microphysical terms. The examples of trained musical perception or accomplishments in Braille is, for Churchland, only a shadow away from the people on the beach listening to their aperiodic atmospheric compression waves.

The important claim here is no longer simply that incoming sensory inputs are

---

[30] Churchland, op. cit., (1988): p. 185.

[31] Churchland, (1988) op. cit., p 177. Elsewhere: 'It is in fact a highly instructive and entertaining diversion to try to perceive the "theoretical" in the "manifest", ... [T]here is the satisfaction of apprehending reality, perceptually, in ways that reflect more deeply and accurately the structure and content of that reality, of coming closer to the ideal of seeing it as it "really is"'. (Churchland, 1979, op. cit., p. 36) And again: '[T]he example of trained musical perception is a straightforward existence proof for the possibility of theoretically-transformed perception in general.' (Churchland, 1988, op. cit., p. 179).

of little consequence for the meaning of observational *terms,* but that inference from theory negates any appeal to the content of our sensations as *sensational* states at all. On Churchland's view, in interpreting one's proximal stimulations sensory inputs can have wildly different contents (recall the infrared cousins). Furthermore, bearing in mind that perception is plastic, it is easy to believe that one can see, hear or feel things in any number of ways given the right theoretical framework. Bearing in mind the case of the caloric cousins, it is also natural to believe that what we once described as 'sensations' actually referred to nothing *contentful* at all. It is from this kind of reasoning that Churchland expects that the theoretically awakened society of the future will no longer talk vaguely and vacuously about the sensational content of their experiences, but will 'perceive the 'theoretical' in the 'manifest'' and 'a new relational order' involving the processes of perception will emerge causing 'an ontological displacement of rather jarring proportions.'[32] The important point is that theory change *writ large* will transform our observational *experiences,* not *just* our observational terms. The position of Churchland here is, in fact, very close to that of Thomas Kuhn when he queries whether, in response to paradigm change, scientists achieve a 'transformation of vision' and so 'pursued their research in different worlds.'[33] Or when Kuhn says: 'something like a paradigm is prerequisite to perception itself.'[34] The tenor of Churchland's claims is no less literal. Churchland has moved deftly from the claim that language and meaning is theoretical in content to the claim that sensory experiences are thus constituted.

Consequences of eliminativism

Does Churchland really expect such a radical move will be undertaken with enthusiasm? Is it, to him, a project that can be implemented in practice? Even he expresses some reservations when he asks about the status we assign to our common-sense conceptual framework, 'if the emerging picture of reality provided by modern-era science is accepted, provisionally, as true?' Churchland acknowledges that 'the common-sense framework is really a loosely integrated patchwork of subtheories, rather than a unified monolith.'[35] Indeed, perhaps only *partial* elimination may be possible.

Churchland's doubts may be read as expressing the general dilemma that no physical description yet seems *prima facie* adequate to map the power of generality that our common-sense picture of reality provides, and certainly this seems to be true. Churchland insists, however, that the view that it could not eventually map the generality of common sense is a misguided view also. To him, the popular position that our physical description must (to be a successful replacement) provide a theoretical analogue for the elements of our common-sense ontology, is a position premised on the conviction that our common-sense ontology needs to be *reduced* by some rival theory, which needs to retain some of the disguised features of the theory that it supplanted. But this strikes him as

---

[32] Churchland, (1979) op. cit., pp. 34.
[33] T. Kuhn, op. cit., p. 120.
[34] Ibid., p. 113.
[35] Churchland, (1979) op. cit., p. 42.

a conviction without ground. It assumes, for one thing, the idea that how we currently conceive of things as being in common experience is the *way things really are,* and this is precisely the sort of conviction that he takes to be false.

The more plausible and likely position is that the common-sense theoretical set that we hold with such trenchancy and passion is not a theory to which all rival theories must bear witness, but merely *'the theory that got their first.'* And, as he makes clear, 'this is hardly sufficient reason to demand that all subsequent theories treat it as the touchstone for their own adequacy.'[36] Churchland point is simply that just because certain parallels may be made between what the theoretical set of modern science describes, and what our common-sense theory tells us, it is no reason to thereby regard this as enforcing or validating the ontological status of the common-sense theory. Rather, the common-sense position (unlike the scientific paradigm) is a proper ontology on parochial historical grounds only, and has less to recommend it in the areas of empirical adequacy, prediction and explanation. The moral, for Churchland, is that reduction is not the means by which 'large scale intellectual progress' is achieved. The means by which an 'awakening' in our perceptual capabilities is ensured is by '[not assigning] to the framework of common sense a significance beyond what it deserves'[37] and opting for 'large-scale' elimination or replacement instead. It would be madness to make it a constraint upon currently acceptable theory that it explain the 'facts', as they may be currently conceived by us, he claims. By analogy: 'The question of what makes the starry sphere of the heavens turn daily ... would never have been disposed of had we ruled out of court any dynamical theory that denied the motion or the existence of that sphere. The "facts", as currently conceived and observed by us, ... may well reveal that we should vacate that starting place as hastily as possible.'[38]

A lot more could be said about all this. There seems to be an important order of difference between hastily departing from our ill-conceived view of the 'starry sphere', and likewise from our beliefs about the sensational aspects of colour and temperature experiences; the former seems a case of conceptual ignorance regarding the mechanisms of the universe; the latter, a fact about how we have evolved and are structured physically as data processing organisms.

Also one could plausibly argue in response to this that *replacing* theories have the same common requirements as *reducing* theories. A successful reduction requires that a theory (T-2) gives an account of the elements of a less sophisticated theory (T-1) in terms of bridge laws and inter-theoretic identity claims for the theoretical terms introduced. This requires the reducing theory (T-2) to *simulate the explanation* that (T-1) provided. A theoretical *replacement* would also seem to require this. Darwin's theory of evolution simulated the teleological explanation inherent in Lamarck's theory without itself being teleological: 'selective pressures' in Darwin's theory simulated the theoretical efficacy of Lamarck's 'acquired characteristics' while avoiding the problems inherent with the latter notion. Moreover, from the perspective of the successor theory, one can accurately assess the efficacy of this simulation. Churchland may well advocate replacement rather than reduction - that neurophysiology

---

[36] Ibid., p. 44.
[37] Loc. cit.
[38] Loc. cit.

replace folk psychology - but it would appear that he still owes an account of how the proposed replacing theory of microphysics could simulate the explanatory features of folk psychology while avoiding its pitfalls in terms of its vagueness and non-specific predictions. But how would a highly developed microphysics plausibly provide an adequate simulation of the general features of the sensational content of experiences such as we have been considering them? Indeed: does it even look as if it *could* provide such a simulation?

This might seem an unfair requirement, given that Churchland thinks that the theoretical basis of folk psychology has *no* explanatory features worth simulating. It would seem, hence, as much a requirement of Churchland to retain simulating characteristics of folk psychology, as it would be for modern geology to retain simulating characteristics of Noachian deluge theory; or astronomy, those of crystal sphere theory etc. In other words, there is no argument on such grounds unless it is already assumed that the theory to be reduced is seen as having useful and valuable explanatory features. And this is precisely the assumption that Churchland is rejecting. So, there would seem to be no logically compelling reason for retaining the existential commitments of folk psychology. (Compare Darwin, who retained the explanatory features of an evolutionary *process,* but not the Lamarckian *mechanism* which was of less explanatory value than the idea of random mutation in conjunction with natural selection.)

This is a partially adequate response, but it puts the onus on those sympathetic with elements of folk theory to justify *their* commitments, and not on Churchland to justify his. It amounts to putting one's metaphysic before one's epistemology, and - as already mentioned - it is open to take the argument in *any* direction, if this broad principle is followed. This would seem to be a recipe for the automatic gain-saying of opponents' positions for no better reason than it conflicts with one's own. This kind of justification for adopting such a radical position clearly will not do.

However, there is another reason why this attitude will not do. Since there is as much a consensus of opinion that folk psychology does have some useful and worthwhile explanatory features as those that say it does not, it is *not* sufficient just to claim that there is no need for a constraint of simulation.[39] The requirement of simulation is still valuable unless it can be shown that there is nothing worth simulating in the case in question. What is needed, therefore, seems to be sufficiently compelling reasons for thinking that folk theory is flawed in every particular. Churchland is, after all, not trying to simply *explain* folk theory of sensational content with a (better) theory of neurophysiology, but is aiming at totally *explaining it away.* The onus is clearly on him to prove his point in this regard. While it is relatively easy to explain away Noachian deluge theory, it is less easy to do the same with the low-level aspects of experiential content. As argued in the previous chapters, there are actually philosophical, perceptual and evolutionary reasons why a sensory order is a feature of the experiences of complex organisms: to simply rule out such contents by fiat is a

---

[39] See, for example, F. Jackson and P. Pettit: 'In Defence of Folk Psychology' pp. 31-54. See also T. Horgan and J. Woodward, 'Folk Psychology is here to Stay', pp. 197-226; and K. Campbell's 'Can Intuitive Psychology Survive the Growth of Neuroscience?' pp. 143-52. For an attack of Patricia Churchland's views along the same lines, see: G. Madell, 'Neurophilosophy: A Principled Sceptic's Response', pp. 153-168.

tall order without adequate justification. But Churchland must do this if he is to claim that there is no necessity to simulate the features of such experiences.[40]

Criticising Churchland

The argument

There are several strands to Churchland's argument. First of all there is the Feyerabendian claim that the meaning of singular statements derives from being embedded in a theoretical belief system. Secondly, there is the Kuhnian claim that theoretical systems naturally change and evolve and can be 'incommensurable' under any comparative criteria. Thirdly, there is Sellars's claim that the nature of our sensory states depends not on such states being phenomenally accessible, but on being imposed and organised from conceptual categories which themselves are culturally transmitted largely through linguistic training. As indicated, all these influences in Churchland are combined and held along with the conviction that the only sensible way that we should refer to experiential content is through the only viable paradigm possible: emerging microphysics. We have seen enough of such a position to see that it is grounded in a number of mutually supporting claims.

The claim that experiential content is inferential in the required sense is supported by the plasticity of perception, its suggestibility to background assumptions and the plausibility of the fictional cases requiring homophonic translation (the 'infrared' case). It is also borne out by a subtle conflation of the theory dependence on observational terms thesis, with a similar dependence of observational experience. The claim that folk psychology as a *theory* needs replacing, is supported jointly by the 'caloric' case and the underpinning of intertheoretic replacement as the motor of theory change. The assumption that these claims are jointly sufficient to legitimate radical replacement eliminativism of sensory content, also demands an acceptance of the Sellarsian point regarding the completeness of explanation as only requiring a treatment in terms of *language*. Each of these points shall be discussed in turn.

The plasticity of perception: ambiguous stimuli and inverting lenses

It is not at all obvious that the plasticity of perception thesis is true. Jerry Fodor has mounted a convincing attack on this claim in the context of his modularity theory of perception and we have already seen the implications of this view for my own thesis in Chapter 8. Fodor's point was that there are some features of perceptual experience which are encapsulated from cognitive penetrability and so, decidedly non-plastic (in the sense required). As we have seen, the existence of informationally local perceptual sub-systems is an important support for the view that not all experiential content can be captured by high-

---

[40] Folk psychology, may, of course, be flawed in some particulars, but not others. I would certainly agree with this, but do not think that the sensational content of experiential states is a case in point, even though it is not a source of epistemic reliability. There is a marked difference between saying that some state is misleading and corrigible, and saying that there is no *sui generis* content to that state at all and that there will be nothing lost by eliminating it.

level features. Low-level aspects of experiences such as colour hues and visual field enlargements do seem to escape such an analysis.

I support this kind of reaction to the plasticity thesis. The claim I have been making with the continuum account is that aspects of experiential content may occur in an amalgam with inferential input, and that there may be *degrees* of such cognitive penetration to the point where there are just 'aspect'-like features. The essential point behind my view is that though inference penetrates experience to a significant degree in most cases, this does not serve to rule out the idea that some features of experiences are not fully captured in such terms.

Churchland cannot afford to make concessions to any kind of encapsularity view of content. On the most plausible reading of his fully inferentialist account of experiential content, we find that he must put forward a convincing case for total perceptual plasticity. (Plasticity, specifically, which is malleable through high-level *cognitive* manipulations). It may, of course, be said that he is advocating a somewhat less extreme claim - plasticity to some degree rather than total plasticity. But the problem with this weaker plasticity thesis is that it does not fit well with Churchland's overall project. To carry through the application of his 'caloric' and 'infrared' cases to normal human experiences, subjects imbued with appropriate theory must be able to *decide* how things look on the basis of internalising a set of cognitive principles. It would not be enough, on his view, that there was always some theory-insulated perceptual content (how then would 'theories bite the dust and ontologies sink into oblivion'?) To draw the eliminativist's conclusion, and to make it compelling, perception must be not just suggestible to cognitive influences at certain levels, but penetrable through and through by them. To be able to swap one set of folk theoretical assumptions about one's perceptual world with neurophysiological assumptions must be because such experiences are outmoded and misleading as to how things 'really are'. But to 'see' them in the radical way that Churchland asks us to, requires that perceptual content be shot through with theory, not just suggestible to it. Churchland thus has to demonstrate that perception is *totally* plastic, not just semi-plastic. I shall call this the *radical plasticity thesis* (RPT).

The case for the RPT has been extensively discussed in the literature. Fodor and Churchland, particularly, have engaged in a dispute over this and it seems to me that Churchland loses this round easily, as indicated below. Some of Fodor's central criticisms of the RPT are adopted in the following discussion.

The claim that perceptual experience can be altered by 'changing one's assumptions about the nature of the object or about the conditions of viewing'[41] is supposed to support Churchland's argument. The example he gives is the case of ambiguous perceptual illusions; the 'assumptions' he refers to are supposed to be the appeal to the theoretical networks in which such integrations can occur. The plasticity of perception is (allegedly) demonstrated when a perceiver can '[learn] very quickly to make the [ambiguous] figure flip back and forth at will'[42] However, it is clear from Fodor's comments that there is another way of assessing such cases, and it does not necessarily support the RPT that Churchland avows:

---

[41] Churchland, 'Perceptual Plasticity and Theoretical Neutrality', pp. 171-172.
[42] Loc. cit.

One doesn't get the duck rabbit (or the Necker Cube) to flip by 'changing one's assumptions'; one does it by (for example), changing one's fixation point. Believing that it's a duck doesn't help you to see it as one; wanting to see it as a duck doesn't help much either. But knowing where to fixate *can* help. Fixate there *and then the flipping is automatic.*
When one becomes sophisticated about laws that govern the way things look, one can finagle the looks by playing the laws. In the most obvious cases: one squints to make things look sharper; one cups one's hand behind one's ear to make them sound louder, etc. It doesn't begin to follow that auditory and visual acuity are cognitively penetrable. Exactly similarly, one learns that one can get the figure to flip by altering one's fixation point (or, for that matter, by just *waiting;* eventually it will flip of its own accord).[43]

Fodor makes the point that there is an important difference between a structurally ambiguous object being seen in multiple ways, and its being determined (cognitively) that an object can be seen in such ways. Fodor's point is that the one claim does not support the other. For the RPT to be true, the subject must not just be able to finagle looks but to *decide* how things look and, in principle, be able to *make things look any way one wants.* (Churchland, after all, wants us to look at things in terms of detailed *microphysical* descriptions.)

However, as Fodor notes, the examples of visual illusion that Churchland offers do nothing to support this latter claim. The RPT is not supported by structurally ambiguous illusions as Churchland supposes, because things patently *cannot* be seen in any way one wants. The Necker Cube never looks like (say) the Sydney Harbour Bridge, a bag of onions or a billiard cue, no matter what cognition brings to bear on perception, though on Churchland's account, there is no principled reason why *any* radical means of conceptual exploitation here would not fit the bill. After all, Churchland wants to replace one interpretation function with another so unlike the original that it would bring about a radical transformation of visual capabilities enabling those who made the change to 'see' solar wavelength distributions and to 'hear' soundwaves. But it is clear that even if one wanted to visually transform the Necker Cube into looking like a billiard cue (or anything else) one could not. Some perceptions are, therefore, immune from *total* perceptual plasticity.[44]

The importance of cognitive influences to perception seems to be overemphasised in Churchland's work; the RPT seems to be far too radical. That there is no demonstration of the cognitive penetration of perception (as opposed to well-rehearsed abilities in fixing certain appearances by squinting and ear-cupping etc.), suggests that there is very little here to support Churchland's case.

---

[43] J. A. Fodor, 'A Reply to Churchland's "Perceptual Plasticity and Theoretical Neutrality"', p. 190-191.
[44] Another very different interpretation of Churchland's point here is not that we can see something in any way we want, but that we can learn to see things *in terms of what our scientific theories tell us about them.* But it is not clear that microphysics tells us *anything* about perception *qua* content, and secondly this kind of interpretation seems to be in tension with the theory replacement doctrine (again, how *could* 'ontologies sink into oblivion') if this kind of story were true?

That one can decide to 'finagle the looks' here is significant. As mentioned earlier, a good deal of what is relevant to the fixation of the various aspects of experiential content is attentiveness: one does decide to concentrate on various features which one notices and so one can accentuate or diminish their importance. The blurry 'look' of the scratches on the window pane, or the lightness of the coloured hue of a painted wall, can be enhanced by degrees of attention-fixing and concentration. One can notice such things over that of the actual window or the wall being looked at. (That's what makes some experiential contents 'aspect'-like and not fully inferentially specified, on my view.) So an adequate account of experiential content must have, built into it, the component of attentiveness: 'finagling the look' of an experience is as much a part of having experiences as imposing a high-level concept or theory on it, or seeing it represented in a different way.

But clearly, noticing the way something looks, or altering its appearance by concentrating on it, is not to *decide* how to see it - confusing these points seems to be Churchland's mistake. Noticing and altering features of an experience do not amount to deciding *what* to experience: it is, rather, merely a matter of attending to various aspects of how an experience is represented. (As Fodor remarks, this amounts to confusing the effect exercise has on one's heart rate with the *decision* to exercise having an effect on one's heart rate.) For fairly obvious reasons, however, one cannot decide how to see things. One may choose how to *describe* things (just as one can choose how to exercise) but, again, this does not amount to choosing how to see what one sees. So, *contra* Churchland, one cannot change how things look by deciding anything; one simply learns to notice certain looks by accentuating and attending to given features of an experience.[45]

Churchland also ignores the various ways that high-level content can influence experience. But cognition need not influence content in an all-or-nothing manner. An experience which has representational content need not have theoretically informational content; an experience need not be propositional linguistic. So even if an experience has certain inferential features, it need not have others. In the case in question, Churchland seems to assume that *every* kind of seeing involves the full penetration of theoretically informational and propositional linguistic content. But even if this is true (Fodor's argument above strongly suggests it is not) this does not enable Churchland to claim that content is fully captured at the higher informational levels. For, on my view, it simply does not follow that if an experience has one kind of content it need not have another kind of content as well (the *complexity* thesis). So even though one represents an experience in a certain linguistically familiar, theoretically informed way, it does not follow that this is the only feature of the experience worth considering. As we saw earlier, even in the case of structurally ambiguous stimuli, aspects of the 'look' can remain the same even when how

---

[45] A recent study on the Schroder staircase suggests that adaptive bias to one or other orientation of an ambiguous figures is modulated by attention. The authors stress in this paper that this effect 'need not imply that attention can alter in a specific manner the interpretation assigned to an ambiguous test figure.' See: 'Attentional Modulation of a Figural Aftereffect', p. 18.

one cognitively *represents* the experience varies.⁴⁶ Even familiar examples of perceptual 'flipping' then do not necessarily support Churchland's assertion of full penetration. Given a multi-level content view, there may be aspects of an experience that simply escape characterisation at the higher informed levels.

There is another thing of importance to note about Churchland's account. Not only can Churchland not demonstrate RPT, but he cannot even allow for look finagling - indeed, on Churchland's eliminativism, there are simply *no looks to be finagled.* There are only proximal stimulations and theories, so Churchland cannot even allow for cases in which how things look is distinct from how one cognitively represents the experience. For Churchland, then, such commonplace experiences like that of hue changes and blurry window scratches must either escape theoretical penetration to some important degree (which would run against RPT), or be experientially incomprehensible. But such low-level experiences seem real enough. It seems provisionally correct then to conclude then that there is something wrong with the RPT.

For Churchland's claims about full perceptual plasticity to be plausible, one should be able to decide the terms of ambiguous stimuli and, moreover, decide what figures are indeed ambiguous. Since an RPT is the means by which Churchland tries to secure an eliminativism of low-level content, there is only one way in which his story about perception must run: he must claim that not only can one notice the 'look' of something, but one can decide how to see it (by swapping one's theory). Anything less would be to weaken significantly the plasticity thesis to a degree which would seriously compromise the applications that this doctrine has for Churchland's philosophy of mind and his rejection of folk psychology.

But, as argued, Churchland does not establish this stronger claim, and only the weaker claim actually seems plausible. The weakened version is that one can decide to attend to aspects of something which looks one way and not another, *not* that one can cognitively determine how something looks. Given the argument Churchland has given for this, it is clear that he has not established the stronger assertion and, at best, it is only the weaker claim that can legitimately be made here.⁴⁷

As a first point against Churchland, he has not established full perceptual plasticity. He has not established that one can cognitively determine how things are seen - not even in the case of structurally ambiguous stimuli. This must be seen as an important point against the thrust of his claims about the high-level dependence of perceptual content. Of course, if the RPT does not go through, then on these grounds neither does radical replacement eliminativism. Premise (3) of Churchland's argument is far too strong. There are, however, reasons for taking Churchland's claims about the radical plasticity thesis to be not just too strong, but *false.* The fact of the matter is that not all content is plastic, despite

---

⁴⁶ Recall Peacocke's 'wire framework' case given in Chapter 5. In this example, the structural ambiguity of the wire cube does not influence the experienced non-representational stability of the figure.

⁴⁷ See Fodor: 'It may be that you can resolve an ambiguous figure by deciding what to attend to. But (a) which figures are ambiguous is *not* something that you can decide; (b) nor can you decide what the terms of the ambiguity are; (c) nor can you decide what further psychological consequences ... the resolution of the ambiguity will entrain. This all sounds pretty unpenetrated to me'. op. cit., p. 191.

Churchland's claims that even the most familiar perceptual features can be radically altered.

I shall take the most dramatic evidence in support of Churchland's thesis to bring out this point. Earlier, we saw that Churchland uses the example of inverting lenses as a case of perceptual plasticity. The case of the inverting lenses demonstrates that one's visual cues can be re-orientated in a dramatic way, yet the organism can adapt to this 'transformation of vision' readily and quickly. Such cases seem an important support for RPT, but the attractions of this view for Churchland's cause are short-lived when the issue of image inversion is considered in more detail.

According to Fodor, there are good ecological reasons why you might expect plasticity of this sort. Plausibly, some degree of plasticity occurs because organisms have to develop and learn to coordinate their spatial and perceptual tasks. As they grow they must 'recalibrate the perceptual/motor mechanisms that correlate bodily gestures with perceived spatial positions (paradigmatically, in the human case, the mechanisms of hand/eye coordination) ... Adaption to inverted (and otherwise spatially distorting) lenses is plausibly an extreme case of this sort of recalibration.' This kind of evidence certainly does not imply that perception is radically plastic:

> The moral of the inverting lens experiment thus seems to be: you find specific perceptual plasticity pretty much where you'd expect to find it on specifically ecological grounds. What Churchland needs to show - and doesn't - is that you *also* find perceptual plasticity where you *wouldn't* expect it on specific ecological grounds; for example, that you can somehow reshape the perceptual field by learning physics. Churchland offers, however, no examples of this. I strongly suspect that's because there aren't any.[48]

Fodor's point is that there is an order of difference between plasticity of (certain) responses to the data of perception, and the plasticity of perception *writ large*. Churchland assumes that support for the first point is automatically support for the second. But Churchland has not actually presented a case for the second claim: all he has shown is that in some cases of image inversion, subjects will recalibrate their perceptual-motor responses; he has not shown that perception itself can be radically rearranged. In fact, the experimental evidence actually runs contrary to his claims even in his own example. The extent to which perception is malleable through artificial image alteration suggests instead that there are some perceptual sensitivities which are not lost through such manipulation. The evidence strongly suggests that perception of some features, such as faces, remains remarkably *insensitive* to image alteration; a finding consonant with some kind of modular view of the perceptual mechanisms, not a

---

[48] Ibid., pp. 193-194. Fodor cites evidence which shows why the perceptual-motor 'growth' factor is very important here. Experimental data have shown that individuals which are 'passively wheeled around but deprived of perceptual motor feed-back' do not adapt the image inversion as smoothly or quickly. (Loc. cit.) See: R. Held and J. Blossom, 'Neonatal Deprivation and Adult Rearrangement: Complementary Techniques for Analysing Plastic Sensory Motor Coordinations', pp. 872-876. See also, C. S. Harris, 'Perceptual Adaptation to Inverted, Reversed, and Displaced Vision,' pp. 419-444.

radical plasticity thesis. Despite apparent image inversion, it seems that perception is not radically 'plastic'.[49]

It is not even clear that Churchland's *exemplar* cases of (alleged) perceptual malleability in learning Braille or in sight-reading music, presents a convincing case for radical plasticity either. It is Churchland's claim that just because some of us have learnt, in recent years, to 'perceive speech by touch' or to 'see music', it follows therefore, that learning and training can produce *any* sort of perceptual information given the right sort of inferential cues. He even suggests at one point that such theoretical conditioning might allow us to think of such familiar experiences in entirely new *aesthetic* terms.[50] But all this is clearly a *non sequitur,* as Fodor notes (impatiently) while paraphrasing Churchland:[51]

> In recent years we have learned to perceive automobiles (not just auditorily but visually). Now the eyes were not evolved for the instantaneous perception of those complex structures. So doesn't their acquired mastery illustrate the highly sophisticated and supernormal capacities that learning can produce in perception?
> Fiddlesticks. Churchland needs, and does not have, an argument that the visual perceptual capacities of people who can read ... differ in any interesting way from the visual perceptual capacities of people who can't. ... The old story is: you read (spot automobiles) by making educated inferences from the properties of things that your visual system *was* evolved to detect; shape, form, colour, sequence and the like.[52]

---

[49] See: R. Kemp, C. McManus and T. Pigott, 'Sensitivity to the Displacement of Facial Features in Negative and Inverted Images,' pp. 531-543. A mainstay of the argument that perception is penetrable by high-level beliefs and theories is the claim that efferent nerve 'descending pathways' of the brain demonstrate that a higher centre can terminate in a lower centre, thus refuting the idea of informational encapsulation in favour of the plasticity thesis. Daniel Gilman has critically evaluated such a claim from a biologist's perspective, and has concluded that none of Churchland's examples given in support of this claim, demonstrate either that high-level information can be transmitted in this fashion, or that the wiring of the brain has any significant bearing for 'a role for beliefs or theories in perception.' See: 'The Neurobiology of Observation', pp. 496-502.

[50] 'Reconceiving musical phenomena in terms of harmonic theory [does not rob] music of its beauty and peculiar identity. On the contrary, such a reconception opens many aesthetic doors that would otherwise have remained closed. P. M. Churchland, 'Some Reductive Strategies in Cognitive Neurobiology', p. 303.

[51] Churchland, (1988) op. cit., p 177.

[52] Fodor, 'Reply' (1988) op. cit., pp. 194-195. On the effects of musical training, Fodor says: 'This merely begs the question, which is whether the effects of musical training are, in fact, perceptual. Churchland adds that 'one can just as easily learn to recognize sounds under their dominant *frequency* descriptions ...[or]...under their *wavelength* descriptions ... What Churchland has to show is, first, that *perceptual* capacities are altered by learning musical theory (as opposed to the truism that learning musical theory alters what you know about music;) second, that it's learning the theory (as opposed to listening to lots of music) that alters the perception; and third that perception is altered in some different way if you learn not musical theory but acoustics. Churchland doesn't show any of these things - he doesn't even bother to *argue* for any of them - and I doubt that any of them are true.' loc. cit.

The point here is simply this: even if one can educate oneself to discriminate perceptual information in different ways, it does not follow that one is reconceiving *what* one discriminates by learning a new theory. Were it true, then illiterates would be visually incapacitated, and automobile spotting would constitute a different form of visual capability of people born relatively recently compared to those of past centuries. Clearly, such a suggestion is absurd.

Fodor's view on this matter is essentially the opposite of Churchland's. Hence, the impatience of the above reply. His claim is that learning new theories does not even *enhance* modularised perceptual content, let alone penetrate it. Perceptual content is, to an important degree, not at all constituted by such learning; fictional caloric and infrared beings notwithstanding. Instead, it is at some level cognitively encapsulated. The role of perception is, partly, to present for the organism certain domain-specific features of the environment which it has evolved to detect. And these features can be strikingly insensitive to theory change as Fodor has noted. That there are such selectively important features as low-level 'looks' is one of the central claims of this book.

If true, this point creates a good deal of trouble for Churchland. If some perception is encapsulated from inferential knowledge, then Churchland cannot claim that low-level sensation is wholly eliminable by large-scale theory change. In fact, if cognitive encapsularity is true, then it is not clear how Churchland's central argument about the redundancy of sensory content can even get off the ground. As we have seen, his arguments for eliminativism involved the imaginative cases of the infrared and caloric beings. Their perceptual discriminations provided analogues of, and reasons for, the homophonic translation of one sensation vocabulary to another. But, if Churchland cannot establish a case for theoretical penetrability and sensory elimination in such *fictional* cases (examples trumped up especially for the purpose of demonstrating this point), he certainly cannot ground the replacement of *our* sensory framework with a better theory on the strength of such examples.

The case for elimination of sensory content plays on the theoretical distance between the perceptions of the fictional beings Churchland imagines, and an accurate ontology of the real world. The way of arriving at an accurate understanding of the way things really are, according to Churchland, is to replace misleading theoretical vocabularies (such as those of the infrared and caloric beings) with better ones. But Churchland can hardly be said to have argued for theoretical penetrability in these fictional cases, if he has not already successfully and unambiguously argued for the RPT. And, on what we have considered so far, he certainly has not done this. Perception, *pace* Fodor, may not be plastic but encapsulated in some sense from inferential cues (learning a new theory alters what one knows about music but not how one hears it). There may well be certain low-level sensory contents (of such things as Fodor suggests above - 'shape, form, colour, sequence and the like'), which are quite resilient to the 'changing of one's assumptions' about objects. Even for the infrared and caloric beings then, homophonic translation of their sensational vocabulary may not capture *everything* about their perceptions, simply because perception is *not* plastic. And if perceptions cannot be radically transformed by learning new theories, then eliminative materialism loses one of its main supports.

This point is encouraged by modularity theory, where the mechanisms involved in perception involve encapsulated, task-specific units which operate relatively autonomously and which feed data into a central processing system. On this view, low-level perceptual content is not influenced at all by the changing of theoretical assumptions, and so the distal outputs of the low-level modules are immune to wholesale elimination. Such a view as modularity theory is certainly not troubled by the off-beat cases of Braille readers and spectral inversions that Churchland offers in support of his claims, and it is certainly not ruled out by the more imaginative cases of caloric/infrared perceivers. For one thing, the former cases are quite different from the cases Churchland needs to support his eliminativism - such cases are actually *consistent* with a modularity view (Churchland needs cases which demonstrate that a change in *theory* brings about these dramatic effects); for another thing, the plasticity of perception thesis, in its most radical form at least, may well be *false*.[53]

In this book an account has been developed which combines a modular view of content with evolutionary considerations. The extent to which high-level cognition can influence or fail to influence experience occurs differentially among species, and also by degrees like a continuum. Perceptual content is also a *complex:* containing multiple levels of content (linguistic propositional, theoretically informational, impurely sensational, etc.) Perceptual content is also *asymmetrical:* always containing low-level, impurely sensational aspects even when high-level, inferential input is present, absent or suspended. Perceptual content, on my view, is certainly influenced by high-level features but even highly representational (and theoretically revisable) features of experience have sensational aspects which resist explanation in such terms. The fact is that perception is not 'plastic' to top-down processing, nor is it altogether immune from inference. Instead, the content of low-level experiences is suggestible, but relatively constrained from such influences. The modularity response to the RPT is essentially in sympathy with this approach if one assumes that encapsulation occurs by degrees.

A question that needs to be asked in connection with the radical plasticity thesis is this. If the RPT is false what then can we make of the cases of perceptual incommensurability that Churchland discusses? In the light of the foregoing, we can reassess hypothetical instances where perception is claimed to be secondary to theory in the following terms: what such examples as the caloric case show is not that caloric *experiences* are theory dependent, but that *caloric descriptions* are - the way the caloric cousins *describe* their experiences is partly constituted by the theory that they have adopted. Descriptions, not

---

[53] It has been pointed out to me that the RPT suffers from an even deeper problem than those already mentioned. Assuming the RPT to be true, Churchland cannot actually provide *objective* evidence in support of the claim. On the RPT how things look depends on one's theoretical commitments. This being so, in the event of a conflict between Churchland and Fodor about how something looks, it would be as equally open for Fodor to claim that *according to his theoretical background* the thing in question does not look the way Churchland says it should. 'Thus, if Churchland's view is right, Fodorians should be able to provide as much evidence for their view as Churchland can provide for his view. This means that if Churchland's view is true, it *cannot* be shown to be superior to its rival. This does not, of course, show that Churchland's account is false, but it does put it out of the domain of rational discussion.' S. G. Couvalis, 'Theory and Observation'.

experiences, are theory-laden.

This seems to be a reasonable claim, but it is not the kind of claim that Churchland wants or needs to defend. He needs to defend a far more inclusive doctrine. Churchland wants to claim that the relevant sense in which theory-ladenness influences experience is not merely at the descriptive level. To support his thesis, he needs language/theory informed descriptions to give way to experiences that are similarly influenced. But again, this does not follow at all. The way that we *describe* our astronomical data is certainly shot through with our theoretical cosmology. But it does not follow that all the astronomical *data*, as experienced, is itself constituted descriptively. If not, then it would not follow that changing of theoretical assumptions, in turn, changes this sort of information. *Contra* Churchland: one simply cannot (using contemporary astronomical theory) see the sun's rising as anything like an earth sink, despite affirmations for this from all (theoretical) quarters. It is even less obvious that the low-level contentful states of colour or heat experiences can be transformable or recalibrated through greater facility with EM wave descriptions, or sound experiences with musical or acoustical descriptions. To make the mistake that just because descriptions are theoretically constituted then so too are experiences, is to make the unjustifiable sleight of hand mentioned in Chapter 3.

The above arguments suggest that we cannot claim that theory change affects perception in any dramatic way. We cannot claim this because (i) perception may not be plastic but suggestible to high-level influences by degrees, and (ii) theories may ultimately only influence how experiences are *described.* So we cannot claim that one can perceive something differently by describing it differently. But, consistent with the continuum account, we can suggest this: EM wave, acoustical and caloric *descriptions* are imbued with appropriate theory, and descriptions *ex hypothesi* are in quite a different domain from low-level content, which is not (exhaustively) imbued with theory. Churchland has not convincingly argued that the changing of descriptions shows that perceptions are plastic through and through, so we are entitled to assert this distinction. I have been brief on this, but it is clear that the radical plasticity of perception thesis has not fared well. But does the general view of a microphysical replacement for folk psychology succeed? In what follows, I suggest that it does not.

Eliminative materialism and psychological nominalism

Folk psychology is eliminable, claims Churchland. It is all a matter of the replacement of common-sense phenomenal vocables with detailed scientific ones. This procedure, according to Churchland, is a holistic one, replacing networks of theory with others better designed to meet the needs of a maturing neuroscience. Is there any justification for this proposal?

Despite Churchland's enthusiasm for the program he proposes, it does not seem that it would work even if he were correct to the letter about the extensional equivalence between our phenomenal vocabulary and its assumed replacement. For a start, it is not even true that one can report physical wavelengths of light reflected from object surfaces in our colour discriminations (and, in the same way, it is not true that one can ever relate the mean kinetic energy of objects with which we come in contact). The reason for this is that there are too many *physically* contingent features involved in such experiences to ever render them capable of being reported without sophisticated equipment designed expressly for the purpose of isolating the feature of interest, a fact that Churchland seems to overlook.

The real situation is thus. In the case of seeing colours, a great number of combined wavelengths are involved in our perceptual judgements; in the case of reporting temperature, the kinetic energy contact with surface molecules of objects and the conductivity of the material in question is also relevant. To take colour perception as one case, Mundle reports that cone pigments in the retina are not responsive singularly to pick out individual wavelengths; rather, the mechanisms of detection of each individual colour involves differential absorption of a number of different wavelengths 'by the one, two or three types of cones affected thereby.'[54] Of course, this complicated process can be detailed, and the variables involved isolated, but it is not without using external experimental means. An actual or possible person in a 'reconstructed' world, such as Churchland imagines, could not itemise such information in singular empirical judgements, no matter how well versed in the relevant colour theory.

Such contingent processes are behind the phenomenon of visual colour illusion, and the phenomenal features that can be induced by, for example, the simultaneous contrast of perceptual cues, or by artificial stimulation. An example might be the phenomenon of the colour white, which can be induced not only by a standard 'white' object, which reflects all spectral wavelengths in incident light, but by the artificial stimulation of the retinal cones with only two specific wavelengths, which, if presented separately, make us see yellow and blue. The point here is that Churchland cannot ignore such contingencies, and it is hard to see how he can avoid them creating problems for his theory. It is not clear that Churchland can cogently argue for his 'brave new world' of perceptually reconstructed human beings, if he cannot get past the empirical difficulties associated with combinations of such data. The fact is that perceptual content, at the physical input level, is actually an *amalgam*, not a series of features which can be itemised individually.[55]

Additionally though, as Goldman notes, a great number of gestaltist considerations bear in here as well. A given perceptual experience depends crucially on the 'state of adaption ... of a subject's visual system, his set and

---

[54] See C.W. K. Mundle, *Perception: Facts and Theories*, p. 52.

[55] Ibid., p. 54. Only in underwater conditions, it is reported that subjects can see what are nearer the 'true' colours of objects. (See: Helen E. Ross, *Perception and Behaviour in Strange Environments*, p. 53.) This is because the phenomenon of 'apparent' colour is always a product of differential absorption of light from surrounding objects. In underwater situations, wavelengths of light from surrounding objects is absent, so an object will appear black. 'Relative wavelength, rather than absolute wavelength is what matters [above the water].' Yet there are circumstances in which sensitivity exposure to one wavelength under such circumstances can yield an enhancement of that perceived or 'apparent' colour. Ross reports that: 'When a diver first opens his eyes at moderate depth in a blue sea, red objects appear a muddy brown: but after a minute or two the red deepens ... an underwater torch appears tinged with red at depth.' Loc. cit. It is clear that Churchland needs an account of both 'apparent' colour, and colour in circumstances of relative wavelength of neighbouring objects - a tall order along strictly neurophysiological lines!

attention, the colours of the surrounding areas and other purely subjective factors'.[56] This point is interesting and relevant for a number of reasons. The first reason concerns the aforementioned amalgam of physical stimuli occurring as indistinguishable inputs. Such experiences involve concurrent surrounding colours and lighting conditions. Another reason, however, concerns how well one is attending to certain features of an experience. One's 'seeing red' in the case of responding to a traffic signal, for example, does seem to have a lot to do with how responsive one may be to road signals and how well one may be concentrating on my vehicular tasks. An adequate account of experience does seem to require a recognition of how purely subjective factors feature in normal human perceptions.

To take up this latter point: it seems fairly clear that one may be having one's retinal cones stimulated with all the right EM waves (in this case, approx. 0.63×10^{-6}m) and yet not 'see red', or, in phenomenal terms, have the light 'appear red' to them. Yet one may be able to *recall* having seen a red light *after the fact*.[57] An experience of this kind does not seem to be simply a case of proximal data being interpreted by one's theoretical assumptions. On the basis of what we have seen of Churchland's argument, he must say in such a circumstance that an experience of this kind is merely uninterpreted stimulus - an experience without theory (and hence, without *content*). But this seems to be both counterintuitive and an oversimplification of the matter. It seems more natural to say of a phenomenon of this kind that it is a kind of low-level experience; an experience which, while contentful, is not dramatically informed by high-level input.

To incorporate such less obvious, but familiar, cases of 'seeing', Churchland needs to either admit the possibility of subsidiary processing units being involved (which register colours yet which do not necessarily allow instant recognition), or admit that high-level input does not fully capture content. This point will be important later. As shown below, the remarks Churchland makes seem to stipulate the necessity of highly sophisticated, language-based interpretative mechanisms, not a structure which allows modification at lower processing levels.

A multiple-level processing view, such as that mentioned above, is clearly consistent with the continuum account. Such a view would allow for experiences to be strongly dependent on the state of adaption of the organism concerned; it would allow for content to feature by degrees of conscious accessibility. In terms used before, one's 'seeing red' might, in this case, amount to being an *unnoticed* seeing. This kind of 'seeing', while clearly contentful in some very primitive sense, is not characteristically a *red* seeing despite the input of all the correct light waves on the retina, and despite being pre-possessed of the relevant background theory (representational and theoretically informational judgments about the colours of traffic signals and about how one should respond etc.) In such a case, the content of such an experience is certainly heavily inferential in many ways, but the subject is

---

[56] A. H. Goldman, 'Epistemic Foundationalism and the Replacability of Observation Language', p. 143.

[57] Especially so in cases of people with 'eidetic' memories. See R. Arnheim, *Visual Thinking*, pp. 102-103.

simply not concentrating on the feature of their experience which is in question. However, the subject's experience clearly has content in this case, as he is able to *recall* having seen the red light later when asked, but not at the time undergoing the experience. (This low-level content may thus be non-functionally epiphenomenal at the time of seeing.) This can be as true of seeing red traffic lights as it is of 'seeing ripe or unripe tomatoes (recall Jackson's example raised earlier). Against Churchland, then, such an experience need not be contentless - proximal stimulus minus socio-linguistically conditioned and theoretically-embedded belief sets - but simply an experience resulting from inattention; an experience minus the subjective factors (noticings, attendings, etc.) that such situations seem to require. If this is true, then Churchland's stress on high-level content as necessary and sufficient features for experiential content is misplaced. 'Seeing red' is a far more complicated notion than a simple theory-heavy account would have us believe, because an experience can be contentful, yet not *noticed*.

If it is implausible to think that the content of experiences can be couched in terms of theoretically descriptive physics, it might be better to insist that an additional level at which experiences are sensed is needed. Content may need to be seen in terms of both the causal, sensory and epistemic orders. And, if so, there may be some basis for thinking that perceptual content is not entirely inferential as Churchland claims and that there is something in the idea that there are aspects of experience which cannot be captured in terms of high-level features. Contentful, low-level experiences arising at several levels of complexity may well be a more accommodating view in the light of these criticisms.

Churchland's reply to this sort of response to his position is entirely predictable. What all this shows is not only how fruitless the enterprise of a thorough-going phenomenology of how things appear to us happens to be, but also how firmly entrenched we are in a long-outmoded theoretical paradigm. His suggestion would be to make the transition from how the colour red 'appears' to individuals to thinking about the context of explanation in terms of physical theory (in terms of EM waves). How one should do this is to forget the idea that phenomenal statements are direct reports of immediate experience and to think of such experiences in terms of non-inferential responses to physical stimulation, which are causally connected to the theoretical context in which terms we are linguistically trained to apprehend. Goldman puts this point in these terms:

> Association of some observation term with some feature of a sensation is not only less important for determining its meaning than the relation of the terms to others in a conceptual system; it is also a product of the subject's indoctrination into the system or theory ... Phenomenal predicates cannot categorize what immediately appears, since *nothing* immediately appears. What does appear is what comes to be reported by [the] use of observation predicates rather than the reverse.[58]

Churchland affirms the point about sensations being conceptualised in terms of

---

[58] Goldman, op. cit., p. 145

observational predicates in these terms: 'our conceptual responses to our sensations ... [are interpretation] functions implanted in childhood as we learned to think and *talk* about the world in the fashion of our elders.'[59]

Admittedly, Churchland's claims and Goldman's reading of them are quite different here. Churchland talks about conceptual *responses* to sensations being under sway of theory; Goldman attributes to him the idea that sensations themselves are under sway of theory. But, Goldman's reading seems the most consistent statement of Churchland's overall position. For only if sensations themselves were under the sway of theory could they be eliminated wholesale. Mere responses being under theoretical sway doesn't necessarily guarantee eliminativism of *content* - which is, after all, what Churchland wants.

Statements like this bring out the central importance of another critical element in Churchland's position: his emphasis on *language*. This is an issue that needs to be treated in some detail as there are several possible interpretations of Churchland's commitments in this context. Language as the bearer of content has already been mentioned as a part of Churchland's argument which can be attributed to the influence of Sellars. However, the idea that high-level, linguistically-mediated conceptualisation, not phenomenal properties, constitutes the only explanation for the way objects appear is, I shall argue, an outlandish claim. Rather than being a premise in an overall argument, such a claim should really make any theorist reconsider the means by which he arrived at such a view.

The emphasis on language being the *bearer* of content is not a matter which can be true in some circumstances and false in others. The claim is either correct or hopelessly misguided. However, it should be noted here that there are two ways that the bearer thesis can be taken: that language occurs *concurrently* with content, or language occurs *prior* to content. Language being the bearer of content is a separate issue to whether language occurs prior to content or whether it is concurrent with it. There is also an asymmetry here. If the bearer thesis is false then it need not mean that either the priority or concurrency claim is false, while if either the priority or concurrency claims are false, then the bearer thesis is false. (If it is not the case that language arises concurrently with content or prior to it, it can't be true that language is the bearer of content.)

I shall call the emphasis on linguistically-mediated descriptions occurring prior to content, the *language-priority thesis*. A weaker interpretation of Churchland's views will also be considered - the possibility that language might arise concurrently with proximal stimulations. This will be called the *language-concurrency thesis*. My claim will be that, on either interpretation, Churchland's view does not establish that language is the bearer of experiential content. Both the language-priority thesis and the language-concurrency thesis are false, so therefore the bearer thesis is false.

Note that Goldman's statement of Churchland's position (above) is neutral on the matter of presentation of language and content, though it clearly affirms the bearer thesis. However, in light of the confusions outlined earlier in this book, the bearer claim itself could be read in two ways: that language is the bearer of *semantic* content (observational terms), or language is the bearer of *perceptual* content (observational experience). It was the conflation of these very separate

---

[59] Churchland, (1979) op. cit., p. 39. Final italic mine.

claims that occupied our attention in sorting out Feyerabend's commitments in Chapter 9. Churchland clearly affirms a bearer thesis of some form in his acknowledgment of the influence of Feyerabend, Hanson, Hesse and Sellars, but his remarks are ambiguous between language as a semantic bearer and language as a perceptual bearer.[60]

Churchland claims that his view is similar to the views of these other theorists 'in essentials', but this does not help us to sort out his stand on the confusion mentioned. As we have already seen in detail, both Feyerabend and Sellars seem to conflate both agendas. Hanson's remarks given here are also explicitly about perception rather than semantic content (see also the epigraph to Chapter 3). Churchland is, however, clearest on this matter in the following passage:

> Our current modes of conceptual exploitation are rooted, in substantial measure, not in the nature of our perceptual environment, nor in the innate features of our psychology, but rather in the structure and content of our common language, and in the process by which each child acquires the normal use of that language.[61]

It shall be assumed from this that, in view of earlier material studied, Churchland (like his predecessors) has confused this issue and aims to support *both* claims. Language, for Churchland, is the bearer of both semantic and perceptual content. Now it needs to be established whether Churchland is an advocate of the language-priority thesis or the language-concurrency thesis.

This separate issue ranking language and sensations in terms of presentation amounts to debating whether theory-embedded *descriptions* of sensations occur prior to content or if content and description arise concurrently. Churchland certainly claims that language is central to making perceptual judgements; his commitments on the presentation issue will be looked at in the discussion below. The language-priority thesis would seem to be the most obvious way by which to secure an eliminativism of low-level content. It is clearly the most fitting interpretation of Churchland's work, given his overall eliminativist motivations. As noted earlier, descriptions are theoretically constituted; observational terms, not observational experiences, are theory-laden. It is also observational *terms* that are radically transformed by changes in theoretical superstructure. I have already suggested that this is a premise in Churchland's argument. If the language-priority thesis is the most accurate position that Churchland is defending, then he cannot afford to lose it, as it is a crucial thread in his overall eliminative materialism. He needs to endorse this claim to support the view that all content is theoretical and revisible.

Churchland is not alone in wanting to affirm a language-bearer thesis. As we saw in the previous chapter, Wilfred Sellars also holds this view:

> [A]ll consciousness of sorts or repeatables rests on an association of *words* (e.g., 'red') with classes of resembling particulars.[62]

---

[60] See his remarks, ibid., p. 37-38.
[61] Ibid., p. 7.
[62] W. Sellars, *Science, Perception and Reality*, p. 289.

Of course, this can be interpreted in two ways: as a language-priority thesis or a language-concurrency thesis. Sellars's arguments for the language-bearer thesis have already been criticised in Chapter 10. Sellars's writing is not clear on the presentation issue.[63] Churchland, however, is explicit about affirming both the language-bearer *and* the language-priority thesis:

> [T]he psychological facts of normal perception ... [are] that children acquire the ability to observe and describe the world in great detail *before* they acquire any significant or explicit awareness of the richness of their sensational life, or even of its existence.[64]

It is certainly clear here that Churchland is talking about perceptual content, not just semantic content. It is also clear that he explicitly adopts the language-priority thesis. However, other remarks that Churchland makes show that his position on this can be interpreted differently. When he introduces his notion of an interpretation function in his 'Argument from Measuring Instruments', for instance, it is unclear what precise relationship language has to content. The idea here is that our sensations are like states of measuring instruments such as ammeters, which 'are of themselves mute, short of an interpretation funded by some theory'; a theory which is mapped onto sentences in a language.[65]

What is really being said here? Can the states occur without an interpretation function, or are such states nothing without it? Perhaps the states are 'mute' only when not combined with an interpretation function afterwards. If the earlier quotation detailing the 'fact' that we describe the world in detail before we are aware of our sensations is anything to go on, then Churchland has language-priority in mind; however, this could easily be read as a concurrency claim too. His position on this is, at best, ambiguous.

But there are other reasons to suspend belief on the more likely interpretation of his views on the presentation issue. Churchland does not, for instance, attempt to produce the 'psychological facts' he claims support language-priority and, without such evidence, we are entitled not to take this claim on its own very seriously. Also, the claim about children acquiring the ability to describe the world before they are aware of the existence of their rich sensational life is not argued for, nor supported empirically. This offhand remark on its own does not add any weight to his argument as it stands. If Churchland is advocating a language-priority thesis, I shall argue that he should not be committed to it for very good reason. Yet he does seem to hold this kind of view in the first passage given above.

---

[63] Sellars seems to think that as adult humans we mistakenly and parochially transpose a structured sensory awareness (a 'logical space') onto prelinguistic infants. This alone, however, is consistent with language-priority or language-concurrency theses. See his remarks: '[W]hen we picture a child ... learning his *first* language, *we*, of course, locate the language learner in a structured logical space in which we are at home. ... But though it is *we* who are familiar with this logical space, we run the danger, if we are not careful, of picturing the language learner as having *ab initio* some degree of awareness - "pre-analytic", limited and fragmentary though it may be - of this same logical space.' ibid., p. 290.

[64] Churchland, (1979) op. cit., p. 39.

[65] Ibid., p. 38.

I have suggested that if either the priority or concurrency thesis is false, then the bearer thesis is false. If Churchland is advocating a priority thesis and this turns out to be false, then he loses his bearer thesis as well. This raises an important dilemma: if Churchland chooses to move away from this strongly nominalist position he shares with Sellars (the bearer thesis), he also moves away from important premises in his overall package which I outlined earlier; if he chooses to retain it, his nominalist position turns out to be false if the language-priority thesis is false. In the passage above, this seems to involve the imposition of language which occurs *prior* to content. I shall suggest in what follows, however, that it is very doubtful that language occurs prior to experience. There is a sense in which something 'immediately appears' without the imposition of language. It will also be suggested that language-concurrency cannot be tenable given Churchland's overall theoretical commitments.

Churchland's claims in support of eliminative materialism are not well supported. The empirical work he offers in support of the plasticity thesis can be much debated as to what they demonstrate. His exhortation that we might be able to learn to internalise detailed physical descriptions (e.g., about colours) is simply implausible. There is no empirical work even offered in support of the language-priority thesis. I strongly suspect that Churchland does not attempt to argue for this premise because he simply assumes it to be true.

For fairly obvious reasons, however, the language-priority thesis simply cannot be true. For one thing, such a view runs up against the developmental and ethological facts. Specifically, the emphasis on language prior to content can be seriously undermined when considering comparative animal and human behaviour. As G. J. O'Brien has argued, Churchland's variety of radical replacement eliminativism (or, as he calls it, 'STEM')[66] amounts to asserting a language-priority form of psychological nominalism: 'the claim that all perceptual awareness is preceded by the acquisition of, and mediated through, language'[67] But such a view, he argues, is clearly inconsistent with documented evidence dealing with animal behaviour. Ethological work on the acquisition of a self concept is one such source of evidence.

Gallop has suggested that the more complicated cognitive concept of 'self' in primates, has pre-linguistic roots as a matter of phyletic necessity. His claim is that this 'may have important implications for claims concerning the evolutionary continuity of mental experience.'[68] The evidence he offers centres upon primates using mirrors to identify marks on their faces. It tends to bear out that a mental concept of self is a feature of infants, apes and other primates from 2-3 days after birth, indicating that, like animal cognition, mental experience is not necessarily a reflective feature of highly-developed organisms equipped with a language. In Gallop's words: 'Man may not be evolution's only experiment in self-awareness.' Of course, if pre-linguistic perceptual features are considered along with very early self-recognitional constructs, it would

---

[66] The *strong thesis of eliminative materialism*, see, G. J. O'Brien, 'Eliminative Materialism and Psychological Self-Knowledge', p. 49-70.

[67] Ibid., p. 51.

[68] G. Gallop Jr. 'Self-Recognition in Primates: A Comparative Approach to the Bi-Directional Properties of Consciousness.' p. 329; See also Michael Lewis and Jeanne Brooks-Gunn: *Social Cognition and the Acquisition of Self*, passim.

seem that the cognitive apparatus prior to inferential input must be quite rich indeed. As added support to this sort of evidence, O'Brien notes that children learn a rudimentary self concept as early as 12 months of age, at least six months prior 'to the first faltering use of personal pronouns in first person ascriptions.'[69]

Katherine Nelson's studies have also found that there are several dimensions in which infants categorise objects before naming or describing them, and one of those is in respect of what she calls 'perceptual properties' of colour, form and texture.[70] Macnamara has provided evidence to suggest that children learn non-linguistic means of object recognition prior to language development, but he eschews 'a complete body of set cognitive structures'[71] in the Kantian mould, arguing that the evidence supports the idea that 'basic [non-linguistic] cognitive structures ... precede the development of corresponding linguistic structures.'[72] This qualification suggests that the cognitive structures in question are not part of a composite of highly intellectual categories which are imposed *en bloc* in perceptual discrimination.

Such developmental findings do not rest easily with Churchland's claims, and the psychological nominalist strand of his argument must be seen to be on shaky ground. For pre-linguistic self awareness to develop, indicates that the stress is misplaced on such early processing being language-governed. Churchland's language-priority theme just does not stand up to the fact of awareness *without* language. Since it does not, the explanation of such phenomena must be put on concepts or structures which are of quite a different nature. O'Brien affirms something like this when he says: 'As a result, therefore, we must posit the existence of conceptual structures underlying the perceptual awareness of young children which are not acquired in a linguistic fashion.'[73]

It seems open to assert in response to all this that the distinction between sensory concepts and descriptive semantic concepts, that has been discussed in previous chapters, might be just what is required here. What O'Brien refers to as 'non-linguistic conceptual structures' which underlie perceptual awareness, might be a requisite feature of having contentful experiences at certain levels. It certainly seems reasonable, at the very least, to insist that this nominalist element in Churchland's package should be reconsidered as being only part of a larger story. It is not the case that the only contentful experiences that are had are fixed through an inferential background of linguistically-mediated theory; some contents seem to be prior to such high-level conceptualisation, and may even constitute its conceptual and evolutionary ground. The ability to have contentful low-level experiences might have developed in response to evolutionary exigencies prior to the ability to filter those experiences with propositional linguistic and theoretically informational judgements. Moreover, this may be understood in entirely naturalist grounds as indicated in this book.

The argument so far, in this and previous chapters, has given some credence

---

[69] O'Brien, op. cit., p. 57.

[70] K. Nelson, 'Cognitive Primacy of Categorisation and its Functional Basis', p. 37.

[71] J. Macnamara, 'Cognitive Basis of Language Learning in Infants,' p.11.

[72] Loc. cit.

[73] G. J. O'Brien, op. cit., p. 59.

to such claims: for it has not been successfully claimed that perceptual experience is entirely plastic to the influence of new theory; nor is such experience entirely explained in terms of the physics of the perceptual situation. Also, it has been argued that the language-priority view does not rest well with the developmental and psychological facts. Further, certain features of perceptual awareness are missed out on when we speak of such content as being, in an important linguistic sense, descriptive. There is, then, room to move on the issue of the relation between experience and high-level content. It may not be a foregone conclusion that experiences are *necessarily* underpinned by mechanisms of high-level inference as Churchland makes out.

There are far better ways of considering the influences on experience than a language-priority nominalism. Empirical and developmental work goes some way toward supporting the limits that must be set on the importance of high-level inferential features to experiential content. The work of Piaget, in particular, shows how infants go through a series of pre-linguistic perceptual motor stages in which they learn by what he calls 'assimilation' and 'accommodation' to interact with and build a discriminatory model of their environment and to formulate an appropriate pattern of behavioural responses to it. In Piaget's work, there is no question that at primitive cognitive stages there is a world being perceived in subjectively contentful form, prior to the imposition of sophisticated forms of language-governed, 'abstract', formal-operational reasoning. Infants interact with the world they experience and organise it in fairly complex ways at later operational levels of development, but the kind of interaction is not initially - on Piaget's view - inferential in any linguistic-propositional, or theoretically informational sense. The type of perceptual consistencies and predictabilities that we, as infants, build out of the world we become assimilated to, is imposed back on the world as anticipatory conceptual invariants later in cognitive stage development, but those invariants are not - at least in the early stages - language governed. Indeed, the early stages of development initially consist of awarenesses far more basic than even the perception of object permanence or size constancy (some of the more rudimentary perceptual integrations on Piaget's account).

In Piaget's theory this developmental process also happens incrementally and by degrees - we don't become sophisticated, theoretically discerning, language-using creatures instantly. It would not be hard at all to see this kind of developmental view, in terms of degrees of increasing inferential perplexity; degrees which include low-level content. It is not suggested here that this kind of view is *established* by a Piagetian kind of account. The point here is simply a matter of inference to the best explanation: if Piaget is right with his developmental view of cognitive competence, then this seems to make Churchland's claim above about language-priority far less appealing:

> This entire process [Piaget's developmental phases] becomes unintelligible if we ... deny perception prior to the acquisition of beliefs and concepts. For it is through interaction with the perceived environment that these early perceptual concepts develop.[74]

---

[74] Ibid., p. 146.

This developmental work would be made even more unintelligible, of course, if perception is denied prior to the acquisition of *language*. (Consider animal and infant perception as an extreme *reductio* of this view.)[75]

There is other evidence to suggest that the language-priority emphasis in Churchland's work is misplaced. Goldman cites evidence suggestive of the informationally sensitive nature of perception at various levels not involving language. He includes, for consideration, face recognition studies (which demonstrate the ability of non-verbal physiognomic cognitions) and studies on congenitally deaf patients who show remarkable perceptual, conceptual and cognitive acuity with no verbal training whatsoever. Any one of these studies is enough to demonstrate that sophisticated, language-governed high-level reasoning is not necessary and sufficient for content. With these and other matters considered, the language-priority attitude which is behind Churchland's eliminativism of low-level experiences must be seen as a very doubtful claim indeed. Contrary to Churchland, some kind of content which is not language-like actually seems to *precede* language.[76]

Churchland need not, of course, fall for the trap of saying that language is prior to content. He can certainly stress the importance of language without making it central to his concerns. Since the language-priority thesis seems such an outlandish claim, possible weaker interpretations of his views will be considered below.

Churchland might claim instead that pre-linguistic content (in the form of proximal stimulations) occurs *in addition* to those sets of theory-embedded concepts which are transmitted through language. Language imposition might arise *concurrently* with such inputs, not prior to them. If so, then he would not be committed to denying content prior to language acquisition. This seems to be Churchland's claim in certain passages. At some points he seems to stress that sensational promptings actually instigate a judgmental response which is already brought to bear on that perceptual situation:

> In the case of perceptual judgements, what the senses do is cause the perceiver to activate some specific representation from the antecedent system of possible representations ... from the conceptual framework - that has been brought to the perceptual situation by the perceiver.[77]

---

[75] Churchland is aware of the dangers in adopting the language-priority thesis, making it unclear again the extent to which he is actually committed to this view. See, for instance, his remarks about language playing no role in the cognitive activities of other animals. Churchland, (1979) op. cit., p. 137.

[76] For further experimental work in fundamental conflict with the language-priority thesis, see: J. Piaget, *The Origin of Intelligence in Children;* E. Gibson, *Principles of Perceptual Learning and Development,* pp. 64-73, 154-60; S. Cary, 'A Case Study: Face Recognition', in E. Walker, *Explorations in the Biology of Language,* pp. 175-201; H. Furth, *Deafness and Learning.* See also work demonstrating that some kind of pre-linguistic content is *necessary* for later language acquisition: E. H. Rosch, 'Natural Categories', pp. 328-350; M. J. Angelin, *Word, Object and Conceptual Development;* J. Bruner and V. Sherwood, 'Thought, Language and Interaction in Infancy', in J. P. Forgas (ed.) *Social Cognition: Perspectives on Everyday Understanding.*

[77] P. M. Churchland, (1988) op. cit., p. 185.

On this view, perceivers bring to the epistemic situation networks of theoretical responses (in the form of sentences) which are then prompted into activation by certain stimuli. This, presumably, is what allows Churchland to claim that the key to an adequate theory of content is to focus not on the sensory states, but on the system of representation that such states bring about. For, on his view, some such systems are simply better than others.[78]

I have one main concern with this interpretation. Even if non-linguistic content may arise concurrently with language-governed theory-imposition, this interpretation does not carry Churchland's eliminativism, unless language *exhausts* experiential content. To claim a concurrency thesis, and not a priority thesis, and *still retain an eliminative materialism,* Churchland must claim that the only content of significance is the theoretically-imbued *linguistic* content. Otherwise, he would clearly be denying premise (2) of his argument that was influenced by Sellars: the endorsement of the propositional/semantic content of an observational statement leaves no experiential residue (the bearer thesis). To suggest otherwise, Churchland would be committed to rejecting the claim that linguistic propositional judgments are the *bearers* of content. But, as mentioned elsewhere, Churchland seems to want this premise as well:

> The meaning of the relevant observational terms, *has nothing to do* with the intrinsic qualitative identity of whatever sensation happens to their non-inferential application in singular empirical judgements. Rather, their position in semantic space appears to be determined by the networks of sentences containing them, accepted by the speakers who use them.[79]

Taken together with the claim that the only legitimate way of securing the matching of observational vocables in response to sensory promptings is by homophonic translation, this means not only that terms get their meaning from a network of surrounding sentences, but judgements about observational data are also dependent on that theoretical network. So a child's use of, say, 'white' in response to the familiar kind of sensation, provides that term with no semantic identity. It acquires that identity by its role in a network of beliefs and inferences: 'Depending on what that acquired network happens to be, that terms could come to mean white or hot ... or an infinity of other things.'[80]

So, whether a language-priority or a concurrency thesis is true, the important thing that must remain on his view of experiential content is *language* as it features in networks of statements (theory), not sensations. However, if all this is true, and if language exhausts both meaning *and* sensations, then how can Churchland allow for content which is non-linguistic?

What is at issue here is whether Churchland can claim a language-concurrency thesis. If he can, then he might be able to allow for cases in which content seems to arise without language. However, it is unclear if Churchland

---

[78] Hence his claim: 'A perceptual judgement, therefore, can be no better, though it can be worse, than the system of representation in which it is constituted.' loc. cit.

[79] P. M. Churchland, (1979) op. cit., p. 11. Italics mine.

[80] Ibid., p. 14. Elimination of sensations, of course, is secured here by homophonic translation of vocables precisely because the content of such vocables have *nothing to do* with sensations.

can have his eliminative materialism of low-level content if he denies premise (2). If he does this, he clearly precludes the possibility of holding premise (4). (Whether (2) is interpreted along language-priority or concurrency lines or not, *once denied* it also denies that perceptual awareness consists of linguistic-conceptual content.) But crucially, since the replaceability thesis *depends* on linguistically-mediated paradigm shifts in the alterations of perceptual gestalts ('the propriety of anyone's perceptual judgments [turns] ultimately on the question of the virtues of the theory in whose terms the responses are made')[81] this seems hardly a way of guaranteeing (6) and (7). So in avoiding the language-priority thesis, the concurrency thesis simply leaves eliminative materialism out of reach! This would certainly be an unwelcome consequence for Churchland. For Churchland, then, the language-concurrency thesis clearly cannot be maintained if language does not *exhaust* content. Otherwise, eliminative materialism would not be an option. However, if language exhausts content, then Churchland *cannot have* content which is non-linguistic - he cannot evade the objection earlier that there is more to content than that which is captured in terms of language.

We can understand, perhaps, how Churchland arrives at this situation. Not only does he explicitly assert the language-bearer thesis, he also systematically conflates the semantic-bearer thesis with the perceptual-bearer thesis. The semantic-bearer thesis is not enough to guarantee him replacement of sensational content (it only gives him replacement of one *language* with another). However, conflating the two enables Churchland to gain elimination of sensations *along with* homophonic translation (because sensations are claimed to have 'nothing to do' with observational terms). So, since Churchland's eliminativism relies on language replacement, he must be committed (even on a language-concurrency thesis) to language exhausting content. However, this leaves us wondering what service proximal stimulations could possibly provide, if they have no content outside language. And, it leaves us wondering what to make of the cases of content already mentioned that clearly seem to precede language acquisition.

This seems to leave Churchland in a paradoxical situation: he needs to show, on the concurrency view, how proximal stimulations can feature in the networks of linguistically-mediated perceptual judgements the meaning of which is fixed into theories. If such judgements had *nothing to do* with proximal promptings, and if radical replacement eliminativism is true and networks of sentences do determine semantic space, then there must be no content outside language. (A consequence which reinforces again premise (2)). Alternatively, the only other way of keeping a concurrency thesis of this form, might be to deny (4) and uphold (2) and to suggest that the proximal inputs in question are not necessary for content. This, however, risks making such stimulations *redundant* to experiences - an outcome, surely, which is inconsistent with any robust materialism.

It is concluded from this that Churchland's premises are mutually supporting; to remove one is to remove the entire deck. Churchland must either have a language-priority thesis (which runs against psychological evidence of content occurring before language) or a concurrency view (which loses his

---

[81] Ibid., p. 37.

eliminativism and his materialism). Since the concurrency thesis leads to a position inconsistent with his overall strategy, the former position is clearly the only tenable one for Churchland. But this leads to the reconsideration of the arguments raised before in relation to this view. Denying premise (2), the Sellarsian premise of his argument, casts doubt on the premise that all content is transformed by linguistically-structured, theoretical networks. On the other hand, upholding the latter with premise (4) requires that (2) is true, and hence that all (significant) content is semantically prior - this again reinforces the language-ladenness proposal. But if the language-priority thesis is the more accurate position, this too seems implausible because some kind of content actually *precedes* language.

Churchland cannot lose any of these premises without abandoning his overall argument. But, because the argument stipulates the necessity of language to occur prior to perceptual structure, this must lead us, ultimately, to abandon Churchland's language-bearer thesis. We must abandon it because the language-priority thesis is simply implausible, and the language-concurrency thesis is simply unable to guarantee eliminativism. Since both the priority and concurrency theses are false in this context, the bearer thesis is false.

Perhaps Churchland is after an even more subtle kind of account, however. Perhaps neither of the above interpretations is what he is after. There is a third possibility that requires consideration. Perhaps the sort of position he has in mind is more along the lines of some kind of Kantian account: experiences are conceptually structured at a high level (partly involving language) while proximal inputs simply furnish the formless raw materials for this 'top down' manipulation. The task of the materialist is to get the most accurate set of interpretation functions to do the job. The relationship between sensing and conceptualising with language, on this view, is just an important part of a critical overall structuring function that cognition performs on meaningless sensory inputs. If we disregard some of the earlier comments made about the essential involvement of language in this process this reading has some support. Some of Churchland's remarks sound very much like he is advocating some kind of *progressive* Kantianism:

> [D]iscriminatory *conceptual* responses to ... first-level [sensory] states, ... are themselves elements in a higher order of activity upon which there are constraints such as consistency and coherence ... [this] has its end, ... in maximising the variety and sheer amount of (putative) information winnowed from the flux of sensory states ... It seeks and continues to seek information in what confronts a perceiver initially as just so much noise.[82]

The trouble with this kind of interpretation is that some of Churchland's claims about sensations and language-priority are in some tension with such an approach. In any case, my views in relation to a Kantian account of content have already been dealt with in Chapter 6. If the most favourable reading of Churchland's views are along these lines, then they remain subject to the criticisms already made of traditional Kantianism.

---

[82] Ibid., p. 42.

Are there any other possibilities Churchland might adopt here? G. J. O'Brien notes that Churchland actually considers making language a 'a relatively peripheral phenomenon' [83] in connection with perceptual experience - a position altogether inconsistent with his earlier affirmations of psychological nominalism. The evidence for this outright repudiation of his earlier views can be found in a passage dealing with language in relation to the cognitive capabilities of our intellectual processes in general. (It occurs along with an apology.)

> To the extent that there is a specifically 'linguistic' mode of intellectual activity then, it is constituted and sustained by a more fundamental mode of intellectual activity .... It may appear to some readers that the position here taken - on the relatively peripheral role that linguistic structures will play in fundamental epistemology - is inconsistent with the ... role ascribed to language as the bearer and shaper of cognitive/perceptual categories.[84]

Churchland's means of reconciling these inconsistent themes takes the form of relegating language as a high-level integration mechanism engaged in exchanging information at or towards the *top* of our information-processing hierarchies.[85] Such a mechanism would integrate 'at a very high level of abstraction' inputs or 'state configurations' derived from the various sensory modalities. By suggesting that it be employed only at this level is, 'quite consistent with the fact that its use must be acquired, sustained and administered by more fundamental information-processing systems of a non-linguistic kind.'[86] So, on this statement of his views, not only is language only one means of understanding content, but there is also said to be more 'fundamental modes of intellectual activity' which underpin the linguistic mode.

Such a manoeuvre may be quite consistent with a materialist account of cognition. For that matter, it is quite consistent with a continuum account of content as well! However, it is flatly inconsistent with the language-priority thesis, the concurrency thesis, the bearer thesis and, ultimately, eliminative materialism. The reason for the inconsistency with psychological nominalism is obvious. (An admission of non-linguistic information-processing is enough to guarantee conflict with his earlier views.) The reason for the inconsistency with eliminative materialism is similar to the remark made earlier in response to the rejection of premises (2) and (4) of his argument: Churchland cannot afford to lose the thesis that language is central to content because linguistically-mediated concepts happen to be the raw materials for theoretical replacement - the nub of Churchland's elimination of experience! O'Brien affirms this point in these terms:

> [I]n abandoning psychological nominalism in favour of more fundamental information-processing systems of a non-linguistic kind, [Churchland]

---

[83] G. J. O'Brien, op. cit., p. 63.
[84] P. M. Churchland, op. cit., pp. 135-137.
[85] Ibid., p. 139.
[86] Loc. cit.

> require[s] an argument ... which indicates that these systems result in our perception being just as theory-laden - and just as revisable - as was the case in the traditional formulation of STEM [the strong thesis of eliminative materialism] utilising as it did a representational system based on natural language. For without such an argument, their endorsement of STEM is clearly undercut by their abandonment of its traditional argumentative support.[87]

Churchland does not provide a satisfactory response to this challenge (see O'Brien for further criticisms). This omission is symptomatic of a failure in his overall theoretical approach.

We have seen cause to reject the inferentialist stress on high-level features such as language now on two counts: it does not fit in with the empirical/developmental facts, and it is not sound to apply such linguistic constraints to all forms of 'awareness' or all 'givens'. (The Sellars chapter earlier placed constraints on this tendency too.) It seems hardly appropriate to accept such a thesis now in the context of eliminative materialism. We can thus discount Churchland's claims above as being insufficient to establish psychological nominalism. And, because of the centrality of this doctrine to his overall views, without this support radical replacement eliminativism is also on doubtful ground.

Thus, Churchland is certainly wrong if he goes beyond the idea that we conceptually organise our sensations, to the idea that there are no sensations without first the acquisition of beliefs and concepts through a facility with (conceptually imbued) language. Such an idea, moreover, should not influence us into thinking that we can collapse the distinction between low-level content and high-level descriptions of content.

None of these counter claims, however, should be taken as suggesting that there is nothing high-level conceptual or nothing linguistic involved in the processes by which we respond to experiences. This would carry things too far, and I have stressed that I am not antagonistic to some degree of inferential influence. It is certainly the case that beliefs about 'how things appear' are linked crucially with the concepts we acquire and the epistemic and linguistic patterns that we accrue because of this. The point here is just that both Churchland and Sellars seem to have the emphasis all wrong. They take all experiential content to be *constituted* by inference at an extremely sophisticated level; specifically, at the level of language and theory. Contentful sensations, in their view, disappear either as proximal stimulations or linguistically-imbued descriptions. But we can avoid making the sensational experiences inferential and a 'linguistic affair', by dropping the idea that the *only* interesting thing about experiences is the epistemic order - the theoretical/linguistic (high-level) content that informs experiences. We can stress equally the kinds of content which do not seem to be captured in such terms, and take such content as informational and ineliminable aspects of experiences. We can stress the *sensory* order. To do so would be to take the continuum account seriously. To claim that no such low-level content exists would be to commit all perceptual experience to be, likewise, inferential, as Churchland, Sellars and others argue.

---

[87] G. J. O'Brien, op. cit., p. 64.

But, as we have seen, this is highly problematic not least because contentful low-level experiences seem to occur as well as high-level mechanisms and sometimes concurrently with them as experiential amalgams (the complexity thesis). Such contents may even constitute an important part in the evolutionary development and realisation of 'selfhood'. Goldman seems to be at least allowing for low-level content to occur when he criticises eliminative materialism in these terms:

> An object's appearing F then, where F is some basic phenomenal property is a non-conceptual, non-epistemic, but psychological fact that enters into the development of perceptual concepts without determining any concepts in itself. If this non-epistemic fact is a necessary condition for forming concepts, rather than the product of acquiring them, then the replaceability thesis becomes far less plausible.[88]

For reasons mentioned earlier in the book, I cannot agree with all of this. I do not think that an aspect-like way in which a thing appears should be understood as being non-conceptual or non-epistemic, even though it may not be characterised exclusively in high-level epistemic terms. A *non-concept* is surely idle in facilitating epistemic concepts, as well as anything else. To suggest that the problem with a strongly inferentialist account is to be resolved by allowing low-level content to be non-conceptual and non-epistemic is simply to reinforce the inferentialist-non-inferentialist dichotomy. It is to admit foundational, incorrigible sense-data. This return to equally doubtful theoretical ground is a consequence that needs to be avoided as much inferentialism.

By contrast, even sensational aspects of experiences must have 'look'-beliefs and being belief-like, they must be informational in some attenuated, low-level sense. The account developed in this book is an attempt to preserve the sense in which experiential content can be said to be conceptually fixed at some levels without implying high-level features. (The view also preserves the involvement of low-level features in various degrees of complexity). The distinction between 'sensory' concepts and 'descriptive' concepts and 'look' beliefs and 'inferential' beliefs and the graduations between them was made in this connection. Though we might disagree with Goldman's claim about the non-conceptual and the non-epistemic, we can agree with that some *prior* perceptual properties might enter into the development of low-level perceptual experiences (such as in Piaget's infants) without being exhaustively determined inferentially.

Is there anything worth keeping of Churchland's argument for eliminative materialism? Clearly, there is. Churchland is right in claiming that by a certain amount of training and concept acquisition and, thereby, reorientation to the world, one can come to experience things that one had not been previously aware. This is an acceptable and agreeable claim. But it does not follow from this that this gives the process of descriptive concept acquisition informational priority. As we have seen, Churchland's arguments have not given decisive reasons for rejecting (eliminating) a multi-level view of experiential content. The sorts of 'purely optical' contents which may, in fact, be resilient to theoretical

---

[88] A. Goldman, op. cit., p. 147.

suggestions are the same sorts of perceptual contents which exhibit implasticity, non-inferentiality, and a non-representative nature. Churchland may be wrong in thinking that this aspect of folk psychology is eliminable.

Low-level content does not seem to be eliminable or fully captured by high-level influences. Goldman's argument to the contrary seems to me to be far more cogent. As he notes: 'If there were no awareness prior to the acquisition of such concepts, it is difficult to see how [high-level concepts] could ever be acquired.' And again: 'one cannot be trained to be conscious *ex nihilo.*' (p. 148.) One may feel, at this point, just like Wittgenstein 'uttering inarticulate sounds' if Churchland's suggestions *were* true, for it is difficult, in the terms of his account, to see how and why consciousness itself could have arisen, if the central factors for observational experience were simply training, education and an inferential background of theory. Evolution itself clearly does not seem to facilitate such jumps in cognitive competence. On the terms of the inferentialist proposal, the naked ape might well have been a language-using beast, but not one that is conscious of his sensations. But things simply did not turn out that way. Because things didn't turn out that way would seem to indicate that, for essentially evolutionary reasons some sort of low-level, sensational experiences may have come before the imposition of various high-level features. The sensory order would seem to precede the epistemic order in terms of informational priority.

Churchland does not separate and distinguish the various elements of high-level inference nor set limits on their application. Obviously, animals do not have very sophisticated concepts or theories, and they don't have language; however they do have qualitative low-level experiences in some sense. Similarly, we do too when we experience colour hues and visual field enlargements and other low-level contentful states. Churchland risks over-emphasising the use of high-level influences on experiences, such as the inculcation of theories and language. And he thereby gives himself no room to move away from the counterintuitive implications of the inferentialist proposal.[89]

Of course, none of the points raised above constitute refutations of Churchland's views. However, it is suggested that neither the eliminative nor nominalist strand in Churchland's argument *necessarily* supports his eliminative materialism.

Churchland's cousins revisited

To return to Churchland's example of the perceptual reports of alien beings, it seems clear where the mistake lies. The mistake is the same as that of the inferentialist proposal generally. Adopting the inferentialist proposal holus bolus amounts to *thesis overkill.* His analysis of one of his own thought experiments was that because one had to look at the visual claims of the

---

[89] Keith Campbell's legitimation of a 'mild enough regulatory role' for observational experience is apposite here: 'A modest philosophy of common sense is content to affirm that, as things have so far developed, there *is* no theory with sufficient authority to discredit the bulk of observational common sense judgements, there does not seem to be any likelihood that such a revolutionary development is just around the corner.' K. Campbell, 'Philosophy and Common Sense', p. 173.

(infrared) aliens expressing temperature reports (rather than colour reports) it follows that the alleged 'phenomenal properties' given in such claims no longer seem to feature in such discourse, except in the form of the semantics of implicative and mutually reinforcing sentences within a theory of some sort, and can really drop out of the analysis entirely.

But Churchland's conclusion certainly begs the important issue. Homophonic translation does not guarantee the redundancy of low-level, sensational contents, even in the case of the fictional caloric and infrared cases. (This is especially so if the RPT and psychological nominalism fail on independent grounds.) That one can trade off one kind of sentence with another for certain experiences, does not say either that there are no such experiences or even that they are theoretically penetrable. *Query:* what *precisely* do the thought experiments establish?

What the examples suggest is that the way one describes one's experiences depends crucially upon the kind of theory that one holds. If one was brought up in a caloric society, one would describe heat experiences in terms of caloric descriptions. But what Churchland wants to show from such examples, is that the theory one learns changes the experiences one is having. This inculcation of theory gives enough principled reasons for the elimination of the 'folk psychology' of sensational experiences. But to this end, the cases offered do not unambiguously corroborate such a view, as Fodor observes:

> The theory neutrality of perception isn't about the impact of one's beliefs upon how one *describes* one's experiences; it's about the impact of one's beliefs upon one's experiences. ... The thought experiment about caloric shows that *some* of the ways that we describe our experiences change with changes in theory.... but what Churchland needs is that *all* of the ways we describe our experiences are (in principle) theory sensitive. In effect, he needs to argue that there can be no theory-neutral observation vocabulary even if there is theory neutral observation.[90]

There is something of a *faux pas* here. At one point, Fodor is saying that descriptions have *nothing to do* with the theory neutral nature of experience; at another point he describes the problem in terms of whether or not the ways we describe our experiences are theory sensitive. Of course, one can hold either of these claims depending on how one places the stress on the problem, and how one understands the theory/observation distinction: Fodor *seems* to oscillate here between taking the neutrality thesis to be a legitimation of positivism; later, he takes it to be a refutation of inferentialism. (On the one hand, the neutral nature of experiential content is not of a descriptive kind at all; on the other, it is not entirely *sensitive* to descriptions). However, knowing Fodor's emphasis in other papers,[91] we can rule out positivism as being the focus, and see the point being about sensitivity to descriptive content.

But there is a further point here: these wildly different claims are thus only on the assumption that inference/non-inference are exclusive and discrete possibilities; and, as argued with the continuum account, there is no *a priori*

---

[90] Fodor, op. cit., pp. 195-197.

[91] J. A. Fodor, 'The Dogma that didn't Bark (A Fragment of a Naturalized Epistemology)'.

reason why this should be true. One can have experiential content without having positivism, and one can have degrees of inferential penetration without inferentialism. So the two options above are not as exclusive as the above criticism makes out.

Peacocke provides a more detailed and telling criticism of Churchland's examples which brings out a different point. What the infrared case establishes, at best, is that the homophonic mapping of the vocabularies is an appropriate means of preserving a certain kind of content in translation. This sort of claim in itself does not say much, for we are able to disagree about the notion of 'content' and importantly whether there is a sense in which one can speak of a critical, but yet *non-translatable* content. The issue is strategic: it is one thing to establish translation at *one* level, and quite another to claim that *all* aspects of informational content are thus preserved homophonically. One could argue that Churchland has established the former, but not the latter. Quite consistent with the imagined case, it could be claimed that there are features of perceptual content which simply cannot be translated in such a manner, because there are aspects of experience which are, in my terms, sensational and non-descriptive. This, precisely, is how a continuum account might reinterpret the point at issue.

> Churchland argues that the word 'hot' applied by ... beings on the basis of their visual experiences, should be given a homophonic translation into our language. I agree with this conclusion, but would offer a different reason for it. Homophonic translation is correct here because when we cannot in translation preserve both mode of presentation and property presented, it is more important for communication and understanding to preserve the latter. (Ideal translation would preserve both). On this position, one can consistently hold that in Churchland's example, homophonic translation is correct, while also holding (a) that types of experience still help to determine the mode of presentation of a property, and (b) that any given physical property presented to us in one way may be presented to other beings in some other way.[92]

For 'types of experience' here, read: impurely sensational content. It is suggested that such content is immune to Churchland's inferentialist approach. The argument here is: Churchland's story about homophonic translation does not unambiguously support the conclusion he wants to support; *ergo* it does not necessarily help his cause. That there may not even be such thing as an ideal translation of the content at issue here is of no moment. In what has been argued elsewhere, all this should be hardly surprising. If there are broadly two different kinds of content to experience, and only one kind can be adequately captured and expressed in terms of descriptions, 'that' clauses, inferential content, theory, etc., then it would be a rather remarkable feat to translate *all* content required in a straight 'homophonic' shift. As argued, however, if there are aspects of experiences which constitute distinct features of experiential content, there may not be a way to express such features in terms which would be required simply to preserve high-level communication. I thus take the point that Peacocke makes as both a rejection of the way Churchland has interpreted

---

[92] C. Peacocke, *Sense and Content: Experience, Thought and their Relations*, pp. 89-90.

the cases in question and as a pillar in support of my own view. Churchland has not established that *all content* is captured by descriptions which can be translated from one being to another; he has, at best, established that the best way of preserving *descriptive* content in this case is to preserve it homophonically. However, my interest here is not what can be preserved homophonically, but what *can't* be so preserved.

If we take the arguments mustered earlier as carrying any weight, it is clear that Churchland has not demonstrated that all descriptions are inferentially labile, let alone that all observational experiences are so sensitive. To suggest that the caloric case advanced could be extended very easily from a useful fiction to a case of fact, is just to beg the issue that descriptive content can be conflated with sensational content, which should instead be kept separate. This is, of course, to beg the question in the other direction, but this has not been done without argument. The point is that even if the caloric case could be extended to us, it would not show anything useful about the content of experience at very low-levels, because we can preserve communication by homophonic translation without translating all of the content of interest. Low-level, sensational content may well be left untranslated. And, as argued in previous chapters, there is a sense in which low-level, impurely sensational content does exist and constitutes an important and valuable feature of experiences.

Churchland's caloric and infrared cases do not unambiguously support his claims. Indeed, the way we view the alien reports gives us reason to react one way or the other to Churchland's scenario. If we take sensational contents to be *post hoc* to detailed inferential descriptions of proximal impingings, then we would react as Churchland does to such a story. On this view, epistemology is the slave of metaphysics and not its arbiter. So, experiential content is secondary or comprehensible only in terms of theory and we have to learn the theory to describe the experience. If, however, we take there to be a distinction between low-level content and its descriptive articulations, then we come to a different conclusion: the descriptions presuppose non-descriptive contents, and that such contents may be experienced in various ways by certain beings physiologically equipped to have such experiences. No justice can be done *describing* the content of such experiences, because the contents of inference and sensation occur at a number of interestingly distinct levels. Even if we are asked to imagine that homophonic translation is to be preserved in this case, the inferentialist view gains no ground: for what constitutes the criterion for asserting and describing is not *ex hypothesi* what constitutes the ground for having certain qualitative experiences on my view. (Of course, the usual proviso here is that, on the continuum theory, there may be a multitude of different degrees in which high-level features and low-level aspects may intersect.)

If this can be granted then it would seem that the import of the cases Churchland offers only creates problems for sensational experiences *if* one assumes the inferentialist proposal. If one assumes a continuum account then they are idle threats. No satisfaction can be had from pursuing this line of approach for either party. Churchland's fictional examples clearly do not rule out a continuum account of content.

Theory change: eliminativism reconsidered

The is another line of criticism that needs to be made on Churchland's views. This is the one that mentioned with respect to his adoption of Kuhn's idea of paradigm shifts as a vindication of radical replacement eliminativism. It was suggested that Churchland has, in embracing a Kuhnian picture of inter-theoretic relations, assumed the very model of which he stands in defence. This claim will now be elaborated. The argument will be that Churchland's understanding of the Kuhnian thesis that he has adopted is oversimplified, and that is really no defence of his position at all.

It is not surprising that eliminative materialists look to Kuhn's book, *The Structure of Scientific Revolutions,* to support their own suspicions about certain theories. The emphasis that Kuhn places on the role of revolutionary change, and (in particular) *incommensurability,* seems very much at the heart of the eliminativist's program. It is precisely these sorts of considerations that justify any form of theoretical eliminativism whatever. If one is to substantiate the claim that the ontological commitments of folk psychology must eventually give way to a superior theory, one must hold a certain view of inter-theoretic relations that embraces theoretical incommensurability, and one must hold that the career of theories is an evolutionary process whereby one theory naturally gives way to another. One cannot, it seems, *be* an eliminative materialist unless one has favoured one or other of these assumptions. (Of course, one can say that these processes *sometimes* go on, and that certain cases fit this model, but this would amount to a significantly *weaker* thesis than that offered by Churchland. It would certainly not be enough to bring folk psychology under such suspicion.)

In a paper by Robert McCauley, the point is also taken that this elimination process can be often quite radical and can extend beyond the simple matter of which theory is better (and which needs to be eliminated) along the lines of certain criteria; in fact, the elimination process often gives rise to a whole new range of data with which theories can be concerned, and which guide further research. McCauley notes:

> The upheaval that follows ... theory replacement is comprehensive, often overthrowing the entire research tradition associated with the older theory - including its accompanying problems, methods and ontology. Attending the new theory is a new research programme whose specifics emerge as the theory develops - generating, in its turn, new problems, new research projects and even new facts.[93]

Such is the flavour of Feyerabend's philosophy of science, and, in effect, Churchland's philosophy of mind. The 'new facts' in the eliminative materialist's program are the data emerging from microphysics. However, it is not obvious that the arguments for Churchland's eliminativism successfully exclude the possibility of alternative accounts. As has been claimed, an inferentialist response is in error in respect of conflating descriptive features with *sensational* features: where the former is a feature of high-level features

---

[93] R. N. McCauley, 'Intertheoretic Relations and the Future of Psychology', p. 81.

such as theories, the latter is not. It thus does not seem to me to be sufficient (or feasible) to eliminate sensational features of experience by overemphasising the importance of the epistemic order. Several reasons have already been given for rejecting some of the themes underpinning this proposal.

Churchland does not pretend that the relation between the theories he has chosen to look at is in any way contiguous; as we have seen earlier he shows that he holds some minor reservations about how exactly the replacement is going to occur between the experiential commitments of common-sense psychology and microphysics and he adds that it is unlikely to occur in any unified way, but in a way which overlaps and meets parts of common-sense psychology, while discarding others. This seems to indicate that Churchland's thesis (by his own admission) must be tempered moderately.[94]

It is clear also, however, that by making this sort of claim, Churchland has a motive: he is trying to account for the rather obvious fact that theories *differ* in the degree to which they are related and are replaced; in many cases, the process here can be straightforward and continuous, but in other cases, relations between rivalling theories make the eliminative procedure difficult to instigate or observe. Certainly, even a brief survey of the history of theoretical advances in science reveals that this is something that Churchland must acknowledge, if his thesis is going to have any bite at all.[95] Churchland seems to assume that the Kuhnian account of intertheoretic relations needs no modification; however, there are reasons to take a more subtle account seriously.

Robert McCauley makes some interesting additions to the usual Kuhnian scheme of things. What he suggests is that all the talk that Churchland makes about inter-theoretic relations and theoretical replacement, is deficient by two considerations: it neglects to include both the notions of *levels of analysis* and *temporality* in theory comparison.

Though we are usually willing to acknowledge levels of analysis in science (we are reasonably willing to uphold the idea that the universe is organised into discrete parts which can be individually studied), it is also true that we tend to

---

[94] 'We must be prepared to count reducibility as a matter of degree. Like translation, which may be faithful or lame, reduction may be smooth, bumpy or anywhere in between.' Churchland (1979), op. cit., p. 84

[95] A good example of theories where this continuous process was easy to observe was between the Lamarckian and the Darwinian theories of evolution. An example of a discontinuous relation between theories is that of Aether theory and Relativity. In the first case, the reason the transformation between theories was relatively continuous and problem free, was probably because the translation of the terms and predictions therein were 'smooth' and the superiority of the one theory could be assessed on the basis of criteria common to both. (The transition from Lamarckian to Darwinian theory was strictly a matter of *partial* replacement; retaining the process of evolution, but changing the mechanism). This was not, however, the case with the (incommensurable?) relations between the theories of the second type. Here, a major transformation in thinking was required a) just to understand the predictions and claims of Relativity over its rival; and b) to see how it offered a more cogent explanation of the physical problems at the time. Additionally, the adoption of bold new concepts (such as the Mass/Energy and the Space-Time equations), the stability of other concepts (the constancy of the speed of light) and the abandonment of others (absolute simultaneity) were necessary conditions of seeing how the new theory offered a replacement at all.

forget this when we read Kuhn. We tend, instead, to think that in a uni-level context, certain theories (say, theories of physics), naturally evolve, change and supplant one another. But we forget that this sort of prediction occurs and makes sense only at a *single* level of analysis *over* time. This does nothing, McCauley notes, to clear up those relations between theories which occur at a *different* level of analysis at the *same* time. McCauley adopts the terms *intra* level, *successional* and *diachronic* to describe the former theoretical relations, and *inter* level or *synchronic* to refer to the second type of intertheoretical context, suggesting that there is good reason to include this broader schema to account for the diversity of actual theoretical relationships.

Good examples of each abound in the history of science and reflect the complexity of the situation, with theories lying anywhere along a continuum within each category, and in some cases overlapping into other categories. The relation between biochemistry and genetics in the 1950s and (earlier) the relation between the Freudian and behaviourist theories of psychopathology illustrate the need for an *inter* level category, as here the theories in question differ contextually along functional and structural lines. But although this shows examples of different levels of analysis occurring at the *same* time, there is also a need for *intra* level contexts as well, where theories of the same level of analysis occur *over* time. A good example of this latter type of context is not hard to find, as it is usually this type of context that is advanced by Kuhnian and post-Kuhnian theorists (like Churchland) to vindicate one or other form of eliminativism or abolitionism. The case of the relations between Aristotelian and Newtonian physics, or Newtonian and Relativistic physics are good cases in point, as these examples show where theories supplant, correct and eventually eliminate (to a greater or lesser extent) one another in the course of a development of a given theoretical level of analysis.

McCauley's point, however, is that while this does go on, there is a 'shallow' and a 'deep' end to both *inter* and *intra* level contexts which are often overlooked, and which depend on the amount of explanatory mapping between rival theories. In many cases of *intra* level contexts for instance, it may not be sensible to speak of an elimination of one theory by another (some argue this with regard to Newtonian and Relativistic mechanics) but instead of a redundancy of *parts* of certain theories by others. This process may occur gradually and inconsequentially, if there happens to be a high degree of explanatory mapping between theories, or (at the other end of the spectrum) a radical replacement process may go on if one or other theory fails to generate any similarity in its predictions at all, and in this case a new paradigm may be born.

On the other hand, within the category of *inter* level contexts (different levels at the same time), substantial explanatory overlap between two theories will not generate elimination or replacement in any degree, but an *accommodation* of one with the other to give a more useful overall picture of some given phenomenon with different levels of analysis. (As is the case with theories such as chemistry and sub-atomic physics or biochemistry and cell biology, etc.) Here it is not sensible to speak of one eliminating the other, but, instead, how they are to be linked in order that a full and complete description of something can be given.

This situation compares unfavourably to an instance of two (or more) *inter* level theories with little explanatory overlap (high incommensurability) which are inherently ontologically discontinuous to start with. These sorts of theoretical contexts are vastly different from the type of contexts that Churchland was trying to describe. His thesis presents a confusion of both levels. According to McCauley, the mistake Churchland has made has been to take the relation between *inter* level (like *intra* level) contexts as providing necessary and sufficient reasons for theory elimination and change. But although this is reasonable to grant in the case of theories which concern themselves with the *same* level of analysis *over* time, it is unwarrantable to expect the same treatment with theories which deal with *different* levels of analysis at the *same* time as the case between 'objective' microphysics and 'subjective' psychology illustrates. The error in this case would be to conflate two different types of theoretical contexts and to treat them as one, and so, to obfuscate the complexities and dynamics of theory choice.

If it can be argued that *levels of analysis* can feature in an important characterisation of explanations generally, then elimination should only proceed, strictly speaking, when the theoretical cases are examples of *intra* level contexts with high incommensurability. However, it may turn out that features of folk psychological explanations are not in this category and exhibit explanatory utility at a different level than microphysical explanations. The thing to note in this revised schema is that: 'the relation of psychology and neuroscience is one (as Churchland has emphasised) between *theories*. The crucial point, however, is that *these theories operate at different levels of analysis.*'[96] If it is plausible to suppose that one can have different theories and take them as accommodating explanations to some phenomena, not as rivals, then Churchland's eliminativism need not work for *every* aspect of common-sense folk psychology (only for parts of it). Furthermore, if Churchland's arguments for perceptual plasticity, psychological nominalism and the theory dependence of content do not work on independent grounds, there is a good chance that low-level content constitutes a part of folk psychological lore that simply escapes elimination for these reasons.

Conclusion

In this chapter the various assumptions that underpin Churchland's eliminative materialism have been considered. It was argued that none of these assumptions necessarily support an eliminative view of content and that other approaches to this matter are worth considering. This brings us full circle to the continuum account. Aspects of experiential content - in particular, subjective phenomenal features - may well stand alongside theories and inferential descriptions of experiences without explanatory dissonance or incoherence. The various aspects of perceptual experience may well have evolved as an organism's functional way of adapting to certain features which are central to its survival. In the next chapter it will be argued that a property dualist account of the mind should be taken seriously.

---

[96] McCauley op. cit., p.196.

12 Experience and subjectivity

Experience is not the sole foundation of our knowledge of the world, but a place must be found for it as part of the world, however different that world may be from the way it is depicted in experience.[1]

Introducing dual-aspect theory

Introduction

Experiential content has been looked at so far in relation to perceptual, cognitive and evolutionary considerations. The position offered in this book is an account that allows for interestingly distinct levels of experience along a content continuum. In this chapter, low-level contents will be looked at in terms of an issue in the philosophy of mind - the subjective qualities of mental states or 'qualia'. Here, the case for taking a 'dual-aspect' theory of the mind will be considered. Nagel's property dualist views will first be outlined and serious problems with them will be exposed. However, it shall be argued that a plausible account of Nagel's position can be given which stands in support of the claims made in this book. The position arrived at will thus stand in support of a revised account of Nagel's views and a continuum theory of content.

The subjective and the objective

Nagel's main concern is with a very traditional polarity; specifically: 'how to combine perspectives of a particular person inside the world with an objective view of that same world, the person and his viewpoint.'[2] It is the traditional distinction between the subjective and the objective that is at issue and the aim is to reconcile the two views so as to make a close-knit metaphysical position. These views occur in his work on a number of levels in relation to a number of

---

[1] Thomas Nagel, *The View from Nowhere*, p. 77.
[2] Ibid., p. 3.

philosophical problems. However, the subject/object dichotomy is the common thread linking each of the problems.

Nagel's aims are most obvious in his famous essay 'What is it like to be a Bat?'[3] where he is concerned with not just the subject/object distinction, but also the traditional problem of consciousness, which he defines as what it is like to *be* a particular organism. To be a 'conscious' human being is to know (subjectively) *what it is like* to be a human being. To be a bat is to be conscious of the subjective features of whatever bats are conscious of. Consciousness is inextricably tied to this feature of knowing *what it is like* to be a particular organism. This feature of consciousness is also described as having a particular *subjective point of view*.

Nagel argues that this definition brings to light a long overlooked assumption: it would seem that any theory of consciousness, be it dualism, materialism or functionalism, must, by necessity, know what it is like in some sense to be conscious, in order to be able to subsume or reduce the phenomenon of consciousness under its explanatory paradigm; it must, in other words, have some gauge of comparison. A reductionist theory of consciousness, for example, must have an idea of what it is that needs to be reduced or else the theory will not work (nor, indeed, will it make sense even to speak of a 'reduction'). As he puts it:

> [W]ithout some idea of what the subjective character of experience is, we cannot know what is required of physicalist theories - any reductionist program has to be based on an analysis of what it is to be reduced.[4]

We must thus treat consciousness as a phenomenon, and not be dismissive of radical new solutions in trying to explain its complex nature - certainly we should not jump on the eliminative materialists' bandwagon too soon. We may be reductionists in our theoretical outlook, but reduction does not entail elimination for precisely the reason that Nagel mentions.

He is hard-lined on this 'ineliminable' aspect of subjectivity for several reasons. It seems to him that if one begins at the outset to embrace a theoretical stance which assumes that mental states are objective (and can be explained by some advanced neurophysiology), then although one may be playing the right cards as far as an *objective* understanding of mind goes, one has nonetheless omitted from consideration something crucial: that is, what mental states are like for the creature that is having them. Experiences *as experienced*, he states, are ultimately nothing over and above the subjective experience of them, and although an experience may have objective aspects to it, it is not the same thing as what one is experiencing subjectively. The issue of bat experiences, of course, is invoked to highlight the issue dramatically: for how is any objective account of such an organism to compare with the radical distinctness of how bats and humans actually experience things? Even though one may be able to develop a very complex objective neurophysiological understanding of both human and bat sensory modalities (and understand precisely how each works), one still could not imagine what it is like to *experience* things as a bat

---

[3] Thomas Nagel, 'What is it like to be a Bat?', Rpt.in *Mortal Questions*.
[4] Nagel, op. cit., p. 167.

experiences them and (presumably) vice versa. The difference here is thus one of subjective points of view, which seems, on the face of it, irreducible to an understanding of objective physiology. Further, the matter is not simply whether or not we (with our sensory modalities) can sufficiently imagine how a bat may experience things; rather, the question is what it is like for the bat itself to experience things. It would seem from this that there is an epistemic divide between objective and subjective points of view, because such viewpoints amount to being qualitatively distinct in some important sense. The two viewpoints are not reconcilable in any conventional way - they amount to being ineliminable and irreducible features of the world.

Does such an analysis beg the question? If this was Nagel's only justification for his position, then it would. But Nagel does present some arguments which will be explored later. First, there are a number of things that Nagel is *not* committing himself to which need pointing out here. A few caveats are in order, before a more critical discussion of the issue:

Caveat 1: First of all, Nagel is not abandoning objectivism as a philosophical proposal: he is, instead, amending it. He says: 'I want not to abandon the idea of objectivity entirely, but rather to suggest that the physical is not its only interpretation.'[5] Elsewhere, he refers to the 'bleached-out physical conception of objectivity' which 'encounters difficulties if it is put forward as the method for seeking a *complete* understanding of reality.'[6] It is clear that Nagel is claiming rather less than that objectivism is false, and rather more than that only some sort of subjectivism can be true.

Caveat 2: What Nagel is suggesting with his subjective/objective distinction is what he calls the 'dual-aspectivity' of mind; a conception of the problem in terms of two distinct features. He is not advocating a dualistic position like that of Descartes, nor is he suggesting that there need be anything mystical about subjective points of view, that no new way of thinking can hope to uncover. Nagel nowhere claims that because mental states, points of view, etc., seemingly cannot be explained by any physiological reduction, that there has to be something non-physical or ethereal about them. In fact, he rebukes this interpretation entirely by claiming that even if we conclude that mental events are not simply physical events, 'it does not follow that we can explain their place in the universe by summoning up a type of substance whose sole function is to provide them with a medium.'[7]

Something non-physical, without mass, energy or spatial dimensions, would make it no easier at all to explain the subjective features of mental content - it would, in fact, make the explanation that much more puzzling. Substance dualism is an implausible thesis. But just as Nagel does not want to embrace dualism of this kind, he does not want to embrace an explanatory physicalism or reductionism either. Physical things can be in states which, according to Nagel, 'cannot, because of their subjective character, be reduced to physical terms.'[8]

Caveat 3: If Nagel is not a dualist in the Cartesian sense, it should also be

---

[5] Ibid., p. 17.
[6] Ibid., p. 15. Italics mine.
[7] Ibid., p. 29.
[8] Nagel, op. cit., (1986), p. 29.

noted he is no 'idealist' either. Idealism, for Nagel, rests upon a mistake as serious as that of physicalist positions. Both assume that one particular point of view and one privileged strategy is *the* strategy for an understanding of what is real about ourselves and the world around us - an outlook which is quite against the dual-aspect line that he advocates. Where objectivist positions try to tell us that the only true way of understanding is a 'view from nowhere'; a view beyond experiential subjectivism to things as they *really are,* Idealism (*pace* Berkeley) tries to tell us that those things are, in effect, an illusion, and have being only insofar as they are integral parts of subjectivity as mind-constituted 'ideas.' But Nagel sees problems with both these approaches and expounds neither. Both, in his view, assume that one 'aspect' alone will do the job of explaining all there is to explain: idealism, to Berkeley, does more than give an account of ideas (it in fact tells us that ideas are all there can be), while objectivism, to the physicalist, attempts more than an explanation of 'physical' phenomena, (it tells us that all there can be are objectively understood physical things and processes).[9] However, it is simply false that nothing exists other than subjective 'ideas' or physical states - the only problem is that neither position is willing to admit that *both* do, and that their positions fail to embrace them. Idealism gives us no way of obtaining an ontology of how things are independent of 'personal experiential perspectives' and leads to scepticism and solipsism; objectivism gives no account of how a 'centreless' world can accommodate subjective points of view. Either way one is faced with difficulties which seem to suggest that both approaches are in error.[10]

Nagel's position, then, is not sympathetic to substance dualism; nor is it sympathetic to objectivism and idealism because all of these positions, in his view, collapse the distinction between what each takes to be *important* ontologically, and what is ultimately real. The contrary suggestion is to acknowledge that both physical things (seen and felt objectively) and mental states (seen and felt subjectively) are real, and what this amounts to is neither a dualism of the kind that a Cartesian would embrace nor an idealism that Berkeley would affirm. The result, for Nagel, is the admission that both the mental and the physical are *features of the world* in some sense. Hence 'dual-aspect' theory.

Caveat 4: Nagel is not suggesting that subjectivity is a private, incommunicable affair. Nagel is quite happy to agree, for instance, with the points made by the later Wittgenstein about public criteria that any language must fulfil. A 'private' language is certainly no language at all, and it makes no sense to say that one has privileged access to one's points of view or subjective experiences *via* such a language. So, Nagel is not on about languages, public or private, in his philosophy, and his position does not at all broach Wittgenstein's central arguments. Moreover, he says explicitly that: 'Mental concepts do not refer to logically private objects of awareness.'[11] It is clear, then, that the claim about the subjective nature of experience is not, simultaneously, a claim about incorrigibility, or privacy for that matter. Despite these points of clarification, it

---

[9] This is why Nagel refers to physicalism at one stage *as a form of idealism*; in his words: 'An Idealism of restricted objectivity'. op. cit., (1986), p. 26.
[10] Ibid., p. 27.
[11] Ibid., p. 37.

is still hard to see what the upshot of this line of thought is in precise terms. This is brought out more clearly in another central text.

The 'View from Nowhere'

Nagel's emphasis in *The View from Nowhere* is to develop the idea that there are irreducible differences between subjective and objective conceptions of self, as suggested previously, but this time through exploring the progressive development of what he calls 'objective' understanding throughout history. This he sees in terms of the following stages. Firstly, an objective outlook begins by seeing perception as caused by the action of the things upon us (and not vice versa, or by a contribution of the two). Secondly, the 'true nature' of such things becomes separable from our perception of them and can thereby be capable of independent manipulation and analysis. Finally, the secondary qualities belonging to our perception of such things (as they appear to us in experience) can then be made to 'crop out of' the analysis, and the underlying primary qualities (the properties such things are thought to possess *intrinsically*) can be comprehended in their own terms. He is here dealing very much with the career of science, which he is calling an analysis of 'objective understanding.' The process of 'detaching oneself farther and farther from the human viewpoint' is a symptom of the long tradition of the method of scientific 'objective understanding' as it has come to be known to us historically.[12]

Nagel acknowledges, without hesitation or regret, that such an understanding has proved, both epistemologically and heuristically, 'extremely fruitful.' He notes that 'understanding of the physical world has expanded enormously with the aid of theories and explanations that use concepts not tied specifically to the specifically human perceptual viewpoint.'[13] This 'detached understanding' is the critical feature of any objective world view, and it stands in dramatic relief to what he has referred to as the 'subjective.' For only the former can be expressed in mathematical terms and can be empirically corroborated, whereas the latter seems immune from any analysis at all. The claim here, however, is that though such an understanding has been extremely fruitful, giving us an unparalleled mastery of nature, it does not seem capable of extension beyond its objective domain. And since it does not do this, it seems, on Nagel's view, to be a less embracing, less exhaustive way of viewing the world than it purports to be. He suggests at several points that such a strategy is inherently limited, and, as a consequence, it should not surprise us if objectivity itself is essentially incomplete.[14] Thus, ... '[any] attempt to give a complete account of the world in objective terms detached from these perspectives inevitably leads to false reductions or to outright denial that certain patently real phenomena exist at all.'[15]

The point is that an 'objective', theoretical understanding is seriously flawed when it comes to trying to illuminate the nature of felt, qualitative experiences. However, such experiential contents are 'patently real phenomena' even if they

---

[12] Ibid., p. 14.
[13] Loc. cit.
[14] Ibid., p. 18.
[15] Ibid., p. 7.

cannot be understood in terms of a scientific, objective understanding, but only 'from the inside'. Nagel withdraws from an 'objective' type of analysis of human subjectivity because he assumes that it is in principle unable to handle the weight of what is the province of sentient human experience. Just as bat experiences and bat physiology are quite different things if one is to be true to either, so all the pursuit of an 'objective understanding' is ever likely to yield is a diluted comprehension of the difference between such conceptions. Thus the possibility of 'explaining' philosophical problems by detaching ourselves farther and farther from our subjective points of view and moving towards an objective view, a 'view from nowhere', is a long-standing trap according to Nagel. What are his arguments for this view?

The arguments (dilemmas of dual aspectivity)

Nagel has some weak arguments to support the view that an objective understanding is inadequate, and one such argument is designed to show that any solely objective view is actually self-defeating. What he notes is that even an objective view itself requires a mental activity in order that such a conception can be formed, and in so far as it does this, an objective view is never wholly objective. Deciding to look at a thing objectively is a mental action, a subjective decision-making, and so an objective understanding always admits of a subjective realm even if it refuses to acknowledge it. (I take it that this is what is behind the remark: 'The subjectivity of consciousness is an irreducible feature of reality - without which we couldn't do physics or anything else - and it must occupy as fundamental a place in any credible world view as matter, energy, space, time, and numbers.')[16] Though this is far from a knock-down argument against reductionism, Nagel hopes it at least points out a certain pragmatic contradiction in the aims of any mono-aspect ontology. More than this, though, the claim is that the success of the strategy of 'detached understanding' has influenced our thinking so that now we see things only in terms of whether or not they can be understood through the rigorous application of the objective strategy. However, perhaps this outlook is a Utopian dream as misguided in principle as Frege's program with formal languages or Kant's program with speculative metaphysics. He is emphatic on this point:

> We flee the subjective under the pressure of an assumption that everything must be something not to any point of view but in itself. To grasp this by detaching more and more of our own point of view, is the unreachable ideal to which the pursuit of objectivity aims.[17]

> Any shift to greater objectivity - that is, less attachment to a specific view point - does not take us nearer to the real nature of the phenomenon: it takes us farther away from it.[18]

Nowhere does Nagel refuse to acknowledge the importance of the 'objectivist'

---

[16] Ibid., pp. 7-8.
[17] 'Subjective and Objective' in *Mortal Questions,* (1979), op. cit., p. 208.
[18] Nagel, (1979) op. cit., pp. 444-445.

spirit *qua* scientific thinking and practice - on the contrary, he says of it that it is 'the only way to expand our knowledge of what is beyond the way [things] appear to us.'[19] But he does not wish to ignore or pay scant regard to how things appear to us and to our subjective viewpoint either. Clearly, such a move does not seem to follow either logically or intuitively from the *usefulness* of objectivist practices, and when it is pointed out in such terms (stripped of the influence of the success of the physical sciences), it seems unreasonable to suppose that it ever could. Putting it another way: the falsity of Cartesian dualism does not entail the truth of objectivist physicalism; and, neither does the truth of objectivism entail the falsity of all forms of dualism. It is not inconceivable that a kind of dualism of *properties* could be true, despite the legitimacy of the 'point of view' of physicalism being acknowledged, and despite the rejection of substance dualism being upheld. Nagel's view trades on this very real hiatus between these familiar conceptions.

By his own admission, his position here is short on argument and long on 'wild speculation.' However, the concern of combining what he takes to be the irreducible subjective point of view with an objective point of view, ultimately, does not get off the ground. He concludes (unhelpfully) that nothing fruitful can be said about how to make this amalgamation at the present time. This is a devastating anti-climax to the grandiose vision that he engages us to imagine.[20] The problem, as he sees it, is how to gain for ourselves some sort of 'general concept of experience,'[21] an 'expanded understanding,'[22] which encompasses all points of view and which reduces none; but how to go about this, Nagel simply tells us, is beyond our comprehension at our current level of awareness, and only time will tell if this awareness is ever possible. It is, then, a futuristic solution on which Nagel's case rests: we will have to wait until philosophy develops more (and, correspondingly, we can understand ourselves better), before that solution is forthcoming. To facilitate this, philosophers should work towards trying to dismantle the types of understanding which fail to acknowledge things as basic as subjective experience and to develop deeper ways of understanding which admit them, but essentially this is complementary to the task rather than decisive for it. The main thing is to wait for a natural evolutionary change in how we see ourselves and the world around us, a change which will come of its own design, and to which we will be receptive when it does. There is plenty of textual evidence that this is the sort of thing he has in mind: what he appears to mean, is that, optimally, we need to move toward some sort of 'generalised objectivity', not a particular (physicalist) version of it. And, just as it is hard now to understand concepts of reality which will be developed five centuries hence, so it is hard now to imagine now what such a 'general concept of experience' would be like. But this shouldn't rule out the idea unless we are already unwilling to 'set the limits of objectivity' beyond our own ordinary viewpoint.[23]

---

[19] Ibid., p. 26.

[20] He forewarns us of this early:'What I have to say about these questions is not unified enough to deserve that title'. Ibid., (1986) p. 3.

[21] Ibid., p. 21.

[22] Ibid., p. 19.

[23] Ibid., p. 22.

Nagel claims that this is the kind of project which is needed for understanding the relation between mind and body. He argues that any correct theory of the relation between mind and body requires 'a new understanding of the phenomena now thought of as physical.'[24]

The main justification that Nagel gives for these kinds of claims is very thin: it appears to be that, although we are currently enmeshed in an objectivist way of thinking, we would never wish to deny that it couldn't be extended beyond its current domain. The history of science has shown that it is quite natural for paradigms to point to, and encompass, things to which they currently do not apply, and we have come to understand ourselves and the things around us better as a result. (As he puts it: 'Only a dogmatic verificationist would deny the possibility of forming objective conceptions beyond our current capacity to apply them.')[25] This is a legitimate claim, of course. The philosophy of science has been instructive in that the way in which any successful scientific paradigm works is to remain open to future developments; if it does not (and to a certain extent all such paradigms have a limited lifetime) then it will sooner or later have to bear the weight of a recalcitrant observation, and be eventually supplanted by a more worthy theoretical successor. Here, however, Nagel is suggesting that because this is *generally* true of scientific paradigms, it is also true of paradigms like 'objectivity', and that, like other paradigms of thought, this too can be extended beyond its current application into areas which it hitherto failed to acknowledge. In other words, because scientific paradigms of thought shift and change, then it is a logical progression for a shift to take place beyond the paradigm of objectivity itself. The claim is that this paradigm will eventually break down into something wider when we eventually realise its shortcomings. The hope is that this process will *include* the subjective, and will breakdown the distinction between first and third person ascriptions regarding points of view. The new way of thinking would presumably be a deeper *experiential* objectivity than we currently possess, and of which we at the moment have absolutely no conception at all.

Nagel's approach here is very unconventional. There are many other ways philosophers have tried to bridge the subjective/objective divide which do not rely on such an evolutionary development of thought. The following are some of the more usual possibilities. One direction in which a dual aspectivity might be maintained at some level is in the tradition of epiphenomenalism - a view which stresses that each mental kind possesses, in addition to its 'appearance' properties, underlying physical causes, which alone are causally efficacious, and which can be discovered empirically. Another kind would be a property dualism (of my own preference), which allows causal interaction from mental kinds to physical properties as well. (The *sui generis* distinctness of low-level sensational content has been argued for in this book as has the idea that such contents have an important causal role.) However, there are also other possible options available here. Materialist accounts also offer a way of bridging the subjective and objective realms. One such solution, along the lines of Davidson's anomalous monism, insists on a dualism in the sense that each mental event satisfying a mental property also satisfies at least one physical

---

[24] Ibid., p. 8.
[25] Ibid., p. 24.

property token (though it is not nomologically nor conceptually reducible to it). A more robust variant, central state materialism, closes the gap by arguing for a strict definitional reduction of mental concepts to physical explanations by means of physical laws. Other less usual options argue that the mental and physical are both products of some *third* property of which they are distinct aspects as both heat and pressure of a gas are the products of the movement of its molecules).[26]

The first two options above are conventional property dualist accounts which claim that the mental is *sui generis* real, in some sense (though they disagree on the extent of the causal powers involved). The third and fourth kinds mentioned are strict materialist options: one an explanatory dualism which merely stresses the theoretical autonomy of mental descriptions (while insisting that the nomological connections between 'mental' and 'physical' can only be realised at physical levels of description); the other allowing the mental only in 'conceptual' terms while insisting on explanatory/theoretical reduction (i.e., the mental has no existential import at all). The final views mentioned are dual-aspect theories in a somewhat less conventional, and more unclear, sense. Nagel will have to offer reasons to distinguish his view from these more orthodox positions, if he intends his own view to be genuinely different. We shall see later that Nagel's views and my own are closely linked.

A problem arises here when some of these options are considered. It is the difficulty of getting at whether Nagel is after an expanded *conception* of the mental and physical, or whether he is after an expanded *ontology* of the two. The options above offer quite different views on this question, and when compared to them even briefly, Nagel's position seems confused: for it appears he does not make it obvious that he sides with any of these alternatives, and yet he seems to employ and conflate all forms to some extent in developing his own view, never clearly distinguishing between them. He seems, in his metaphysically lighter moments, to want to identify mental and physical properties in a way which some future ontology will recognise, while somehow retaining their distinctness as conceptions in some sense. But, in his heavier moments, he acknowledges that all the orthodox relations between physical and mental properties do not exhaust the possibility that there might be a stronger ontological distinctness between the two kinds of features. His remarks about bat experiences, for instance, seem to suggest this stronger claim. It is never obvious, in other words, the extent to which he sides with any standard form of bridging the gap between the mental and physical and to what degree he succeeds in articulating his own:

> Is [Nagel] identifying each human self with the human brain or is he identifying the *property* of being a self with the *property* of having a brain of the same physical kind as the human? ... In some places Nagel appears to commit himself to the stronger thesis... But [this] undermines his own

---

26 This final kind of view might, for example, stress some abstract place holder as the bearer of distinct mental properties (as, for example, Strawson's conception of a person as a bearer of both material and mental presupposing properties; or Russell's neutral monism). More obscurely, it might be a way of legitimating Spinoza's panpsychism (in which mentality is somehow an essential feature of all physical entities - so the mental and physical turn out to be properties of some third kind of material that manifests both kinds of features).

insistence on the irreducibility of mental phenomena; for natural kind concepts precisely *do* admit of reduction to concepts specifying the empirical essence of the kind. Pains would be C-fibre stimulation in the way that heat is molecular motion. What it is like to be a bat might turn out to *be* a neural configuration. And so mental objectivity would be reducible to physical objectivity after all. The only way to block this result is to deny that mental kinds could be identical with physical kinds, ... [which] allows for a duality of 'aspects' only in the sense that the *conceptions* are distinct; but this is not enough to frustrate physical reduction.[27]

The sense in which 'conceptions' is being used here, clearly concurs with such views as central state materialism, where mental descriptions can be reduced to physical descriptions by means of laws of psychophysical correspondence. Here, 'conceptions' means 'ways of understanding and theorising/explaining the mental.' Central state materialists certainly think that the mental is distinct in *this* sense. Anomalous monists, by contrast, would allow for a reduction at the physical level but disallow strict psychophysical laws (claiming that mental descriptions nonetheless *presuppose* strict nomological connections). Of course property dualists, who regard the mental as a *sui generis* realm, would not regard this distinction of conceptions to be essential. In this view, features of 'the mental' are not simply at matter of theorising/explaining; it is more than conceptual difference - it is a difference in *content*.

The issue is important, and some of Nagel's claims clearly do indicate an ambivalence on this matter. A selection of examples will give the flavour of some of the quite different positions suggested here, and how he vacillates on them:

> [D]ual aspect theory is committed to ... the picture of appearances as part of reality... The mind is after all a biological product. When the cat hears the doorbell, there must be something going on, literally in his head, not just in its furry little mind.[28]

> The subjective features of conscious mental processes ... cannot be captured by the purified form of thought suitable for dealing with the physical world.[29]

> [T]he mental properties would be at least supervenient on the physical - a particular type of physical process being a sufficient but not inevitably a necessary condition of a particular type of mental process.[30]

> [A]ccording to dual aspect theory both the mental and the physical properties of a mental event are essential properties of it - properties which it could not lack ... Presumably something similar would have to

---

[27] C. McGinn, 'The View from Nowhere', (Review) in *Mind,* 96 (1987): p. 266.
[28] Nagel. op. cit., (1986), p. 31.
[29] Ibid., p. 15.
[30] Ibid., p. 48.

be true if mental processes had physical properties. ... Both must be essential components of a more fundamental essence.[31]

Some of these passages admit merely a distinction in *conceptions* as being the crucial thing and the claim about supervenience seems, oddly, to make substantial concessions to a type-type identity theory, a position which Nagel completely eschews elsewhere. The theme of a distinction between conceptions, however, is consistent with most accounts of the mental and physical (as mentioned, even central state materialism allows for a distinction between 'conceptions'). However, it is clear that while in places Nagel seems to suggest a dualism of conceptions, elsewhere he suggests something quite different. In other places he refers to essential properties which are products of brain functioning, suggesting that some kind of property dualism is what he is after. However, the last passage - with its admission of a 'fundamental essence' - sounds decidedly Spinozian, and seems to admit a more basic level wherein 'subjective' and 'objective' might feature as distinctly existing aspects of some 'deeper' reality. These last points suggest more than a difference in conceptions, they suggest a difference in ontology. It certainly does not help in getting a grip on Nagel's position when he slips between alternatives so readily, and particularly when the options would seem to be inconsistent with each another.

Moreover, adopting the view of the 'expanded understanding' that he seems to advocate doesn't help us in forming a clear opinion on what he is after either, for the notion of 'understanding' in relation to the above views is itself ambiguous: does a change of understanding in Nagel's sense mean a change of *ontology*, or a change in *conceptions?* Some of his statements seems to support the former; some the latter. Nagel does not disentangle these questions and seems to assert both claims. At some points the confusions even occur in the same passage:

> I have distinguished between reality and objective reality, and also between objectivity and particular conceptions of objectivity. ... [I]f we admit that there are things which cannot be understood in this [latter] way, then other ways of understanding them must be sought. One way is to enrich the notion of objectivity. But ... [r]eality is not just objective reality. ... the truth is not to be found by travelling as far away from one's personal perspective as possible.[32]

It is hard to know what Nagel means here by 'reality is not just objective reality' or what he means by 'enriching the notion of objectivity'. If it is *conceptions* that are being considered here, then how does a (non-reductive) form of objective understanding rule out (say) a Davidsonian account of mental events in terms of an ontological monism combined with a theoretical and explanatory dualism of conceptions? If it does not rule this out, then why the rebuke about the 'purified form of thought' of physicalism? The problem is that if the notion of the mental that is required here is only a more highly developed 'form of

---

[31] Loc. cit.
[32] Ibid., pp. 26-7.

understanding' (as opposed to a new-look view of what 'the mental' is), then one can have this without compromising a physicalist ontology. But if it is a new-look *ontology* that is required, then why does Nagel not offer unambiguous support for this claim? The text harbours a number of possibilities. Something like a Spinozian view would seem to be the most suitable candidate for the stronger position, yet his comments are not unqualified on this. (Claims such as 'there is more to reality than what can be accommodated by the physical conception of objectivity'[33] lend credence to this interpretation of his views, yet, there is some evidence that his position is much *weaker*, leaning simply on a development of a conceptual understanding). To deepen the mystery, Nagel's punchline is that, by taking on an 'expanded understanding', we 'come as near as we can to living in the light of truth.'[34] It is not clear how such claims clarify matters.

There is a subsidiary problem here. Not only is Nagel unclear about what sort of philosophy his 'dual aspect' theory is, it is also the case that he is unclear about how the category of subjective experience is supposed to feature in it. What we gain from Nagel is that experience and subjectivity are crucially linked and that we cannot approach a conception of this sort of experience 'from the outside' as it were. But this sort of reaction to dual aspect theory is assisted by a number of substantial confusions with respect to what is actually meant in the text by subjective *points of view*. Norman Malcolm has highlighted these confusions:

> The conception is perhaps best expressed by saying that a particular person is a point of *viewing*, for the *Self* or *I* that inhabits that person. Nagel's conception deepens perplexity. One feels bombarded by questions such as the following: (1) If the *I* that normally resides were to move out, would TN lose consciousness? (2) Nagel says that the *I* that occupies TN 'receives the experiences' of TN (ibid., p. 62). Does this mean that a single experience of TN is had *twice* - that in TN there are *two* experiencing subjects? Or does TN *have* the experiences and the I *only apprehend* it? (3) If TN is the point of view from which the *Self* or *I* observes and acts on the world, does not TN *himself* observe and act on the world; or do TN and the *I* do it in unison? One hopes that they will not fall into disagreement.[35]

The dualism of *things* here (the 'I' and 'TN') issue from taking Nagel's *ontological* theme very seriously. As Malcolm implies, the consequences should make one want to reassess the position that made one arrive at such a view. But this interpretation amounts to suggesting something very close to a Cartesian position, which Nagel has repudiated elsewhere. It is hardly surprising that such questions have been asked here, given the confusions mentioned. Nonetheless, I am sure that this is not Nagel's position, though it certainly needs to be made more clear what the focus of his interest is, if it is not this one.

---

[33] Ibid., p. 15.
[34] Ibid., p. 231.
[35] N. Malcolm, 'Subjectivity', *Philosophy,* 63, (1988): pp. 158-9.

The query here is urgent, for there is at least one fallacious move arising from Nagel's whole treatment of points of view. The problem is that the identification of the 'subjective' with what can be thought about by using concepts (when standing to the world in a certain way and not another) can be read *without* the commitment to an 'expanded understanding' that he seems to want us to consider. We might say that Nagel, in fact, makes a question-begging jump here from a *way of conceiving* such a perspective to a claim about the perspective itself. This, as Peacocke notes, amounts to a sense/reference slip:

> A greater or lesser degree of objectivity has in the first instance to do with *ways of conceiving* of the world. It is a further step to suppose that differences in modes of conception correspond to differences in reality, a step corresponding to the difference between sense and reference .... When he writes 'The fact that mental states are not physical states because they can't be objectively described in the way that physical states can' (p. 29) there is a jump: from modes of description to the things described.[36]

Peacocke does qualify this objection by suggesting that differences in objectivity of conception may correspond to differences in the reality thought about, if additional arguments could be offered for this difference in reality. 'The sense/reference gap would be bridged, for example, if it could be established that some state or object characterised at the relatively subjective level is a state or object which could not be thought about with concepts of the more objective level.'[37]

These points will be taken up later. It will be argued that there is a way of joining a continuum account of experiential content with a Nagelian view of mind. For now, the criticism is that Nagel does not build this bridge between the subjective and objective, and so leaves his thesis open to other interpretations *weaker* than the position he seems, in places, to be maintaining. Some of the familiar options one might take on this have been indicated: notably, anomalous monism, central state materialism. It is crucially important that Nagel distinguish his position from these others, as his claims about the irreducible difference between subjective and objective perspectives (e.g., about bats) simply do not hold with some of these other views of mind-body relations (e.g., anomalous monism). However, if there *can* be a way of showing that the subjective and the objective can be understood as being at two exclusive and distinct levels, then dual-aspect theory may still be a tenable position, even if some of Nagel's arguments for it are not. Moreover, it might be a position which can rest with a physicalism of substance, yet disavow a physicalism as a fully *explanatory* thesis. A more coherent account of Nagel's position will later be suggested which avoids the confusions mentioned.

We need to get a grip on the most *consistent* position put forward in Nagel's writing. Perhaps a place to start would be to see how Nagel repudiates the more orthodox possibilities. An important argument which goes some way to rejecting the more familiar views above can be found in 'What is it like to be a

---

[36] C. Peacocke, 'No Resting Place: A Critical Notice of The View From Nowhere by Thomas Nagel', p. 68. Page reference to Nagel (1986).

[37] Ibid., pp. 68-9.

Bat?', when he claims that 'the subjective character of experience is not captured by any of the familiar, recently devised reductive analyses of the mental, for all of them are logically compatible with its absence.'[38]

This 'absent qualia' argument is an old objection which has been well rehearsed in the literature. Jackson has raised a similar kind of argument which brings out the problem.[39] He asks us to imagine a brilliant scientist called Mary who *ex hypothesi* knows all there is to know about the physics and physiology of colour perception, but who has continually lived in the confines of a colourless room. In this example, a reductive understanding of colours in terms of light waves and retinal stimulations is insufficient to capture essential qualitative features of colour experiences - demonstrating that any view of content which 'misses out' on such features is essentially misguided.

Both of these arguments may be said not to work, and for standard reasons: it begs the question in favour of the thesis being defended. Janet Levin, in her paper, 'Could Love be like a Heatwave?' argues that there is an 'equivocation' in such examples, and claims that they presuppose that 'knowledge' in such circumstances involves a practical task, 'in Nagel's case, the ability to imaginatively project oneself into another point of view.' But the problem is that this doesn't show that one's *theoretical* knowledge is deficient. Levin explains by suggesting that 'although sufficient experiences of the sort had by bats may be required for knowing what it is like to be one, it does not follow that this experience is the only source of any theoretical knowledge about bats.' Hence:

> [T]hough Mary may not know what it is like to see colours without actually having seen them, it does not follow that she is missing any theoretical knowledge about colours or colour experience. Thus it does not follow that there are facts about experiences that no objective theory can describe.[40]

The problem with this suggestion is that Levin trades on an ambiguity in the phrase 'theoretical knowledge'. For her, observational knowledge itself is 'theoretical' in her sense, as is knowledge *that* (as opposed to knowledge *how*). The ambiguity in the phrase allows Levin to assert that Mary is not missing anything. But clearly she is missing certain *kinds* of 'theoretical knowledge' (in Levin's sense); namely, the kinds of experiences that bats have. By trading on this ambiguity, Levin does seem to concede substantial ground to Nagel and Jackson. There may be no *theoretical* facts missing from the physicalist account, even though there are certain aspects of the sensational experience, or certain *observational* facts, which are. But this kind of reply allows us to see Nagel's claims in an important light. Nagel might be able to have a dual aspectivity of the 'subjective' *as experienced* as against the 'objective' *as described by theory*. Dual-aspect theory may be read as the thesis that certain facts about subjective *experiencings* cannot be captured in terms of theoretical descriptions.

---

[38] Nagel, op. cit., (1979), p. 166.
[39] Frank Jackson, 'Epiphenomenal Qualia,' *Mind and Cognition: A Reader*, p. 471.
[40] Janet Levin, 'Could Love be like a Heatwave?', Rpt. in Lycan, *Mind and Cognition: A Reader*, op. cit., p. 479.

Nagel never explicitly words his views in precisely this way, but at base, it does seem to be his central point. If this is so, then distinctions between Nagel's position and some of the more orthodox kinds of dualist and materialist accounts mentioned earlier can be made. The difference between his position and others would come down simply to a matter of emphasis. What makes the 'subjective' and the 'objective' genuinely distinct in Nagel's view is that one, but not the other, can be captured in terms of the objective descriptions offered by science. The 'objective' mode of description reveals certain facts or truths because it offers certain 'perspective-less' truths; whereas the 'subjective' mode of experiencing can offer certain 'perspectival' truths - truths as experienced 'from the inside' by perceivers. This stress, combined with his insistence on the 'speculative synthesis' of subjective and objective perspectives, helps distinguish Nagel's account easily from that of the other accounts. In short, it is quite different from Davidson's account (Davidson claims that physical descriptions *can* capture the ontology of the mental). It is also quite different from the more traditional dual-aspect accounts offered by Spinoza, Russell and Strawson (who do not make the explicit distinction between descriptions and experiencings). And it is quite different from the account offered by the epiphenomenalist (who does not aim for a 'speculative synthesis' as Nagel does). It is certainly different from central state materialism which disavows any explanatory autonomy of 'the mental' from physical descriptions. Nagel's account seems to be closer to a property dualism of my own variety - where certain *contents* of one's perspectival experiences contain aspects which escape being captured at higher informational levels.

If this kind of understanding of Nagel's property dualist account can be maintained, it may be enough to get past Peacocke's point that to make the sense-reference jump, one needs to show that a state characterised at the subjective level cannot be thought about with concepts of another level. It may simply happen to be the case that the nature of objective descriptions of contentful experiences cannot capture experiences *as had* by perceivers. As will be shown later, this is one way of reading Nagel's philosophy of mind. It is a helpful reading too, as it enables some connections to be made between a continuum theory of experiential content and a dualist account of mind. It will later be pointed out that a continuum account of content actually coheres with Nagel's thought and provides reasons why his account might be true.

There is a need to develop this kind of account of Nagel's philosophy. The remarks Nagel makes in justification of his position are notoriously unclear and ambiguous. He neither attempts to offer a coherent account of the nature of mind nor distinguish his views from more traditional accounts, as attempted above. Moreover, his treatment of the 'expanded understanding' required to integrate the subjective and objective perspectives often amounts to little more than vague, metaphysical flag-waving. There are no immediately engaging reasons offered for suggesting that a non-reductive 'expanded understanding' is required, so here he really gains no ground on the physicalist/reductionist. As for the claim about transcending objectivity, this also amounts to serious question-begging on Nagel's part: it does not seem to me that because we expect scientific theories to break down and be replaced, it necessarily follows that the physicalist conception of objectivity needs to be replaced with the sort of experiential schema that he proposes. Clearly, he needs to offer more cogent reasons for us to accept this claim. However, there is more plausible support for a dual aspect view in his treatment of the problem of *realism,* which will now be outlined briefly. This will integrate the suggestions mentioned earlier and enable us to make far more sense of how his 'speculative synthesis' features in his philosophy of mind.

Limits of understanding

Nagel describes realism as a thesis which is not about the kinds of things we know, but about 'how far our thoughts can reach.'[41] He also tries to defend the view that in some very strong realist sense 'the world extends beyond the reach of our minds.' Idealism is juxtaposed to this as the view that what there is, is what we can think about or conceive of, or what we or our descendants could come to be able to think about or conceive of; the view that there is something we *could not* think about or conceive of makes no sense.[42] Nagel claims that more orthodox forms of realism and idealism depend on this more general dichotomy.

Nagel tries to present a case for realism in this specified sense. He argues that, if it is possible that certain forms of human beings can 'constitutionally lack the capacity'[43] to conceive of some things which we can conceive of (like blind people or congenitally permanent nine-year-olds), it is equally possible that *we* could be constitutionally limited in comparison to higher order capacities. Moreover, it is not necessary that such capacities be *realised* in certain creatures, just as it would not be necessary for *us* to exist for the congenital nine-year-olds to have genuine limitations in what they could conceive and understand. Nagel pushes the point further, and tries to imagine a congenitally permanent nine-year-old philosopher with an interest in the issue of *realism* wondering if there were real things of which he/she was incapable of understanding. The point being, of course, that if this sort of being can be sensibly said to suppose a real world which is beyond the reach of his/her conceptual powers, it is equally reasonable that *we* could do the same. We could have an articulable realism of things which we could not, in principle, understand. And we could both be *right* about it in an important sense, even though we could not conceive the kind of things in question.

Despite the artificiality of this example, it has a lot of force. Unless we are prepared to rule out a realism of what we cannot understand on the basis of that which we can understand, we must be prepared to admit this kind of realism as a possibility. And the only basis on which we can rule it out, it seems, is by some sort of *translatability* argument: it is only possible to conceive of things if they are at least translatable into our language, current concepts and descriptions; something which we could not even *in principle* understand cannot be said to be 'real' because to conceive of it we would have to, in some sense, formulate it in terms and concepts we could understand, in order to speak of it. Nagel's argument anticipates this kind of objection:

---

[41] Nagel, op. cit., (1986) p. 90.
[42] Loc. cit.
[43] Loc. cit.

> Suppose Realist Junior (speculates) [about] beings, with capacities that the nine-year-olds lack, who could understand aspects of reality that are inaccessible to them, ... it seems very artificial to deny that someone in this position could believe something we know to be not only significant but true: that there are concepts usable by other types of minds, ... but which cannot be translated into his language or any other language that he can understand. Wouldn't a nine-year old Davidson who arose among them be wrong?[44]

The burden of *denying* that we could consider a reality which lies beyond our understanding seems to rest with those who say it is unintelligible. And, as Nagel points out, limitation of translatability seems to be a lame argument. The analogy with a lower being seems to have a familiar ring about it - though Nagel is quick to point out that just because reality can be extended here and does not have a 'built-in limitation,' does not mean that anything *corresponds* to our conception of what this reality is like - only that we have no reason to believe that *nothing* does, and every reason (by analogy) to think that *something could*.[45]

The procedure of specifying the legitimacy of conceptions beyond our understanding should seem familiar: Nagel tells us it is precisely the sort of procedure which is considered legitimate in disciplines like physics, so it should not be considered odd: '[It]... exemplif[ies]... a theoretical step that is commonplace elsewhere. We can form the idea of phenomena that we do not know how to detect. Once the conception of a new physical particle is formed, defined in terms of a set of properties, those properties may then allow experiments to be devised which will permit its detection.'[46] The important point for conceptions of realism is this: if Nagel is right, then there could be a real world in some robust sense which is beyond our theoretical comprehension, but which we can be right about *in the same sense* that a congenitally permanent nine-year-old philosopher can be right about the world beyond him or her. And if this sort of realism can be a legitimate realism, then it means that we need to take issue with much of Kantian and post-Kantian metaphysics which claims that we cannot form conceptions beyond our capacities to understand them.

Nagel does just that by agreeing with Strawson ('in denying that we know things *only* as they appear to us'), but also agreeing with Kant ('in holding that how things are in themselves transcends all possible appearances or human conceptions'). According to Nagel, our knowledge of the world is partly knowledge of the world as it is in itself, and partly knowledge of how things appear to us. However, there is no identity relation here. Our knowledge 'includes things of which we cannot and never could conceive, no matter how far the human understanding is expanded.'[47]

Of course, thinking about things that we cannot fully understand or conceive of amounts, in part, to thinking about things we cannot *describe* in the

---

[44] Ibid., p. 96-7.
[45] Ibid., p. 98.
[46] Ibid., p. 24.
[47] Ibid., p. 101.

theoretical and conceptual terms available to us. Again, Nagel can be read here as claiming that some phenomena just cannot be understood in ways which can be *captured* by (current) theoretical descriptions. As he points out though, this does not mean that such phenomena do not exist, for there just may be things (or properties of things) which we cannot know about in this way 'no matter how far the human understanding is expanded.' However, even though there may be some things that we just cannot conceive of in this way, it still makes sense to talk about such things, and it still might be plausible that such things (however imperfectly conceived) might constitute the actual nature of the world. The anecdote about the nine-year-old realist underlines this point.

This view, of course, coheres with Nagel's treatment of the problem of mind argued for earlier. In his view, the 'subjective' nature of the mental just cannot be understood in terms which we use to describe 'objective' physical states. In some important sense, the *contentful nature of the subjective* seems to escape such an analysis. Similar to the realism example, however, it might even be possible for a 'wider' conception of subjectivity and objectivity to be possible, wherein the 'subjective' features along with the objective descriptions, but we *constitutionally lack the capacity* to conceive of such a possibility. The dual aspects of the 'subjective' and 'objective', that he has been considering, might ideally occur 'by combining into some conception of a single world those features of reality that are revealed to different perspectives at different levels of subjectivity and objectivity.'[48] But, because of our imperfect conceptual grasp on the world, this composite-type analysis may forever be beyond our understanding:

> [W]e must ... admit that the world probably reaches beyond our capacity to understand it, ... and this admission ... can be expressed only in general concepts whose extension is not limited to what we could in principle know about.[49]

We might call this kind of claim Nagel's *speculative integrationism*. This could be defined as the thesis that speculative higher order views, which we currently cannot understand, can assist in reconciling philosophical problems. This is an important, though often overlooked, part of Nagel's thought. It provides a way of clearly distinguishing Nagel's philosophical outlook from more traditional views. His 'intellectual optimism' for this kind of approach rests on the plausibility of cases such as the nine-year-old realist forming coherent higher order views about the kind of world that exists which he or she could neither understand nor describe. The implicit point is that this kind of strategy might well be useful in the consideration of other matters as well.

When this sort of analysis is couched specifically in terms of points of view and we reconsider the initial problem of Nagel's unclear relationship between the subjective and the objective, it would make sense then to have the following picture: dual aspect theory, according to Nagel, specifies an irreducible difference between two kinds of ways of looking at the world - ways in which we can describe and understand, and ways in which are simply experienced and

---

[48] Ibid., p. 8.
[49] Ibid., p. 24.

'felt' and which cannot be fully captured by descriptions. Such an understanding of Nagel's philosophy also makes coherent sense of his remarks about bat experiences. For Nagel, the ways in which we may describe and understand bats 'objectively' do not capture the kinds of unique sensations that bats experience 'subjectively'. Since this reading of Nagel seems to fit with so much of his writing (about bat experiences, about the issue of realism, about the subjective/objective dichotomy), I shall take this to be the substance of his philosophy of mind. We can avoid the confusions mentioned earlier by making his argument hinge on the difference between *describing* and *experiencing*. Nagel's account is certainly a property dualist account, but it differs from other such positions because of the stress that he places on precisely this point. But Nagel is a property dualist with another important difference. Unlike other property dualist accounts, Nagel allows for the possibility that the intrinsic nature of the subjective and objective can be *combined* somehow in some 'higher order' view, which transcends such personal experiential perspectives and objective descriptions.

This reading of his views has implications. Importantly, it means that Nagel's philosophy of mind is an *ontological* thesis, not merely a conceptual one. His claim is that what is ontologically salient does not simply amount to the kinds of things that one can *understand* - what exists is not just tied to a certain way of conceiving and describing. A physicalist approach to explaining what exists is certainly one useful manner of understanding - it is an understanding that is preoccupied with *describing* the world in 'objective' terms. But Nagel makes two points here: firstly, that not all ways of explaining what exists are of this kind. There are some ways of understanding which amount to a *non-descriptive* grasp of some state of affairs which makes sense speculatively (as in the 'realist junior' example). Secondly, some features of the world cannot be understood just by being described; they cannot exist in any other way than as *subjective experiencings,* so properties of subjective experiencings must escape an objective analysis. Despite the evident confusions with respect to Nagel's way of understanding the subjective and objective divide, a consistent position can be assumed from all this. Let us contrast it briefly with Davidson's account.

Davidson claims that descriptions at the mental level are descriptions of events that can also be described and explained at the physical level, even if there may be no tight nomological/conceptual ties between the two descriptions. Nagel, contrariwise, assumes that the appropriate terms of *any* translation here are beyond our (current) explanatory devices. This amounts to saying that there should be no compromise on what the terms of the explanation are when it comes to the nature of the mental. Nagel's move is to accept that the only substances in the world are physical, whilst denying that 'physical' provides an adequate and complete explanation of the mental, as it is experienced. Moreover, he seems to suggest that *until* one has a correct and adequate vocabulary to harness subjective experiencings and objective descriptions, it is deflationary to suggest one to which the two are (ultimately) reducible. It is then best to treat them as *sui generis* aspects of reality.

In the scenario scouted earlier, Davidson Junior was wrong to insist that there was only a 'real world' which could be couched in conceptual terms he could understand. Realist Junior was right to speculate on a different conception of 'real world' even though he couldn't describe it. The example shows just how there can be a truth of the matter about the kind of things in the world, without the necessity that we might be geared to knowing what this truth is. The point seems to be that *some* truths, even closer to home, are the *perspectival* truths arising out of the actual experiencings derived from subjective points of view, which we have no adequate physical explanation for, and which cannot be captured in descriptive physical terms.

This should be read as an interpretation of Nagel's dual-aspect theory. It is a way of understanding several themes in his writing: his emphasis on the radical distinctness of sensory and objective conceptions, his speculative integrationism and his rejection of orthodox accounts of the mind. The way in which Nagel articulates his position is sometimes quite unclear. However, the interpretation above seems to amount to the most plausible and coherent account of his views.

As stated earlier, other traditional accounts of the mind can't be like his account, or else Nagel would have to agree with them. And, on my reading, there does seem to be a difference in views here: anomalous monism (to take one) is a *conservative* thesis: it tries to canvass 'understanding' in terms already appreciated for their heuristic and explanatory value; namely, the concepts and descriptions of the physical sciences. This account leaves room for a conceptual dualism, but not an ontological dualism, because on this view, there is no more in an account of experience than that described by science. Central state materialism, to take another example, is an even bleaker view: it, likewise, tries to canvass understanding itself in wholly 'objective' terms; terms which can be identified and *described* in their physical details. This view regards even *concepts* as being physical in nature too, so although there is room here for a conceptual distinction between the mental and the physical, the kinds of things that mental concepts describe are just physical things. On this view, the 'mental' collapses into being descriptions of contingently identifiable brain states.

Such 'descriptive' accounts are, of course, a very common way of treating the mind-body problem. Indeed, it has been the exclusive preoccupation of physicalist philosophers with 'objective' features generally, that allows them to treat conscious experience in terms of mental *descriptions* and, therefore, as alternative descriptions of physical (objective) events. This has been a self-justifying business, and something of a tradition. Setting adequacy requirements for accounts of mind-body relations to fulfil these kinds of 'objective' understandings is to isolate the terms of the inquiry in advance. On such criteria, only theories which admit that the 'mental' can be objectively described are considered worthy theoretical positions. So, seeing the mental in terms of descriptions spawns many different ways in which such descriptions can be made: behavioural, functional, conceptual, type-nomological, token-nomological and so on. Hence, the multitudinous varieties of materialism and the reason why the philosophy of mind is dominated by so many of these positions. Instances of such descriptive materialist accounts are, of course, just versions of the 'objective' strategy which, Nagel claims, has allowed secondary qualities to 'drop out of' the analysis of the world. It is this vicious cycle in the philosophy of mind that he sees himself as breaking.

But a materialist account of mind *of any kind* might be a tall order if Nagel is right about the ontological distance involved here: it might be wrong to base an (ultimate) account of things in terms of wholly objective *descriptive* understandings, even if it is acknowledged and agreed upon by all concerned that all there is a physical world. Davidson's conservative position only takes as serious explanations those conceptions which can be physically described; Nagel's position is more agnostic. According to Nagel, however, it may be premature to speak in terms exclusively physical according to our current conception of 'physical'. His claim is that the *content* of subjective experiencings needs to be considered, along with physically describable contents, as serious features of the physical world. And the conception of the mind that would do this successfully, would no longer capture only features of the world which can be described; it would also capture the 'felt' contents of subjective experiences. As far as I can see neither Davidson, nor any other dual-aspect view advanced actually claims as much, so Nagel's view is genuinely different.

If this interpretation can be attributed to Nagel's writing in view of the confusions mentioned earlier, then we can now say this: the program of combining these 'perspectives' is difficult, not just because of a conceptual difference between them, but because the *content* of such orders is of an entirely different ontological *character*. This seems entirely consonant with Nagel's dual-aspect theory in how it has been interpreted here. This point will be developed later in relation to the concerns of this book. Before this, however, another crucial feature of Nagel's work needs to be addressed.

Expanding objectivity

Nagel aims to include the subjective and the objective in an 'expanded form of objectivity'. But there is an ambiguity in this idea which should be noted. On the one hand, Nagel is aiming for a new position in which the traditional forms of 'objective' and 'subjective' can be seen in terms of a higher-order view; a view sufficiently 'far out' from one's perspectival centre to make sense of both polarities in terms of a 'new' conception containing 'mutually irreducible essential properties.'[50] Such a view is expressed as a kind of 'objectivity' in Nagel's work. This kind of objectivity is stressed as part of his program to transcend the objectivist ontologies which limit us. At one point, for instance, he suggests we should work at 'form[ing] a new conception that includes a more detached understanding of ourselves, of the world, and of the interaction between them....[where] objectivity allows us to transcend our particular viewpoint and develop an expanded consciousness that takes in the world more fully.'[51] This kind of objectivity features again when he says: 'to acquire a more objective understanding of some aspect of life or the world, we step back from our initial view of it and form a new conception which has that view and its relation to the world as its object.'[52]

On the other hand, there is also the emphasis on objectification, which suggests that the viewpoints are *not* features of such an understanding:

> A view or form of thought is more objective than another if it relies less on the specifics of the individual's make-up and position in the world, or

---

[50] Nagel, op. cit., (1986) p. 31.
[51] Ibid., p. 5.
[52] Ibid., p. 2.

on the character of the particular type of creature that he is. The wider the range of subjective types to which a form of understanding is accessible - the less it depends on specific subjective capacities - the more objective it is.[53]

These claims are antagonistic. They assert *two* forms of objectification: an 'Absolute' objectification in which 'a great deal is left behind in the process, since at every stage we separate into a category called "appearance" something which earlier was conceived as part of "reality"' and a 'Hegelian-like' objectification where 'nothing is left behind in the new analysis ... every aspect ... is retained, though maybe somewhat altered, in each of its successors.'[54] However, Nagel does intimate that the dimensions of the 'subjective' and 'objective' should actually be plotted on a continuum:

> [T]he distinction between more subjective and more objective views is really a matter of degree, ... We may think of reality as a set of concentric spheres, progressively revealed as we detach gradually from the contingencies of the self.[55]

The general aim here is to make use of objectivity as a broader notion than 'the physical', and opting for an expanded form of it. The specific aim is to seek a 'method of understanding' to make sense of subjective experiences without compromising their distinctness. The suggestion here is to treat 'objectivity' as a contextually *relative* notion: what is properly 'objective' depends on the fixation point of *belief;* and one can either ride roughshod over the localised perspectives with the 'Absolute' conception of 'objective', or accommodate them with the 'Hegelian' version. Following from the imagined case of the nine-year-old philosopher, of course, it is legitimate to fix one's belief about subjective and objective points of view in terms of an 'expanded understanding' about both, even if one is conceptually distant from such an understanding. It is to allow the fixation point of belief to *transcend* both standpoints. Nagel articulates this point with reference to a fictional being actually capable of such leaps of imagination claiming that a 'being of total imaginative flexibility could project himself directly into every possible subjective point of view, and would not need such an objective method to think about the full range of possible inner lives.' However, being limited in this regard, we are invited, instead, 'to think of ourselves from the outside - but in mental, not physical, terms .... a natural objective understanding of the mind along these lines would be - an understanding as objective as is compatible with the essential subjectivity of the mental.'[56]

This kind of suggestion does not seem helpful; indeed, it seems quite mystifying. The fable of the nine-year-old philosopher wrestling with the problem of realism suggests that we might be constitutionally inept at such an understanding. The same seems to be the case, likewise, with the interminable

---

[53] Ibid., p. 4.
[54] Jonathon Dancy, 'Contemplating One's Nagel', pp. 2-3.
[55] Nagel, op. cit., (1986), pp. 4-5.
[56] Ibid., p. 17.

dilemma of the subjective and the objective. But unlike the 'realism' case, there is a deeper problem here: to absorb our minds as well as our bodies in such an understanding amounts to combining the *contents* of subjective sensory states and objective physical states simultaneously, in some unified sense, without explanatory reduction and without considering the sensory states only as descriptions. But on Nagel's account, the contents of the 'objective' stance are geared to capture descriptions and the contents of the 'subjective' precisely cannot be captured in such terms. Furthermore, the subjective perspective, being the localised perspective from which we view the world, is central to our being: we cannot project ourselves imaginatively away from it as easily as the nine-year-old could project himself into considering the issue of realism. Is this 'expanded understanding' possible then? This is Nagel's challenge. What is clear is that whether we can 'explain' what it is like to have certain sensational contents as well as we can explain certain objective, descriptive events is a real problem for any authentic philosophical account of the kinds of informational exchanges we have with the world. As the problem is expressed here, however, it seems unlikely that this can be achieved beyond the making of suggestive metaphors and assertions.

To quale or not to quale?

Fortunately, one can reach some positive and informative conclusions about all this. What one can say about Nagel's work is that there must be certain properties of low-level experiential states which are lost in a physicalist analysis of those states. Concentrating on 'objective' descriptions of the world allows physicalist philosophers to treat the 'mental' in (descriptive) physical terms. But *pace* Nagel, an emphasis on objective, descriptive concepts makes them miss out on something crucial: the nature of the experience itself, as it is had by the perceiver. On Nagel's view, there must be more to the story than merely 'objective' descriptions of the world, because the subjective perspective presupposes *experiencings* of sorts. And experiences *qua* experiences are *sui generis* distinct features of the world, and particular features of human beings as data-processing organisms. To say this commits us to the view that the way the world is structured at one level of 'objective' inquiry is very different from how experience is structured at another level of 'subjective' inquiry. And, because there are differences in how this occurs, there must be a corresponding distinction in the ontological nature of the informationally complex, perceiving and inquiring human being, which seems to carry on at both levels. The human being escapes being scientifically described - just as much as he is captured by such descriptions. So he is both a scientific and *trans* -scientific creature.

Earlier we have seen Peacocke stipulating that if it can be shown that concepts of one level of 'subjectivity' cannot be thought about using the concepts or descriptions of the higher 'objective' level, then we *can* make an ontological claim of interest. On the argument of this book, and on Nagel's view of the nature of mind, it seems that we can show this. As argued, there *is* a divide between the lower and higher level of man-in-the-world in respect of the contentful structure of experience and the contentful nature of descriptions. The content that is employed in inferential integrations of experience cannot be translated onto the low-level sensory integrations. The 'inferential' is *sui generis* to aspects of experience which are low-level sensational.

This is close to what has been argued throughout this book. It is a view which, to some extent, both supports and receives support from Nagel's philosophy. On my view, and Nagel's, one can say that there are *qualia:* 'felt' properties of experiences which are ineliminable. There are felt properties of experiences because experiences cannot be captured in high-level conceptual terms by 'objective' descriptions. There are *sui generis* properties of such experiences because not all conceptual content can be accounted for in descriptive or inferential terms.

However, in saying this, unorthodox reasons are appealed to which are not available on Nagel's analysis. The claim made in this book is that it is plausible that low-level sensational features occur if experiential content is organised, for essentially evolutionary reasons, at a number of different perceptual levels. This point is consistent with the claims made regarding animal and infant experience: low-level similarities and differences, 'aspects' of content, must be *felt* properties of experiences, for there is little else for some organisms to go on. This is not to say, however, that descriptive concepts do not feature in subjective perspectives at all. Experience itself, though always perspectival and subjective, may be more-or-less theoretically (objectively) informed, even if it cannot be fully captured in such terms. It is to this multi-level kind of view of content that the continuum account applies.[57]

The reason why there might be 'felt' aspects of experiences has only been dealt with briefly in this book. The continuum account sees mental content being usefully informed by contentful experiential qualia because such features do seem to have a selective advantage. It is important for organisms, which do not have well-developed *descriptive* capacities, to have experiential *states* of some kind, and these also assist in transmitting some features of perceptual information fast. It is not implausible to think that sensational content might have some survival value over and above that of being the principal means of informational exchange with the 'objective' world. Further, conscious sensory states are efficacious in bringing about what might be called 'laying down procedures' - while undergoing some mechanical routine, conscious awareness of some external disruption can bring an organism to undergo new action patterns or aversive behaviours. If elimination of low-level sensational features of experience was not satisfactorily achieved by those philosophers discussed in the previous chapters, then a continuum account along the lines being sketched, or a dual-aspect view along the lines Nagel is suggesting, may be a more plausible story. The dual-aspect theory of the mind is essentially compatible with a continuum account of content.

There is a rider to be added to this. Nagel's subjective/objective distinction is not to be equated exactly with my distinction between low-level and high-level content. This is a mismatch. Even Nagel's 'subjective' stance encompasses theory-loaded (but perspectival) explanations. The 'I' in Nagel's subjective point of view is itself theoretically informed to some extent. The precise point, for my thesis, is that Nagel's subjective stance *also* encompasses low-level,

---

[57] In adult humans (and some animals), there may be several kinds of content that inform experience, so experience is not exclusively subjective. There may be degrees of high and low level content, as I have mentioned elsewhere.

contentful, non-descriptive grasping of a sensational nature. It has been the aim of this work to suggest that this level is an essential part of contentful experiences. Moreover, it is this level of contentful, non-inferential grasping that, in my view, *enables* both theorised subjectivity and scientific objectivity in creatures like us.

In the final analysis, is Nagel's 'dual-aspect' position plausible? I think that with the above clarifications it is. It, at least, requires a serious audience. To suggest that there are two discernible *contents* to how we integrate features of the world informationally seems to me an entirely respectable view (The claim here is that there are, in fact, *several* non-exclusive contents). To suggest further that such a problem ultimately might have a solution which is forever beyond our comprehension is, admittedly, an obscure notion, though the criticism that it is obscure or inadequately argued does not in itself show that the suggestion is wrong. The matter of a speculative integrationist account deserves further investigation than can be attempted here.

Some objections

Dual-aspect theory faces standard objections which prevent it being considered as a reputable theory of mind and content. This is the place to briefly mention some of those objections.

The panpsychism objection: The problem here is that if one allows certain physical entities to have mind-like properties then there's no reason not to allow *all* physical entities (e.g., rocks and other inanimate objects) to have such properties. And, the idea of all entities having mind-like properties is implausible.

I agree that panpsychism is implausible. But I would deny that a property dualist account of the kind I am espousing necessarily leads to it. All that has been claimed is that certain contents can't be captured in high-level terms. It *hasn't* been claimed that low-level contents are an ubiquitous feature of the world, as panpsychism does. Moreover, the account given here provides for low-level contents only where evolutionary sophistication allows it, and this is an empirical matter to be borne out (or refuted) in individual cases. Property dualism might entail the logical *possibility* of panpsychism, but there is clearly no evidence for panpsychism being true. It is fairly clear that rocks etc., do not exhibit low-level contents. As it is not self-evident, nor a entailment of my view, I shall not discuss it. My point is only that we need a more subtle explanatory focus on the matter of low-level content - and a property dualist account best provides this for *most* experiential amalgams. This is not to say, of course, that there mightn't be a better theory of mind and content down the track (this much is acknowledged by Nagel himself).

The non-sequitur objection: It has been pointed out to me (by Chris Mortensen) that though it is right to point out that contents need not necessarily be linguistic, it need not follow that any state involved in the informational process can avoid being a propositional attitude. And, if this is the case, then 'property dualism is no threat since qualia disappear in favour of [such] contents ...[and while] any propositional attitude will have aspects which are non propositional, it will need a further argument to show there are mental or qualia-like ... That some aspects of mentality are non-verbal doesn't entail dualism, in other words.'58

I agree that property dualism is not entailed by the existence of non-propositional contents. But, in fairness, it hasn't been claimed that there is an entailment relation here. I've only claimed that if low-level contents can't be captured in high-level terms, that the property dualists' position is at least *plausible*. This is quite a different matter from claiming an entailment. On Mortensen's first point, I am not persuaded that qualia 'disappear' in favour of non-verbal propositional attitudes - though this requires arguments that cannot be attempted here (it seems to me that the whole *problem* of qualia is precisely that they escape *any* sort of characterisation, and not just of the propositional variety). In any case, what can it mean to say that propositional attitudes can have aspects which are non-propositional? A plausible account of non-propositional aspects which are simultaneously not quale-like is called for here.

Nor does it seem obvious that propositions always occur in all experiences. It doesn't seem clear in some of the several species of 'look'-belief given in chapter 4, for instance, that propositional attitudes occur in each case. Seeing, for example, 'the third house on the left' seems to have propositional content, for sure. But in recalling the third house on the left from an experience in which the third house on the left was *not* initially noticed, what are we to say? How is this kind of content to count as a full-blown propositional attitude? A proto-attitude maybe - but this suggestion hardly seems better than keeping qualia at the one end of the continuum; unless, of course, a story could be told about attitudes which are simultaneously not quale-like. It is hard not to think that the notion of a propositional attitude is being made to bear a heavy load here.

Mortensen wants to tell a story in which 'qualia are contained by propositional attitude operators' in some way. Non-verbal beliefs leave qualia 'semantically bracketed and ontically sanitised' in his view. Though this is consistent with a robust materialism it doesn't get us (ontologically speaking) much further than opting for a dualism which is sympathetic to speculative integration with some future materialist theory (as Nagel argues). Unless, of course, the *way* in which quale can be so contained is told in such detail that rules out the dualist account by fiat. And, as far as I know, no such story is yet available. In any case, the idea that propositional attitudes might have aspects which are non-propositional seems to me to be a substantial enough concession to get from any propositionalist; certainly enough, I think, to make property dualism at this point an *equally* plausible story.

I am certainly not persuaded - as Mortensen is - that unsophisticated organisms can best be described as have 'propositional attitudes in some attenuated sense' rather than experiences. If it's hard to admit low-level experiences in very unsophisticated organisms, it's surely harder to admit that they have propositional attitudes - unless by it we mean something *very different* from Brentano-like high-level beliefs, intentions, wantings, and so on. And, if one means something very different then I don't how it helps to call them 'propositional attitudes' rather than experiences - unless it is to save some kind of tacitly-held inferentialism. Contents might well be proposition-like some way up the continuum as I have admitted, but admitting this is a far cry from

---

[58] Chris Mortenson, pers. comm. See also his: 'Mental Images and Neurophysiology' in *Computers, Brains and Minds: Essays in Cognitive Science,* passim.

admitting that there are propositions all the way through, which is what I deny.

The 'failure of closure' objection: Frank Jackson has pointed out that my account does not allow the possibility that the physical world might be causally closed. If some contents can't be captured in the high-level terms of the physical sciences then dualism must entail a failure of explanatory closure.

Property dualism may entail a failure of closure if a dualist account *on its own* was the only game in town. But I haven't claimed that it is the only game. I have argued for a story which provides for a number of levels of explanatory influence. Again, the continuum suggestion provides for *sui generis,* not causally inexplicable contents, and the mechanisms of such contents mostly have features which *are* explicable in a causal sense: on one level, low-level features are *quite* explicable in evolutionary terms (one would expect such contents if they help to tell a selective story). On another level, such contents are *quite* explicable in terms of a modular view of perception (one would expect processing to occur at different levels). Both of these levels of influence are part of a larger story which is entirely causal. If a partly causally closed account of certain *aspects* of low-level content can be obtained, then I can't be said to be *denying* closure. True, not all aspects of content might admit of closure so easily, but that's not necessarily a philosophical problem. The role of a property dualist theory, instead, might be to provide a conceptual framework in which it might make sense to say that such contents are legitimate features of the world. As a metaphysical story, perhaps that's all we can expect from it. (After all, whoever expects a single theory of *anything* - even a straight physical theory - to provide full explanatory closure?) A perfectly legitimate line to take here is to insist that mental contents *are themselves causes* and to stress the rather old view that some kind of interactionist story is true. This should not, of course, be seen as an interaction between 'ghostly substances' and the physical, but an interaction between the physical states of organisms of certain evolutionary complexity and *properties* of those states which can't be captured in high-level terms. That a story of this kind is yet to be told in a fully satisfactory way is not necessarily an indication of a failure of explanatory closure, only an indication of a failure of *current* explanatory closure. In principle at least, closure is possible if we get our theoretical understanding right. The 'failure of closure' objection, I conclude, is not a serious one.

Conclusion

In this chapter some of the problems with Nagel's 'dual-aspect' theory of the mental and the physical have been outlined. Despite my reservations regarding Nagel's account, it is suggested that his theory can be read in a way which legitimises and reinforces the continuum view of experiential content. The continuum account also offers some reasons why a dual-aspect view of mind might be true. The dualist account is that 'objective' descriptions of experiences, in physical terms, do not capture the sense in which some experiences have low-level, non-descriptive 'aspects' which are subjectively felt. So there must be a sense in which any wholly physicalist view of experiencing organisms is inadequate. The reason why this might be true is that mental content, as much as any other feature of the world, is a property and a product of complex evolving systems.

13 Experiencing the 'manifest' image

> To deny the reality or logical significance of what we can never describe or understand is the crudest form of cognitive dissonance.[1]

There is a long-standing dilemma in philosophy concerning the nature of man, perhaps best summed up by Sellars:

> The philosopher is confronted not by one complex many-dimensional picture, the unity of which, such that it is, he must come to appreciate; but by two pictures of essentially the same order of complexity, each of which purports to be a complete picture of man-in-the-world, and which, after separate scrutiny, he must fuse into one vision.[2]

The view put forward here is bewildering at first blush. How can a view of man-in-the-world which incorporates the vocabulary and ontology of feelings, beliefs, desires, sensory quale, be 'stereoscoped' along with a view of man as an essentially physiological creature, explicable entirely by means of the ontology of the empirical sciences? The task would seem hopeless unless one is prepared to reify one view at the expense of the other. Yet this is not what the statement of the problem asks us to consider. It engages us to consider somehow combining the two without allowing either to be 'overwhelmed in the synthesis.' Yet, it is not clear how this can be done without compromising the appeal and integrity of each.

I have been concerned with two orders of complexity of man's nature in this book. The issue examined has, to some extent, run parallel to the conflict between these two views of man. The issue has been whether or not a full and adequate account of experience and content can be given along high-level lines, employing the familiar categories of high-level concepts, theory and

---

[1] T. Nagel, 'What is it like to be a Bat?' in *Mortal Questions*, pp. 170-171.
[2] Wilfred Sellars, 'Philosophy and the Scientific Image of Man', in *Science, Perception and Reality*, p. 19. For the following quotations, see pp. 5-37.

background knowledge. Against the direction of eliminativism, reductionism and inferentialist accounts generally, it has been claimed that it cannot. It was argued that the dichotomy between experience being dependent in any necessary and sufficient way on such high-level conceptions (the inferentialist proposal) and experience arising via non-inferential action on the senses (the observational account) needed to be overcome by a more subtle and enriched view.

The alternative account presented incorporated a continuum thesis: there are several levels of content including varying degrees to which high-level influences can be present in experience. It also incorporated a complexity thesis: experience is best understood in terms of an amalgam of content, both high- and low-level, which can be simultaneously present in every experiential complex. Finally, it also incorporated an asymmetry thesis: that while there are more or less degrees of sensational content in every high-level experience, there are no high-level features in very low-level experiences. The claim has been that the continuum account is a better account of perception, and that high-level features alone will not capture experiential content - in fact, inferentialism is false even for sophisticated experiences, though it does isolate some important and necessary elements in high-level perception.

An attempt to fuse the two views of man-in-the-world, of course, is an enterprise of a somewhat different kind. The interest here is in combining the deliverances of sense with the explanation of the sensory world offered by science in terms of neurophysiological events. However, the treatments overlap here to some extent: both approaches suggest accounts which emphasise the nature of high-level descriptions over the contentful nature of sensations. The neurophysiological approach tries to canvass the relation between one view and the other in terms of available or potentially available empirical conceptions. Some philosophers even attempt to effect a reconciliation between the two kinds of images by compromising the level of sensation with the level of neurophysiological description.

Similarly, the inferentialist proposal turns to available descriptive features - representational states, concepts, background knowledge, propositions or theories - to account for the nature of perception. It likewise tries to canvas the relation between experience and content in terms of sophisticated 'high-level' conceptions. The emphasis on high-level cognitive factors in my case thus parallels the emphasis on complex empirical realisations, as determined by science, in Sellars's case. Any attempt to combine the two kinds of content - the descriptive and the sensory - is thus of intrinsic interest. I want to consider, in concluding, just how the two views of experiential content might be 'focussed into one vision', just like Sellars's two views of man-in-the-world.

When the problem of the two views of man was originally expressed in terms of a clash of two 'images', it was not intended to refer to the traditional dualism-materialism polemic. Here, the question is whether man can be understood in terms of a special substance or set of substances, in addition to how he is characterised by science. The two images did not refer to an essentially 'naive' (as opposed to a 'sophisticated') way of thinking about human beings. Rather, they referred to different ways in which human beings have evolved intellectually. The human beings' view of themselves was conceived to be prompted by certain historical forces and it had developed and evolved with those circumstances to bring about a functional way of looking at the world. Sellars's terms for these ways of relating to the world are the 'manifest' and 'scientific' images. The essential dualism 'is not that between mind and body as distinct substances but radically different ways in which the human individual is *related* to the world.' Each of these 'images' was seen to have historical roots: the 'manifest' image evolved as man came to 'recognise or encounter himself' as a *person,* not merely as an object - specifically, a person enmeshed in a network of rights and duties. This originated essentially as pre-scientific speculation; firstly, about man against nature; then about man against man, and finally man against community. It was in these stages that an 'irreducibly new' level of conscious awareness about himself developed from his organic nature: a move characterised by essentially 'correlational' procedures, drawing upon introspectible and perceptual knowledge of himself and the world around him. By contrast, the 'scientific' image evolved as our 'postulational' capacities developed; where we came to explain phenomena of the world by assuming, and then describing, imperceptible mechanisms underlying the physical and chemical nature of certain entities. Chronologically, of course, the manifest image is the most ancient while the scientific image is of relatively recent origin. Each 'image' has central importance for our nature, yet both are idealisations in something like the sense that a frictionless body or an ideal gas is an idealisation.

What came to be well appreciated by philosophers, of course, was that for the purposes of *explanation,* the scientific image was the best image to go by; while for the purposes of seeing oneself as a consciousness - a person - living in a world of rights and duties, the manifest image was essential. To be a *person,* one needed to be seen in terms of rehearsing intentions - it was not sufficient to be described in terms of a scientific specimen. Likewise, as a consciousness, one was related to the world in a way which was very different from how one was related to the world as an object of scientific discovery. While both images are important to the development of human beings' understanding of themselves, one image constituted a 'conceptual framework of persons'; the other, a 'symbolic tool.' However, it was recognised equally that these images needed to be conjoined in some way, if people were to fully understand their complex nature. And, since both images seemed equally important and essential to human functioning - each did purport to be a *complete* picture of man-in-the-world - they needed to be somehow kept as compatible accounts. The manifest image needed not to be simply *reconciled* with the scientific image, but *joined* to it. Both images on their own were essentially incomplete. Sellars himself did not attempt to do this joining; he merely ventured to point out that the 'dualism of the manifest image and the scientific image of man-in-the-world' was a dualism which could be ultimately 'transcended', even if only in thought.

Sellars may well be right in the historical details about the origins of the manifest image and the scientific image. He may also be right that the essential dualism of the 'manifest' and the 'scientific' can be transcended in something like the way he suggests. But the dilemma of how to go about joining the two is not just a matter of fusing different *images,* even if 'only in thought'. The issue is how the levels of explanatory analysis articulated by those very different views can fit together. And here, the project traditionally strikes a snag. No scientific 'image' has succeeded in explaining - using only the 'postulational' vocabulary of science - what it is like for an organism to have certain qualitative sensations; to have 'felt' aspects to its experiences. This is certainly part of the 'essential tension' which any account of man must face. And it is really the point of most conflict in the clash of the images. This point of conflict has been the central concern of this book.

Materialist responses to the conflict between the images generally suggest that 'the scientific image is not yet complete' and that 'when the chips are all down' the manifest and the scientific conception of both sensations *and* conceptual thinking would fit into a 'synoptic view as parallel processes'. On most contemporary accounts of this problem, the former would be seen and understood as occurring only in connection with complex physical processes which, in essence, *is* the scientific image. However, most philosophers (eliminativists excluded) opt for the 'primacy' of the scientific image in the restricted sense, which also allowed for the person to be seen in terms of membership of a 'community' and in the business of rehearsing intentions. Few philosophers want to rule out the conceptual importance of the manifest image for day-to-day life, though they certainly hold that the manifest image would be understood in the more familiar empirical conceptions which the 'scientific' image will, eventually, *describe* in detail.

Yet we have seen in this book reasons for doubting the optimism of this entire approach. We have seen that some aspects of man-in-the-world cannot be fully captured by high-level factors. More specifically, they cannot be fully captured just by being described. The having of qualitative sensations is also not merely a matter of an 'image' of man looked at 'synoptically', or otherwise; it is a feature of certain experiences with an evolutionary function which stands in need of explanation. Moreover, we have seen that there is a case for claiming that a framework of sensory content is a requirement for any adequate view of the nature of perception. Low-level aspects, we saw, cannot be ruled out of an account of experience and content. Any attempt to suggest that the scientific image is more primary than the manifest image has to contend with the problem that some features of man-in-the-world simply escape a full and complete scientific characterisation.

At this point any similarities between the clash of the images and the concerns in this book disappear. Any characterisation of the issue treated in terms of rival 'images' is misleading - it suggests that it is just a matter of combining, at a theoretical level, what is essentially a conceptual outlook on the nature of man which has developed over time. However, as argued, the content of experiences is not merely part of a conceptual outlook understood by way of a certain theory; it is, in other words, no mere 'idealisation.' It is essentially a difference in the way we go about processing the world at different levels. If what has been argued in this book is plausible, then one of those levels cannot, by its nature, be captured in descriptive terms. So, saying that the 'manifest' is, at bottom, what the 'scientific' will eventually describe is fundamentally to presuppose that such content will eventually be captured by descriptions. And this is to invoke the terms of the inferentialist proposal which has here been called in question. If successful in this project, then philosophers' claims for the scientific over the manifest cannot be achieved, and another way of joining the descriptive and the sensational must be sought. This new way must take the sensory aspects of the 'manifest' as being genuinely *contentful* - and, at some level, non-descriptive and non-reducible. To see the problem in this way makes joining the two features harder, but perhaps makes for a more authentic account of man-in-the-world. On the view presented here, the contentful nature of the sensory stands in as much need of an account as the empirical nature of the descriptive.

The low-level/high-level dichotomy - the distinction between sensational and inferential content - does not in any way correspond to the distinction between the 'manifest' and the 'scientific' images. I have not intended to claim here that it does. The scientific image is not the same thing as a perception informed by high-level reasoning. Even my key example of high-level reasoning - Sherlock Holmes's experience of the cigar-band near Jones's body - is framed in terms of the manifest image; in fact, the manifest image is wholly constructed from ordinary (i.e., scientifically unsophisticated) perceptions. The scientific image, by contrast, is a *world view* derived from scientific experimentation: it is not usually a conceptual element in experience (except, perhaps, that of scientists in laboratories). It does not describe a world of experience, but a world as understood in terms of scientific theory, postulates of theory and entities corresponding with the results of experimentation (electrons, quarks and so on). The scientific image is thus not equivalent to inferentialism in perceptual content, nor is the manifest image equivalent to sensational content (though it often describes such content in terms of that image). The claim here is certainly not to forge a connection between the two images of man-in-the-world and the two levels of perceptual content.

The important point - and the reason for making this comparison - is that there is a connection between how philosophers traditionally try to resolve the problem of the two images and how the inferentialist proposal treats the issue of experiential content. The inferentialist proposal, we saw, tries to capture experiential content in high-level terms - it suggests that high-level influences are either *necessary* for experiences, or are necessary *and sufficient* for them. On any inferentialist view, there is no contentful experiential content outside the imposition of high-level categories. On this view, the nature of the sensory ends up being fully captured in terms of the descriptive facilities common to the various features of high-level inference.

How philosophers customarily treat the problem of the two images is explicitly part of this tradition. Their way of overcoming the dichotomy of the manifest and the scientific images is to capture the one image with the descriptions of the other. The content of the manifest image does not escape the explanatory mechanisms of the scientific image because it can actually be described by them 'when the chips are all down.' So most materialist philosophers make *the same sort of mistake* as that made by inferentialists, namely, that experience can somehow be *fully captured* by descriptions.

This way of resolving the dilemma arising between the manifest and the scientific is not uncommon. The inferentialist myth is pervasive in the treatment of many philosophical problems, as I have tried to show. Sellars's attempt to capture the sensory or the manifest in terms of what can be described by science is specifically a first step in the program of *reductionistic physicalism* (i.e., the *exclusive* primacy of the 'scientific image' over that of the 'manifest image'). This program consists firstly in the reduction of experience/perceptions to concepts and beliefs, and then the reduction of those concepts and beliefs to actual physical events, a manoeuvrer common to many materialist philosophers.

This book has tried to attack the first step of this program, making less plausible the claim that the descriptions of the scientific image can fully capture the contentful nature of experiences. My view - essentially in sympathy with Nagel's - is that the explanatory *primacy* of the scientific image in the context of experience and content is overstated.

While this is a reason for rejecting the inferentialist myth, this book does not take a stand on the specific dichotomy between the manifest image and the scientific image. I have not attempted a fusing of the images in *this* sense, nor do I attempt to connect this problem with the problem of experience. The continuum account is, at best, a metaphor for a new way of thinking about experience and content; it does not bear the weight of a new theory of man-in-the-world, although implications may carry over for it. Even if my rejection of the inferentialist proposal were false, the 'essential tension' between a world of conscious experiences and a world of whirling, colourless particles would remain. This problem remains despite placing stumbling blocks in the path of the inferentialist. Nagel's 'subjective' and 'objective' bind is basically Sellars's 'manifest' and 'scientific' tension, not to mention Eddington's 'two tables' problem revisited. No solution is offered for this dilemma.

However, it has been argued that the inferentialist proposal is false. It has also been suggested that the first stage in a physicalist-type reduction of experiential content will not work any more than it will for the fusing of the 'manifest' and the 'scientific' images - both presuppose that content can be captured by high-level descriptions, theory, and so on. But I have attempted more than just a negative critique: I have also tried to replace the standard views with a more subtle account.

In concluding, it remains to say a few words about what the alternative account amounts to in the broadest sense. As shown, admitting the 'aspect'-like features of experiences along with the descriptive, conceptual level is a matter of incorporating into the world features about ourselves as sophisticated data-processing organisms. It is to admit certain ways in which we structure the world perceptually; it is to admit levels of contentful *experiencings* along with levels of descriptions and theorisings. Certain aspects of experiential content, on this view, have 'look'-like features - and these are as much a part of our experiences as the representational, propositional and theory-embedded features which may be expressed and described in high-level scientific terms.

The alternative account presented in this book tries to 'fuse' the various contents of experience into one vision. A fusion is needed between the two levels because both kinds of content are ways in which we do go about processing the world as experiencing organisms. A single vision is also needed because the failure to give an account of low-level content often leads to misleading and impoverished philosophies. Failure to recognise 'the sensory' leads to what Nagel describes as 'outright denial that certain patently real phenomena exist at all,'[3] and, hence, to the legitimation of various forms of reductionisms, eliminativisms and physicalist accounts, which confuse the *having* of an experience with the *describing* of it.

It seems highly likely that an entirely naturalist account can be given of sensational content, however. Any concern that a repudiation of inferentialism

---

[3] T. Nagel, *The View from Nowhere*, p. 7.

in the context of experience will legitimate various sense data theories, relativisms and positivist accounts is unwarranted. The view adumbrated in this book insists that an adequate account of experience must include sensational features as contentful experiences for basically evolutionary reasons. Such features have a distinct informational function which enables 'something that it is like' for creatures to have certain experiences. And this function both *personalises* the experience and makes it available for later, more detailed processing. By way of reconciling the competing intuitions to keep such content, I opted for a property dualist account of man, along with a view of the evolution of perceptual systems which enables some aspects of experiences to be *felt,* rather than just described or conceptualised in high-level terms. Unavoidably, this position has required a rejection of the views which stress only high-level, descriptive conceptualisation as an explanation of felt experience, just as it has required a rejection of the strict formulation of the theory dependence of observation thesis. Ruling out such hardened philosophical precedents has meant that I have had to abandon 'inferentialist' accounts along the lines of Churchland, Sellars, Feyerabend and Armstrong, as well as the emphasis behind much of contemporary rationalist thought. It has also required that I make substantial modifications to the orthodox interpretation of Kant's epistemology. The aim has been to arrive at an account of experience and content which incorporates the idea that experiences admit of inferential features as well as 'optical' or felt features. There are, on my view, several important levels of perceptual analysis worth considering, and they constitute *sui generis* aspects of content.

In sum, the position argued for in this book carries over naturally to an account of man. For if low-level *experiencings* are admitted along with the 'postulational' and 'descriptive' vocabulary of science, then there is forever more to the nature of man than the descriptive scientific image that philosophers discuss. There is also more than what is simply 'manifest'. The nature of man, just like the nature of his experiences, is multi-faceted. The approach given here suggests that a certain view of man must be the end result of any adequate account of experiential content. Like the two images of man-in-the-world, it is very much in sympathy with the project of uniting the postulational and correlational vocabularies. Unlike this issue, however, it aims not just to reconcile what is described by science and what is sensed by man, but to reconsider the way in which we look at the relationship between 'descriptions' and 'sensings' as they arise in the context of experience and content.

Bibliography

Armstrong, D. M. (1961), *Perception and the Physical World*, International Library of Philosophy and Scientific Method. Routledge and Kegan Paul: London.
_____ . (1968), *A Materialist Theory of the Mind*, International Library of Philosophy and Scientific Method. Routledge and Kegan Paul: London.
_____ . (1973), *Belief, Truth and Knowledge,* Cambridge University Press: Cambridge.
_____ . (1992), 'A World of States of Affairs', Unpublished Manuscript.
Arnheim, R.(1969), *Visual Thinking*, Berkeley: University of California Press.
Bach-y-Rita, P. et al, (1969),'Vision Substitution by Tactile Image Projection', *Nature*, 221, pp. 963-4.
Bechtel, W. and Abrahamsen, A. (1991), 'Beyond the Exclusively Propositional Era', in *Epistemology and Cognition*, J. H. Fetzer (ed) Kluwer Academic Publishers: Dordrecht.
Beck, J. (1972), *Surface Colour Perception*, Cornell University Press: London.
Bennett, J. F. (1971), *Rationality*, Studies in the Philosophy of Psychology Series. Routledge and Kegan Paul, Humanities Press: London.
Berkeley, G. (1948), *The Works of George Berkeley,* Collected Works, Vol. 2, A. A. Luce and T. E. Jessop (eds) Nelson and Sons: Edinburgh.
_____ . (1973), 'A New Theory of Vision', *Philosophical Works*, M. R. Ayers, (ed) London.
Bird, G. (1962), *Kant's Theory of Knowledge: An Outline of One Central Argument in the Critique of Pure Reason,* International Library of Philosophy and Scientific Method. Routledge and Kegan Paul: London.
Bishop, J. (1980), 'More on Thought and Talk', *Mind*, 89, pp. 1-16.
Blakemore, C. and Cooper, C. F. (1973), 'Development of the Brain Depends on Visual Experience', *Vision Research*, 13, pp. 535-58.
Boden, M. (1979), *Piaget*, Brighton, Harvester Press: Sussex.
Boghossian, P. A. and Velleman, J. D. (1989), 'Colour as a Secondary Quality', *Mind*, 98, pp. 81-103.
_____ . (1991), 'Physicalist Theories of Color', *The Philosophical Review*, Vol. C. No. 1, pp. 67-106.
Bohr, N. (1934), *Atomic Theory and the Description of Nature,* Cambridge University Press: Cambridge, UK.

Bravo, M. and Blake, R. (1990), 'Preattentive Vision and Perceptual Groups', *Perception,* 19, pp. 515-522.
Brown, H. I. (1977), *Perception, Theory and Commitment: A New Philosophy of Science,* Precedent Publishers: Chicago.
Cam, P. (1990), 'Insularity and the Persistence of Perceptual Illusion', *Analysis,* 50, pp. 231-43.
Campbell, K. (1988), 'Philosophy and Common Sense', *Philosophy,* 63, pp. 161-174.
_____ . (1988), 'Can Intuitive Psychology Survive the Growth of Neuroscience?', *Inquiry,* 29, pp. 161-74.
Cary, S. (1978), 'A Case Study: Face Recognition', in E. Walker (ed) *Explorations in the Biology of Language,* Harvester: Hassocks.
Chalmers, A. H. (1982), *What is this Thing Called Science?,* Queensland University Press: St. Lucia.
Churchland, P. M. (1979), *Scientific Realism and the Plasticity of Mind,* Cambridge University Press: New York.
_____ . (1984), *Matter and Consciousness,* M.I.T Press: Cambridge, Mass.
_____ . (1986), 'Some Reductive Strategies in Cognitive Neurobiology', *Mind,* 95, pp. 303-309.
_____ . (1988), 'Perceptual Plasticity and Theoretical Neutrality', *Philosophy of Science,* 55, pp. 167-187.
Churchland, P. S. (1983), 'Consciousness: The Transmutation of a Concept', *Pacific Philosophical Quarterly,* 64, pp. 80-95.
Conan-Doyle, A. and Dickson Carr, J. (1954), *The Exploits of Sherlock Holmes,* Butler and Tanner: London.
Cooper, L. A. and Shepard, R. N. (1973), 'Chronometric Studies of the Rotation of Mental Images', in W. G. Chase, (ed)*Visual Information Processing,* Academic Press: New York.
Couvalis, S. G. (1989), *Feyerabend's Critique of Foundationalism,* Gower Publishing Company, Avebury Series: Aldershot, UK.
_____ . (1992), 'Theory and Observation', Unpublished Manuscript.
Cottingham, J. (1978), 'A Brute to the Brutes?: Descartes' Treatment of Animals', *Philosophy,* 53.
_____ . (1986), *Descartes,* Basil Blackwell: Oxford, New York.
Dancy, J. (1988), 'Contemplating One's Nagel', *Philosophical Books,* Vol. XXIX, No 1, pp. 1-15.
Davidson, D. (1975), 'Thought and Talk', in S. Guttenplan (ed) *Mind and Language,* Wolfson College Lectures. Clarendon Press: Oxford, UK.
_____ . (1980), 'Mental Events' in *Essays on Actions and Events,* Clarendon Press: Oxford, New York.
Dawkins, R. (1988), *The Blind Watchmaker,* Penguin, London.
Dennett, D.(1988), 'Quining Qualia', *Consciousness in Contemporary Science,* A. Marcel and E. Bisiach, Oxford University Press: Oxford, New York.
_____ . (1991), *Consciousness Explained,* Little, Brown and Co: Boston.
Dretske, F. I. (1969), *Seeing and Knowing,* International Library of Philosophy and Scientific Method. Routledge and Kegan Paul: London.
Falkenstein, L. (1990), 'Kant's Account of Sensation', *Canadian Journal of Philosophy,* 20, pp. 65-88

_____. (1991), Kant's account of Intuition', *Canadian Journal of Philosophy*, 21, pp. 163-195.
Feyerabend, P. K. (1955),'Wittgenstein's Philosophical Investigations', *Philosophical Review* 64. Revised and Rpt. in P. K. Feyerabend, Philosophical Papers, Vol. 2.
_____. (1978), *Science in a Free Society*, NLB: London.
_____. (1981), 'Science Without Experience', in *Realism, Rationalism and Scientific Method*, Philosophical Papers, Vol. 1. Cambridge University Press: Cambridge, N.Y.
_____. (1981), 'An Attempt at a Realistic Interpretation of Experience', in *Realism, Rationalism and Scientific Method*, Philosophical Papers, Vol. 1. Cambridge University Press: Cambridge, New York.
Fodor, J. A. (1983), *Modularity of Mind: An Essay in Faculty Psychology*, A Bradford Book. M.I.T. Press: Cambridge, Mass.
_____. (1984), 'Observation Reconsidered', *Philosophy of Science* 51, p. 23-43.
_____. (1985), 'Precis of The Modularity of Mind', *The Behavioural and Brain Sciences* 8, pp.1-42.
_____. (1987), 'Meaning and the World Order' in *Psychosemantics : The Problem of Meaning in the Philosophy of Mind*, Explorations in Cognitive Science Series, 2. M.I.T. Press: Cambridge, Mass.
_____. (1988), 'A Reply to Churchland's 'Perceptual Plasticity and Theoretical Neutrality', *Philosophy of Science,* 55, pp. 188-198.
_____. (1991), 'The Dogma that didn't Bark (A Fragment of a Naturalized Epistemology)', *Mind*, Vol. 100, pp. 201-220.
Forgas, J. P. (1981), (ed) *Social Cognition: Perspectives on Everyday Understanding*, Academic Press, London.
Furth, H. (1973), *Deafness and Learning: A Psychosocial Approach*, Wadsworth Pub. Co: Belmont, California.
Gallop, G. Jr. (1977), 'Self-Recognition in Primates: A Comparative Approach to the Bi-Directional Properties of Consciousness', *American Psychologist*. May, pp. 329-337
Geach, P. T. (1957), *Mental Acts: Their Contents and their Objects*, Humanities Press. Routledge and Kegan Paul: London.
Gibson, E. (1969), *Principles of Perceptual Learning and Development*, Meridith: New York.
Gilman, D. (1991), 'The Neurobiology of Observation', *Philosophy of Science* 58, pp. 496-502.
Glover, J. (1989), *The Philosophy and Psychology of Personal Identity*, Penguin: London.
Goldman, A. H. (1982), 'Epistemic Foundationalism and the Replacability of Observation language', *Journal of Philosophy*, LXXIX, pp. 136-154.
Gould, S. J. (1980), *The Panda's Thumb*, W.W. Norton and Co: New York.
Gregory, R. L. (1963), *Concepts and Mechanisms of Perception*, pp. 65-129. (Reprint of a monograph by R. L. Gregory and J. Wallace, 'Recovery from Early Blindness: A Case Study.')
_____. (1972), *Eye and Brain: The Psychology of Seeing*, 2nd Ed. Weidenfeld and Nicholson: London.
Griffin, D. (1981), *The Question of Animal Awareness: The Evolutionary*

Continuity of Mental Experience, Rockefeller University Press: New York.
Guarniero, G. (1974), 'Experience of Tactile Vision', *Perception,* 3, pp. 101-104.
Hampshire, S. (1959), *Thought and Action,* Chatto and Windus: London.
Hanson, N. R. (1958), *Patterns of Discovery: An Enquiry into the Conceptual Foundations of Science,* Cambridge University Press: Cambridge.
Hardin, C. L. (1988), *Color for Philosophers; Unweaving the Rainbow,* Hackett Publishing Co: Indianapolis and Cambridge.
_____. (1990), 'Color and Illusion', from, *Mind and Cognition: A Reader,* William Lycan (ed) Basil Blackwell: Oxford, Guildford.
Harman, G. (1974), 'Epistemology' in E. C. Carterette and M. P. Friedman, *Handbook of Perception,* Vol. 1; Academic Press: New York.
Harris, C. S. (1965), 'Perceptual Adaptation to Inverted, Reversed, and Displaced Vision', *Psychological Review,* 72, No. 6. pp. 419-444.
Hegel, G.W. F. (1929), *Hegel's Science of Logic,* W. H. Johnson and L. G. Struthers (eds) Muirhead Library of Philosophy. Allen and Unwin, Humanities Press: London.
Heider, E. R. and Oliver, D. C. (1972) 'The Structure of the Color Space in Naming and Memory for Two Languages', *Cognitive Psychology,* 8, pp. 337-496.
Held, R. and Blossom, J. (1961), 'Neonatal Deprivation and Adult Rearrangement: Complementary Techniques for Analysing Plastic Sensory Motor Coordinations', *Journal of Comparative and Physiological Psychology,* 56.
Hirsch, H. V. B. and Spinelli, D. N. (1970), 'Visual Experience Modifies Distribution of Horizontally and Vertically Orientated Fields in Cats', *Science,* 168, pp. 969-71.
Horgan, T. and Woodward, J. (1985), 'Folk Psychology is here to Stay', *The Philosophical Review,* XCIV, No. 2, pp. 197-224.
Hume, D. (1988), *A Treatise of Human Nature,* L. A. Selby-Bigge (ed) Clarendon Press: Oxford.
Hunt, S. (1994), 'A Realist Theory of Empirical Testing: Resolving the Theory-Ladenness/Objectivity Debate', *Philosophy of the Social Sciences,* 24, No. 2, pp. 133-158.
Jackson, F. (1977), *Perception: A Representative Theory,* Cambridge University Press: Cambridge; New York.
_____. (1990), 'Epiphenomenal Qualia', *Mind and Cognition: A Reader,* William Lycan (ed) Basil Blackwell: UK.
_____ (1991), 'What Mary Didn't Know', *Journal of Philosophy,* 83, 1986. Rpt. in *The Nature of Mind,* D. M. Rosenthal (ed) Oxford University Press: Oxford, New York.
Jackson, F. and Pettit, P. (1990), 'In Defence of Folk Psychology', *Philosophical Studies,* 59, pp. 31-54.
Jahoda, G. (1971),'Retinal Pigmentation, Illusion, Susceptibility and Space Perception', *International Journal of Psychology,* Vol. 6, pp. 199-208.
Jennings, H . S. (1904), *Contributions to the Study of the Behaviour of Lower Organisms,* Carnegie Institute Publication No. 16: Washington, Gibson Bros.
Kant, I. (1781 and 1787), *Critique of Pure Reason,* Hartknoch, Riga.

_____ . (1922), *Prolegomena Gesmmelte Schriften,* Kant's Collected Writings. Academy edition, Vol. 4; De Gruyter and Predecessors: Berlin.

_____ . (1933), *Critique of Pure Reason,* N. Kemp Smith trans. 2nd imp. Macmillan: London.

_____ . (1958), *Critique of Pure Reason,* N. Kemp Smith *Trans.* Random House: N.Y.

_____ . (1968), *Inaugural Dissertation,* (1770) G. B. Kerford and D. E. Walford Trans. 'Kant's Pre-Critical Writings', M. U. P: Manch.

Katz, D. (1935), *The World of Colour,* Kegan Paul, Trench, Trubner and Co. Ltd: London.

Keil, F. C. (1981), 'Constraints on Knowledge and Cognitive Development', *Psychological Review,* 88, No.3, pp. 197-227.

_____ . (1984), 'Mechanisms of Cognitive Development', in *Mechanisms of Cognitive Development,* W. H. Freeman and Co: New York.

Kemp, R. et al (1990), 'Sensitivity to the Displacement of Facial Features in Negative and Inverted Images,' *Perception,* 19, pp. 531-43.

Kosslyn, S. M. (1980), *Image and Mind,* H. U. P: Cambridge, Mass.

Kottenhoff, H. (1957), 'Situational and Personal Influences on Space Perception with Experimental Spectacles', *Acta Psychologia,* 13, pp. 79-97.

Kuhn, T. (1962),*The Structure of Scientific Revolutions,* University of Chicago Press: Chicago.

Levin, J. (1986),'Could Love be Like a Heatwave?: Physicalism and the Subjective Character of Experience', *Philosophical Studies,* 49, No. 2. pp. 245-261

Lewis, M. and Brooks-Gunn, J. (1979), *Social Cognition and the Acquisition of Self,* Plenum Press: New York.

Liberman, A. et al, (1967),'The Perception of the Speech Code', *Psychological Review,* 74, pp. 431-461.

Locke, J. (1965), *An Essay Concerning Human Understanding,* J. W. Youlton, (ed) Everyman Library. London.

Lorenz, K. (1962), 'Kant's Doctrine of the A Priori in the Light of Contemporary Biology', *General Systems Yearbook,* Vol. 7. pp. 23-35.

_____ . (1977), *Behind the Mirror A Search for a Natural History of Human Knowledge,* R. Taylor, trans., Methuen and Co: New York.

Mackie, J. (1976), *Problems From Locke,* Clarendon: Oxford, UK.

Macnamara, J. (1972), 'Cognitive Basis of Language Learning in Infants', *Psychological Review,* Vol. 79, No. 1, pp. 1-13.

Madell, G. (1986), 'Neurophilosophy: A Principled Sceptic's Response', *Inquiry,* 29, pp. 153-68.

Malcolm, N. (1972), *Thought and Knowledge,* Cornell University Press: Ithaca.

_____ . (1988),'Subjectivity', *Philosophy,* 63, pp. 147-160.

Marslen-Wilson, W. (1973), 'Speech Shadowing and Speech Perception', Ph.D thesis. M.I.T.

McCauley, R. N. (1986), 'Intertheoretic Relations and the Future of Psychology', *Philosophy of Science,* 53.

McGinn, C. (1983), *The Subjective View,* Clarendon: Oxford, UK.

_____ . (1987), 'The View from Nowhere', (Review) in *Mind,* 96, pp. 263-272.

McGinn, M. (1990), 'On Two Recent Accounts of Colour', *The Philosophical Review,* Vol. 41, No. 164, pp. 316-324.

Meglitsch, P. A. (1981), *Invertebrate Zoology,* 2nd. Edition; Oxford University Press, New York.

Merbs, S. L. and Nathans, J. (1992), 'Absorption Spectra of Human Cone Pigments', *Nature,* 356, pp. 433-435.

Morgan, M. J. (1977), *Molyneux's Question: Vision, Touch and the Philosophy of Perception,* Cambridge University Press: Cambridge, UK.

Millar, A. (1985),'What's in a Look?', *Proceedings of the Aristotelian Society,* New Series, 86 pp. 83-97.

──────── . (1991), 'Concepts, Experience and Inference', *Mind,* 100 pp. 495-505.

──────── . (1991), *Reasons and Experience,* Clarendon Press: Oxford, UK.

Mortensen, C. (1989), 'Mental Images: Should Cognitive Science Learn from Neurophysiology?' in *Computers, Brains and Minds,* Peter Sleazak and W. R. Albury (eds) Kluwer Academic Publishers: Dordrecht.

Mortensen, C. and Nerlich, G. (1986), *Aspects of Metaphysics,* Unpublished Manuscript.

Milne, L. J. and Milne, M. (1963), *The Senses of Animals and Man,* Deutch: London.

Mundle, C. W. K. (1971), *Perception: Facts and Theories,* Oxford University Press: London; New York.

Muscari, P. G. (1985), 'The Subjective Character of Experience', *The Journal of Mind and Behaviour,* Vol 6, No. 4, 1985. pp. 577-598.

Nagel, T. (1986), *The View from Nowhere,* Oxford University Press: New York:

──────── . (1974), 'What is it like to be a Bat?', *Philosophical Review,* LXXXIII, pp. 435-451.

──────── . (1979), *Mortal Questions,* Cambridge University Press, Cambridge, New York.

Nelson, K. (1973), 'Cognitive Primacy of Categorisation and its Functional Basis.' *Merrill Palmer Quarterly of Behaviour and Development* , 19, pp. 21-39.

Newman, E. and Hartline, P. (1982), 'The Infrared "Vision" of Snakes', *Scientific American,* 246, March, pp. 98-107.

Newton-Smith, W. (1981), *The Rationality of Science,* International Library of Philosophy. Routledge and Kegan Paul, Boston: Mass.

O'Brien, G. J. (1986), 'The Observation-Theory Distinction Revisited', Unpublished Manuscript.

──────── . (1987), 'Eliminative Materialism and Psychological Self-Knowledge', *Philosophical Studies,* 52, pp. 49-70.

Peacocke, C. (1983), *Sense and Content: Experience, Thought and their Relations,* Clarendon Press: Oxford, New York.

──────── . (1989),'No Resting Place: A Critical Notice of The View From Nowhere by Thomas Nagel', *The Philosophical Review,* Vol. XCVIII No. 1, pp. 65-82.

Pendlebury, M. (1990), 'Sense Experiences and their Contents: A Defence of the Propositional Account', *Inquiry,* 33, pp. 215-30.

Piaget, J. (1954), *The Origin of Intelligence in Children*, Basic Books: New York.
Pippin, R. (1982), *Kant's Theory of Form: An Essay on the Critique of Pure Reason*, Yale University Press: New Haven.
Popper, K., and Eccles, J. (1977), *The Self and its Brain: An Argument for Interactionism*, Springer and Verlag: Berlin.
Quine, W. V. O. (1961), 'Two Dogmas of Empiricism' in *From a Logical Point of View*, 2nd ed; Harvard University Press: Cambridge Mass.
Radner, M. and D. (1989), *Animal Consciousness*, Prometheus: Buffalo.
Reid, T. (1895), *Essays on the Intellectual Powers of Man*, Thin: Edinburgh.
Rivers, W. H. R. (1905), 'Observations on the Senses of the Todas', *British Journal of Psychology*, Vol. 1. pp. 321-96.
Robinson, W. S. (1975), 'The Legend of The Given' in *Action, Knowledge and Reality: Critical Studies in Honor of Wilfred Sellars*, H. N. Castaneda (ed) Bobbs-Merrill Co: Indianapolis.
Robinson, J. O. (1972), *The Psychology of Visual Illusion*, Hutchinson: London.
Rock, I. (1975), *Introduction to Perception*, Macmillan: New York.
Rollins, B. E. (1989), *The Unheeded Cry: Animal Consciousness, Animal Pain and Science*, Oxford University Press: New York.
Rosch, E. et al. (1976), 'Basic Objects in Natural Categories', *Cognitive Psychology*, 8, 1976. pp. 328-50.
Ross, H. E. (1974), *Perception and Behaviour in Strange Environments*, Allen and Unwin: London.
Routley, R. (1981), 'Alleged Problems in Attributing Beliefs and Intentionality in Animals', *Inquiry*, 24, pp. 385-417.
Samet, J. (1986), 'Troubles with Fodor's Nativism.' in Peter A. French et al (ed) *Midwest Studies in Philosophy*, Vol. X. Uni of Minnesota Press: Minneapolis.
Schilpp, P. A. (1953), (ed) *Albert Einstein, Philosopher-Scientist*, Harper: NY; Evanston.
Sellars, W. 'Empiricism and Abstract Entities.' (1963). *The Philosophy of Rudolph Carnap*, P.A. Schilpp, (ed) The Library of Living Philosophers, Vol. 11. Open Court: La Salle, Ill., USA.
_____ . (1963), 'Empiricism and the Philosophy of Mind', in *Science, Perception and Reality*, Routledge and Kegan Paul: London.
Schiano, D. J. and Jordan, K. (1990), 'Mueller-Lyer Decrement: Practice or Prolonged Exposure?', *Perception*, 19, No. 3, pp. 307-316.
Shaw, D. (1989), 'Natural Selection and Epiphenomenalism', in *Issues in Evolutionary Epistemology*, K. Halweg and C. Hooker (eds) State University of N.Y. Press: New York.
Shoemaker, S. (1991), 'Qualia and Consciousness', *Mind*, 100, pp. 507-524.
Sibley, F. N. (1971), *Perception: A Philosophical Symposium*, Methuen and Co. Ltd: London.
Siegel, S. and Petry, S. (1991), 'Evidence for Independent Processing of Subjective Contour Brightness and Sharpness', *Perception*, 20, pp. 233-241.
Strawson, P. F. (1966), *The Bounds of Sense: An Essay on Kant's Critique of Pure Reason*, Methuen and Co. Ltd: London.

Sternberg, R. J. (1984), (ed) *Mechanisms of Cognitive Development,* W. H Freeman and Co: New York.

Stereley, K. (1989), 'Fodor's Nativism', *Philosophical Studies,* 55, pp. 119-141.

Stich, S. P. (1979), 'Do Animals have Beliefs?', *Australasian Journal of Philosophy,* 57, pp. 15-28.

Townsend, A. (1979), 'Radical Vegetarians', Critical Notice, *Australasian Journal of Philosophy,* Vol. 57, pp. 85-93.

Warnock, G. J. (1965), 'Seeing' in *Perceiving, Sensing and Knowing,* Reprint with *Postscript.* Robert J. Swartz (ed) Anchor Books: Garden City, New York.

Westphal, K.(1987), *Colour,* Basil Blackwell: Oxford, UK.

Wittgenstein, L.(1961), *Tractatus Logico Philosophicus,* Routledge and Kegan Paul: London, UK.

———. (1980), *Remarks on the Philosophy of Psychology,* Vol. 1. G. E. M Anscombe and G. H. Von Wright (eds) Cambridge University Press: Chicago.